Pinay Power

Pinay Power

Peminist Critical Theory

Theorizing the Filipina/American Experience

Edited by Melinda L. de Jesús

ROUTLEDGE
NEW YORK AND LONDON

Published in 2005 by
Routledge
Taylor & Francis Group
270 Madison Avenue
New York, NY 10016

Published in Great Britain by
Routledge
Taylor & Francis Group
2 Park Square
Milton Park, Abingdon
Oxon OX14 4RN

Library of Congress Cataloging-in-Publication Data

Pinay power : peminist critical theory : theorizing the Filipina/American experience /
[edited by] Melinda L. de Jesús.
    p. cm.
    Summary: "Pinay Power: Peminist Critical Theory is a collection of peminist (Filip-
ina American feminist) cultural criticism by and about Filipina Americans. It features
essays by female scholars and writers who tackle issues such as gender, decolonization,
globalization, transnationalism, identity, sexuality, representation and spirituality. It also
features examples of peminist artwork." —Provided by publisher.
    ISBN 0-415-94982-3 (hardback : alk. paper) — ISBN 0-415-94983-1 (pbk. : alk.
paper) 1. Filipino American women—Social conditions. 2. Filipino American
women—Intellectual life. 3. Feminism—United States. 4. Feminist theory—United
States. 5. Critical theory. I. De Jesus, Melinda L., 1965-
E184. F4P547 2004
305.48'89921073—dc22   2004021270

Taylor & Francis Group
is the Academic Division of T&F Informa plc.

Visit the Taylor & Francis Web site at
http://www.taylorandfrancis.com

and the routledge Web site at
http://www.routledge-ny.com

To my Pinay sisters throughout the diaspora
To my students and colleagues
To my family
And to the memory of my father, José M. de Jesús Sr.—because he wanted to learn more about "women's studies," and because he helped me become the *peminist aktibista* I am today

Contents

18 *Sino Ka? Ano Ka?*: Contemporary Art
by Eight Filipina American Artists   291
VICTORIA ALBA

19 Theory in/of Practice: Filipina American Feminist
Filmmaking   309
CELINE PARREÑAS SHIMIZU

20 Resisting Appropriation and Assimilation via
(a)eromestizaje and Radical Performance Art Practice   327
GIGI OTÁLVARO-HORMILLOSA

21 The Herstory of *Bamboo Girl* Zine   341
SABRINA MARGARITA ALCANTARA-TAN

22 Through Our Pinay Writings:
Narrating Trauma, Embodying Recovery   351
MARIE-THERESE C. SULIT

23 Filipinas "Living in a Time of War"   373
NEFERTI XINA M. TADIAR

    Contributors   387

    Permissions   393

    Index   395

List of Illustrations

Acknowledgments

Pinay Power: Peminist Critical Theory, Theorizing the Filipina/American Experience was by no means a solo endeavor, but came about from the cooperation and support of many. First, I would like to thank all of the contributors for their faith and patience as I struggled to put this anthology together. It was truly a privilege to engage with their inspiring essays and artwork. Next, I would like to thank the following friends and colleagues for their support of this project: Karen Leong, Karen Kuo, Wei Li, Maddie Adelman, Jackie Martinez, Lisa Anderson, the Wakonse "Bad Kids" (Dan Brouwer, Scott and Liz Okamoto, Nick Ray, and Thomas Walker), Roisan Rubio, Karen Wolny, Trisha Lagaso, Mark Johnson, Katie Gilmartin, and Bob Tinsman. Many thanks to my resident "Feline Americans," Zoyd, Ninjette, Pickle, and Buster, for providing furry companionship and distraction as I edited this book.

Maraming salamat po to: Michelle Malonzo, my amazing undergraduate intern who came to my office out of the blue in November 2003 to offer her help with source checking and editing, and to Mary Fran Draisker and Janet Soper of Arizona State University's College of Public Program's Publications Assistance Center, for all their help with formatting and manuscript preparation.

A 2001 Arizona State University Women's Studies Summer Research Grant supported this work.

Introduction: Toward a Peminist Theory, or Theorizing the Filipina/American Experience*

Origins

In October 1998, while an assistant professor of Asian American studies at San Francisco State University, I was invited by university art gallery director Mark Johnson to create and facilitate a panel discussion about Filipina American issues as a closing event for *Sino Ka? Ano Ka?* (Who are you? What are you?), a landmark exhibit featuring the work of eight Bay Area Filipina American artists. I titled the symposium "The State of Filipina America" and invited fellow Filipina American scholars and cultural activists Penny Flores, Neferti Tadiar, and Celine Parreñas to speak.[1]

The auditorium is packed and buzzing with good energy. After the thought-provoking presentations by Penny, Neferti, and Celine and amid a stimulating series of questions from the audience, one of my male colleagues, a fellow instructor of Filipino American studies, slips quickly into an empty seat in the back and attempts to hijack the proceedings. He missed the papers presented earlier and clearly is uninterested in the topics we're discussing. "Dan" speaks of his longtime community activism and how we "feminists" are too busy "intellectualizing" and "doing theory," whereas he and his brothers have been "doing reality" since before I was born. Furthermore, he asserts, this symposium's focus on gender "dilutes" focus on racism against Filipinos—read: Filipino men. Looking out into the audience, I see my students staring back at me with looks of discomfort, outrage, concern, and fear; some slink deeper into their seats,

---

*A note regarding the dual usage of "Filipina/American" and "Filipina American" in *Pinay Power*: these terms appear throughout the anthology, with the majority of contributors preferring the latter. My preference for "Filipina/American" in this introductory chapter references two things: first, my initial use of this term in my 1998 article "Fictions of Assimilation: Nancy Drew, Cultural Imperialism, and the Filipina/American Experience" (reprinted in this anthology as chapter 3), which employed "Filipina/American" to underscore the fluid nature of Pinay identities as *both* Filipina *and* Filipina American; and also Sarita See's specific usage of the term in 2000 to problematize our understandings of Filipino/a American culture and identity as rooted in U.S. colonization and imperialism. Please see the following for more information: Sarita See, "An Open Wound: Colonial Melancholia and Contemporary Filipino/American Texts," in *Vestiges of War: The Philippine American War and the Aftermath of an Imperial Dream, 1899-1999*, Angel Shaw and Luis Francia, eds. (New York: New York University Press, 2000), Note 1.

hiding. This isn't the first time Dan and I have clashed about gender issues, but it is definitely a very public attack and now directed toward my Pinay colleagues. I'm angry that our singular attempt to discuss Filipina American experiences is being denigrated by the same tired, sexist, cultural nationalist rhetoric. Trying to be a gracious facilitator, I interrupt Dan's long-winded diatribe, saying that his comments are not related to the subject of our panel discussion and that we are moving on. He interrupts me again and I cut him off. Audience members clap. The discussion continues while Dan leaves in a noisy huff.

At that moment I decided we needed an anthology of Filipina American feminist theory—and now, after seven long years, you hold it in your hands. But my yearning to know more about my own history, and that of other Filipinas, has much deeper roots:

The arrogant white feminist professor chiding me that I shouldn't "ghettoize" myself and my academic training by "just doing Asian American Studies." Searching This Bridge Called My Back *in vain for writing by Filipina Americans.[2] Fourth grade classmates taunting me as the "Oriental coffee bean." My parents telling me that "Filipinos had no culture before the Spanish came." And always, this recollection: I'm about nine years old, and I'm sitting in the back of my family's Ford LTD station wagon, facing out the back window as my father drives our car up Eaton Avenue. I am suddenly aware of how our car moves through space and time, passing the familiar houses and landmarks of my neighborhood. Then I notice the nothingness left in our car's wake—how space and time rush in to swallow up where our car has been, every second of its motion is devoured, leaving not one trace. We're traveling but there's no sign of our having been on the road at all; our presence is erased as soon as it is made. Somehow, I connect this sense of motion and simultaneous erasure to my family's history—how we operate in the very American "perpetual present," eschewing any link to our Filipino past.[3] I learn to forget that my parents have accents, that they speak a language I don't know—a language they did not teach me. I learn that it's better to be "here" than "back home," that bad stuff happened during "the war." And because my parents have so many dreams for my American future, I learn to distance myself from my history. When asked, I say, "My parents are from the Philippines, but I was born here." So this is the American Dream—living in the perpetual present, moving through life without a past, swallowed whole, invisible, but unable to deny the lingering ache of absence . ...*

Legacies of Erasure

According to the 2000 U.S. census, Filipino Americans are the second fastest growing Asian/Pacific Islander community in the United States today (constituting 18 percent of the total Asian/Pacific Islander population), but we remain invisible, underrepresented politically and culturally.[4] Too often marginalized within both mainstream and academic conceptions of the term *Asian American*, Filipino Americans also suffer from the effects of colonial mentality: our complicated relationship with the United States and its imperialist legacy has had a tremendous impact upon our sense of history and identity. Thus, many hegemonic cultural and political forces conspire to transcribe us within narratives of amnesia or forgetfulness.

The themes of lost identities and histories dominate Filipino American cultural studies. Many critics delineate how a heritage of dual colonizations (first by Spain and then by the United States), coupled with American cultural imperialism, has left an indelible mark on the Filipino American psyche. E. San Juan Jr. writes that the "reality of U.S. colonial subjugation and its profoundly enduring effects—something most people cannot even begin to fathom, let alone acknowledge" has created "the predicament and crisis of dislocation, fragmentation, uprooting, loss of traditions, exclusions and alienation" for Filipino Americans.[5] Likewise, Oscar Campomanes contends that the crisis of Filipino/American identity is rooted in the "United States' imperial nationality," which demands that we forget our own colonization: as "objects of powerfully amnesiac acts," Filipino Americans are transcribed by and within "powerful acts of forgetting and impressions of formlessness."[6] Eric Gamalinda describes Filipino American alienation as one consequence of this amnesia: "Many Filipino Americans still regard their own culture as inferior (that is, compared to America's), which further reinforces the Filipino's invisibility. It is no wonder that second- and third-generation Filipino Americans feel they are neither here nor there, perambulating between a culture that alienates them and a culture they know nothing about or are ashamed of."[7]

The Need for Pinay Power

Despite our ubiquitous presence throughout the diaspora, Filipinas remain contingently visible: as nameless, faceless overseas contract workers, sex workers, and mail-order brides scattered across the globe. We are seen as objects of a sexist, imperial ideology, yet we remain invisible as subjects and agents. Filipinas are simultaneously everywhere and nowhere. This section explores our historical invisibility.

For Filipina Americans, the legacy of imperialism, colonization, and alienation is further complicated by the patriarchal bias of both Asian American and Filipino American studies, which has dictated the marginalization of Filipina voices and concerns and ignored our attempts to transform these disciplines through incorporating feminist and/or queer theory. For example, foundational Filipino American historiographies—like Fred Cordova's *Filipinos: Forgotten Asian Americans—A Pictorial Essay*—reflect an overly heterosexist, androcentric rendering of the Pinay experience that relegates us to the narrow roles of mothers, wives, and daughters. As Cordova has noted, "The heart and soul of the development of the Filipino American experience were personified in Pinays—particularly first-generation women, including those separated from their men, and their second-generation daughters, who tried to emulate their mothers. Pinays have been the yeast that set their men and children rising and the leaven that got their communities producing."[8] Asian American feminist theorists note how the historical antiracist focus of Asian American studies overall has contributed to this sexism. Shirley Hune writes, "In Asian American Studies, race is the organizing category and the master narrative remains male-centered. Hence the historical significance of women is rendered invisible when their lives, interests and activities are subsumed within or considered to be the same as those of men."[9] Meanwhile, Yen Le Espiritu maintains that "the anti-racism agenda has homogenized differences among Asian Americans, assuming heterosexuality and subordinating issues of gender and social class."[10] Today, patriarchy maintains its insidious hold: renowned Filipino activist Ninotchka Rosca writes that Filipino anti-imperialist activism often disregards sexism,[11] while Asian American feminist theorist Rachel Lee notes that as Asian American political critique has become increasingly sophisticated, it still retains its propensity to subordinate gender issues.[12]

Mirroring the invisibility of Filipinas within Asian American and Filipino American studies is the underrepresentation of Filipinas within the field of feminist studies. The last thirty years have seen an explosion of writings by U.S. women of color, including groundbreaking anthologies by and about Asian American women—for example, Asian Women United of California's *Making Waves* and *Making More Waves*, Sonia Shah's *Dragon Ladies*, and Linda Vo and colleagues' *Asian American Women: The Frontiers Anthology*.[13] Until recently, however, there has been relatively little published by and about Filipina Americans.[14] This critique is not meant to dismiss these important Asian American feminist works but is an attempt to further contextualize the invisibility of Filipina/Americans among our own allies. Beyond the necessary criticism of East Asian hegemony in Asian America, which has lead to constructing and signifying Asian American women as of solely Chinese, Japanese, and/or Korean descent, these crucial questions remain: Why have we Filipinas silenced ourselves? And what/whom does our silence, our self-erasure, serve?

These are the realities Filipina Americans face as we struggle to create Pinay herstory. Clearly, as Mitsuye Yamada notes, "To finally recognize our invisibility is to finally be on the path of visibility. Invisibility is not a natural state for anyone."[15]

Defining Peminism

I first heard the term *peminism* as a graduate student at the University of California–Santa Cruz in the early 1990s when a classmate used it to describe a specific form of feminist theory rooted in the *Filipina American* experience—an experience very different from the implicit (and thus explicit) subject of white liberal feminism. *Peminism* describes Filipina American consciousness, theory, and culture, with the *p* signifying specifically *Pinay* or *Pilipina*, terms used in referring to ourselves as American-born Filipinas.[16] It demarcates the space for Filipina American struggles against the cultural nationalist, patriarchal narratives that seek to squash our collective voice in the name of "ethnic solidarity." Some Filipina American critics prefer the terms *pinayism* or *Pinay studies* to describe Filipina American feminist theorizing; despite the differences in terminology, each form describes Filipina American struggles against racism, sexism, imperialism, and homophobia and struggles for decolonization, consciousness, and liberation. *Peminism* thereby signifies the assertion of a specifically Filipina American subjectivity, one that radically repudiates white feminist hegemony as it incorporates the Filipino American oppositional politics inscribed by choosing the term *Pilipino* over *Filipino*.[17]

Most important, peminism is about loving ourselves and other Pinays, loving our families and communities. Indeed, peminism is an inextricable part of our decolonization as a people: far from being a slighting of Filipino American men or Filipino American culture in general, attention to Pinay voices and perspectives demonstrates our commitment to the liberation of *all* Filipinos.

Conceiving *Pinay Power*

Initially, my goals for this present volume were three-pronged: (1) to delineate a body of peminist theorizing oppositional to the patriarchal bias of Filipino American Studies—my altercation with "Dan" only brought home its necessity; (2) to situate peminist theorizing, particularly by American-born Filipinas, in relation to Asian American feminism that has often ignored or marginalized Filipina perspectives; and (3) to theorize peminism in relation to U.S. feminisms of color to ascertain the similarities and differences characterizing their methodologies and issues. However, over time, my vision of the anthology's purpose and scope evolved in ways I did not anticipate.

As an American-born Pinay trained as an Asian American and feminist scholar, I was very aware of the limited number of Filipina American resources I might draw upon in my own research and teaching. My voracious reading of creative and theoretical work by U.S. women of color—for example, Gloria Anzaldúa, Barbara Christian, bell hooks, Maxine Hong Kingston, Chela Sandoval, Merle Woo, and Mitsuye Yamada—led me to conclude that Filipina American theorizing would exhibit similar themes and concerns. Initially,

I was adamant that the anthology privilege the voices of Filipina *Americans*—as opposed to Filipina *Filipinas*—because I wanted to carve out a distinctive space for the hybrid Filipina American experience. However, in editing *Pinay Power,* I began to comprehend how my own identity crisis as an American-born Filipina led me to privilege a split between peminists that does not exist.[18] I found that, indeed, peminist theorizing shares many similarities with feminisms of color and Asian American feminisms—for example, the negotiation of the "borderlands,"[19] the emergence of mestiza consciousness,[20] the simultaneous struggle to fight racism in the women's movement and sexism in our ethnic communities, as well as the pressure to "pledge allegiance" to *either* culture *or* gender, but not both. And I found that the analysis of the legacy of American imperialism in the Philippines unites peminist discourse.

Thus, what distinguishes *Pinay Power: Peminist Critical Theory* is the gendered analysis of imperial trauma—the Philippines' dual colonizations by Spain and the United States—and the articulation of Pinay resistance to imperialism's lingering effects: colonial mentality, deracination, and self-alienation. The authors included in *Pinay Power* compel us to recognize rather than reject this history, for to acknowledge and theorize its violence and its exponential repercussions is to take the first steps toward decolonization and empowerment.

Claiming the Peminist Space

Pinay Power: Peminist Critical Theory is an interdisciplinary collection of critical essays about the contemporary Filipina/American experience organized around the themes of peminist consciousness, theory, and culture. It strives to answer the following questions: What is the state of Pinay America? What are our issues? How do we theorize our lives? What does our cultural production look like? How do we imagine our futures? Resisting the silencing and erasing of Filipina American voices, the essays presented here demonstrate innovative linkings across and through American ethnic and postcolonial studies, third world feminist, queer, and Asian American and Philippine feminisms. They push for our acknowledgment of how prevalent Asian American studies' models have unwittingly limited our full comprehension of the ramifications of the neocolonial relationships between the United States and the Philippines and, in turn, challenge us to question our investment in the term *Filipina American* itself.[21]

Gathering together for the first time new and previously published essays by and about Filipina Americans, *Pinay Power* is not necessarily "comprehensive" as much as it is a selective and thematic charting of the parameters of peminist theorizing today. Because this volume privileges American-based Pinays writing about the Pinay experience from a humanities/cultural studies perspective, there are a number of gaps in terms of covering themes addressed therein (for example, Pinays and aging, labor stratification, education, mental health, popular culture, and political participation). Nevertheless, *Pinay Power* provides an overview of the issues Pinays face in the new millennium and, as such, it is just the beginning of many necessary conversations we must have about the future of Pinays everywhere.

Haunted by the ghosts of colonization and imperialism, *Pinay Power* manifests common themes throughout: alienation, invisibility, trauma, healing, and resistance. Stylistically, many of the authors here employ talk-story or autoethnography as a methodology for theorizing the intersections of the political and personal experience of being Pinay. Indeed, one unique feature of *Pinay Power* is the significance of mestiza Filipina American theorizing advanced by mixed-race writers Sabrina Margarita Alcantara-Tan, Gigi Otálvaro-Hormillosa, Linda M. Pierce, and Michelle Remoreras Watts. As testimonies of Filipina American agency, creativity, and resistance, the twenty-three essays included here "speak" to one another throughout the collection, weaving a powerful and dense web of feminist resistance. In ordering the essays, I sought to group together works whose themes resonated very strongly with one another; however, the subsections reflect just one way of mapping the terrain of contemporary peminist thought.

Pinay Power opens with part I, "Identity and Decolonization." Drawing upon autoethnography and family history, the essays in this section underscore the intersections of personal and communal struggle in confronting our imperial and colonial legacies as Filipina/Americans. Leny Mendoza Strobel's "A Personal Story: On Becoming a Split Filipina Subject" maps the Filipina/American's painful process of internal colonization and her struggle for decolonization through critical indigeneity. Similarly, Linda M. Pierce's "Not Just My Closet: Exposing Familial, Cultural, and Imperial Skeletons" draws upon work by Strobel and others to interrogate—from a mestiza's perspective—her family's history in relation to its investment in whiteness. Pierce underscores that the scars she and her family bear are not unique, but rather exemplify the pervasive colonial mentality that plagues Filipino/American culture itself. Like Pierce, I draw upon my mother's family history in "Fictions of Assimilation: Nancy Drew, Cultural Imperialism, and the Filipina/American Experience" to explore how the dynamics of cultural imperialism and racism radically complicate what girls of color learn from their negotiations with the ideologies promulgated within the seemingly benign *Nancy Drew Mystery Series*. Ending this section is Rachel A. R. Bundang's "'This Is Not Your Mother's Catholic Church': When Filipino Catholic Spirituality Meets American Culture," which explores the connections among identity, consciousness, and decolonization and posits peminist "syncretic spirituality" as an important space for our community's growth and transformation.

The essays in part II, "(Re)Writing/Peminist Sociohistory," provide important interventions against Filipina American invisibility. In "Asian American History: Reflections on Imperialism, Immigration, and 'The Body,'" Catherine

Ceniza Choy interrogates the future of Asian American historiography through the story of her developing a multidisciplinary, international methodology for understanding Filipina nurses, immigration, and imperialism. Her essay underscores the "imagination and creativity" needed "to conceptualize alternative historiographies" that can theorize the increasingly complex intersections of gender, race, work, migration, and globalization in the twenty-first century. Sociologist Rhacel Salazar Parreñas takes up Choy's charge in "Migrant Filipina Domestic Workers and the International Division of Reproductive Labor"; her analysis of "the international transfer of care-taking," a three-tiered system in which "migrant Filipina domestic workers hire poorer women in the Philippines to perform the reproductive labor that they are performing for wealthier women," delineates the dynamics of race and gender as aspects of reproductive labor under global capitalism and emphasizes the often-concealed personal and familial costs Filipina domestic workers must reconcile as they continue to work "in the middle." Finally, a study of a relatively unknown cohort of second-generation Filipina Americans, "Beauty Queens, Bomber Pilots, and Basketball Players: Second-Generation Filipina Americans in Stockton, California, 1930s to 1950s," by Dawn Bohulano Mabalon, outlines how Stockton Pinays "carved out new spaces for them-selves, and created new conceptions of Filipina womanhood ... through peer networks, community organizing, social events, and through their labor as well as leisure activities." Mabalon's article offers an important representation of Filipina Americans as active agents in their own histories.

Part III, "Peminist (Dis)Engagements with Feminism," explores the com-plicated relationship between peminism and hegemonic or white liberal femi-nism. "Pinayism," one of the first attempts to theorize the contemporary Pinay experience, describes Allyson Goce Tintiangco-Cubales's struggle to define a Pinay-centered theory that would transcend the limitations of Filipino Ameri-can cultural nationalist and mainstream feminist theory. Reminding us that "Pinay + ism = Pain + Growth" in her analyses of the competition and distrust that often inhibit Pinay collective unity and activism, Tintiangco-Cubales proffers a bittersweet reflection on how social transformation begins with loving and respecting ourselves and our sisters. Greatly expanding upon Tintiangco-Cubales's analyses, Frank L. Samson's "Filipino American Men: Comrades in the Filipina/o American Feminism Movement" offers an innova-tive reflection on why and how progressive Filipino American men should integrate aspects of Pinayism into their personal politics and also develops one of the first analyses of how Pinayism intersects with—and could develop fur-ther through incorporating aspects of—Philippine feminisms. This section of *Pinay Power* ends very fittingly with Delia D. Aguilar and Karin Aguilar-San Juan's "Feminism across Our Generations." Aguilar and Aguilar-San Juan, mother and daughter scholar-activists, present a dialogue organized around their differing generational, political identities in relation to "feminism ... as a theory and as a political practice"—a conversation offering insights pertinent to everyone engaged in feminist activism. Aguilar and Aguilar-San Juan's dialogue not only emphasizes the interconnections between Filipina American and Philippine feminist thought but also describes where and how Filipina American youth might best focus their efforts to further their generation's own decolonization.

The prevailing Catholicism of much of Filipina/American culture renders expression and discussion of female sexuality—particularly sexuality outside prescribed Catholic, heterosexist, homophobic norms—taboo, resulting in guilt, confusion, and fear for many Pinays. The essays organized in part IV, "Theorizing Desire: Sexuality, Community, and Activism," demonstrate how and why Pinay sexuality remains a crucial site for peminist struggle. In "Tomboy, Dyke, Lezzie, and Bi: Filipina Lesbian and Bisexual Women Speak Out" Christine T. Lipat, Trinity A. Ordona, Cianna Pamintuan Stewart, and Mary Ann Ubaldo break the silence around Pinay queer identities and discuss coming out, creating community, and fighting invisibility as well as the changing climate toward lesbian and bisexual Filipina/Americans over time and through different generations. M. Evelina Galang's "Deflowering the Sampaguita" problematizes Pinay heterosexuality as constructed within repressive patriarchal and religious expectations of female behavior. Playing with the mutual significations of the Holy Communion and heterosexuality, Galang's cautionary plea to parents emphasizes that the schizophrenia evident in the silence about, yet policing of, sexual activity robs Pinays of the chance to explore the profound spiritual aspects of sexuality and leads to a female legacy of shame, confusion, and alienation from one generation of Pinays to the next. Trinity A. Ordona's "The Long Road Ahead" offers a very timely discussion of Filipina American lesbian realities given the recent focus on same-sex marriage in the U.S. media. Here Ordona underscores how coming out for most Filipina Americans entails renegotiating all family relationships.

Part V, "Talking Back: Peminist Interventions in Cyberspace and the Academy," offers examples of peminist intervention online and within the ivory tower. Perla Paredes Daly's "Creating NewFilipina.com and the Rise of Cyber-Pinays" describes how her outrage about the Internet's prevailingly negative stereotypes of Filipinas led her to create the NewFilipina.com website and how, in turn, this act of cyberspace activism profoundly impacted her feminist and nationalist identity, her commitment to community organizing, and her own spirituality. Similarly, Emily Noelle Ignacio's "Ain't I a Filipino (Woman)?: An Analysis of Authorship/Authority through the Construction of Filipino/Filipina on the Net" explores the significations of "Filipina" in the soc.culture.filipino newsgroup. Tracing how Filipinos across the diaspora resorted to promulgating sexist stereotypes of Filipinas in an effort to assert nationalism and anticolonialism, Ignacio exposes how the newsgroup posters' invocations of the "good" Filipina versus "bad" Westernized/American woman advocate sexism while effectively silencing Filipina Americans who challenge these stark dichotomizations. The next two articles explore peminist interventions in the academy. My essay, "'A walkin' fo' de (Rice) Kake': A Filipina American Feminist's Adventures in Academia, or A Pinay's Progress," contrasts my experiences as a "diversity initiative" postdoctoral and an Asian American studies faculty member to delineate the limitations of both multiculturalist and cultural nationalist discourses as well as the changes that must be made in order to transform the academy into a more welcoming space for all women of color. Likewise, Michelle Remoreras Watts's "Not White Enough, Not Pilipino Enough: A Young Mestiza's Journey" describes Watts's journey to claim her identity as a Pinay mestiza and how this struggle led to her becoming a student and community activist. Negotiating the significations of "mestiza-ness" to her fellow activists, Watts critiques Pilipino American identity politics and sexism and reclaims the power of the erotic in the service of love for herself and her community.

The essays in part VI, "Peminist Cultural Production," highlight the theoretical and artistic work of contemporary Pinays; in essence, they model peminism in action, offering us glimpses of the peminist future. Victoria Alba's essay for "*Sino Ka? Ano Ka?*: Contemporary Art by Eight Filipina American Artists," the first exhibition by Filipina Americans, contextualizes the work of innovative Bay Area–based artists Eliza O. Barrios, Terry Acebo Davis, Reanne Agustin Estrada, Johanna Poethig, Stephanie Syjuco, Lucille Tenazas, Catherine Wagner, and Jenifer Wofford. It also problematizes the diversity of aesthetic responses to and representations of the Pinay experience today. Filmmaker Celine Parreñas Shimizu's "Theory in/of Practice: Filipina American Feminist Filmmaking" describes her journey as an artist and the development of her Filipina American feminist film aesthetic. Writing her own filmography, Shimizu traces the evolution of her work from Filipina-centric to Pan-Asian feminist and details how it addresses the themes of invisibility, identity, sexuality, stereotypes, violence, and racism. Shimizu's story is an inspiration to other Pinays who strive to create multidimensional representations of Filipina American realities and to all female artists who labor in male-dominated fields. The next two essays proffer peminist theory informed by mestiza and queer realities and, like Shimizu's, situate art and culture as powerful agents of change. In "Resisting Appropriation and Assimilation via *(a)eromestizaje* and Radical Performance Art Practice," performer and writer Gigi Otálvaro-Hormillosa delineates how her mestiza roots (Filipina and Colombian) and queer identity inform the notion of "*(a)eromestizaje*"—the aesthetic that grounds her provocative works *Inverted Minstrel* and *Cosmic Blood*—and how *(a)eromestizaje* itself enables a decolonizing, liberatory performance practice committed to empowering its audience to question U.S. society's racist, sexist, and heterosexist status quo. Similarly, "The Herstory of *Bamboo Girl* Zine," by Sabrina Margarita Alcantara-Tan (a.k.a. Bamboo Girl), echoes the confrontational aesthetics of *(a)eromestizaje* as well as Perla Daly's accidental foray into cultural activism. Here Alcantara-Tan delineates how her personal struggle to define her identity as a queer Filipina mestiza, to learn her cultural history, to fight back against racist/sexist street harassment, and to critique the homophobic and racist punk scene results in the discovery of her own voice and her capacity for activism and advocacy. Finally, Marie-Therese Sulit's and Neferti Xina M. Tadiar's essays explore the themes of trauma and war in literature by Filipina/Americans and model how Filipina American cultural productions themselves provide opportunities for mediation, transformation, and resistance. In "Through Our Pinay Writings: Narrating Trauma, Embodying Recovery," Marie-Therese C. Sulit plumbs the intersections of trauma studies and Filipina American studies in the peminist renderings of the Philippines/U.S. imperial encounter in texts by Elynia Mabanglo, Lara Stapleton, M. Evelina Galang, and Merlinda Bobis. Sulit writes, "Narratives of trauma … become narratives of resiliency. Embodied in this resiliency lies the promise of recovery and of peace"—an apt metaphor for *Pinay Power* as a whole. Neferti Xina M. Tadiar's "Filipinas: 'Living in a Time of War'" is a very appropriate closing essay. This provocative example of peminist theorizing draws upon poetry by Pinay authors Elynia S. Mabanglo and Joi Barrios, art from the *Sino ka? Ano ka?* exhibition, and research about the experiences of Filipina overseas contract workers and challenges us to move beyond seeking simply further representation of Filipinas worldwide to examine the violent processes that create our circumstance as Pinays—even the ways in which we regard one another. To radically change these modes of seeing/understanding/relating, Tadiar claims, is to change our collective destiny as "fodder in a never-ending war."

Coda

In March 2004, I listened to my colleague A. Yemisi Jimoh deliver a powerful address, part of which read,

> Diaspora consciousness is a profound recognition of being part of an immense and harrowing breaking away … a mass psychological, perhaps even corporeal, desiderata for recovery of the missing parts. A New World state of mind, an Old World forgetting—to disremember, to be disremembered … dismembered—yes. And the blood …. It is not about the blood; it is not solely in the blood. It is beyond the political, cultural, or biological hybrid. Yet it is not simply in the mind either.
>
> Diaspora consciousness exceeds the binary, the double located in the one dark body, abandons the singular and personal struggle between self and power—empire, imperialism, colonialism, supremacy … instead, diaspora consciousness seeks to reconstruct the

disparate parts in order to revise, though refusing to forget, the old narrative that was inscribed upon the minds, scattered and, yes, scarred minds. Diaspora consciousness gives precedence to that embattled part of the divide—the sundered part within each dark body that is striving for its existence and against domination—and seeks to occlude the breech that separates the one dark body from others similarly besieged—divided, severed, ruptured, dispersed, though connected.[22]

Jimoh's evocative words touched me deeply as I recognized the similarities between her rendering of the African diaspora consciousness and the Filipina experience of diaspora that we have yet to claim—an experience we Filipina Americans try so hard to forget. I invoke Jimoh here because her words underscore why and how diaspora consciousness undergirds our continuing process of decolonization and becoming: relinquishing our reliance upon the schizophrenia of the perpetual present; resisting colonial mentality, deracination, and heteropatriarchal silencing; and refuting the model-minority stereotype of the obsequious, submissive, and/or exotic erotic. Indeed, the peminist essays in *Pinay Power* model diaspora consciousness to emphasize the commonalities of Pinay experience worldwide: how our identities, bodies, labor, art, activism, representation, sexuality, spirituality, family, community, and nation have been co-opted by a myriad of forces and how we have the power still to reclaim them. Thus, to reclaim and reconnect across/despite our diversity of experiences will be the best evidence of *Pinay Power* as Filipinas across the globe continue to resist and heal the fragmentation of imperial trauma, reimagining our future and "re-visioning" the Filipina image from the suffering, submissive Maria Clara to the twenty-first century peminist *babaylan* (priestess and healer).

In short, *Pinay Power* asserts the peminist presence—"loud, brown, and proud"—and signifies only the beginnings of the peminist revolution. May the essays here inspire you as you live the next chapters of our collective Pinay herstory. *Mabuhay!*

Melinda L. de Jesús
Phoenix, Arizona

Notes

1. Art critic Victoria Alba's exhibition essay for *Sino ka? Ano ka?* (accompanied by images by the artists Eliza Barrios, Terry Acebo Davis, Reanne Estrada, Johanna Poethig, Stephanie Syjuco, Lucille Tenazas, Catherine Wagner, and Jennifer Wofford), as well as essays on the exhibition by Neferti Tadiar and Celine Parreñas Shimizu, are included in this volume.
2. This monumental anthology, edited by Cherrie Moraga and Gloria Anzaldúa, is regarded as a foundational narrative of U.S. third world feminisms or feminisms of color; see Cherrie Moraga and Gloria Anzaldúa, eds., *This Bridge Called My Back: Writings by Radical Women of Color* (Latham, NY: Kitchen Table: Women of Color Press, 1983). Anzaldúa's subsequent anthology *Haciendo Caras: Making Face, Making Soul* includes two essays by Filipina

Americans; see Gloria Anzaldúa, ed., *Haciendo Caras: Making Face, Making Soul* (San Francisco: Aunt Lute, 1993). See also Chela Sandoval, "Mestizaje as Method: Feminists of Color Challenge the Canon," in *Living Chicana Theory,* ed. Carla Trujillo (Berkeley: Third Woman, 1998), 351–70, for a cogent history of U.S. third world feminist theory and a comprehensive bibliography of key writings by U.S. feminists of color.

3. Meena Alexander notes, "We have an ethnicity that breeds in the perpetual present and I think this is our great enticement and our challenge as Asian American artists." Alexander, quoted in Augie Tam, "Is There an Asian American Aesthetics?" in *Contemporary Asian America: A Multidisciplinary Reader,* Min Zhou and James V. Gatewood, ed. (New York: New York University Press, 2000), 629.

    Moreover, in his 1981 lecture "Postmodern and Consumer Society," Frederic Jameson asserts that "our entire contemporary social system has little by little begun to lose its capacity to retain its own past, has begun to live in a perpetual present" and compares the experience of the "perpetual present" to schizophrenia. See Jameson, "Postmodernism and Consumer Society," in *The Anti-Aesthetic: Essays on Postmodern Culture,* ed. Hal Foster (Port Townsend, Wash.: Bay, 1983), 125, 118.

4. Asia Source, "Asia Today Special Report: Asian Americans and Census 2000 Results, 30 May 2001" (New York: Asia Society, March 13, 2003; updated May 26, 2004). Available online at http://www.asiasource.org/news/at_mp_02.cfm?newsid=53011.

5. E. San Juan Jr., "The Predicament of Filipinos in the United States: 'Where Are You From? When Are You Going Back?'" in *The State of Asian America: Activism and Resistance in the 1990's,* ed. Karin Aguilar-San Juan (Boston: South End, 1994), 206.

6. Oscar Campomanes, "The Empire's Forgetful and Forgotten Citizens: Unrepresentability and Unassimilability in Filipino-American Postcolonialities," *Hitting Critical Mass: A Journal of Asian American Cultural Criticism* 2 no. 2 (1995): par. 37, 24–26 (online version). http://socrates.berkeley.edu/!crimass/v2n2/campomanesprint.html

7. Eric Gamalinda, "Myth, Memory, Myopia: Or, I May Be Brown but I Hear America Singing," in *Flippin': Filipinos on America,* ed. Luis Francia and Eric Gamalinda (Philadelphia: Temple University Press, 1996), 3.

8. Fred Cordova, *Filipinos: Forgotten Asian Americans—A Pictorial Essay* (Seattle: Demonstration Project for Asian Americans, 1983), 153.

9. Shirley Hune, "Introduction: Through 'Our' Eyes: Asian/Pacific Islander American Women's History," in *Asian/Pacific Islander American Women: A Historical Anthology,* ed. Shirley Hune and Gail Nomura (New York: New York University Press, 2004), 2.

10. Yen Le Espiritu, *Asian American Women and Men: Labor, Laws and Love* (Thousand Oaks, Calif.: Sage, 1997), 2.

11. According to Ninotchka Rosca, "A way has to be found to integrate the struggle against racism and sexism with the struggle for worker's emancipation … and with the struggle against imperialism." See Rosca, "Living in Two Time Zones," in *Legacy to Liberation: Politics and Culture of Revolutionary Asian Pacific America*, ed. Fred Ho (New York: Big Red Media, 2000), 87.

12. Lee writes, "What troubles me about this exciting debate over the changing grounds of Asian American political critique is that gender issues may take a secondary place, considered irrelevant or less important than these global debates over whether diaspora, exile, postcoloniality, or transnationalism shall replace the nation as an alternative identity formation for border-crossing Asians." See Rachel Lee, *The Americas of Asian American Literature: Gendered Fictions of Nation and Transnation* (Princeton, N.J.: Princeton University Press, 1999), 10.

13. See Asian Women United of California, ed., *Making Waves: An Anthology of Writing by and about Asian American Women* (Boston: Beacon, 1989); Elaine H. Kim, Lilia V. Nillanueva, and Asian Women United of California, eds., *Making More Waves: New Writing by Asian American Women* (Boston: Beacon, 1997); Sonia Shah, ed., *Dragon Ladies: Asian American Feminists Breathe Fire* (Boston: South End Press, 1997), and Linda Vo and Marian Sciachitano with Susan H. Armitage, Patricia Hart, and Karen Weathermon, eds., *Asian American Women: The Frontiers Anthology* (Lincoln: University of Nebraska Press, 2004).

14. While two Filipina/American literary anthologies have been published recently—Nick Carbo and Eileen Tabios, eds., *Babaylan: An Anthology of Filipina and Filipina American Writers,* ed. (San Francisco: Aunt Lute, 2000), and Marianne Villanueva and Virginia R. Cerenio, eds., *Going Home to a Landscape: Writing by Filipinas* (Corvallis, OR: Calyx Books,

2003)—Rhacel Salazar Parreñas's *Servants of Globalization* (Stanford, Calif.: Stanford University Press, 2001) and Catherine Ceniza Choy's *Empire of Care: Nursing and Migration in Filipino American History* (Durham, N.C.: Duke University, 2003) are the first book-length critical studies about Filipina/American migration and are crucial correctives to this invisibility. M. Evelina Galang's 1996 collection of stories, *Her Wild American Self* (Minneapolis: Coffeehouse Press, 1996), was one of the first literary representations of the Filipina American experience. Parreñas, Choy, and Galang each have essays in this volume.

15. Mitsuye Yamada, "Invisibility Is an Unnatural Disaster," in *This Bridge Called My Back: Writings by Radical Women of Color,* ed. Moraga and Anzaldúa, 40.

16. *Pinay* is Tagalog slang for "Filipina woman"; however, this term is used interchangeably with *Filipina* by Filipina Americans. In an e-mail to me (March 18, 2003), historian Dawn Mabalon traced the term's history:

> The origins of "Pinay" can be traced to the early migrations of Filipina/os to the United States … . [The term] has historically been used by Filipina/o Americans to denote Filipina/os either living in or born in the United States … . The term was/is in constant use in Filipina/o American communities from the 1920s to the present, and seemed to be particularly reclaimed and politicized by Filipina/o American activists and artists in the FilAm movements of the 60s/70s … . In more contemporary times, "Pinoy" and "Pinay" [are] used as slang by Filipina/os in the Philippines and the US to identify anyone of Filipina/o descent … . It's interesting how that term traveled from the United States back to the Philippines, and the controversies surrounding its usage in the 60s and 70s point to the ongoing issues surrounding class in Filipina/o American communities … . I LOVE the term "Pinay" because it's a term created by Filipina/o Americans early in the 20th century as a way to differentiate their identities and experiences from Filipina/os in the Philippines, and it's a very positive and affirming term in my own experiences.

17. *Pilipino/a* is a political and regional choice of self-naming grounded in the third world student movements of the late 1960s. The *p* over *f* choice may appear to be pedantically semantic; nevertheless, although specifically a California-based, working-class-identity politics, the renaming signifies the claiming of what is perceived to be the native *p* sound in resistance to the colonizer's *f* sound. Anthony Pido writes, "None of the seven major linguistic groups in the Philippines have an 'f' sound; the people refer to their country as *Pilipinas* and themselves as *Pilipino*." See Pido, "The Macro/Micro Dimensions of Pilipino Immigration to the United States," in *Filipino Americans: Transformation and Identity,* ed. Maria P. P. Root (Thousand Oaks, Calif.: Sage, 1997), 37 n. 1.

    Linguistically, the *f* sound derives from the Spanish colonizers that named the islands "Las Islas Filipinas" (after Philip of Spain); the American takeover of the islands in 1898 reinforced the imposition of the *f* sound via the Anglicizing of that term to "The Philippine Islands." For further discussion of this issue, see Campomanes, "The New Empire's Forgetful and Forgotten Citizens," nn. 17, 18, 22. http://socrates.berkeley.edu/!crimass/v2n2/campomanesprint.html

18. The fact of American imperialism in the Philippines distinguishes and complicates Filipino American history in relation to Asian American history because Asian American and Filipino American historiographies preclude or elide critical analyses of U.S. imperialism to privilege the immigrant narrative of "becoming American." This stance is very ironic, considering that the earliest Filipino immigrants, subjected to American cultural imperialism since the Philippine-American War, entered the United States as wards and nationals of the United States. See E. San Juan Jr.'s pointed and provocative critique of the Filipino American cultural nationalists' desire to "claim America" in "The Predicament of Filipinos in the United States."

19. Peminism resonates with U.S. third world feminist theory, as it is grounded in the exploration of the borderland space articulated by Gloria Anzaldúa and many other contemporary U.S. feminists of color. Anzaldúa maintains that "mestiza consciousness" offers new ways of being that transcend the oppositional forces/narratives that would divide us: "The new *mestiza* copes by developing a tolerance for contradictions, a tolerance for ambiguity … . She learns to juggle cultures. She has a plural personality, she operates in a pluralistic mode … . Not only does she sustain contradictions, she turns the ambivalence into something else." See Gloria Anzaldúa, *Borderlands: La Frontera* (San Francisco: Aunt Lute, 1987), 79.

20. I explore aspects of Filipina mestiza identity in "Liminality and Mestiza Consciousness in Lynda Barry's, *One Hundred Demons*," *MELUS Journal* 29, no. 1 (2004): 219–52.
21. Sarita See deftly summarizes these issues:

> I use the term "Filipino/American" to indicate both the presence of Filipinos in the United States and the imperial presence of the United States in the Philippines. This term encompasses minority racial status, colonial status, and the postcolonial legacy of invisibility produced by the amnesia that distinguishes U.S. history in relation to empire. Conceiving of the term Filipino/American solely as a designation of racial minority status risks repeating the erasure of a history of colonization, a massive omission that too typically characterizes many historical treatments of U.S. imperialism at the turn of the century. I would even argue that the terms "Filipino-American" and "Filipino American" are misleading and tautological, for being "Filipino" in some sense also means being "American," or to be more precise, a racialized subject of a U.S. colony. (The asymmetry of the rhetorical relationship between "Filipino" and "American" becomes clear when one realizes the inverse is ludicrous: being "American" emphatically does not always also mean being "Filipino".)

> See Sarita See, "An Open Wound: Colonial Melancholia and Contemporary Filipino/American Texts," in *Vestiges of War: The Philippine American War and the Aftermath of an Imperial Dream, 1899–1999*, ed. Angel Shaw and Luis Francia (New York: New York University Press, 2000), 396, n. 1.

22. A. Yemisi Jimoh, Plenary Panel, MELUS (Society for the Study of Multiethnic Literatures of the United States), University of Texas–San Antonio, March 2004.

I
Identity and Decolonization

1

A Personal Story:
On Becoming a Split Filipina Subject[1]

LENY MENDOZA STROBEL

Ever since Mount Pinatubo erupted in 1991, I have been trying to paint in my mind the new landscape of my hometown. The images of a merry childhood—the days of playing under moonlit nights, chasing each other's shadows—have come to this. Lahar changes the land and it changes the people. N. V. M. Gonzalez, a Filipino American writer, calls the Philippines "a lahar of colonizations."[2] The Filipinos tremble at the wrath of Apu Mallari, the god who dwells in the belly of the earth. And they call for repentance.

In the 1950s, San Fernando, Pampanga—a town fifteen miles southwest from Mount Pinatubo, ten miles south of Clark Air Force Base (the largest U.S. military base in Asia), and fifty miles north of Manila—was a growing rural town surrounded by farming and fishing barrios. We lived a mile away from the *municipio*, the town plaza, which was like any other plaza built during the Spanish colonial period. The Catholic church and its big courtyard faced the municipio. Outside the courtyard, in the open wet market, the fishermen and farmers brought their fresh catch and fresh produce and competed for the attention of the mother who carried a basket in one hand and a baby in the other. Across the wet market, the shoe, dry goods, and grocery stores owned by the Chinese merchants served the needs of the local elite who sought refuge inside the bazaars from the melee outside.

By the time I was born, the Methodist church had built a small church across the town plaza. It had no domes or turrets like the Catholic church—only a plain wooden cross without the crucified Christ atop the wooden scaffold beams where bats made their home by day. By night they hovered around the heads of Sunday night worshippers. I grew up in this church.

I was raised with white, middle-class, Protestant values in an animistic context by a Catholic mother and a Methodist father, both of whom had Chinese and Spanish ancestors. I didn't know it then but we were poor. But we had "class and good taste" and lived as genteel a lifestyle as possible, according to what we were taught by our colonizers was genteel and civilized. Thus, we had Friday evening concerts with music by Johann Sebastian Bach and Wolfgang

Amadeus Mozart, my mother on the piano and my brother on the violin. My sisters and I sang in harmony with Cole Porter and Irving Berlin.

Before we had television, our radio was always tuned in to Frank Sinatra, Nat King Cole, and sometimes to the Voice of America. Our reading fare was Hans Christian Andersen fairy tales, not Tagalog comics. We read English-language newspapers and magazines, not *Liwayway* and *Bulaklak*, which were read only by the *bakya* crowd, the common folk.[3]

We lived this lifestyle in the midst of a neighborhood where every afternoon the women sat in their front steps picking each other's lice while they talked about the latest *tsismis* (gossip)[4] and where the men squatted on the sidewalk stroking and cuddling their fighting cocks, drinking beer, smoking cigarettes, and telling ribald jokes punctuated by obscene words and gestures. Soap operas on the radios blared through open windows, for the women and men liked to keep track of their favorite soaps while they created their own in their huddles. Dogs, cats, and pigs roamed freely in this little hamlet and the horses that pulled the *calesas*, the horse carts, were fed in stalls built right outside the ten-foot-high cement walls of our backyard. Many of our neighbors were calesa drivers.

My world was inhabited also by spirits, superstitions, and omens. I heard ghost stories of visits from departed relatives or spirits possessing those who offend the gods. And then there were superstitions. When the cat washed itself, we were told to expect company. When our palms itched, we were told to anticipate money. When I swept the floors and moved the dirt toward the door, my mother scolded me for driving away good fortune.

My father drove this animist world underground. As Protestants, my father said, we were not to believe in these things. They did not exist; they were not real. Every night he led us in Bible readings and prayers. And every day my mother reminded us to be careful not to offend the spirits, not to cross their paths without asking permission, for she believed that the hills and the big narra trees were home to gnomes and dwarves. And the mythical *tikbalang* or the *aswang* would come and get little girls if they were not home by sundown.[5] These otherworldly creatures played an active role in our fearful imaginations as they were invoked in order to make us behave.

The shadow of Clark Air Force Base and the mystique of its isolation and separation by miles of barbed-wire fences and guarded military outposts awed us. Filipinos were allowed inside the base only once a year, on the Fourth of July. The one year when my family boarded one of the army buses for a tour of the base was highlighted by the gift of a brown lunch bag with an apple, an orange, and a hamburger wrapped in star-spangled blue and red.

In the 1960s, Peace Corps volunteers appeared in my high school. There was Mr. Sheehan, tall, pale, and lanky and full of condescending kindness on the little brown children who tugged at his sleeve as he walked to school every morning. There was Mr. Patrick, who had asked my older sister to teach him the famous bamboo dance, the *tinikling*. We still have a picture of him and my sister dancing … dancing his way into our hearts. *Oh, isn't that nice*, the ladies sighed, *that they are so interested in our folk dances.*

My mother had a pen pal, Miss Rose B. Mann, from Pennsylvania. I do not know how they came to correspond, but every year we looked forward to our Christmas package of old Christmas cards, secondhand clothes, bags, and old magazines. Packages from the States smelled fresh, earthy, and musky, and we sniffed and sniffed that odor out of the package. The States smell good and clean, we told ourselves. It must be heaven.

May is fiesta time. In San Fernando it was May 30. Evening processions of the Santo Nino and Virgen de los Remedios, of murmured Hail Marys and the pitter-patter of wooden *bakya* clogs on the asphalt pavement always silenced the onlooker. The light of flickering candles in the dark, veiled heads, and hands wrapped in rosary beads evoked feelings of awe and eeriness at the same time. Protestants didn't believe in saints, much less in processions and chanted prayers, so we watched "them" with the self-righteousness of the Pharisees.

Fiesta brought wanted and unwanted guests in the neighborhood—except to our home. Father forbade my mother to cook and forbade all of us from inviting relatives and friends. "Fiestas are for worshipping the saints," he said, "and we do not worship saints." And for many years, May was the saddest time of the year.

Things changed one day. My sister, who had been teaching Filipino culture at the dependents' school at Clark Air Force Base, met a Yankee from Maine. He was the school administrator. Unbeknownst to us, they had been dating. We eventually found out when my sister insisted that we should have a telephone. He kept the phone ringing. The mystery of this white man unraveled when my sister asked if she could invite him to the town fiesta.

Perhaps it made my father glad that this very important white man was interested in my sister. Although he relented cautiously about breaking a family nontradition, he soon found himself making plans to roast the pig he had been raising in the backyard. You see, my father raised pigs to supplement his income. In June, when school opened, he would sell the pigs so we could pay our tuition. That year, Junior the pig became the sacrificial one to honor the white man.

I was assigned to make sure the house was clean—especially the toilet and the toilet bowl. When no amount of muriatic acid would erase the yellow-stained bowl, my sister handed me a copper penny. Here, she said, use this to scrape the stain. I sweated for hours on my knees scraping the yellow. Yellow isn't good enough. Only white will do. I think this left a mark in my soul that I wouldn't understand for many, many years.

And so I made sure that I was liked by all the white missionaries and Peace Corps volunteers who came to visit us. Miss Hetty, a very old lady with silver hair, stood six feet tall. When she paid us a visit, she looked down on the bamboo floor and wondered if the thin slats would hold her up; they looked so frail and precarious. So she tiptoed ever so slightly and sat on a chair at the dining table, holding her weight up for fear that if it pulled her down she would fall through the floor. I do not remember if I liked her or not, for she did not smile very much. But I remember the white of her hair and the pale of her wrinkled skin.

This was the kind of regard and fascination I held toward the missionaries and the Peace Corps volunteers. My young adult life became a series of attempts to approximate whiteness and the symbols of that whiteness. I developed a taste for American fashion, food, music, and movies. I started calling my father and mother Mom and Dad instead of Tatang and Ima. We spoke in English even outside the classroom. My friends and I set ourselves apart from the bakya and we made sure that the dark and ugly did not become a part of our *barkada,* our circle of close friends.

Reaching out to white folks, hoping for whiteness to rub off, and testing one's self and measuring it by how well you could maintain their friendship and interest while waiting to hear some affirmation of your friendliness and the infamous "Filipino hospitality" became a full-time preoccupation. And sometimes you were rewarded by an invitation to their homes for dinner, for a ride in their cars (always on the way to a religious meeting), and sometimes to the exclusive country club surrounded by high walls and open only to white folks.

And so it came to pass. My American (mis)education became complete when I married a white man and came to live in the master's house. But this beginning also became the beginning of the end. A deafening dissonance was produced by shattered expectations and the failure of religious structures and cultural Christianity. Dissonance was produced by white folks' looks and malicious questions: Are you married to a GI? (read: Are you a prostitute?). Are you a mail-order bride? (read: Are you for sale?) Do you know of a maid? (read: Are you a domestic worker?). And when I was not mistaken for a Filipina, I was glad—Chinese, French Vietnamese, Japanese, or Korean but not Filipino, thank God!

There was nothing in my Protestant upbringing that prepared me for the silence of God to many of my questions. If I'm a child of God, why do I feel intimidated by white people who are better educated, talk faster, laugh louder? If I'm a child of God, how come white Christians do not treat me like one? How come they do not ask me intelligent questions? And why do they assume I'm a mail-order bride or married to a GI? If I'm a child of God, why am I not satisfied with spiritual answers to my questions?

There was no one to turn to and no one to talk to. My sister, who married the other white man, said, "It will take time. Don't worry, someday you will feel better." If I had waited passively for that day I would have ended in a mental asylum. I became angry at what I didn't understand, blamed myself, and blamed God for betraying me. How could He have brought me to this land only to shatter me and condemn me to live in confusion and utter despair amid a sea of white people who are as cold and distant as the gaze in their eyes? These people whom I have been taught to love, imitate, cherish, respect, envy—they had all betrayed me.

Do I not recite the pledge of allegiance? Do I not sing the "Star Spangled Banner"? I knew the Gettysburg Address by heart in fourth grade. Do I not know "Oh! Susana," "Michael Row Your Boat Ashore," "I've Been Working on the Railroad"? I even named my son after Dustin Hoffman. I adore Julie Andrews and Robert Redford, eat at McDonalds, and shop at K-Mart. Isn't that what being American is all about? Why then do you stare at me and ask me where I learned to sing your songs, to speak your language—not to mention George Frideric Handel's *Messiah* or the hymns of Charles Wesley?

> Remembering is never a quiet act of introspection or retrospection. It is a painful remembering, a putting together of the dismembered past to make sense of the trauma of the present.
>
> —Homi K. Bhabha, "Interrogating Identity:
> The Postcolonial Prerogative"

Nine years ago, in a conversation with a famous Christian writer, who I thought by virtue of his having lived as a missionary to Africa would understand my confusion and answer my questions, he said, "America is the greatest country in the world; therefore, third-world peoples look up to the United States; we become a frame of reference for everybody." My tacit agreement with this conclusion drove me farther into the abyss of feeling inferior and intimidated. From then on, there was nothing but the pressure to assimilate, act, and talk and walk like a white person. The resulting feelings of alienation were too heavy a price to pay. I stopped paying. I had to look elsewhere for the answers.

The thought of my grandmother often visited me in those days. Perhaps she was watching over me and wanted to remind me that I was loved. I thought of her and saw her in my mind as she strung the fragrant buds of sampaguita.[6] "Always gather the buds at dusk when their fragrance is not wasted in the heat of the sun," she said. And while I helped her string the fragrance, she would reach into her pouch and assemble her *maman*—betel nut, lye, and a green leaf as wrapper. She chopped the betel nut, spread a thin layer of the lye on the leaf, wrapped it, and put it in her mouth. And then she told stories.

I thought of my mother, a strong-willed woman with a quiet spirit. My mother does not talk much, perhaps because for fifty years my father has been doing all the talking for both of them and sometimes he even forgets to speak for my mother. In what other ways does my mother speak for herself? My mother has an independent spirit, a sense of self that is quiet and unobtrusive but knows how to have her way when she wants to. She will never give up teaching piano lessons, for that is her space. Making music and teaching music are hers alone. My father does not make music.

Thus, even while in the master's house, I learned to create a space where I was at home with my mother and grandmother. I rewrote their stories in my memory so I could see them in a new light. How did my mother create a life, paint her boxed-in world where the ancient spirits never died? How did my grandmother raise seven children by herself when her husband died young? How did my mother resist the negation of her Catholic faith and of her voice in a patriarchal home?

And what about my father? Will he ever find a place for himself outside the colonial gaze? Is there a space in himself where he is truly reconciled and at peace? Why, when he had the chance to live in the master's house, did he decide to go back home? Perhaps he, too, came face to face with the white master and shuddered at the thought of who he had become. He would resist by going home and making a promise never to set foot in the master's house again.

Slowly it dawned on me that I was tapping into an inner resource through my memories. This source was yet unnamed, but it whispered many things to my tired soul. The voice said, *Before there were Spaniards and Americans, there were peoples who sang, danced, lit the fire by night; and they told each other stories about Malakas at Maganda, about Biag-ni-Lam-Ang. There were women who healed, the* babaylans *and* katalonans, *women who tilled the land alongside the men, wove baskets, and cast bronze and silver into earrings and necklaces, armbands, and anklets.*

But these memories were faint. I do not remember much because these memories were buried underneath an avalanche of foreign words. What I knew and felt in my bones there was no word for—not in English, anyway. Is it possible? Is it possible that before we were colonized and were called people in the dark, lazy, backward, primitive, or monkeys we already knew the wisdom of the ancients and lived under the guidance of our *anitos,*[7] that we already knew who we were, until by the threat of hell and of guns, they told us we were not who we said we were and that we had better believe their definitions of us or they would kill us?

You are wild, they said. You need to be Christianized. You must get rid of your anitos, your superstitions. We will teach you how to become like us. We will unite your divided selves by giving you our language. We are your fathers; you are our children. By the grace of God, we will make you civilized yet!

And so we became like them.

I did.

There is freedom in that confession, that indeed the self that was constructed by the colonizers was a false self. I came to see that the damaged culture described by the colonizers was really a projection of their own failure at this grand imperial experiment. And I understood that when white people judge me harshly, it was because I reminded them of their own darkness, their own failure to heal the split in their own selves.

Now I laugh when I look at the sea of brown and yellow faces that stare back at the white man. The hordes they have condemned have followed them back into their own house, where there is no retreat, no escape. Go ahead, order your brides from the catalogs. You think that Filipinas are the last dream girls in the world? How naive you are! No one has learned how to subvert and resist the colonial gaze better than the mail-order bride. She will wise up eventually, if you don't kill her first; she will make sure you pay. Pay for what? Pay for your debts; your false promises. And she will offer herself as a sacrifice while she atones for the sins of those who came before her and died without repentance.

Yes, I know—there is anger and defiance in my voice. How can I help it? I have not spoken for centuries. I didn't know I had a voice. I didn't know I could speak. Must I now beg forgiveness for such outrageous rantings and ravings? Let me for a moment listen to my own voice and hear the timbre and resonance of my own truth, which has been denied for so long. Perhaps soon the anger will be spent and I will be able to move on.

Move on—to where? There is no place I could go where there is an escape from my split self. For I know the white father has become a part of me and I am in his shadow. I couldn't return the projected darkness without being torn apart. But I am learning not to internalize those dark projections anymore.

I am aware that in writing this autobiographical essay I am both unmasking the past without being free from the nostalgia of that past. My memory is selective, for there were wonderful moments in my childhood that I will always treasure. The wounds of its oppressiveness have been healed, but scars remain. There are wounds that still await justice and there are wounds that are better forgiven. But now the memory of the past can be informed by a consciousness that resists further mutilation.

This is also an attempt at simultaneous re-presentation: indigenization and multiculturality, the latter anchored in indigeneity in order to keep it centered and keep it from being dragged into the margins. Indigenization as a process, not as a complete return to a precolonial past, recognizes that—in a sense—"you can't go home again," but the process itself that requires the grasping of the process of psychological colonization/marginalization and the reconstruction of your own personal history means that now "you can take home with you wherever you are." It transforms consciousness.

In the collective consciousness of Filipinos, dislocation is assumed to be a natural state. We have learned not to take our identity crises seriously. We have learned instead to laugh, and sing, and dance, for it seems that these are the only permissible ways of asserting an identity. We often question ourselves on the worthiness of the struggle and resign ourselves to the hands of the gods. This is where the Catholic and Protestant Churches have attained a measure of "success," for by preaching sin and hell, churches appeal to the fatalistic and frightened consciousness of the oppressed. The promise of heaven becomes a relief for their existential fatigue. The more the masses are drowned in a culture of silence, the more they take refuge in churches that offer pie in the sky by and by. They see the church as a womb where they can hide from an oppressive society. In despising the world as one of vice, sin, and impurity, they are in one sense taking revenge on their oppressors. This directs their anger against the world instead of the social system that runs the world. By doing so, they hope to reach transcendence without passing the way of the mundane. The pain of domination leads them to accept this anesthesia with the hope that it will strengthen them to fight sin and the devil, leaving untouched the real source of oppression.[8]

What remains of the indigenous religious consciousness is played out in the realm of a surreal and metaphysical clinging to the spirit world while embracing its symbols now expressed by saints with Caucasian features and other catholicized animist rituals.[9] Their prayers are a desperate plea for miracles that will wipe out their oppressive poverty, only to be answered by the wrath of nature. The repression of the indigenous religious consciousness keeps them from making the connection between the wrath of nature and the actions of men who have raped the land and the people. What is then thought of as irreconcilable in this split is relegated to the sphere of the mysterious, where no one is responsible and no one is accountable.

Still, one must not discount the influence of indigeneity at the unconscious level, for even though, on the one hand, the colonization of Filipinos seems to be total, there remains an unarticulated/intuited sense of primordiality in their sense of self, something deeply rooted—the understanding of which is still in the process of being articulated. There is now a movement to return to our oral traditions and folklore in order to displace colonial narratives with our own. With a return to Filipino language(s) to define who we are on our own terms, it is now possible to reconstruct ethnic identity. Thus, the study of *loob* (the core of being), *kapwa* (the shared inner self), *diwa* (psyche), and other indigenous concepts has facilitated the articulation of Filipino values, displacing the colonizer's definitions of Filipinoness such as *hiya* (sense of shame), *utang na loob* (reciprocity), and *pakikisama* (smooth interpersonal relationship).[10] The use of Filipino language(s) as a framework opens up the access to the symbolic order where the historical determinism of colonialism is deconstructed.

How does a return to indigenous values facilitate multiculturality? How could it help Filipinos and Filipino Americans navigate in a pluralistic society?

The concept of borderlands, its multiple boundaries, interconnectedness, fluidity, and creativity, can be useful to Filipino Americans. There are many tongues, many geographic differences in customs and traditions, many class and generational differences. There are at least three kinds of Filipinos—the urban, the provincial, and the tribal. Filipino Americans derive a part of their identities from one of these groups. The other part of their identities is derived from white America—whether middle class, working class or upper middle class. Add to these the cultural characteristics passed down through miscegenation from the Chinese, Spanish, Japanese, Muslims, Americans, and other cultural groups. But the indigenous consciousness expressed in diva, kapwa, and loob is what finally gives shape to Filipino character, cultural values, and traditions. In the U.S. context, to be effective in navigating the borders, Filipino Americans must first undergo the decolonization process through the reclamation of indigenous values.

Colonization has overdetermined Filipinos from without. We are not only born split, but we are also born on the border. But perhaps the resiliency, the will to survive, the ability to sing and make merry comes from this indigeneity. In the Western context, where responses to the colonizer have been judged inadequate, ineffective, marginal, or born of obsequiousness, resistance and defiance undergird it. Whether this is connected to a metaphysical belief in cosmic justice, to existential fatigue, or to the strength of the indigenous imagination can be ascertained only by Filipinos themselves. Perhaps it is all of these.

Filipino psychology and philosophy studies assert that Filipinos have a holistic worldview that is derived from the sense of the self as a whole. We perceive ourselves as holistic from an interior dimension operating under harmony (*loob*). We perceive ourselves as people who feel, people who will, people who think, and people who act as a whole. Many Filipino languages are nonlinear and vertical; there is no separation of subject and object and there are usually no gender distinctions. Filipinos uses poetic speech, which is rooted in a spiritual consciousness that is affective and nondiscursive and where objective and subjective reality, the world and the soul, coexist separately.[11] The core concept of *loob* has dual dimensions—*loob* (interiority) and *labas* (exteriority); these dimensions are deployed, often as accomodative tools under colonization.

This articulation of Filipino psychology is empowering and liberating. What was before known only intuitively is now validated by discourse. What has seemed impossible—due to the lahar of colonizations—as the ethnic identity project has become possible by reclaiming the indigeneity of our own tongues. The narrative of the colonizers that has dominated our colonial history and educational system is being displaced by a decolonized discourse. The past twenty years in the Philippines have seen the rise of postcolonial writings and the indigenization of the social sciences.

In the United States, a growing sense of cultural nationalism among Filipino Americans as a result of having access to indigenous psychology has been a way of suturing the split self—not only a suturing but also a defiant way of resistance to total assimilation. While remaining conscious of the limits to assimilation imposed by racism and applying the learned strategies of navigating in the dominant culture, a reconstructed identity replaces the obsequious, inferior identity, which before had no conscious access to its own strength and integrity.

The reconstruction of Filipino American identity through indigenization positions itself within the emerging transformation of the dialectics between master and slave, center and margin, and subject and other. The return to ethnicity/indigenization as an antidote to alienation of the colonized self is facilitated and mediated by this process while at the same time participating in the creation of new spaces that would transform the dominating culture.

The Filipino American's ability to maintain a *both/and* sense of belonging to a homeland and to an adopted culture is born out of the holistic sense of self that enables one to live on the border without becoming schizophrenic. This ability is aided by the break from historical determinations and psychological definitions imposed from the West and its grounding on an indigenous, albeit syncretic, culture. The reclaimed sense of ethnic self must be nurtured lest it be obliterated by the new discourses of postmodernity, where fluidity is always privileged. One must question the emerging concepts of deterritorializations of space, cultures, and nations.

Who is advocating deterritorializations, and for whom? How would these proposed reconfigurations empower third world peoples who are still fighting for their rights in their own territories? We must always be suspicious of concepts formulated by Western anthropologists, in the name of interdependence and interconnectedness, as we must also be wary of the same tendencies of emerging economies in Southeast Asia to exploit the weaker economies and natural resources in the same region.

We must also question whether it is really possible at this historical moment to have no grounding reference to a determining culture or history in the postmodern experiment. In the Philippines (in a postcolonial context), where the displacement of colonizers' narratives is a fairly recent development, new narratives formulated by Filipinos for ourselves must be allowed to sink and take root in the collective consciousness of the people without losing track of how the postmodern dialogue is trying to erase notions of rootedness and transcendence.

Growing ethnic awareness must also give way to a broader understanding of power differences within the local context, as well as within the context of an emerging global culture. The cultivation of the ethnic self is only one of many strategies for positioning oneself in the fluid borders that are still constrained by dominant structures. The stabilization of ethnic identity for Filipino Americans has a healing and transformative potential in the memory of a people who had been deeply violated.

On a global scale, the international diaspora of Filipinos must be seen in the context of our search for a home. For many, the economic conditions of the Philippines can hardly be called home—pushing hundreds of thousands of men and women (primarily) to seek economic relief elsewhere in order to provide a home for the families they left behind in the Philippines. This diaspora must also be seen in the historical context of our imbalance as a result of colonialism/imperialism and the displacement of the self through negation by the master's narratives. That this diaspora is perceived by the Philippine government as its own version of "foreign aid" is symptomatic of a consciousness that remains uncritical of its marginal situatedness. The paradox of the "colonized taking care of the colonizer" is being played out in hospitals and convalescent homes, where Filipino nurses abound; in Europe and in the United States, where Filipino nannies and domestic workers are taking care of other people's children It is evident in Japan's Filipino entertainers and in Denmark and Australia's Filipino mail-order brides, who provide caretaking services, especially to men. This is the most stark and depressing legacy of colonization as a patriarchal legacy—the exploitation of women.

The drive to live in the master's house is also symbolic of the desire to become like the master. Our colonized consciousness has convinced us that *to be* is *to be like the master*. To be Filipino is not good enough—or so we we have been taught (or coerced) to believe. It is a reflection of the internalization of the dark shadows projected by the colonizer onto the colonized. These are shadows from which there is no escape, shadows that will keep haunting until they are withdrawn, atoned for, and integrated within the colonizer's self.

Just as the lahar from Mount Pinatubo is expected to bury most of the surrounding areas within a ten-mile radius in the next five years, the lahar of colonizations that has buried the Philippines for centuries still drowns many Filipinos in colonial consciousness. Where there is hope, however, is in the growing indigenization movement, which reconstructs a strong sense of identity and ascribes that identity with its own integrity so that it may take its rightful place in the global community. It is also this sense of self that enables it to reject the projections of the colonizer without the effect of reversal. This self does not negate itself, but accepts its difference from others. It has a voice and it speaks in its own language.

Mount Pinatubo slept for six hundred years. While it slept, it provided a home for the Aetas, the first inhabitants of Luzon. On its slopes they planted, hunted, and lived undisturbed for centuries. In the lowlands, the volcano also provided a home for Clark Air Force Base and an entire city that supported this vast colonial/military enterprise—mostly by catering to the instincts of men. Mount Pinatubo's eruption displaced both the Aetas and the air base. This rupture, literally and metaphorically, brings about an ambivalent struggle that calls for negotiation. Now that the tribal peoples have been forced to the lowlands, should they now assimilate? Or should they be relocated (assuming space is available) and allowed to continue a tribal existence? Can they go home again?

The Americans were finally ejected, not by political negotiation but by the wrath of nature. Filipinos see this as poetic justice. But the question cannot be ignored: What will replace the displaced economy? And there is still an even bigger question: Now that Filipinos no longer have the master to blame, will we make it on our own? The master may have left, but he also left behind a long colonial legacy.

Within a postcolonial context, Filipinos must continue to undo the colonial gaze. Within the postmodern context, Filipinos may yet find ourselves navigating the fluid borders with resilience (as we have always done) and with a newly reclaimed sense of integrity in a decolonized consciousness.

Notes

1. The following articles helped me in coming to terms with the decolonization process: Akhil Gupta and James Ferguson, "Beyond Culture: Space, Identity and the Politics of Difference," *Cultural Anthropology* 7, no. 1 (1992): 6–23; Dagmar Hoffman-Axthelm, "Identity and Reality: The End of the Philosophical Immigration Officer," in *Modernity and Identity*, ed. Scott Lash and Jonathan Friedman (Oxford: Blackwell, 1992), 196–217; David Lloyd, "Race under Representation," *Oxford Literary Review* 13, nos. 1–2 (1991): 62–94; Lisa Malkki, "National Geographic: The Rooting of Peoples and the Territorialization of National Identity among Scholars and Refugees," *Cultural Anthropology* 7, no. 1 (1992): 24–42; George Marcus, "Past, Present and Emergent Identities: Requirements for Ethnographies of Late Century Modernity Worldwide," in Scott Lash and Jonathan Friedman, eds., *Modernity and Identity*, 309–30; R. Radhakrishnan, "Ethnicity in an Age of Diaspora," *Transition*, no. 54 (1991): 104–15; Brackette Willliams, "A Class Act: Anthropology and the Race to Nation across Ethnic Terrain," *Annual Review of Anthropology* 18, no. 1 (1989): 401–44.
2. Nestor V. Madale Gonzalez, "Even as a Mountain Speaks," in *The Novel of Justice: Selected Essays 1968–1994*. (Pasig City, Philippines: Anvil Publishing, 1996), 105.
3. *Bakya* are wooden clogs, practical footwear for warm and sunny days as well as for rain and flood weather. The notion of the bakya crowd as a means of describing the common folk has its origins in these clogs.
4. In an oral, highly contextual culture, *tsismis* symbolizes many levels of interacting, social bonding, or an indirect manner of communicating—more than just gossip.
5. The *tikbalang* is a tall, hairy, half-horse, half-human creature that inhabits the forest; the *aswang* is usually a female creature that can sever her upper body from her lower body, grow batlike wings and fangs, and fly around at night stalking victims for blood and revenge.
6. The sampaguita is the national flower of the Philippines, a tiny, white, usually single-petaled flower often strung into a necklace; it has a very delicate, sweet fragrance.
7. The *anitos* are the pantheon of gods in the kingdom of Bathala (God), and also one's spirit ancestors.
8. Paulo Freire, *The Politics of Education*, trans. Donaldo Macedo (New York: Bergin and Garvey, 1985).
9. Melba P. Maggay, "The Indigenous Religious Consciousness," *PATMOS Magazine* (Manila: Institute for Studies in Asian Church and Culture) 96, no. 2 (1990).
10. Virgilio Enriquez, *From Colonial to Liberation Psychology* (Quezan City: University of the Philippines Press, 1992).
11. Leonardo Mercado, *Elements of Filipino Philosophy* (Tacloban City, Philippines: Divine Word University Press, 1976).

2

Not Just My Closet:
Exposing Familial, Cultural, and
Imperial Skeletons

LINDA M. PIERCE

> To decolonize is to tell and write one's own story, that in the telling and
> writing others may be encouraged to tell their own.
>
> —Leny Mendoza Strobel, "Coming Full Circle," 66

During a conference last year, I was told that identity politics were no longer relevant—that strategic essentialisms had been replaced with color-blind academic theory, in what I can only assume to be a research-based meritocracy. This implied dichotomy between the politics of identity and a "valid" base of theory and research invokes the classic divide between the personal and the political. Although women's studies scholars first debunked this split decades ago, this deconstructed knowledge needs to be consistently reiterated in order to combat its hegemonic opposition. Feminist and critical race studies scholars concerned with U.S. decolonization must continue to emphasize the connection between personal and cultural histories in order to underscore the notion of privilege and accountability. Thinking about how my personal or family history relates to my cultural history begs questions of nationalism, imperialism, global capitalism, patriarchy, militarism, colonization, and white supremacy. Ignoring the politics of my identity only exempts me from social responsibility, prevents me from examining my own complicity in status quo structures of imperialism, and slows the movement for change. And theorizing the politics of my identity effectively initiates a process of decolonization that is critical to my ability to survive and thrive in the United States.

Claiming an Inheritance

Being a Filipina American, or Pinay, means being colonized—first by Spain and then by the United States—and although you may not have been alive or present for the process of colonization, you experience the fallout nonetheless.

31

In her introduction to *Filipino Americans: Transformation and Identity*, Filipino studies critic Maria P. P. Root explains, "The traumas associated with colonization that lasted almost 400 years scarred us all, regardless of our nativity, language, class, or gender. Trauma fragments and fractures the essence of our being and self-knowledge; it disconnects us from each other."[1] Regardless of your nativity, your memories are colonized. You are born into trauma without an initial understanding of or hermeneutic for your fragmented self and you must work diligently just to explain your own life—to recognize and name your scars, to educate yourself about your specific cultural history and uncover its connections to your subjectivity. The ideologies of your family are colonized, and even your own thoughts and actions are colonized, despite your initial unawareness of the systematic forces at work in the simple procedures of your daily life.

Being born into a colonized family, you inherit the ideals and learn the narrative of colonization; as you come into consciousness, you are immersed in the promises of each colonizer, from the benefits of Spanish patriarchy, aristocracy, and religious authority to the promises of U.S. education, opportunity, and meritocracy. Author and activist Nilda Rimonte describes the powerful influence of Spanish colonial ideologies in her article "Colonialism's Legacy: The Inferiorizing of the Filipino." Referencing the lasting effects of the mythologies justifying religious imperialism, Rimonte explains, "So pervasive and persistent is this golden legend that anyone growing up in the Philippines breathes it in with the air itself."[2] Your parents and grandparents, having inhaled the air in the Philippines with slow and deep breaths, raise you with certain "givens"—known variables that are less of a conscious understanding and more of a subtle awareness—like the act of breathing itself. Whether these givens are transplanted or born onto U.S. soil, they develop and change along with new, previously unknown variables. Your understanding of gender, economics, race, and immigration comes with an acute awareness of U.S. privilege that is at once critical and optimistic—you are defined by this contradiction, simultaneously Filipina and American, simultaneously pessimistic and hopeful.

Being a Filipina American means being postcolonial—after colonization, but certainly not over colonization. It means constantly negotiating neo- and postcolonial identities and filtering out latent Spanish colonial ideals and inherited American colonial ideals from the ideals that you struggle daily to prioritize intellectually. Being Pinay means learning how to decolonize your mind, from the necessary steps involved both in beginning and continuing that process. In her article "Coming Full Circle: Narratives of Decolonization among Post-1965 Filipino Americans," Filipino studies critic Leny Mendoza Strobel notes, "Decolonization is a psychological and physical process that enables the colonized to understand and overcome the depths of alienation and marginalization caused by colonization. By transforming consciousness through the reclamation of one's cultural self and the recovery and healing of traumatic memory, the colonized can become agents of their own destiny. Decolonization is a necessary phase in the development of a healthy Filipino American cultural identity in the United States."[3] Being Pinay thus means having a relationship to decolonization: whether active or passive, engaged, conflicted, opposed, or in denial, the relationship is automatic (and sometimes uninvited) by virtue of living in America. It means a constant awareness of "Philippine-ness" in America, awareness of systems of colonial imperialism, awareness of which generation you or your family members were American born, awareness of the obstacles that your family has had and continues to face, awareness of your relationship to others.

Finally, being mestiza means struggling between physical and metaphysical cultural borders, struggling to maintain a consistent and coherent identity despite the fact that the dominant culture attempts to disaggregate you and recognize only what it considers the most "valuable" parts of yourself at every given turn. You personify the colonizer at the same time that you are colonized; you participate in the colonization of yourself; and, as Filipino studies critic Vicente Rafael points out in his acclaimed book *White Love, and Other Events in Filipino History*, you "invoke the legacy of the ilustrados" grounded in elitist structures of Spanish colonialism.[4] You embody privilege, which is considered either detestable or enviable—and sometimes both at once—depending on your audience. Root explains that part of the mestizo identity is being "regarded as less authentic by some, yet enviable by others."[5] Your enviable status derives from privilege and marks you as complicit in hegemonic structures of racial and economic oppression. Your light skin serves as a daily reminder of your privilege and accountability, of your complicated status as "woman of color," of your responsibilities as scholar and activist.

Through the process of decolonization, you come to realize that the aspects of your identity that you had long taken for granted are actually tied to global discourses of colonial imperialism. As you recover colonial history, you are startled at how easily it explains pieces of your life. As Root notes, in a passage that would seem to explain pieces of my own life, "Four hundred years of combined colonization, first by Spain and then by the United States, widened the Filipino gene pool with the possibility of lighter skin, hair, and eyes. The tools of colonization gave meaning to the variation in physical appearance among Filipinos. Spain introduced colorism; preferential treatment was clearly associated with lighter skin color. Centuries of this education primed the Filipino for vulnerability to internalize American rules of race. Colorism and then racism inculcated the notions: 'White is beautiful,' 'White is intelligent,' and 'White is powerful' in the psyches of many brown-hued Filipinos, thus inferiorizing the Filipino."[6] You come to understand that your life, your family, your day-to-day interactions that were once so personal are actually part and parcel of particular social constructions of race, gender, class, and nation. You inherit these struggles by virtue of being born. And then—only after processing painful emotions, uncovering relevant historical context, and recognizing your relationship to others in the trajectory of the past and present—you begin to comprehend your life. You are exhausted. But now you are ready to begin.

Decolonization: Piecing Together Fragments of a Personal History

I developed an internalized understanding of the systematic privileging of whiteness in Pinay culture long before I was capable of intellectualizing it. In fact, long before I was born, the privileging of whiteness occupied a distinct place in the cultural memories I would soon inherit—memories both general and specific, systematic and personal. My late grandfather, Papa, was half German, half Irish and noted in the family for his dashing good looks; there had always been an unspoken consensus that Mama, a Filipina of both Spanish and Tagalog descent, had "married up." As it was always already present in our family's collective consciousness, I was born into this consensus and inherited the memory as if it were my own. She had snagged an American, a handsome, young, blonde-haired, blue-eyed American soldier near the end of World War II, and she was "lucky" to get him because he was seven years younger and she was a widowed mother of two.

In his article "The Quiet Immigration: Foreign Spouses of U.S. Citizens, 1945–1985" Michael Thornton explains, "Following World War II, marriage rates between people of various cultural, national, and racial heritages increased dramatically."[7] The marriage of white American men to Filipino women increased in particular, in part because of the U.S. military presence in the Pacific. However, in 1944 when my grandparents wed in the Philippines, U.S. antimiscegenation laws were still in full force, Filipina/o immigration was capped at fifty persons per year, and acceptance of interracial and cross-cultural marriages was not prevalent. Mama told me that she married him, in part, because she felt she owed him a debt of gratitude for saving her from the Japanese. She points to one of my aunts, my *titas*, who still bears the scars on her body that remind her of Japanese occupation. The Schmidt-Douglas household that raised Papa wholly agreed that Mama was lucky to get him; they helped shape the family's consensus that she had married up by rejecting the union and refusing to accept the brown woman and her brown children who existed only in a faraway place. He was so young and handsome; he was throwing away his life, they said. The marriage probably wasn't legitimate any-way, they protested, since it occurred in the Philippines. No one would hold him to these obligations, no one would blame him for his youthful mistake. He could come back now and still undo the damage. The message was clear: she was not worthy. But there was definitely hope for the offspring of the deLeon-Douglas clan; he would make us worthy.

The desire to "outmarry" is not unique to my *pamilya* (family): the yearning to move up and the move that equates "up" with "out" of one's race is endemic to the colonial complex. In "Images, Roles, and Expectations of Filipino Americans by Filipino Americans," Filipino/a community activists Allan L. Bergano and Barbara L. Bergano-Kinney cite a young Filipina American living on the East Coast; in a personal interview, the young woman explained, "Because of the American colonization process, Filipinas are being taught that 'marrying up' means 'marrying white.'"[8] When consistently faced with messages that you are backward, inferior, barbaric, and uncivilized—and then promised that there is an alternative—it is tempting to opt for that alternative, at first. However, the alternative—assimilation—implies assimilation *into* something, some normative standard or ideal. Socially, politically, and historically that ideal has been to assimilate to whiteness; when dealing with "outmarriage," such assimilation promises to be an actual possibility. In her book *Racially Mixed People in America*, Maria P. P. Root has problematized the notion of outmarriage by arguing that the term itself reflects "the internalization of dichotomous rules regarding group belonging."[9] To move *out* of a group implies that there exists some sort of contained place *within* the group, invoking notions of racial purity or ethnic legitimacy defined by constructed racial borders. The problems with the term *outmarriage* become further complicated within the Philippine context; Filipinas longing to "outmarry" with white Americans occupy a unique position informed by ideologies, education, economics, and politics—specifically those colonial and neocolonial. One cannot discuss Filipina outmarriage without considering the colonial context; for many Filipinas, marrying "out" meant out of an economic caste, out of an institutional, internalized, colonial sense of inferiority, and out of the Philippines.

Moving out of the Philippines was another one of those familial "givens"—as soon as Mama married the American soldier, it was known that the family was bound for the States. The U.S. government shared in this consensus: given the increased U.S. military presence in the Philippines during the war, the government recognized the propensity for Filipina–American intermarriage and changed immigration quotas to accommodate the Filipina war bride. Mama was then able to come to the States with her husband, and their children were born "half American." As Root explains, "[F]ollowing World War II, and particularly the Korean War, the Filipina war bride entered the United States exempted from immigration quotas through the Soldier Brides Act of 1947. During this period of time, a generation of Filipinos, many of whom were born in the Philippines of white American fathers, emerged.[10]

Mama and Papa's children would hold dual citizenship until the age of twenty-one, when they would be forced choose an allegiance, declare loyalty to one nation under God, and forfeit their claims to another. When Papa's family refused to recognize his new brown wife, however, the soldier turned temporary expatriate and decided to stay in the Philippines as an act of defiance. He immersed himself in Filipino culture, learned to speak Tagalog "like a native," and raised eight children with Mama over the next twenty years. The six children that they bore together grew up with the consciousness that they were "half American" and, although nobody said these specific words out loud, it was understood that the significance was found in the meaning: "half American" meant "half white." Being American carried some distinctive virtues—promises, mostly—such as the promise of economic opportunity, the promise of equal treatment under the law, and the promise of each individual's right to pursue happiness. Of course, these promises are inextricably tied to the value of whiteness; the history of the United States is a long and repetitive narrative of the inaccessibility of the promises of the American dream to many people and communities of color. Being "half white" had specific social and economic value for Mama and Papa's offspring, of which the children themselves developed an acute and internalized awareness from their earliest days. Of all of their children, my mother turned out to be the most fair-skinned, a quality that brought national notoriety, movie stardom, and economic success.

By the time she was a teenager, my mother was already an icon in the Philippines: first discovered at a Halloween Dance-o-Rama contest, she later won the title of Junior Miss Philippines at the tender age of thirteen—a contest that narrowed down the finalists to "the ten fairest." Like something straight out of a Disney film—and no less important, a cartoon—young Filipinas were competing to be "the fairest of them all." The virtues that afforded my mother success in Philippine beauty pageants were distinctly tied to the genes inherited from her blue-eyed American father. As my mother catapulted to success in Philippine film, becoming a wildly popular movie star, the news clippings described her best assets as having "mestiza beauty," being "fair and lovely," and even "statuesque," towering over her Filipina costars at her staggering height of five foot four.

My mother was not only praised but also rewarded for her fair skin—socially as well as economically. She was taught to protect it, carry an umbrella to shield her skin from the hot tropical sun, and never stay outdoors for too long. She went to great lengths in order to preserve this most valuable asset, and she carried these values with her as she migrated to the States. When I was growing up in the cloudy state of Washington, I remember her leaving a towel in the car in order to shield her left arm from any sun that might color it when she sat in the driver's seat. A natural performer, she would only agree to sing karaoke with the family if the microphone had an "echo" function that would hide her accent. And when she visited me years later in Tucson, Arizona, during a summer high of 125 degrees, she wore long pants at all times rather than expose her legs to the browning effects of the sun. Most of these subtle acts had become normalized in my adolescence, a routine part of growing up that I always found curious, but I had yet to intellectualize them.

What I had still to learn were the ways in which these seemingly individual experiences in my personal history were located within a larger history. As Leny Mendoza Strobel explains, "Decolonization is the ability to tell one's story in a manner that makes sense and makes meaning out of all the experiences of the past. To locate one's personal history within the history of the community is to find the relationship between the self, the nation, and narration. The story of the self contains the narrative of the nation. To tell one's story is to allow the fragments of consciousness to be sutured and healed so that the Filipino story can be told in its wholeness."[11] Piecing together the fragments of my own story helped me to understand the narratives of community and nation critical to colonization (and, subsequently, decolonization). The politics of my identity are meaningful when understood as belonging to more than just me or my pamilya and extending beyond the life histories of my grandparents and great-grandparents into a colonial history spanning four hundred years.

The project of piecing together fragments of my personal history was made easier in the context of others' histories. In her article "Mestiza Girlhood: Interracial Families in Chicago's Filipino American Community since 1925," Barbara M. Posadas narrates the descriptions of Filipino adolescence revealed in personal interviews with families in Chicago. Posada explains, "[A]s adolescents they spent their summers avoiding the darkening effects of the sun."[12] Allan L. Bergano and Barbara L. Bergano-Kinney's article "Images, Roles, and Expectations of Filipino Americans by Filipino Americans" adds testimony from a personal interview conducted with a Filipina from the East Coast, now living in Manila. Their subject explains, "Marrying a white man for Filipinas is a step up … socially and economically. Mixed children by white men here [in the Philippines] are thought of as more valuable, precious, and better prepared for modern society. This mentality isn't new. Many of the elders here believe 'White is right.' All white boyfriends, husbands, and mixed children are shown off here as trophies."[13]

My mother's status as mestiza helped launch her as the ultimate "trophy": the movie star. Seeing reflections of my family history in the stories of other Filipina Americans betrays the larger trajectory of colonialism and the ways in which it has collided with my life experiences. Moreover, understanding how colonialism's privileging of whiteness extends into non-Filipino communities of color helps us, as Strobel has noted, "find the relationship between ourselves, the nation, and narration." The importance of theorizing our personal histories is crucial, not only to understanding ourselves but to the larger project of decolonization. Contextualizing my mother's seemingly instinctive privileging of whiteness within larger, oppressive economic and colonial structures effectively moves the discussion away from the demonization of the colonized, toward positive strategies for change.

Giving Voice to the Skeletons

Although I was beginning to understand my mother's experience by situating it within these larger frameworks, it was slightly different for me. As Michael Thornton has found, "The largest proportion [of multiracial children] lie in Asian White households."[14] As a multiracial child born in the United States, I am closer to the white cultural norm to which my *pamilya* had been taught to ascribe. I don't have an accent; I am the beneficiary of the American public education system; there is no apparent reason why I should not succeed. At first, success meant the same thing in America as it had for the *pamilya* in the Philippines: beauty. Among my cousins I was "the fairest of them all," so the pamilya declared me the next Miss America. I was uncooperative in this venture, preferring instead to bury myself in books. When I began to have serious boyfriends during college, the first question was always, "What color eyes does he have?" The goal was a blue-eyed grandchild; this would be the ultimate testament to the *pamilya's* success in America.

Even in middle school I knew there was something wrong with this privileging of whiteness, and although I was an obvious recipient of such privileging in my family, it made me uncomfortable. The fact that I was so explicitly privileged in this way only elucidated the ways in which my mother, my older brother, my grandmother, some of my cousins, and many of my titas and uncles were disadvantaged for the very same reasons. It was personal: I could only enjoy my privilege at the expense of the people I loved, those who raised me, sacrificed for me, and taught me the value of family. I began to understand why these ideas were "curious"—in fact, quite problematic—and I struggled to unlearn these normative values. It took me a while, however, to begin this process, as I did not yet understand the systematic nature of my family's problems. I understood how my family had internalized notions of racial inferiority and subsequently viewed miscegenation as some sort of salvation, but I thought this phenomenon was unique to my family. I felt anger and shame, which initially silenced me—I didn't want anyone to know about the way my family privileged whiteness. It was wrong, it was an embarrassment; it was a skeleton in our closet.

It was not until I entered the university system that I began to unpack some of these issues. In her book *Outlaw Culture: Resisting Representations*, acclaimed critic bell hooks describes her work as "a kind of theorizing through autobiography or storytelling."[15] I needed to theorize my autobiography in order to acquire meaning that was historically contextualized rather than merely self-indulgent. Seeking out this theoretical framework, I turned to postcolonial studies; to my surprise, foundational critics like Aimé Césaire, Frantz Fanon, and Albert Memmi wrote narrative and theory that was not only compelling but also seemed to apply directly to my life.[16] Memmi suggested that although colonized peoples traditionally respond to their oppressive situation in two different ways—assimilation or revolt—the attempt at assimilation is particularly complex and problematic given that the colonized would have to "adopt his own condemnation" in order to assimilate.[17] It became clear that we had all, in fact, been adopting our own condemnation, and this realization was accompanied by a conscious drive to decolonize. Providing historical context and connections, bell hooks explains how the Black Power movement of the 1960s had also turned to postcolonial theory; specifically, "Reading Frantz Fanon and Albert Memmi, our leaders began to speak of colonization and the need to decolonize our minds and imaginations .... That meant establishing a politics of representation that would both critique and integrate ideals of personal beauty and desirability informed by racist standards, and put in place progressive black standards, a system of valuation that would embrace a diversity of black looks."[18] Notions of "personal" beauty with which I had been struggling were, in fact, overtly political and tied to a politics of representation that is steeped in the context of global imperialism. I realized that maintaining my silence—keeping my skeletons in the closet—only served to help mask this larger context. So I began to talk.

During my undergraduate years, a Filipino American Student Association (FASA) chapter formed at my university; this space changed everything, for it was here that I started talking to others about my family, and I quickly met with the startling realization that I was not alone. My friends had such similar experiences growing up—especially in mixed families—that I finally began to see how we were implicated in a larger system, how my family values were connected to centuries of colonialism and how they fit into critical race theory. Most of all, I began to understand the need to decolonize. As Strobel explains, "To decolonize is to be able to name internalized oppression, shame, inferiority, confusion, anger."[19] Once I could name my shame and recognize its constructed origins—recognize that the skeletons in my closet did not belong to me alone—I could reject internalized notions of superiority and inferiority, sort out my confusion, and find constructive methods for channeling my anger into proactive work.

Of course, this realization was bittersweet; I felt validated by the fact that there were others like me but angered by the fact that there were others going through similar or worse experiences. My anger served to motivate me to read, theorize, and talk. I read Gloria Anzaldúa, Chrystos, Jessica Hagedorn, and bell hooks. I theorized my personal history and began to understand my family in a whole new way. I talked to other women of color and found that this privileging of whiteness (or "lightness") exceeded not only my own family space but my cultural space as well. My Ethiopian roommate in college explained to me that she, too, carried umbrellas, wore long sleeves in the summer, and stayed out of the sun on beautiful days because her mother had always privileged her mocha skin and warned her to protect herself from getting any darker. I felt compelled to explore more critical race discourses to help develop my sense of the systematic elements of this process. Before long, I was drawn to Nobel Prize–winning author Toni Morrison.

In her novel *The Bluest Eye* Morrison tells the story of a young African American girl's desire for blue eyes in early 1940s Ohio.[20] In her afterword, Morrison explains that the novel was written based on an actual desire expressed by a peer in elementary school. Morrison found this desire problematic even as a child, and writes that "twenty years later I was still wondering about how one learns that. Who told her? Who made her feel that it was better to be a freak than what she was? Who had looked at her and found her so wanting, so small a weight on the beauty scale?"[21] This spoke to me: "better to be a freak than what she was." Better for my mother to wear a towel on her arm while driving, better to wear heavy jeans in 125-degree heat, better to layer on white foundation makeup than to simply be who she was. Although I had certainly noticed the privileging of whiteness and recognized that it was problematic, I had never before asked Morrison's important question: who made her feel this way? Once, my mother had forgotten to replace the towel in her car after she had taken it in for a washing; it was a sunny day, and my usually pale mother's arm turned brown in a matter of hours. "See? I told you," I remember her saying. "I have to be careful about this. I can get brown very easily." Where did she learn that brown was somehow less desirable? "Who told her?"

The question became bigger than my familial experience when I read more about others' experiences. In her article "Filipino American Identity: Transcending the Crisis," scholar Linda A. Revilla notes, "The irony of mixed-heritage Filipinos not being accepted as Filipinos is exposed when one considers the pains that Filipinos in the Philippines and abroad take to maintain a standard of appearance that has its roots in colonization: for example, keeping out of the sun so as not to get 'too dark' or pinching the nose to make it less flat."[22]

Staying out of the sun and pinching the nose were all too familiar practices, but the discovery was that these practices extended beyond the scope of my experience. That these "standards of appearance" have roots in colonization reinforces bell hooks's assertion that notions of personal beauty are steeped in a politics of representation. The question is much bigger than "Who told my mother that brown was less desirable?" The question is "Who told *us all?*" *The Bluest Eye* is Morrison's attempt not only to highlight these problems and ask these questions, but also to answer them. She explains, "The assertion of racial beauty was not a reaction to the self-mocking, humorous critique of cultural/racial foibles common in all groups, but against the damaging internalization of assumptions of immutable inferiority originating in an outside gaze."[23] An outside gaze, of course—we were not born with an instinct to privilege whiteness; this was a learned phenomenon.

Morrison's fiction provides multiple sources for this gaze, from the actual gaze emanating from people who have internalized notions of superiority to the manufacturing of dolls, billboards, plastic cups, and Hollywood movies that valorize representations of whiteness. Morrison writes, "Adults, older girls, shops, magazines, newspapers, window signs—all the world had agreed that a blue-eyed, yellow-haired, pink-skinned doll was what every girl child treasured."[24] Even candy wrappers represented whiteness. As Morrison explains, "Each pale yellow wrapper has a picture on it. A picture of little Mary Jane, for whom the candy is named. Smiling white face. Blond hair in gentle disarray, blue eyes looking at her out of a world of clean comfort. The eyes are petulant, mischievous. To Pecola they are simply pretty. She eats the candy, and its sweetness is good. To eat the candy is to somehow eat the eyes, eat Mary Jane. Love Mary Jane. Be Mary Jane."[25] This "simply pretty" picture of blond Mary Jane on candy wrappers, representing the "sweetness" essentially characterizing little girls, is emblematic of the colonized subject's inability to escape racial representations, even in seemingly arbitrary packaging. Of course, the packaging is anything but arbitrary; the picture of Mary Jane is explicitly tied to the historical convergence of racism and capitalist imperialism.

The wrapping and packaging of soap, biscuits, tea, and chocolate by enterprises like the nineteenth-century, British-owned East Africa Company serves as a cultural predecessor to the twentieth-century Mary Jane candy wrapper. In his book *Representation: Cultural Representations and Signifying Practices*, noted critic Stuart Hall explains that the owner of the East Africa Company believed that the spread of commodities would make "civilization in Africa inevitable …." The gallery of imperial heroes and their masculine exploits in "Darkest Africa" were immortalized on matchboxes, needle cases, toothpaste pots, pencil boxes, cigarette packets, board games, paperweights, and sheet music. "Images of colonial conquest were stamped on soap boxes," Hall notes, "[on] biscuit tins, whiskey bottles, tea tins and chocolate bars …. No preexisting form of organized racism had ever before been able to reach so large and so differentiated a mass of the populace."[26] The mass marketing of racism employed by enterprises of colonial imperialism produced multiple effects: it initiated the systematic devaluation of people of color; it fused the binary opposition of "civilized" versus "primitive" to constructions of race; it tied successful capitalist marketing strategies to techniques that reinforced and exploited existing racial categories; and it reproduced these images en masse so that they became globally pervasive.

The move from the nineteenth to the twentieth century included the slow transition from the minstrelesque images on soap wrappers, tea tins, and chocolate boxes to the oppositional representation of Mary Jane. After a century of hegemonic representations of "primitive" inferiority, certainly enough time for some of these images to become internalized, the twentieth century has mass-produced images largely invested in the prescribed "alternative": the valorization of whiteness. How do we then begin to deconstruct such a powerful, ubiquitous gaze as this?

As I began searching for an answer to this question, I discovered an article in *Filipinas* magazine called "Do the White Thing," which described the skyrocketing sales of skin-whitening creams in the Philippines. As one of Allan L. Bergano and Barbara L. Bergano-Kinney's interview subjects confirms, "I cannot tell you how many products are advertised and sold here [in the Philippines] to 'whiten' our skin."[27] The story in *Filipinas* was especially significant, first because it explained that the success of skin whiteners reflects a lingering colonial mentality; second, because as long as these products have been in demand, there has also been staunch resistance from Filipino social reformers; and third, because despite initial imperialist sympathy from critics in the United States, once news of these products hit CNN, the whitening creams were in demand in America as well. The article points out that, although "the manufacturers say surveys show that most Filipino women would rather have whiter skin … it's hard to find a woman who'll admit to using their products."[28] This denial is significant in that it underscores the fact that there is a level of awareness that the desire for lighter skin is problematic—women are reluctant to admit their use of the product because they know their desire is somehow fraught. Again I thought of Morrison's question, "Who had looked at her and found her so wanting, so small a weight on the beauty scale?"[29] Why would a Filipina pay to bleach her skin, despite the possibility of hazardous side effects? Presumably she thinks the risk is worth it, but where did she learn this? Who had looked at her and found her so wanting? Why would she take this risk, then hide the secret in her closet?

Denial of one's internalized oppression helps sustain the colonial complex. The systematic, imperial whitewashing occurring globally is so difficult to deconstruct, precisely because it is global; since the outside gaze is panoptic, an oppositional gaze or gazes of resistance are necessary on a broad base. I revisited my initial reaction—silence—and realized that the first step away from denial was to help break that silence on a larger, institutionalized scale. I started openly talking about this cultural phenomenon, writing about it, incorporating it into the classes I teach and raising the issue at conferences, often in the face of those who frowned upon my discussion of "identity politics." In my classes, students were relieved to be addressing some of the complex issues surrounding race, privilege, and systems of power. Students of color expressed to me that they, too, had thought this was their family's "skeleton in the closet" and were stunned to find that they were not alone, that these notions originated in an outside gaze, and that the gaze was in fact systematic. These realizations were bittersweet for my students, much like they were for me—the moment these students realize that they are not alone, shame dissipates but then quickly turns into anger, rage, and frustration. I try to steer my students into the types of spaces that the FASA chapter was for me—spaces where they feel comfortable talking about these experiences, problematizing, discovering, and rediscovering themselves together. I tell them to keep talking about it, to begin healing, to take action. When we give voice to the skeletons in our closets, they speak volumes—announcing why they are silent and who silenced them in the first place. And unless we give voice to these skeletons, they will stay closeted, along with the shame and confusion that can accompany family secrets.

Decolonization is a painstakingly slow process, often because the path is not quite linear: denial, lack of information, and the stronghold of colonial ideologies can slow the process to such an extent that new levels of consciousness for the colonized are often accepted only provisionally at first. As Memmi explains, "So then, no doubt provisionally, the colonized admits that he corresponds to that picture of himself that the colonizer has thrust upon him. He is starting a new life but continues to subscribe to the colonizer's deception."[30] The "start" of decolonization, then, is often coterminous with contradictory colonial ideologies. Often, decolonization begins with one step forward and two steps back, but there are spaces—in our classrooms, in our literature, and in our honest conversations with one another—where it can begin. As Strobel explains, "To decolonize is to ask: Where do I go from here?"[31]

Where I go first is out of my closet, bringing my skeletons along with me and interrogating the reasons why they were hidden in the first place. I insist on giving voice to these skeletons, in part by seeking out others' stories and acknowledging that the skeletons are not mine alone; I insist on examining the politics of my identity, and what is more, I insist that you examine yours. Only when we have all uncovered our location in the trajectory of colonial imperialism, when we have theorized our life experiences, considered our positions of complicity, and begun implementing strategies for resistance can we heal the traumas that have, variously, affected us all. As Strobel suggests, "To reclaim memory at the personal level is to engage in the process of creating a collective memory of a people's history."[32] The project of decolonization is both personal and political; it hinges on identity politics, interrogated and contextualized. Once we recognize these skeletons as existing not just in our own individual, familial, or even cultural closets, we can begin to expose them as for what they are: imperial skeletons encouraging silence and self-loathing. It's time to start cleaning out our closets.

Notes

1. Maria P. P. Root, ed., *Filipino Americans: Transformation and Identity* (London: Sage, 1997), xi.
2. Nilda Rimonte, "Colonialism's Legacy: The Inferiorizing of the Filipino," in Root, ed., *Filipino Americans*, 40.
3. Leny Mendoza Strobel, "Coming Full Circle: Narratives of Decolonization among Post-1965 Filipino Americans," in Root, ed., *Filipino Americans*, 64.
4. Vicente Rafael, *White Love, and Other Events in Filipino History* (Durham, N.C.: Duke University Press, 2000), 165.
5. Root, "Contemporary Mixed-Heritage Filipino Americans: Fighting Colonized Identities," in Root, ed., *Filipino Americans*, 83.

6. Ibid., 81.
7. Michael Thornton, "The Quiet Immigration: Foreign Spouses of U.S. Citizens, 1945–1985," in *Racially Mixed People in America,* ed. Maria P. P. Root (Newbury Park, Calif.: Sage, 1992), 64.
8. Allan L. Bergano and Barbara L. Bergano-Kinney, "Images, Roles, and Expectations of Filipino Americans by Filipino Americans," in Root, ed., *Filipino Americans,* 202.
9. Root also complicates her argument by discussing the implications of the term *outmarriage* for multiracial persons: "From some perspectives, almost all marriages for multiracial people will be outmarriages in some sense." See Maria P. P. Root, "Back to the Drawing Board: Methodological Issues in Research on Multiracial People," in *Racially Mixed People in America,* ed. Maria P. P. Root (Newbury Park, Calif.: Sage Publications, 1992), 188.
10. Root, "Contemporary, Mixed-Heritage Filipino Americans," 85.
11. Strobel, "Coming Full Circle," 70.
12. Barbara M. Posadas, "Mestiza Girlhood: Interracial Families in Chicago's Filipino American Community since 1925," in *Making Waves: An Anthology of Writings by and About Asian American Women,* ed. Asian Women United of California (Boston: Beacon, 1989), 278.
13. Bergano and Bergano-Kinney, "Images, Roles, and Expectations," 202.
14. Thornton, "The Quiet Immigration," 74.
15. bell hooks, *Outlaw Culture: Resisting Representations* (New York: Routledge, 1994), 209.
16. Aimé Césaire, *Discourse on Colonialism* (New York: Monthly Review, 1972); Frantz Fanon, *Black Skin White Masks* (New York: Grove, 1967); Albert Memmi, *The Colonizer and the Colonized* (Boston: Beacon, 1965).
17. Memmi, *The Colonizer,* 121.
18. hooks, *Outlaw Culture,* 173.
19. Strobel, "Coming Full Circle," 66.
20. Toni Morrison, *The Bluest Eye* (New York: Plume, 1993).
21. Toni Morrison, "Afterword," in *The Bluest Eye,* 210.
22. Linda A. Revilla, "Filipino American Identity: Transcending the Crisis," in Root, ed., *Filipino Americans,* 107–8.
23. Morrison, "Afterword," 210.
24. Morrison, *The Bluest Eye,* 20.
25. Ibid., 50
26. Stuart Hall, "The Spectacle of the 'Other,'" in *Representation: Cultural Representations and Signifying Practices,* ed. Stuart Hall (London: Sage, 1997), 240.
27. Bergano and Bergano-Kinney, "Images, Roles, and Expectations," 202.
28. Mynardo Macaraig, "Do the White Thing," *Filipinas,* March 1996, 57.
29. Morrison, "Afterword," 210.
30. Memmi, *The Colonizer,* 137.
31. Strobel, "Coming Full Circle," 66.
32. Ibid., 73.

3

Fictions of Assimilation: Nancy Drew, Cultural Imperialism, and the Filipina/American Experience

MELINDA L. DE JESÚS

I was raised a parochial-school, steel-town girl, the third of four sisters, in one of the "gritty cities" of eastern Pennsylvania in the 1970s. My girlfriends and I, like countless others across the United States, shared a love of Abba and the Bay City Rollers, *The Brady Bunch* and *The Partridge Family,* Leif Garrett and Andy Gibb, clogs and Bonne Bell Lipsmackers. We held myriad sleepovers where we never really slept, logged endless hours talking on the phone; we hated our piano teachers, babysat, and shopped at the mall. We read *Seventeen* magazine and religiously attended Girl Scout meetings. Forever clad in our boring parochial-school plaid uniforms (complete with Peter Pan–collar blouses), we were besotted with our young female lay teachers who wore stylish platform shoes and let us try them on. We were into *Godspell* and Catholic Youth Organization activities and some of us wanted to be nuns.

Between third and fifth grades we began that awkward transition between girlhood and womanhood and our first inklings of adolescence were characterized by anxiety over menstruation, bras, body hair, and breasts. Moreover, what had once been a relentless competition *with* boys for academic and athletic superiority turned into a confusing competition *between* girls for a boy's attention. In response we immersed ourselves in the world of Nancy Drew: unflappable, sophisticated Nancy always outsmarted the boys and got things done. She exhibited the supreme confidence that we lacked yet so desired.

Our love for Nancy bordered on obsession: we reveled in the minute details of her life and would devour each of her mysteries, frantically trading them with each other while keeping careful track of which mysteries remained unread. We were devout fans of her television show and used our Nancy Drew lunch boxes with pride. Thus, Nancy Drew mystery books provided a communal experience for us preadolescents. Through the familiar, lulling surety of these formulaic mysteries—Nancy's predictable "adventures" were always capped with her triumphant successes—we vicariously explored adulthood even as we clung, however tenuously, onto the more neatly delineated life we were leaving behind—the safety of girlhood.

However, there is an interesting complication to these wistful reminiscences. My fellow acolytes in the cult of Nancy Drew—Joni, Cindy, Mary Jo, Tina, Patti, Diane, Suzanne, Pam, Carla, and Molly—were all of Pennsylvania Dutch, Irish, Italian, German, or Slovak descent. I was the only Filipina—indeed the only girl of color in my parochial elementary school, my family the only "nonwhite" family in my entire neighborhood. Thus, I am forced to ask, how did the specificity of white consciousness impact the construction of our girls' culture? Did race make a difference in terms of my relationship to Nancy Drew? I believe so. While my girlfriends and I gleaned important messages about female agency through reading Nancy Drew books, my close identification with the girl supersleuth had a specific impact upon my psyche as a Filipina, which I will explore in this essay.

Feminist assessments of the fictional teen detective Nancy Drew depict her as an important role model for generations of American women. Like many girls, my love of Nancy Drew was a maternal legacy; however, my mother is a Filipina raised during the American regime in the Philippines. What enabled both my mother and me to identify so strongly with this blond, blue-eyed sleuth and her exciting adventures? Below I explore the parameters of my mother's and my own investment in Nancy Drew. Highlighting the Filipina/American experience and drawing upon Filipino American history and feminist criticism, I delineate how the *Nancy Drew Mystery Series*—a cultural phenomenon steeped in and intent upon defending white Anglo-Saxon Protestant (WASP) values, introduced to the islands via the imposed American educational system—furthered the aims of "benevolent assimilation" in the Philippines through American cultural imperialism and internal colonization.[1]

In the Shadow of the "Famous Girl Detective"

As my sisters had done before me, from about third through fifth grades I was obsessed with reading every single volume of the *Nancy Drew Mystery Series*. Like many generations of American girls, I would voraciously devour one satisfyingly hair-raising mystery a day, content in the knowledge that my idol, the shrewd, fashionable, "titian-haired" Nancy, along with trusty sidekicks Bess and George, would be around tomorrow with yet another mystery to solve. Moreover, after grueling indoor soccer practices on Tuesday nights, I remember begging my father to rush me home so I would not miss the new *Hardy Boys/Nancy Drew* television program. During this period, prior to moving on to the infamous Judy Blume books, I read several other detective series—those of the Bobbsey Twins, the Hardy Boys, Cherry Ames, Vicki Barr, Judy Bolton, and the Dana Girls—yet Nancy reigned supreme. She held an important place in my imagination and became an impossible role model of brains, guts, and honor combined with impeccable manners and style. So great was her imprint upon me that as an angst-ridden sixteen-year-old, I wrote the following poem:

Fuck off, Nancy Drew
Fuck off, Nancy Drew
and your famous father, Carson Drew
the prominent lawyer of River Heights
and your housekeeper, Hannah Gruen
who has loved and cared for you since your mother died
and your perfect boyfriend, Ned Nickerson
the scholar athlete of Emerson College
Were you ever suicidal?
Did you ever shoplift?
Ever run off to Phillipsburg, NJ
to drink Molsons in the parking lot of some dingy warehouse?
What did you do when your blue roadster broke down
or when there were no more mysteries to be found?
You had all the answers—
but the questions aren't the same anymore!
You outsmarted Mrs. Tino,
saved Bess from the abductors
And never smeared your mascara.
Your clothes were always impeccable
though your hair changed like the weather—
titian, strawberry blond, auburn.
You deceived me—
you and your two best friends,
Bess and George, the sycophants.
Life was one big party for you, Nancy
But not for me.
All your problems solved within two hundred pages.
Did you ever lose your virginity?
Did you ever get drunk and throw up?
Did you ever fight with your dad and wish he were dead?
Nancy, you never told us
that detectives could feel so shitty.
I always believed that you were real
But you never lived outside "The Nancy Drew Mystery Series."
Now I'm left to solve it all by myself
Me, famous girl detective
In my own shiny blue roadster
Without a damn clue at all.

While certainly melodramatic, the poem illustrates how my strong identification with Nancy turned to bitter disillusionment about her and her simple world as I aged. Outgrowing and discarding childhood idols is a part of adolescence; however, in retrospect, given my training as a literary and cultural critic, an Asian American feminist and scholar, it seems improbable that I could have identified so deeply with Nancy Drew. Thus, the real mystery alluded to in the last four lines of my poem would be the following: how did a brown Pinay like myself come to identify so much with this WASP girl detective?[2] Furthermore, how could my valorization of Nancy Drew as role model ever lead me to a coherent sense of self as a Filipina American feminist? These are not rhetorical questions when one begins to consider the intense cultural dominance of the United States in the Philippines and how the *Nancy Drew Mystery Series*, imported as part of the American-imposed educational system, functioned as one aspect of "social engineering" in the Americanization of Filipino culture.[3]

Importing the Stars and Stripes: Education and Cultural Imperialism

As civilian government replaced military rule in the islands after the Philippine-American War, the U.S. government enacted an intensive program of social engineering. Its goal, the complete Americanization of the entire population, was promulgated by the arrival of hundreds of American teachers to the islands (called "Thomasites") whose mission was "to impart Western civilization to Filipinos under a policy of 'benevolent assimilation' and political tutelage."[4] The American public school system introduced throughout the islands revised existing Filipino educational models and curriculum and mandated English as the official language of instruction.[5] Thus, "infected with colonial culture and with grand illusions about the United States, Filipinos soon started to migrate to what they had been taught to think of as the land of opportunity and fair play."[6] These Filipino laborers, recruited in the 1920s and 1930s for cannery and fieldwork, unlike most Asian immigrants, were thoroughly Americanized.

Unfortunately, the optimistic *manongs* arrived in the United States during a period of intense anti-Asian sentiment and, although wards and nationals of the States, at the time found themselves subjected to the same patterns of Asian exclusion suffered by Chinese, Japanese, Koreans, and Asian Indians before them.[7] Politically disenfranchised—denied land ownership, citizenship, and education—and mired at the bottom of the labor market in "stoop labor," *manongs* endured racist stereotyping as "savages" or "sex-crazed monkeys" who threatened white female purity and thus were subject to miscegenation laws.[8] Author Carlos Bulosan, in his 1943 novel *America Is in the Heart*, sums up the harsh discrepancy between the Filipino dream of America and the reality of Filipino reception in America.[9] Fraught with images of deracination, homelessness, despair and loneliness, poverty, and disillusionment, Bulosan describes the migratory, violent lives of the manongs through a mind-numbing catalog of place names, murders, beatings, and riots. It fascinates me to think of Bulosan and my mother as contemporaries of sorts, subjects of the same Americanization process that engenders within them the same dream. While she, a well-to-do mestiza in Baguio, dreamt of becoming American, Bulosan, subjected to the brutal migratory life of the manong farmworker, continued to search for the America he had been promised back in the islands.

Nancy Drew, Mom, and Me

My mother, Eloisa, passed on her love of Nancy Drew to my sisters and me. We all admired Nancy Drew's image as the smart, levelheaded, feisty girl detective that was fearless, gracious, and well-dressed. For my mom, especially, the image of American girlhood freedom was especially attractive: Nancy drove herself about unchaperoned and lived an exciting, adventure-filled yet wholesome life far beyond the reality of patriarchal Filipino society (which dictated Filipina responsibilities to home and to the Church), beyond the realities of the Japanese occupation. Underscoring these qualities, however, my mother insisted that Nancy had one overriding attraction: She was American, and everyone wanted to be American.

However, Mom's family had not always embraced Americanization. Her maternal great-uncle, Maximo Angeles, fought alongside Emilio Aguinaldo, leader of the Filipino revolutionary nationalistic group *Katipunan,* for Filipino sovereignty, first against Spain (1896) and later against the United States in the Philippine-American War (1898–1901). By the time of my mother's childhood in Baguio (1932–1944), the family's legacy of resistance had changed radically. Her father, José Domingo, was a staunch supporter of American innovation, investments, and culture. Mom attended a private school run by the Belgian Missionary Canonesses of St. Augustine; there she raided the school's library for the Bobbsey Twins and Nancy Drew mysteries and later for those by Zane Grey, Louisa May Alcott, Frances Hodgson Burnett, and Sir Walter Scott. Mom was discouraged from reading vernacular Ilocano or Tagalog magazines and fondly remembers reading the *Saturday Evening Post.*

My mother's family's paradigmatic shift from resisting the imposition of American culture via imperialism to valorizing/reifying the importation of American culture, I believe, is cemented in the following story. After the liberation from Japanese occupation, U.S. soldiers came by to ask my grandfather what his children might need. The next day, service men returned with American cultural artifacts: V-discs (special records shipped to the troops), magazines, and books. It is telling that my mother remembers being thankful not for the food and clothing the Americans would supply, but for the American culture denied her during the occupation. Here the process of Americanization is completed: recapturing the Philippines, Americans reestablished cultural supremacy and the war-weary Filipinos were thankful.[10]

Mom taught English and home economics at Holy Family College in Baguio before her marriage and relocation to the United States in 1958. In this sense, what had been for my mother a desired, imagined construct (Nancy Drew's American lifestyle) became a reality for me: as part of my family's first American-born generation, the literal terrain of the *Nancy Drew Mystery Series* became my own. Indeed, the fictional River Heights could easily be my own hometown along the Lehigh River, complete with the requisite winding back roads, quaint towns, and mysterious mansions. Thus, mom's vision of American girlhood was truly realized for her daughters; her sharing of her love of Nancy Drew mysteries only reinforced this fact.

Recently I asked my mother if she remembered being bothered by Nancy's being a "white girl." Mom maintained that she never noticed Nancy's whiteness; she "just became her." For me, however, growing up in a racially segregated community, my reading and identifying with Nancy Drew entailed complex negotiations with my American and Filipino identities that resulted in the negation of myself as Filipina in order to be the "American girl." For both of us, then, identifying with Nancy Drew entailed an erasure and subsuming into whiteness, an integral process of internal colonization, which I will outline herein.

Fictions of Assimilation: Nancy Drew and Hegemonic Feminism

Carolyn Heilbrun writes, in "Nancy Drew: A Moment in Feminist History," "[Nancy's] class and the fact of her ready money and upper-middle-class WASP assumptions are what make her an embarrassment today. The question is, should we therefore dismiss her as predominantly an embarrassment, a moment in the history of feminism of which we are now ashamed?"[11] Answering her own question, Heilbrun admonishes that "there is a danger that we critics, with our close analytical machinery and our explorations of social and economic conditions, will damage the original Nancy Drew books … looking for things that they do not and cannot offer, while failing to see and praise their real qualities."[12]

Thus, she and other authors in Carolyn Stewart Dyer and Nancy Tillman Romalov's collection *Rediscovering Nancy Drew* maintain that we can appreciate Nancy Drew for what she inspired, and that what might be construed as Nancy's shortcomings in our current political climate should not negate our love for her. As Heilbrun notes, "By the 1990s we have learned that no woman can speak for all women. Certainly Nancy Drew cannot speak for women of color or poor women."[13] Nevertheless, reading the *Nancy Drew Mystery Series* as a tool of American cultural imperialism, a fiction of assimilation imported to the Philippines as part of the "civilization" process, radically complicates such feminist desire for nostalgia. Indeed, how benign are these texts when they are employed to inculcate a desire for American culture and whiteness? Given the reality of forced cultural assimilation in the Philippines, how can we begin to assess the value of Nancy Drew as a feminist role model for Filipinas or other women of color?

I contend that Heilbrun's recuperation of the image of Nancy Drew, while seeming to gesture toward consciousness of race and class differences, once again inscribes the imperialistic stance of the United States in relation to the Filipina/American experience. The ease of this racist stance is compounded when we consider how the realities of Filipina/American culture often conspire to prevent recognition and resistance to modes of hegemonic feminist domination. Pinay feminist Delia D. Aguilar writes, "What I am attempting to stress here is that our colonial mentality makes it almost second nature for us to assume the persona of our colonizer. Consequently, our susceptibility to conceptions of shared sisterhood among all women merely acts to reinforce our neocolonial standing …. This can explain our inability as Filipinos, unless residence in the United States and elsewhere has educated us, to discern racism in the conduct of those whose mission is to uplift and enlighten us."[14] Aguilar exhorts Filipinas to reject the "colonial predisposition toward self-erasure," as well as the "unrehabilitated colonial outlook," which "makes us very vulnerable to the influx of ideas … the uncritical acceptance of which could signify nothing more than a feminist replication of neocolonialism."[15]

Through her pointed consideration of Filipina/American realities, Aguilar emphasizes how Filipina feminism demands a mode of vigilance and resistance to both internal colonialism (colonial mentality) and a hegemonic feminism that seeks to incorporate us and erase our very existence within its blinding whiteness. Moreover, Aguilar underscores that feminists like Heilbrun must begin to acknowledge how simplistic invocations of "sisterhood" merely accentuate hegemonic feminism's complicity in maintaining white dominance. Thus, a truly "global" feminist theory would incorporate attention to the circulation of ideologies as well as to the complex personal negotiations we ourselves make within competing modes of power—for example, patriarchy, white supremacy, compulsory heterosexuality, classism, and imperialism.

Thus, for Filipinas, Nancy Drew books, circulated by the grade school and public libraries established by the American-imposed educational system and also readily available in local bookstores, become the means by which the Americanization of Filipino culture is accomplished. As fictions of assimilation, created and imported by American colonizers to promulgate American cultural dominance in the islands, Nancy Drew books inculcate affiliations with and yearnings for an American femininity implicitly valorized as "white." Emphasized throughout these books is the pervasive positing of WASP culture and values as normative. In this sense, it is easy to see how Nancy Drew functions as another facet of cultural imperialism through engendering childhood identifications with and strong desires to *be* Nancy Drew.

Revisiting River Heights: Rereading *The Mystery at Lilac Inn* and *The Clue of the Leaning Chimney*

Scholars of children's serial detective fiction have analyzed the *Nancy Drew Mystery Series'* place within the "Stratemeyer Syndicate." Founded by Edward Stratemeyer in the early 1900s, this virtual empire of serial children's novels was produced with factorylike efficiency by the syndicate's hired stable of ghostwriters (this same process continues today).[16] The Stratemeyer Syndicate created almost all of the most popular children's series books (those of Nancy Drew, the Hardy Boys, and the Bobbsey Twins), thus controlling the series-fiction market as well as the imaginations of generations of ten- and eleven-year-olds. The implicit goal of Stratemeyer series books was to inculcate American children into middle-class values and behavior, even as librarians decried their "racy" plots. However, how did these same goals translate to colonies of the United States? What are the implications of these texts within the economy of cultural persuasion in the Philippines, which was based on capitulation to American ideologies? Specifically, what vision of America is available in the *Nancy Drew Mystery Series*? How did/do Nancy Drew books promulgate American cultural values and expectations of social relations?[17]

Bobbie Ann Mason, in *The Girl Sleuth,* sums up the world of Nancy Drew as follows: "[T]he original Nancy Drew series—the first thirty-five or so volumes which accumulated throughout the 1930s, 1940s, and 1950s—portrays a fading aristocracy, threatened by the restless lower classes .... When minorities know their place, Nancy treats them graciously .... Nancy's job is to preserve the class lines, and for her the defense of property and station are inextricably linked with purity and reputation. She defends beautiful objects, places, and treasures from violence."[18]

Mason's reading seemed harsh until I myself reread *The Mystery at Lilac Inn.*[19] Seeking to discern the overall vision of America and American girlhood in the *Nancy Drew Mystery Series*, I was astounded by what I found versus what I had remembered. My gentle remembrance of Nancy—as a thoughtful, modest, young woman—was replaced by the image of a snobbish, icy, Daddy's girl. Less American girl-next-door than Carson Drew's confidante and hostess, she epitomizes WASP privilege and its wealthy suburban lifestyle. *The Mystery at Lilac Inn* details not only Nancy's search to find Emily Crandall's stolen fortune in jewels but also describes the sleuth's irksome search for a temporary housekeeper.

Nancy's interactions with possible housekeepers demonstrates how the series' authors reinscribed the racist politics of the period: white is right and non-WASPS are unattractive or suspicious. The first example is a very stereotypical description of an African American woman whom Nancy dismisses in disgust; we read, "As she opened the door her heart sank within her. It was indeed the colored woman sent by the employment agency, but a more unlikely housekeeper Nancy had never seen. She was dirty and slovenly in appearance and had an unpleasant way of shuffling her feet when she walked."[20] The second applicant for the housekeeping job, Mary Mason, is described as "a tall, wiry, dark-complexioned girl who was obviously the one sent from the agency. She had dark piercing eyes and stared at Nancy almost impudently."[21]

Again, Mason succinctly describes the significance of this characterization, noting, "Appearances are never deceptive in Nancy's Ivory-pure life. Good and evil are strictly white and black terms. Criminals are dark-hued and poor …. Piercing dark eyes are the most common characteristic of Nancy's foes. Their greedy eyes are piercing because they are disrespectful, gazing threateningly beyond their station, perhaps seeing through the façades of the gentry whose power they crave."[22] Thus, readers of the series come to recognize that Mary's "dusky" complexion, "piercing eyes," and impudent manner clearly mark her as a criminal in the world of Nancy Drew.

Similarly, in "Nancy Drew and the Myth of White Supremacy," Donnarae MacCann delineates the white supremacist consensus concerning the natural inferiority of African Americans, which she then contextualizes to the overtly racist depiction of the black caretaker in *The Secret of the Old Clock*, the original volume of the Nancy Drew series penned by Stratemeyer himself. She writes, "The author presents him as a drunkard, a liar, a person who has constant run-ins with the police, an unreliable employee, and a fool. As you watch the details of the character emerge in just a few pages of text, you feel as if you have been transported to a blackface minstrel show and are watching a skit in which the actors blackened their faces and drew huge white mouths as a way to ridicule the African American."[23]

Moreover, other people of color are reduced to similar racist representations throughout the original series. For example, revisiting *The Clue of the Leaning Chimney*—one of my perennial childhood favorites and one of the few that prominently featured Asian characters and culture—provides a compelling vision of the structure of American cultural values and social relations in the Nancy Drew worldview.[24] The novel recounts Nancy's efforts to locate a mythical site of precious clay, free the imprisoned Chinese artisans Eng Moy and Eng Lei, and bring wily dealers of fake Chinese porcelain to justice. When Nancy first visits Mr. Soong, the River Heights "retired Chinese importer" who plays a leading role in the mystery, she notes that his study "reflected the cosmopolitan tastes of a widely traveled Chinese gentleman."[25] Furthermore, he is described as "a short gentle-faced Chinese with spectacles and a tiny goatee. He wore a richly brocaded mandarin coat and beautifully embroidered Chinese slippers."[26] Readers know immediately from these descriptions that "cosmopolitan" Mr. Soong—coupled with his many valuable "Oriental" objets d'art—is a definite good guy in the class-conscious world of Nancy Drew.

In contrast, Mr. Soong's compatriots, the missing Engs, are pitiful, tragic figures. These Chinese artisans are kidnapped by evil biracial brothers and forced against their will to create fakeries of priceless Chinese potteries. Prevented from learning English and hidden away in an abandoned Civil War iron mine and smelter, they are completely at the mercy of their captors. The Engs' only modes of resistance are to hang the Chinese characters for "Help!" on the leaning chimney and to try inscribing their names into the faked vases in the hopes that someone might recognize them. Surely these pitiable creatures are deserving of Nancy Drew's help! Lucky for them, Nancy Drew has learned from Mr. Soong to "read" Chinese.

The most telling construction in *The Clue of the Leaning Chimney* is the characterization of its villains. Here, the bad guys are mixed-race Chinese American brothers who take advantage of their biracial/bicultural status for evil ends. Again, the series' stock depictions of "others" clearly paint the men as criminals. For example, Ching, Mr. Soong's deceitful employee, is described as "a short, inscrutable-looking Chinese servant" who takes after his Chinese mother.[27] David Carr (alias John Manning), Ching's brother and partner in crime, is described as "a man with black hair and dark skin. But the most striking thing about him was his eyes. They seemed to stare from his head like two small glittering black marbles."[28] The opposite of his brother, Carr "resemble[s] his [American] father."[29]

The depiction of biracialism here plays into the fears of miscegenation that were prevalent at the time; likewise, it precludes any positive space for biracial/bicultural people.[30] What does this say to Asians like me who also are culturally American? Ching and Carr "pass" as both Chinese and American; both also pass off fake Chinese art to gullible consumers. They violate set racial/cultural boundaries and therefore must be punished. In contrast, Nancy Drew crosses cultures—by learning Chinese—but only for the express reason of apprehending the criminals. Her actions thus exemplify the only kind of cultural crossing sanctioned throughout the series: Nancy seeks out, then utilizes, her knowledge of Chinese only to reinforce and maintain WASP hegemony. Any intimacy with non-WASP cultures then must complement Nancy's tireless efforts to defend the status quo and its beautiful accouterments.

The mystery ends with Nancy's daring escape and her return (with police reinforcements) to save the Engs and Mr. Soong from the clutches of Ching and Manning. Nancy receives a precious souvenir for her work on this mystery. The grateful Engs, unable to express their gratitude in English, create a commemorative vase that depicts Nancy as a cross between St. George and St. Joan of Arc, defending the meek Engs and Mr. Soong from the villains: "Against a soft green background was pictured a slender, golden-haired girl in a suit of armor, pitting a lance at a scaly green dragon. Behind her stood a Chinese girl and two men in long Oriental robes."[31]

Thus, *The Clue of the Leaning Chimney* neatly delineates Nancy Drew's tireless efforts "to preserve the class lines ... [and defend] beautiful objects, places, and treasures from violence"[32]: in short, to maintain the status quo. The lesson seems to be the following: the Carr/Manning brothers, suspect mixed bloods, try to confound systems of racial/cultural purity by taking advantage of their dual identities. They transgress set boundaries, pimping Chinese culture by selling copies of stolen authentic Chinese antiques to unsuspecting Americans. Like all the criminals in the Nancy Drew world, Ching and Carr threaten WASP societal conventions and therefore force Nancy's actions to defend the crumbling aristocracy as well as to maintain the market value of "Oriental" heirlooms in River Heights and its environs.

As I reread my old Nancy Drew books, I wonder where my mother situated herself and how she dealt with the stereotypical depictions of nonwhites as laughable and stupid, evil villains or household help. Rather than evoking nostalgia, revisiting River Heights forced me to relive my own discomfort upon reading these passages as a young girl, while simultaneously underscoring the complex negotiations I made as a reader in order to enter this world. With whom should I have identified—the smart, fearless girl detective, whom I aspired to be, or the inscrutable Asian, the dark complexioned villainess, or comical "darkie" who *looked* like me? Given the realities of cultural imperialism and colonial mentality, legacies of my family and my culture, these "choices" were never really choices at all.

Reading Nancy Drew: Strategies and Questions by Women of Color

Bobbie Ann Mason writes that the Bobbsey Twins were "the source of many of my ideas, prejudices, and expectations. They were like cookie cutters on my imagination."[33] Did reading Nancy Drew mysteries have the same "cookie cutter" effect for women of color in the United States? I believe so. In our aspirations for a feminist role model in the girl sleuth, we were also forced to take in the cultural baggage of white supremacy inherent in the series' depictions of American girlhood and its possibilities. This valorization of whiteness often leads to the denigration or negation of self and whole communities of color.

For example, Pinay playwright and novelist Jessica Hagedorn describes how her reading of Nancy Drew, juxtaposed to more high-culture texts such as those of Honoré de Balzac, is an integral part of what she sees as the "chaos" of colonialist Filipino culture:

> I was taught to look outside the indigenous culture for inspiration, taught that the label "Made in the USA" meant automatic superiority; in other words, like most colonized individuals, I was taught a negative image of myself. In school, classes were taught in English, Tagalog was taught as a foreign language ... and the ways of the West were endlessly paraded and promoted .... My lopsided education in Anglo ways was

> sophisticated; by the age of nine or ten, *while enjoying the cheap thrills provided by adolescent Nancy Drew mysteries*, I was already reading Walt Whitman, Emily and Charlotte Brontë, Honoré de Balzac, Edgar Allen Poe, Charles Dickens, and Jane Austen.[34]

Similarly, Dinah Eng, in "Befriending Nancy Drew across Cultural Boundaries" cites Nancy Drew as providing a model of compassion but, most important, of assertiveness and questioning of authority—qualities Eng felt she herself lacked as an Asian American.[35] Disturbingly, Eng describes how her desire to be white, to be Nancy Drew, created self-conflict and erasure of herself as Asian. Her remembrances illustrate how the Nancy Drew text functions as a site of colonization: how "absence" (not seeing her own image), coupled with the pervasive white hegemony of American culture in general, leads to psychological conflict and self-obliteration. "When we don't see ourselves on television, in the newspaper or other media, it's as though we don't exist," she writes. "As a child, I think that translated into the feeling that I wasn't really Asian. I could look in the mirror; I could see that my face was different from everybody else's, but inside I felt that I was white. I felt like I was Nancy Drew at times …. I had constant cultural conflicts to resolve."[36]

Unlike Eng, in "Fixing Nancy Drew: African American Strategies for Reading," Njeri Fuller notes that her process of identifying with Nancy Drew involved making Nancy "a black girl like me …. I began imagining that I was Nancy Drew. I would also make some of her friends black."[37]

Fuller's positive "colorizing" of Nancy certainly indicates her own positive self-image as a girl of color; nevertheless, her successful negotiation of Nancy Drew and racial identity should not diminish the fact that *all* girls of color need heroines with whom they can identify. Like Eng, Fuller objects to the erasure of people of color in the revised editions of the series. She writes, "The Nancy Drew books didn't destroy me. But I have to ask: when will there ever be books we can call classics in which I am represented in a wonderful way? And when will such books become as accessible in libraries and bookstores as are their mainstream white counterparts?"[38] In addition to highlighting the political implications of the absence of "color" in the revised Nancy Drew mysteries, her comments introduce salient questions concerning marketing and availability of responsible, multicultural texts.

As Fuller has noted, the Nancy Drew revisions have removed racial and ethnic stereotypes to the extent that no people of color exist within the series. Donnarae MacCann comments on this obliteration and also raises important questions concerning the messages and politics inherent in children's literature today, and how these texts affect children of color. "What do children of color feel when they see themselves excluded from such an important cultural phenomenon as literature?" she asks. "What do they feel when they see their language and culture reduced to inferiority? What happens when the so-called mainstream white child sees black characters as incapable, insignificant, or unattractive? And what happens when young people who are white see racism receiving approval in children's literature? What kind of society is it that entertains one group of children at the expense of another?"[39]

I contend that this process of "whiting out" both manifests and demonstrates the racist rhetoric of the *Nancy Drew Mystery Series* itself. Stratemeyer scholar Carol Billman, in *The Secret of the Stratemeyer Syndicate*, unwittingly collaborates my stance through her analysis of the revision phenomenon:

> In the early years of the series, it has been well documented, Nancy Drew exhibited a distinct prejudice against ethnic and racial minorities—blacks, Jews, Italians, and Irish, most obviously. Now the egregious bigotry has disappeared, but fundamental beliefs about social propriety remain the same. The value system inherent in the Drew books is nicely summed up by one of the most prevalent images in the series: the great house now in decay and overgrown by unruly shrubs and weeds. It is part of Nancy's role as detective to do the "landscaping" necessary to restore the fine old house to its former glory and its rightful owners.[40]

Billman's diction here is chilling: whether intended or not, the phrases "great house," "former glory," and "rightful owners" breezily invoke images of the "good old days" of the antebellum South and, consequently, offer a very telling commentary on how white supremacy clearly underscores the Nancy Drew mysteries' "fundamental beliefs about social propriety." As such, the Nancy Drew mystery itself must be read as a site of colonization: explicitly valorizing an all-American, all-WASP world, this beguiling text seeks to persuade readers (particularly readers like Eng, Fuller, and myself) to embrace "whiteness" and to be subsumed within its lulling "normalcy."

Moreover, Billman contends that reading serial fiction gives children important skills and tools that they may then apply to reading other texts. She writes that "readers do not simply abandon those books they once regarded so highly, taking with them only fond memories of their favorite heroes and heroines. They also carry over the confidence gained from stories about successful young discoverers and a literary template—a sense of how stories are constructed and proceed—that will be helpful later. Schooled in the elementary virtues of fiction and having fully discovered all the secrets of the series mysteries for themselves, they are ready, in both senses of the word, to explore what is beyond."[41] Billman implies, then, that reading serial fiction like Nancy Drew mysteries provides the reader with the helpful "literary templates" of racism and classism. When viewed within the larger economy of U.S. cultural imperialism in the Philippines and elsewhere (as well as within the internally colonized United States itself), I shudder to think how these books relentlessly continue to mold expectations of how all "stories"—nationalist narratives and personal histories alike—"are constructed and proceed" and, thus, in actuality impede readers from exploring what is truly "beyond."

Voilá! Unmasking the Real Villain

In my analysis of female acculturation via Nancy Drew books from the Filipina/American perspective, I hope to have underscored the importance of recognizing the hegemonic forces embedded not only within popular culture but also in current modes of critical analysis; by this I mean exploring how cultural capital and ideology circulate in order to discern the roots of their power, their modes of persuasion, and their desired effects upon intended subjects. Euro-American feminist theorists, rather than making the obligatory references acknowledging "differences" among women, thus need to radicalize feminist praxis: to utilize a conscious feminist analytical process that can recognize and engage with the reality of white dominance as pervasive in all economic, political, social, and cultural contexts. Such a stance is a necessary corrective to naive and dangerous visions of sisterhood, which can only reinscribe, in this case, American imperialism.

In her poem "To Live in the Borderlands," Gloria Anzaldúa uses the metaphor of white bread to describe the process of assimilation and deracination:

> the mill with the razor white teeth wants to shred off
> your olive-red skin, crush out the kernel, your heart
> pound you pinch you roll you out
> smelling like white bread but dead.[42]

This pervasive "whitening" is enforced by the media, the educational system, libraries, our families, and Filipino culture itself. Recognizing and resisting the hegemonic forces of assimilation and deracination can entail the creation of more positive images of people of color in children's literature; more urgently, we need to develop strategies of cultural resistance that will enable Pinays (as well as other girls of color) to resist the debilitating colonial mentality that characterizes Filipino American culture.

Sometimes as I speed along winding, tree-shaded country lanes in my own blue roadster, the ten-year-old in me who imagined herself as a famous girl detective reappears. I can easily recall the sense of excitement that fueled my love of Nancy Drew mysteries: the danger, anticipation, and assurance of that inevitable happy ending, complete with the requisite blurb describing the next mystery to be solved. However, writing this piece—which I've nicknamed "The Case of Pinay Acculturation"—I realized that Nancy trained me to look for the wrong kind of criminal. Rather than the stock, beady-eyed, "swarthy" thugs of the past, the true villain is Nancy herself.

Notes

1. In the "Proclamation of December 21, 1898," President William McKinley used the term "benevolent assimilation" to characterize American colonial policy in the Philippines: "Finally, it should be the earnest and paramount aim of the military administration to win the confidence, respect and affection of the inhabitants of the Philippines by assuring them in every possible way that full measure of individual rights and liberties which is the heritage of a free people, and by proving to them that the mission of the United States is one of benevolent assimilation, substituting the mild sway of justice and right for arbitrary rule" (Epigraph to *Benevolent Assimilation*). See Stuart Miller's *Benevolent Assimilation* (New Haven, Conn.: Yale University Press, 1982) for a cogent history of the Philippine-American War (1898 to 1901) and its aftermath.
2. *Pinay* is the Tagalog (Pilipino) word for "Filipina."
3. Glenn Anthony May defines "social engineering" as "an effort to mold, and often to restructure, a society"; see May, *Social Engineering in the Philippines: The Aims, Execution, and Impact of Colonial Policy, 1900–1913,* Contributions to Comparative Colonial Studies vol. 2 (Westport, Conn.: Greenwood, 1980), 1.
4. Sucheng Chan, *Asian Americans: An Interpretive History* (Boston: Twayne, 1991), 17.
5. See May, *Social Engineering,* and Bonifacio Salamanca, *The Filipino Reaction to American Rule 1910–1913* (Hamden, Conn.: Shoe String Press, 1968) for curiously unpoliticized accounts of the American educational system in the Philippines, 1900–1913.
6. Yen Le Espiritu, "Filipino Settlements in the United States," in *Filipino American Lives* (Philadelphia: Temple University Press, 1995), 3.
7. *Manong* is a Tagalog term denoting respect, as in "older brother."
8. See Chan, *Asian Americans*; Espiritu, *Filipino American Lives*; and Ronald Takaki, *Strangers from a Different Shore: A History of Asian Americans* (New York: Penguin, 1989) for cogent histories of Filipinos in the United States. Geoffrey Dunn, prod., and Mark Schwartz, dir., *A Dollar a Day, Ten Cents a Dance: An Historic Portrait of Filipino Farmworkers in America* (San Francisco: National Asian American Telecommunications Association/Cross Current Media, 1984; videocassette) is a poignant documentary of the experiences of Filipino farm workers during this period.
9. Carlos Bulosan, *America Is in the Heart* (1943; reprint Seattle: University of Washington Press, 1993).
10. David Joel Steinberg claims that burgeoning Filipino nationalism prompted the people's rejection of Japanese claims to be "fellow liberating Asians" who came to "emancipate the Filipinos, drive out the wicked white rulers and establish a true bond with the Filipinos"; see Steinberg, *The Philippines: A Singular and Plural Place*, 3d ed. (Boulder, Colo.: Westview, 1994), 102. Filipino writer and activist E. San Juan Jr. views this situation very differently; he contends that the Filipino guerrilla war against the Japanese invaders is yet another aspect of American imperialism and colonial mentality:

   The much-touted U.S. legacy of schools, roads, public health programs, artesian wells, "democratic" politicians, and "the most gregariously informal backslapping imperialist rulers known to history" serves to explain, for Stanley [Karnow], why Filipinos cherish a "deferential friendship" for Americans. Does this then explain why Fred Cordova, in his pictorial essay *Filipinos: Forgotten Asian Americans* boasts that "an estimated one million innocent Filipino men, women and children died while defending Americanism during World War II from 1941 to 1945?" Indeed isn't the appropriate question: Are so many Filipinos really so screwed up that they would make such a sacrifice? Think of it: one million natives defending the cause of [the] Lone Ranger and Charlie Chan. One million dark-skinned natives sacrificing their lives for Americanism.

   See E. San Juan Jr., "The Predicament of Filipinos in the United States: 'Where Are You From? When Are You Going Back?'" in *The State of Asian America: Activism and Resistance in the 1990s*, ed. Karin Aguilar-San Juan (Boston: South End Press, 1994), 214.
11. See Carolyn Heilbrun, "Nancy Drew: A Moment in Feminist History," in *Rediscovering Nancy Drew*, ed. Carolyn Stewart Dyer and Nancy Tillman Romalov (Iowa City: University of Iowa Press, 1995), 18.
12. Ibid., 19.

13. Ibid., 20.
14. Delia D. Aguilar, "Gender, Nation, Colonialism: Lessons from the Philippines," in *Sentena-ryo/Centennial: The Philippine Revolution and Philippine-American War,* ed. Jim Zwick. Available online at http://www.boondocksnet.com/centennial/sctexts/dda_95a.html; also published in Nalini Visvanathan, Lynne Duggan, and Lau Nisonoff, eds., *The Women, Gender, and Development Reader* (London: Zed, 1997).
15. Aguilar, "Gender, Nation, Colonialism."
16. See Carol Billman, *The Secret of the Stratemeyer Syndicate: Nancy Drew, The Hardy Boys, and the Million Dollar Fiction Factory* (New York: Ungar, 1986) for a detailed history and analysis of children's series fiction in the United States. I find it ironic that Edward Stratemeyer's first best-seller was the volume *Under Dewey at Manila* (1898), the first of the Old Glory Series. Billman glibly notes, "Then there was the lucky coincidence of Dewey's attack and Stratemeyer's war novel for boys" (18).
17. See Dyer and Romalov, eds., *Rediscovering Nancy Drew,* and Billman, *The Secret of the Stratemeyer Syndicate,* for comprehensive readings of how the Nancy Drew mysteries were revised beginning in 1950 in order to eliminate ethnic and racial stereotyping. My mother read the original mysteries; I read both the original and revised versions.
18. Bobbie Ann Mason, *The Girl Sleuth: On the Trail of Nancy Drew,* ed. Judy Bolton and Cherry Ames (Athens: University of Georgia Press, 1995), 73.
19. Carolyn Keene, *The Mystery at Lilac Inn* (New York: Grosset and Dunlap, 1930).
20. Ibid., 16.
21. Ibid., 18.
22. Mason, *The Girl Sleuth,* 68–69.
23. Donnarae MacCann, "Nancy Drew and the Myth of White Supremacy," in Dyer and Romalov, eds., *Rediscovering Nancy Drew,* 132. MacCann's study purports to describe the American racial climate (social/political setting) up to the publication of the first Nancy Drew mystery in 1930; unfortunately, her work is limited to an analysis of black/white relations. She does not include any references to the virulent anti-Asian violence of this same period, nor does she describe parallel Latino and Native American struggles.
24. Carolyn Keene, *The Clue of the Leaning Chimney* (New York: Grosset and Dunlap, 1949).
25. Ibid., 10, 14.
26. Ibid., 14–15.
27. Ibid., 14.
28. Ibid., 182.
29. Ibid., 130.
30. See the film *Slaying the Dragon* (exec. prod. Asian Women United and KQED; dir. Deborah Gee; San Francisco, Calif.: National Asian American Telecommunications Association/Cross Current Media, 1987; videocassette) for an analysis of how fears of Asian American unions were manifested through popular films of the period.
31. Keene, *The Clue of the Leaning Chimney,* 209.
32. Mason, *The Girl Sleuth,* 73.
33. Ibid., 33.
34. Jessica Hagedorn, "The Exile Within: The Question of Identity," including an interview by Karin Aguilar-San Juan, in Aguilar-San Juan, ed., *The State of Asian America,* 174; emphasis added.
35. Dinah Eng, "Befriending Nancy Drew across Cultural Boundaries," in Dyer and Romalov, eds., *Rediscovering Nancy Drew,* 140–42.
36. Ibid., 141.
37. Njeri Fuller, "Fixing Nancy Drew: African American Strategies for Reading," in Dyer and Romalov, eds., *Rediscovering Nancy Drew,* 137.
38. Ibid., 139.
39. MacCann, "White Supremacy," 134–35.
40. Billman, *The Secret of the Stratemeyer Syndicate,* 114. Billman also notes that the revisions themselves were motivated not only by the Civil Rights movement, but by marketing: modernizing the Nancy Drew plots, descriptions and characters invigorated the mysteries' "up-to-date" outlook—an essential component to their enduring popularity (146).
41. Ibid., 155.
42. Gloria Anzaldúa, "To Live in the Borderlands," in *Borderlands/La Frontera: The New Mestiza* (San Francisco: Spinsters/Aunt Lute, 1987), 195.

4

"This Is Not Your Mother's Catholic Church": When Filipino Catholic Spirituality Meets American Culture[1]

RACHEL A. R. BUNDANG*

Introduction

On the bitter-cold day I turned twenty-six, I was at a conference for both lay and ordained Catholic ministers, listening to Joan Chittister deliver one of the keynote addresses. I honestly do not remember anymore what her exact topic was, but one of her punch lines really stuck with me: "The Trinity is more than two guys and a bird!" For me, the words may as well be apocryphal. However, upon reflection, they are also telling. For all the mystery I was taught to accept and appreciate without question or critique, I still seek to make sense of the mystery within the bounds of my knowledge, perception, and lived experiences.

There indeed lies my starting point, as I seek to articulate my understanding of spirit and spirituality, especially in relationship to ministry and community. Spirituality, for me, is rooted in a sense of whole, deep, and rich community. It is this community that affirms and sanctions, gives shape and censures. It is this community that calls forth my gifts to be used in its service, for the sake of empowerment and liberation.

As I was preparing this essay, this string of thoughts occurred to me: It took twelve years of Catholic school and living—socially and economically—at the edge of a Filipino community in the Deep South to initiate me rudely and painfully to issues of class. It took the four years of my undergraduate career (at Princeton University) plus the four years of work out in the world to make me viscerally conscious of the double-edged sword of race and ethnicity, of multiculturalism and the politics of "brownness." Now it is this struggle to jump through all the hoops that Harvard University places before me—in order to win and not just survive, to be competitive as well as competent—that is pushing me to tie it all together, to grapple consciously and concretely with

*This article has been edited from its original version which appeared in *Brown Papers*, 3, no. 1 (1996): 1–14.

what it means to be a (not *the*) "1.5 generation" Filipina living in America. As a Master of Divinity candidate, I seek to do this by peering through the lens of lived religion, where faith and culture, the personal and communal all intersect. So it continues. Such is the process and history of my conscientization. I have been eaten but not consumed.

Although I have had the "requisite" experiences that feminists would claim as central to developing a feminist consciousness, the notion—and language—of feminist liberation (in terms of spirituality, theology, ministry, and other religious life) is really quite new to me. On many points, my thoughts and interests fall within the domain of feminist discourse and action; this is most clearly the case when I think about the dynamics and ethics of interpersonal relationships. However, to be perfectly honest, despite my work as a Young Feminist Network organizer for the Women's Ordination Conference, feminism as such is simply not at the forefront of my identity or consciousness —especially outside the ordination question or perhaps an occasional inclusive language dilemma.

I am certain that I have grown up in a more permissive milieu than I would have had in the Philippines, where I was born. I am of the generation immediately following *This Bridge Called My Back*[2]—suspicious of the white, Euro-American feminism that does not always speak to or even listen to me and other women of color, yet cognizant of its power, impact, radical potential, and effects. While I appreciate feminism's goals and achievements as a movement if not always as an ideology, somehow it simply has not figured into my personal-identity politics as a distinct and separate strain. For want of a better term, I have sometimes considered myself *culturally, situationally,* or *de facto* feminist. I simply cannot imagine any girl growing up in America for the past twenty-some years without absorbing feminist messages. It is in this sense that feminism has made itself part of my worldview, my framework, and my own language.

Experience, though, leads me to believe—firmly and honestly—that my participation and social location in American society is more affected by my immigrant background (despite my naturalized status), my racial/ethnic affiliation, and my class than by my gender; hence, my uneasy relationship with feminism exixts. It is on the former grounds more often than the latter that my dignity, humanity, competency, and worthiness of respect have been questioned. How can I take up, address, and incorporate one without losing my grounding or footing in another? How can I fight on all fronts effectively without burnout, without martyrdom?

On trying to articulate the nature of her struggle, the *mujerista* (womanist) Maria Antonietta Berriozábal writes, "As a woman of color, I have spent most of my life living in a society that does not understand my reality, the essential wedding of personal and community responsibility, of faith and community. But, like many sisters of color, I have not sat by, hoping that others would effect this integration for us. Each of us has sought in her own way to act on her reality."[3] These words are very real for me. There is a deep, messy, and rich interconnectedness between what is personal and public (or communal), what is spiritual and secular, what is political, and what is for its own sake. One of the effects of living as a postcolonial, as a third-world woman in the heart of the first world, is that we have a dual luxury and burden of being limited by categories and yet flowing among them—even transcending them—as we skate along the margins. However, if all we do is manipulate and maneuver to make space for ourselves, how do we ever really overturn the existing order? How desirable and possible a goal is that?

Spiritual Identity

I must start by critiquing a few sweeping generalizations about and expectations of feminist spirituality, leadership, and ministry that were laid out in the abstract for this essay.

First, religion is an expression of humanity's ultimate concern—an articulation of longings for a center of meaning and value. It will persist. More than ever, women need to participate in redefining spiritual values for the new millennium.

As long as women have been making choices, I seriously doubt that they have ever not defined and abided by their own ethics and nurtured their own spiritual lives. It is more a matter of whether those choices were made freely or compelled by circumstances, as well as whether those choices were recognized and respected by the powers that be.

Second, women of the world still struggle with violence, subjugation, misogyny in fundamentalist religions, and the deaths of their children in ethnic wars. Clearly, the male-dominated model of spiritual leadership has not created—but rather, hindered—the solutions to these human struggles.

However true that may be, feminist spirituality, thought, and method are not necessarily the sole or correct responses, either. In failing to challenge internalized notions and habits of hierarchy effectively, feminism has been blind to its own faults and prejudices, forcing itself upon poor women and women of color, as if they could not articulate their own needs, as if they were incapable of being agents of their own destiny, and as if they were always to be subsumed without being heeded first.

There is rampant egotism and a frustratingly rigid tyranny of orthodoxy within white, liberal, Euro-American feminism, particularly as I have encountered it in my graduate studies—not just in the texts, but also in the students and professors who would adhere to it. It falls short by seeing parity and equality as sameness, uniformity, and even being identical to men rather than making room for differences within equality. In the drive for unity, for "sisterhood," it wants to overlook, erase, and even sacrifice other particularities to the exclusion of gender difference alone. It is insufficiently self-critical about how it participates in oppressive systems, processes, and practices. In the quest for an all-inclusive sisterhood, ongoing controversies and questions about what constitutes responsible appropriation will persist. In trying to be everywhere and do everything, it can lack the focus and sensitivity it holds so dear. It denies that there are other ways of identifying and being oneself.

Difference should not, and does not, automatically call for hierarchical relationship. So often we forget that difference is not just physical; it is also experiential. In short, if the feminism you mean is one that does not make room for me and my complex, multifaceted betweenness, then I want no part of it. A feminism that does not practice what it preaches about right relation, mutuality, and power-with—that does not make room for other ways of seeing and being in the world—is fundamentally hypocritical and dishonest.

This is not to say that other categories also do not have their own limitations. For instance, race and ethnicity, as defined in mainstream America, do not address individuals and peoples who fall between the cracks. Who are you, if you are neither black nor white? And within individual communities, there is the dirty, bound-and-gagged secret of class that no one wants to address. Why the sycophantic, unquestioning acceptance of all things capitalist? Are you perhaps more American if you've made money, if you've bought into and achieved the American Dream? And between race and class is also complicity. Are racial/ethnic minorities destined to never be "American enough" by virtue of not being white, no matter their accent, no matter their birthplace or residency, and no matter how much they earn or achieve? This is not just rhetoric. All these issues are exacerbated within postcolonial communities, particularly here in the United States.

Granted, some brands of feminism try to be more inclusive and, sometimes, they are well articulated.[4] But these messages are not what filter into the mainstream/malestream. Especially among poor women and women of color—two groups with much overlap—feminism faces a huge credibility gap.[5] Regardless of the reality, the image of the radical, rather than the reconstructionist, feminist is the one that dominates the imagination. What has it really done for them/us/me, anyway? What are we doing now that we weren't doing before or already? One would find that so many of these women would not identify themselves primarily as feminists. While recognizing that identity and affiliation depend heavily upon context, the dominant paradigm of difference in America is based on race. My own spirituality is challenged to grow, to resist this racialization, to begin articulating something more consonant with the experiences and needs of women like myself whose voices have never been heard. In this context particularly, I see my role as threefold—mirror, prophet, and teacher—leading us as an uprooted, immigrant people, exiled both by choice and by circumstance, through critical reflection and especially bringing memory and hope home to those of my generation.

Third, there is a perception that feminism will make women abandon their roles as nurturers and facilitators of passing on the spiritual values of a culture. At least that is noted as a perception. However, women should not have these roles exclusively; they do not nor have they ever, I suspect. The members of a culture and a community each play their own roles, according to their gifts and skills, as guardians of the values and ethics they hold dear.

Beneath the overlays of Chinese, Spanish, and American cultures, one finds a surprising degree and strong tradition of mutuality in Filipino male–female relationships. For all the differentiation within my multiple communities (Filipino and otherwise) and the challenges they face, I cannot entertain and will not participate in a feminism that simply discards men. Men and women alike contribute to the life of a culture and a community, although perhaps in different ways—ways both constructive and sometimes detrimental, too. I am reminded of the part of Alice Walker's classic definition of "womanist" as one who is "[c]ommitted to the survival and wholeness of an entire people, male and female. Not a separatist, except periodically, for health."[6] Everyone is valued. Everyone is called to participate.

Spirit is breath, purpose—that which brings us life and instills in us knowledge of ultimate meaning. We are most alive when we seek that spirit, that thing we most desire, that thing which would satisfy us most profoundly when we are hungry and replenish us when we are dry and empty. It is in this quest, this pursuit, that spirituality is born and developed.

My own spiritual life/spirituality exists on two levels. First, there is the personal. Even a cursory survey of Asian American literature, from the writings of Carlos Bulosan to those of Jessica Hagedorn and others,[7] shows that two themes, in particular, arise again and again. One is that of being in exile, a resident alien—no matter how long one has been here, no matter if one was born here or back in the motherland. It is a sense of being rooted elsewhere and, sometimes, "else-when."[8] At this level, mine is a wilderness spirituality— although I am sometimes tempted to call it a spirituality of the (apparently) absurd. This spirituality is rooted in my experience of alienation—being in an alien nation, being an alien in a nation, being a (former) resident alien as an immigrant and as one who lives in that no-man's-land between America's strict racial paradigm of black and white. Even with the survival mechanisms I have developed—being fluidly multicultural and multilingual and, especially, cultivating multiple modes of affiliation and identification—I am painfully conscious of living in exile and often ask myself, "How can I sing my songs in this strange land?"

The other recurrent theme is what W. E. B. DuBois classically calls "double consciousness": the duality, the transculturality, the fluidity of moving back and forth in between "mainstream white consciousness" and a more racialized consciousness. Some have also less charitably—or more playfully, depending on how you look at it—called this "cultural schizophrenia."[9] This racialized consciousness is what takes precedence for me and it encompasses whatever else I feel, know, and experience in terms of class and gender. With every choice I make, I weigh the price and the process of assimilation and integration. I have to question and reshape, time and again, my identity, authenticity, and integrity as a woman in the diaspora; and I do this, conscious of what has come before me and what may result from my actions.

My other level of spirituality is the communal. What do we call our community of accountability and how do we constitute and sustain that community? In other words, who shares in these experiences of alienation and what does it take for us to "come home"? What binds us together? When do we affiliate primarily as women, or as Filipinos, or as Asian Americans, or as people of color? What do we seek? What do we need? What do we treasure? How do we claim voice, claim presence, claim power? In this essay and in future work, I would like to explore further the relationships between the individual and the community, the interplay between faith and culture, and the construction of multiple identities and multiple modes of affiliation to suit a multiplicity of contexts.

It is probably clear by now that I identify myself in a whole host of ways. With the projects I have been working on for the past two years, I have been thinking about what it means to be a Filipina, an Asian Pacific woman, in North America. Scholar and activist E. San Juan Jr. ruefully notes that we often—silently and secretly—ask ourselves the same questions that non-Asians often ask us: "Where are you from? When are you going back?"[10] Indeed we are a people of the diaspora, dislocated by choice, chance, or need. We occasionally struggle with our identity politics, our restless rootlessness, and our sense of exile. We find ourselves wondering about or even longing for a "home" we may know only through books and family stories, not through personal visits. We try to gauge our authenticity and seek to forge our integrity as persons, as a people that are never allowed to forget their "otherness." We must ask ourselves again and again: What do we consider our community—or communities—of accountability, and why?[11] What are our criteria for authenticity, for integrity, for belonging—and should we even have them or operate on them? In our living, to what and for what does our doing and being matter?

The void into which we seem to keep throwing these questions is reflected in the absence of literature on Filipino religious experience in the diaspora, even in the United States. Further beyond that, Fil-Am life and culture in general is subsumed under the vast, yet limited, umbrella of Asian American studies. This, in turn, consists of writings on "the big three": Japanese, Chinese, and Korean Americans. In addition, those that would include Filipinos under the aegis of Spain might argue for a better fit historically and culturally. The truth is that we can be both and neither.

Theologies and study of Asian Americans' religious experiences in the United States are not yet at a point where they can even deal with trying to settle on a name like *womanist, mujerista,* or *teología de conjunto* (collaborative Hispanic Protestant theology), as empowering as that might be. (Post) colonial implications of naming and speaking aside, I do not think that naming, in this case, is as important as the struggle to articulate what is yet unspoken, unseen, unknown. Especially as we branch out and forth from our individual nations into Asian America—and the world—we still have to contend with questions of language, practice, and origin: Which do we use, and how? When? Why? We have to understand the history, dynamic, and legacy of the colonialism that introduced us to Christianity and then was even better at subjugating us with it.

Devout woman that she is, my own mother raised me Filipina and Catholic from birth. By the time we emigrated to the United States, I had, at the age of two, already received the sacraments of baptism and confirmation. Looking back on this memory—one that I learned rather than actually lived and remembered—twenty-five years later, I see just how much Roman Catholic Christianity is part of my family's legacy to me, as well as my identity as a Filipina American. Its beliefs, practices, and values are so deeply woven into the cultural fabrics that clothe me.

However, I cannot ignore the rough seams between the two strains of Catholicism—Filipino and post–Vatican II American—in me. Because I am a woman and, consequently, cannot be ordained to the priesthood as it exists within this particular denomination, the American part of me wrestles constantly with two large "whys": Why should I remain Catholic? Why should I pursue a theological education—albeit in a very liberal institution—if ordination is a moot point? For all its faults and limitations, though, the Catholic theological, verbal, and spiritual idiom has made itself at home deep within me; maddening as it is sometimes, in its obstinacies and inconsistencies, I respect tradition even as I contest it, disagree with it, and subject it to critique. Faith and theology aside, Catholicism's cultural significance and its ties to who I am as a Filipina are thick as blood itself. My experience of the Church cannot be encapsulated in a single sticking point and is greater than one sole controversy.

I am often asked, "Why don't you just switch denominations so you can get everything you want—ordination, marriage, family?" While I recognize the presence of other denominations and religions within Filipino and Filipino American communities, the overwhelming majority are still Catholic—whether in practice, worldview, or—at the very least—culture, imagination, and symbol.[12] I cannot help but see Allan Figueroa Deck's characterization of Latino theology as similar to my own stance and project. He writes, "Among Latinos the unity of the Church does not revolve around the resolution of differences of creed or doctrine. While Latino theologians are generally not disloyal to the normative teachings of their respective faith traditions, the commitment out of which they write and teach is not so much the confessional, doctrinal faith-stance typical of mainline religion as much as the cultural and social class commitment of their communities, their gente, their pueblos."[13]

I find myself at turns standing either in solidarity or tension with the Filipino faithful, as well as with others whom I claim as my own. For me to walk away from, and turn my back on, the Church would, for all intents and purposes, be the same as walking away from and turning my back on my people—male or female, Catholic or not, rich or poor, schooled or illiterate. While I have my opinions, I neither pretend nor claim to be an expert in all things Filipino/Asian/American.[14] But, in short, it is the pull of the people and the call of community to solidarity that continues to engage me here, that continues to keep me living in creative tension at the intersections of these two worlds.

At the most fundamental level, though, the main reason why I remain Catholic and pursue this master of divinity degree even as I plan to continue for both ministry and doctoral study at some point is that I am called to make a particular faith journey with a particular road map, for reasons I can neither explain nor understand fully. According to Chung Hyun Kyung, there are three rhythms to an Asian woman's spiritual growth: (1) impasse: living death, (2) choice for life: discovering the true self, and (3) reaching out: building a community. These rhythms are not a one-time, absolute event, but rather occur again and again as part of a pattern and process of transformation—as natural and inevitable as life itself.[15] I find myself in this spiral, this cycle of growth that keeps leading me back and back and back to familiar territory that is yet never the same as I last left it.

Chung also notes other characteristics of Asian women's spirituality that may illuminate the remainder of this discussion. According to her, this spirituality is:

1. concrete and total: rooted in real, everyday, lived experience;
2. creative and flexible: adaptive and adaptable; able to envision and make a way out of no way and to use what fits and is liberative;
3. prophetic and historical: committed to realizing radical, fundamental peace and justice for all;
4. community-oriented: inclusive in its vision and approach to the liberation struggle, particularly in seeing the problems, as well as devising solutions;
5. pro-life: meaning, in a much broader sense than in the American abortion debate, committed to comprehensive nonviolence and embracing peace as a lifestyle choice;
6. ecumenical and all-embracing: it seeks wholeness and respects integrity; draws from the range of available faiths, traditions, and cultural

resources; and accepts (with a critical eye) the value and possibility of syncretism as a liberative act or response; and

7. cosmic, creation-centered: the natural goodness of creation is trusted ultimately to outweigh the impact of "the fall"; hence, one must make choices that consistently affirm life rather than choose death and destruction.[16]

Even in the broad brushstrokes I have used up until now, I have, to varying degrees, clearly found these aspects true or useful for beginning to make sense of what Asian American religious experience is and how, or whether, it includes and addresses people like me with a complex web of multiple affiliations. They also help me discern to what degree, and in what ways, I may legitimately claim to be feminist.

Maybe my spirituality is feminist after all—feminist in that I cannot help but speak from my own experience and cast that story out into the public domain, whether as part of the chorus or cacophony. That specification of context is one of the cornerstones of feminist theory and pedagogy. In my family, and in the Filipino community where I grew up, I saw so many mixed messages in the practices of Catholicism—very traditional, very Spanish Catholic, very pre–Vatican II. Of course we went to mass; many a Wednesday evening we were dragged to rosaries and novenas. We often observed the first Friday and/or first Saturday of each month. Year-round, the Santo Niño traveled a circuit from house to house, marking the anniversaries of loved ones' deaths with novenas. We had the Santacruzan processions in May, with all the juicy character parts doled out to the daughters and sons of "the beautiful people" (i.e., the professionals, the wanna-bes, and the social climbers). In the dark chill of winter (or what passed for winter in Florida), we walked the path of *el Nazareño Negro*, the Black Nazarene. Nearly all these activities, of course, ended up with food and fellowship in the house or the social hall.

But there were many times when this fellowship excluded rather than included. Many a Sunday I would sit blankly or resentfully at mass, hating having to go rather than really wanting to be there and instead feeling like a hypocrite in the process. Without meaning to level offense, the God my parents worshipped surely did not speak to me. I wanted more "I and thou." I wanted a God who did more than sit as a distant object of fear and devotion, bestowing mercy or inflicting punishment. I wanted a God who could be [an] adult with me, not as a parent but as a mentor/companion—a God who is equal parts fierceness and compassion; who respects toughness and independence as much as gentleness and community; who would let me act and not just be acted upon; who challenges with and is challenged by humor, sassiness, anger, and madness; who would allow me full agency—mistakes and all. I wanted a God with whom I could wrestle (like Jacob) and argue (like Job) and collaborate (like Mary). I wanted a God-at-home-in-body. And I must also admit that sometimes I want a God who is healer, comforter, and deliverer.[17] I find myself saying "yes" to Judith Plaskow's reinterpretation of God's otherness as "moreness without domination … divinity in what the dominant powers despise."[18]

Sure, religious practice, faith, devotion … all these things may strengthen you, sustain you, and embolden you, but when do they hold you back? When do they oppress, rather than liberate? When do they deny the fullness of humanity? When are they vehicles of human hubris rather than of genuine offerings to God? When and why does the purpose of a religious observance get subordinated to cultural demands and expectations?

For instance, when I was growing up, I did not fit the values that activities such as the Santacruzan and others espoused and promoted, whether tacitly or explicitly. I was "just working class," not rich, or at least certainly not a child of the professional class; nor was I beautiful, not in the exquisitely mestiza pageant-princess perfect or absolutely exotic way that these girls almost always were. Rather, I was the academically and musically talented one, the reliable prop trotted out only for their amusement or convenience. Against their disdain, I defended myself with an equal and opposite disdain. In the Filipino community where I grew up, the practice of Catholicism slid back and forth sharply on a continuum between escapist fiestas and rituals on the one hand and unquestioning, uncritical expressions of *bahala na* fatalism and infantilizing dependency on the other.[19] Without meaning to sound uncharitable, it was especially these latter parts that, in my mind, seemed to let a passive–aggressive element fester in both the God/person and God/community relationships, to their ultimate detriment. With the energy and vitality sapped out, the spirituality that was lived and manifested was consequently at least stunted—and stunting—if not altogether destructive. The traditional expressions of faith that I witnessed all around me often seemed out of place, anachronistic, woefully irrelevant to the reality of this community living in exile, as it were. Other than the obvious social purposes of trying to bring a community together and passing on shared values and cultural practices, what purpose did sustaining these memories serve? Where was God in all this? How could we continue to invest these practices and beliefs with meaning justifiably, without reducing it to mere parading and profiling?

After I finished my undergraduate degree, I went through four difficult, incredibly trying years of wilderness—complete with a descent into hell, an epiphany, and redemption. As a minister/theologian in training, graduate school itself has been a process of being led—perhaps even being called—to greater depths within myself and uncharted territories beyond my ken. In the process, one thing has become clear: my studies have confirmed my deep conviction that while spirituality may need silence, solitude, and space to blossom, it—like theology—is not and cannot be born in a vacuum. It also needs the context of community—a community of accountability—to give it

shape, structure, and dimension. Thinking, for example, of the route liberation theology has taken into seminary classrooms, one wonders whether the
academy is, can, or even should be held accountable to the communities from
which it receives ideas. What constitutes a truly ethical relationship between
theory and praxis here? How does and should this question affect our preparation and work as theologians and ministers? What does this mean for the laity
engaged in their own spiritual development?

I think it is entirely possible to have a spiritual life outside institutional
religion. As for me, I stepped out of the Catholic Church for a while—not
because of any deep doctrinal differences, but rather because it was not speaking to my needs (i.e., where I was at that very difficult, angry, and painful time
in my life). I wanted maximal autonomy at that point and the last thing I
needed was another person, another institution telling me what to do and how
to do it. If I had no part in fashioning the box, I certainly did not want to fit
into it.

During that period of almost three years, I dabbled in other ways of articulating my spiritual self. I looked at feminist/goddess spirituality; I looked at
Buddhism; I looked at New Agey/pop psych/soc-anth writings; I even looked
at Gnostic and mystical traditions within various religions. But I was very
alone—and all too aware of my lack. I was hounded by ghosts and demons
whose names and tricks I never knew. I felt a deep sense of alienation, homelessness, rootlessness, and restlessness. But the thing is that we want to find a
home, to come home wherever we are, to be there and really belong for always,
unconditionally.

Spiritual identity is, for me, inseparable from community. I hungered for
the common language, the shared values and ethics, and the collective experience of worship. I am at a point and a place now where I am fed and sustained
by my participation in an intentional, thoughtful, active, and progressive
Catholic community. This congregation is reasonably mixed, middle-class,
quite well-educated, and deeply (almost physically) engaged in its faith—how
to deepen and strengthen it, how to live it out daily, how to share it with others,
and how to integrate it fully.

As much as I enjoy all that, I think about how I would, or even could, bring
these notions, experiences, and ideas back to the Filipino American community in a way that is respectful, meaningful, and liberating. I was discussing
this presentation with a friend of mine, a Mexican American priest. He lit up
with recognition when I told him that for me, spirituality is also rooted in
community. "But," he asked me, "if you critique the rituals and practices that
you find detrimental, how do you have community without all that stuff?
What will you put in its place?"

He voiced my own question. How can we reshape that body of experience?
What is culturally compromised and what is preserved? What can we include,
discard, refashion, or reinterpret? How else can we as a people, with a shared

history and a shared experience, articulate that and continue to live as a community? How else can we envision cultivating a common identity that would yield and sustain a strong, vibrant spirituality?

To his query I do not yet have an answer that would effectively address the communal dimension of spirituality. All I can offer is my own journey, my own exercise in critique and syncretism—drawing upon the lessons I have learned from everyone and everything everywhere, not just Catholics and Filipinos, but also especially from the women of PANAAWTM and my African American, Latino/a, and Jewish brothers and sisters.[20] They have taught me—and still continue to teach me—new/old ways of imagining and relating to God and community as right here in my face and not just off and away somewhere—of being within myself and being out in the world, of integrating spirituality and ethics into full personhood.[21]

Toward a Liberative Ministry

What spirituality and ministry both share is their need of, and focus on, relationship—be it with God or someone else. In this sense, they both require community. Of all things, spirituality and ministry—just like the theology clothing them—need to be constantly in touch with the everyday lives of everyday people in order to keep them honest and in order for them to have shape, purpose, and meaning. If nothing else, Catholicism—and particularly this hybrid of Filipino and American strains that I have lived and that embraced me—has, in my case, instilled in me strong and particular notions of Church, of discipleship, of community, and of ministry; and these notions inform the choices I make in pursuing my own theological education.

Those of us in the bridge generation are looked upon to play Janus: being in the present, minding the past, and looking ahead to the future. As I share with you my thoughts on how to imagine a liberative ministry and how we can engage in that work, please keep in mind that these are thoughts in progress and in process.

If spirituality describes a state or condition of relationship, however fluid or static, however solitary or populated, then the work of establishing, cultivating, and sustaining those relationships that give meaning and purpose to spirituality, whether individual or collective, constitutes ministry. As I have written and said in other contexts, ministry is certainly more than being ordained and working as a pastor of a parish. There are as many different kinds of ministry as there are ministers, settings, communities, and paths. I think that at the very least ministry must begin as faith made manifest in outward action. It is life in service, grounded in commitment to another's well-being and compelled and informed by faith—whatever one's tradition, whatever one's theology.

However, let us make one thing absolutely clear: service is not the same thing as servitude. Service in this sense respects the dignity, integrity, and personhood of all those involved. As an action, it honors what is right, just, and holy in both the people and the situation. It is with this understanding of service that we have the foundation for even talking about ministry.

Ministry starts at the intersection of self and community. Ministry requires not only a great deal of time, energy, and commitment, but also faith, hope, and (of course) love—in and of the people, the work, the mission, and the God who asks us to honor in others that which we would treasure for ourselves. Just as much as we need to understand ways in which we are oppressed and need liberation, we also cannot remain trapped in that wound-edness. We must then envision and design a different reality, an alternative future in which we achieve that healing, that wholeness, and that integrity both in person and in community.

With the apparent glibness of these words, I do not mean to say that good ministry is always as easy or smooth. Nor, by liberation, do I mean some upwardly progressive spiral at whose apex is an inevitably comfortable life-style, achievable only by some and not others. The aim of liberative ministry is to enable us all to live with full human dignity. It is a call for justice, just as much as it is a call for peace or love, and because it is a call that crosses lines of class, race, gender, and generation, it recognizes the necessity and worth of struggle just as much as the value of rest and celebration.

Ministry demands a conscious commitment to making sure that our work is honest, accountable, and empowering to our respective communities, in academia and beyond. Without this commitment, it cannot be fully and truly liberative. Moreover, ministry is not liberative if it does not touch everyone, if it does not transform things radically. And a radical transformation does not have to be drastic; it can surely be subtle—and always handled with care and sensitivity, love and clarity (of purpose, if not always vision). However, that subtlety does not detract from the profundity or worth of the change.

As a Catholic student in a non-Catholic school, I have had plenty of time and opportunities to reflect upon the relationships among the Church, culture, and ministry and how these have made an impact on my faith. It is really only in the Church, though, where gender has been an unavoidable problem—the only place where I can point to concrete sexism. No matter how liberal the community, parish, or diocese—no matter how well intentioned the leadership or the congregation—there still exists a limit to how far I can go. Rosemary Radford Ruether notes that

> a recognition of sexism as sin requires a radical redefinition of ministry and church. The grace of conversion from patriarchal domination opens up a new vision of humanity for women and men, one that invites us to recast and re-create all our relationships. Psychologically, one cannot affirm a feminist identity against the historical weight of patriarchal oppression by oneself. Theologically, it is essential to understand

redemption as a communal, not just an individual experience. Just as sin implies alienation and broken community, so rebirth to authentic self-hood implies a community that assembles in the collective discovery of this new humanity and that provides the matrix of regeneration.[22]

At the very least, the sexism calls for a situationally feminist response in order to address the injustice. But where I differ with Ruether is that I seem to find more space in the Church than she does to be who I am and who I can be(come). While I recognize the shortcomings of Church structure, I am not so reluctant to give up Catholicism or Christianity. Aside from its role as provider of framework and vocabulary for my system of faith and belief, it still has value for me insofar as it constitutes part of my cultural grounding and my cultural self. On a larger scale, I still have hope that it can be redeemed, restored, and transformed to be more inclusive. What Ruether calls "liberated zones" are created and do exist, even flourish.[23]

I reflect upon the relationship between spirituality, theology, and ministry. My bias, as a Catholic woman who cannot be ordained, flashes back and forth between two sides. On the one hand, most people—men or women—who graduate with a master's degree from my institution will not end up teaching in a seminary setting. Chances are that they will be employed, whether lay or ordained, in some other organization, doing things with real, everyday people that affect real, everyday people's lives. However, I do not want to discount the desirability and necessity of proper theological preparation and grounding. So how does mindful, honest, constructive dialogue take place between the two camps? How can theologians serve effectively in the ministry of writing and representation, and how can ministers be pastor, prophet, and priest all at once, whether ordained or not? How can both groups be true to their communities of accountability?

As a student, there are three main and intertwined components of my ministry at present: (1) physical presence—through action; pastoralness, or visibility in service to (and leadership of) the community; (2) psychic presence—through speech and preaching; learning to become a prophet in a very public way, learning to wield and convey appropriate moral and spiritual authority; and (3) engagement—through interpretation of Scripture and tradition, according to the culture, context, and needs of the community of accountability.

None of these is quite polished yet, but I am learning and I approach the task of becoming prophet, poet, and priest with both joy and awe.

Filipina and American, as well as post–Vatican II Catholic: the push and pull among these poles demand that I respond with a feminism that I resist, because I have not really needed it elsewhere. I have learned, unfortunately, to respond first to race. Moreover, one of the consequences of this racialization is that my vision of ministry (except in the broadest of terms) is not yet fully inclusive and is not yet global. Despite my universalistic tendencies, I feel that the particularities still need to be respected, even if not entirely understood. There is a strong tension between essentialism and being subsumed. I am still learning to love *fully* and *clearly*—and those are not two words that one normally sees associated with love. I can see the connections to other struggles, but my struggles have been here, on this ground, on this turf, and in this place. Until I feel sufficiently strong and sufficiently established here, I am not sure how effective I would be elsewhere. I need to develop resources and the tools—personal and professional, emotional and intellectual, and spiritual and social.

In what events—or narratives, if you will—that are now proceeding in contemporary world history shall we participate? Is it a narrative of assimilation and integration, or a narrative of emancipation and national self-determination? Is there a universalizing or transcendent multiracial narrative, a global narrative that subsumes and guarantees our self-empowered, if long-delayed, ethnogenesis?[24]

As a people in exile, a people of the diaspora, the most liberating ministry we can undertake right now is the act of decolonization. How can we heal the scars of colonization—"decolonize our souls," as some have asked? From what or whom do we seek deliverance: ourselves, someone or something else?

I do not think that the answer lies in forgetting culture, heritage, or tradition but rather in transforming it. If you are interested in "women's internal liberation," for instance, what devotions should we revisit, reinterpret, or even discard? What would a Filipina feminism that achieves integrity within the spheres of both faith and culture look like?

Moreover, what religious and spiritual resources do Filipino Catholicism and culture offer for liberation? Here I cannot help but think about the essentialist claims of some Afrocentric thought in comparison. What sense does it make to appeal to a history—that so few know—especially in an immigrant community like ours, especially as time passes from one generation to the next? How do we respond to the realities of Fil-Am culture, Fil-Am experience? How honest and inclusive can we be, say, of other Asian Americans' experiences; of those of other people of color; of those who belong to other faiths or none at all; of men and children; and of gays, lesbians, bisexuals, and the transgendered? What lies at the heart of our identity as a Filipino American community, and how is that manifested in our faith lives?

Our faith can be incorporated into the spiritual and cultural jazz, the *mestizaje* (mixedness), or the syncretism—and not just be assimilated or integrated—that we resort to time and again as individuals and as a community.[25] A liberative ministry in this context would let me draw from the breadth and depth of my experience, my being, to connect with others, to respond to their needs and desires, and to empower them. In other words, syncretic spirituality requires a syncretic ministry. This, then, is challenged to grow and change as it respects and observes tradition, while interpreting and transforming it with thought and care to ensure it fits in new contexts and responds to new situations.

Notes

1. This essay is based on a presentation for the Women and Spirituality panel at the Filipino American Women's Network national conference, Minneapolis, August 10, 1996.
2. Cherríe Moraga and Gloria Anzaldúa, eds., *This Bridge Called My Back*, 2d ed. (Latham, N.Y.: Kitchen Table/Women of Color, 1983).
3. Ada Maria Isasi-Díaz, "Mujeristas: Who We Are and What We Are About," with responses by Elena Olazagasti-Segovia, Sandra Mangual-Rodriguez, Maria Antoinetta Berriozábal, Daisy L. Machado, Lourdes Arguelles and Raven-Anne Rivero, *Journal of Feminist Studies in Religion* 8, no. 1 (1992): 105–25; Maria Antoinetta Berriozábal, response to Ada Maria Isasi-Díaz, "Mujeristas: Who We Are and What We Are About," *Journal of Feminist Studies in Religion* 8, no. 1 (1992): 117.
4. For example, see Elisabeth Schüssler Fiorenza, *But She Said: Feminist Practices of Biblical Interpretation* (Boston: Beacon, 1992); and *Discipleship of Equals: A Critical Feminist Ekklesialogy of Liberation* (New York: Crossroad, 1993). See also the introduction to *Weaving the Visions: New Patterns in Feminist Spirituality*, ed. Judith Plaskow and Carol Christ (San Francisco: Harper and Row, 1987), 1–14; Mary Grey, "Claiming Power-in-Relation: Exploring the Ethics of Connection," *Journal of Feminist Studies in Religion* 7, no. 1 (1991): 7–18; and Pamela K. Brubaker, "Sisterhood, Solidarity, and Feminist Ethics," *Journal of Feminist Studies in Religion* 9, nos. 1–2 (1993): 53–66.
5. The following is merely a sample of the literature on that tension: Ada Maria Isasi-Díaz, "Mujeristas: Who We Are and What We Are About," with responses by Elena Olazagasti-Segovia, Sandra Mangual-Rodriguez, Maria Antoinetta Berriozábal, Daisy L. Machado, Lourdes Arguelles and Raven-Anne Rivero, *Journal of Feminist Studies in Religion* 8, no. 1 (1992): 105–25; Asian Women United of California, eds. *Making Waves: An Anthology of Writings by and about Asian American Women* (Boston: Beacon, 1989); Anzaldúa and Moraga, eds., *This Bridge Called My Back*; Gloria Anzaldúa and Cherríe Moraga, eds., *Haciendo Caras/Making Face, Making Soul* (San Francisco: Aunt Lute Foundation, 1990). bell hooks also has written extensively on this subject.
6. Alice Walker, *In Search of Our Mothers' Gardens* (Orlando, Fla.: Harcourt Brace Jovanovich, 1984), xi.
7. See, for example, Jessica Hagedorn, "The Exile Within: The Question of Identity," in *The State of Asian America: Activism and Resistance in the 1990s*, ed. Karin Aguilar-San Juan (Boston: South End, 1994), 173–82.
8. Even the title of E. San Juan Jr.'s essay "The Predicament of Filipinos in the United States: 'Where Are You From? When Are You Going Back?'" in Aguilar-San Juan, ed., *The State of Asian America*, 205–18, represents this phenomenon all too well.
9. Hagedorn, "The Exile Within," 176.
10. San Juan, "The Predicament of Filipinos," 205.
11. I first encountered this term when Rita Nakashima Brock delivered a lecture, "Interstitial Integrities," in April 1995 at Harvard Divinity School, Cambridge, Massachusetts.
12. *Special Edition* 2, no.1 (1993–94), "Religion, Fil-Am Style," devoted to Filipino-American spiritual and religious lives, is based on a survey, generically phrased to include Catholics and non-Catholics alike. Ninety-six percent of the participants identified themselves as Roman Catholic (see pp. 10–12).
13. Allan Figueroa Deck, "Latino Theology: The Year of the 'Boom,'" *Journal of Hispanic and Latino Theology* 1, no. 2 (1994): 60.
14. For further discussion on the ethics of representation, see Rachel A. Bundang, "The Gospel According to the Third World Intellectual: Prophetic Cultural Criticism," January 12, 1996, unpublished.
15. Chung Hyun Kyung, *Struggle to Be the Sun Again: Introducing Asian Women's Theology* (Maryknoll, N.Y.: Orbis, 1990), 86–91.
16. Ibid., 91–96.

17. For a fascinating discussion on how we imagine and relate to God as male or female, see Catherine Madsen, "If God Is God, She Is Not Nice" with responses by Starhawk, Emily Culpepper, Arthur Waskow, Anne C. Klein and Karen Baker-Fletcher, *Journal of Feminist Studies in Religion* 5, no. 1 (1989): 102–17.

18. Elizabeth Bettenhausen, "Theology and Spirituality: What's the Difference?" *Brown Papers* 1, no. 3 (1994): 11.

19. *Bahala na* roughly translates as "whatever," in the sense of just letting the chips fall where they may. Here it indicates an abdication of any sense of agency in one's relationship with God. For a historical perspective on and critique of Filipino religiosity, see Behn Cervantes, "Hungry for Miracles," *Special Edition* 2, no. 1 (1993): 40–45.

20. PANAAWTM stands for Pacific/Asian and North American/Asian Women in Theology and Ministry.

21. The work and examples of other women of color and U.S. minorities, theological or otherwise, has been integral to my growth and thought. Latina and mujerista thought in particular have been important because they come from the same cultural matrix: colonization by Spain. Womanist work has been important, too, because we share the experience of exploitation and captivity by American capitalism, not to mention racism.

22. Rosemary Radford Ruether, *Sexism and God-Talk: Toward a Feminist Theology* (Boston: Beacon, 1983).

23. Ibid., 205.

24. San Juan, "The Predicament of Filipinos," 216.

25. For more on the relationship between syncretism and mestizaje, especially in Latino theology, see Deck, "Latino Theology," 50–63.

II
(Re)Writing Peminist Sociohistory

5

Asian American History: Reflections on Imperialism, Immigration, and "The Body"

CATHERINE CENIZA CHOY

Speaking the Truth

It is May 1999. As my first academic year as an assistant professor comes to an end, I am filled with optimism about the state of Asian American studies at the University of Minnesota–Twin Cities. University faculty with research interests in Asian American studies formed an Asian American studies planning group this year. Recently our group received two university grants to coordinate and strengthen our Asian American studies research and course offerings.

However, while watching a local news program, my optimism is shaken. The newscaster reports that Minnesota governor Jesse "The Body" Ventura has created an audio version of his autobiography, *I Ain't Got Time to Bleed. More hype for our governor who claims that he speaks his mind and tells it like it is,* I think. Then the news program plays an excerpt of the audiobook, in which Ventura says, "I loved the Philippines. I was stationed at Subic, and I loved going into Olongapo. It was more like the Wild West than any other place on earth. In Olongapo, there's a one-mile stretch of road that has three hundred fifty bars and ten thousand girls on it every night .... To the kid I was then, it was paradise."[1] I wonder, *Am I listening to an advertisement for a sex tour in the islands?* I immediately reject this sound bite as another example of orientalist, colonial nostalgia in American popular culture, but then hesitate to dismiss it so quickly. Representations of the Philippines on American television are so abysmally few that Ventura's excerpt (small as it is) has a potentially powerful impact. The power of Ventura's publicized memory of the Philippines is compounded by the fact that he is a national as well as local celebrity whose fame crosses the boundaries of politics, show business, and sports. He is known as the "refreshing" Independent Party governor who attributes his shocking political victory to his ability to "tell the truth."[2] Given his appearances on the *Today Show, Live with Regis and Kathy, Late Night with David Letterman,* and the *Tonight Show with Jay Leno*, I cringe when fathoming the tens of thousands of people he has reached with his version of truth telling.

I realize that by opening this essay with Ventura's orientalist depiction of the Philippines, I may be reinscribing the very stereotypes that I wish to reject. What does "The Body" have to do with my work on Filipino nurses, imperialism, and immigration, anyway? However, Ventura's excerpt has inadvertently reminded me of an important agenda for the future of our discipline: analyzing the legacies of American imperialism and colonialism and their connection to contemporary U.S. immigration and labor. As George J. Sanchez argued at the 1998 American Historical Association annual meeting, "It is time for American scholars in general, and immigration historians in particular, to recognize the imperial origins of many of the racialized issues now confronting American immigration."[3]

What is equally important about Ventura's representation of the Philippines is what it excludes as well as includes. The use of Filipino women to embody a Philippine "paradise" for American men is a central part of this depiction. Invisible are the colonial and neocolonial relationships of inequality between the United States and the Philippines and, more specifically, the history of U.S. military presence in the islands and its legacies of prostitution, disease, and environmental destruction. Erased once again is the history of American imperialism. As William Appleman Williams observed more than forty years ago, "One of the central themes of American historiography is that there is no American Empire."[4]

Another salient interrelated theme of Ventura's excerpt is the privileged role of Ventura as an American adventurer. Ventura "goes into" Olongapo, which functions as an extension of the American West. In this familiar narrative, the movement of adventurers is unidirectional. Might we think of Filipino nurses, for example, migrating to the United States as adventurers? Probably not. In the celebratory narratives of western expansion, invisible are the migrations of Filipinos east into the United States; many of them thought of America as a paradise—yet another legacy of American colonial education in the Philippines—but became disillusioned by its exploitation, racism, and violence.

As we enter a new millennium, it is time for historians to vigorously engage with American imperialism and colonialism and its legacies. The future of Asian American history is to speak this truth.

The Personal and the Professional

One of the major arguments I make in my work on Filipino nurse migration to the United States is that this contemporary phenomenon is inextricably linked to early-twentieth-century American colonialism in the Philippines.[5] The establishment of Americanized nursing training in the Philippines during the U.S. colonial period laid the professional, social, and cultural groundwork for a feminized, highly educated, and exportable labor force. And just as American colonialism in the archipelago needs to be understood in an international context of U.S. imperial power, so too does Filipino nurse migration. In the late twentieth century, the Philippines has been the *world's* top exporter of nurses, sending significant numbers of nurses to the Middle East and Canada as well as the United States. However, I did not originally approach my research with these perspectives. In this essay I chart the challenges I faced during this project and hope that this intellectual journey will reveal important insights for the future of our discipline.

My work has been, and continues to be, informed by personal experiences as well as diverse academic literatures. Growing up as a second-generation Filipino American in New York City in the 1970s and 1980s, I had observed that many of the Filipino women living in my apartment building were nurses. They worked in the cluster of hospitals that was within walking distance of my Lower East Side neighborhood: Beth Israel, Cabrini, the New York Eye and Ear Infirmary, and Bellevue. These Filipino women in their white uniforms were arguably the most visible group of the growing Filipino-American immigrant community.

The scholarly literature on Filipino nurse migration to the United States confirmed my childhood observations. Beginning in the late 1960s, the increasing numbers of Filipino nurses ended decades of numerical domination by foreign-trained nurses from European countries and Canada. Paul Ong and Tania Azores have estimated that at least twenty-five thousand Filipino nurses migrated to the United States between 1966 and 1985.[6] They have gone so far as to suggest that in the United States "it could be argued that a discussion of immigrant Asian nurses, indeed of foreign-trained nurses in general, is predominantly about Filipino nurses."[7] Because foreign nurse graduates are more likely to be employed as staff nurses in critical care units of large metropolitan and public hospitals, the numbers of Filipino nurses are especially significant in urban areas. In New York City, Filipinos constitute 18 percent of registered nurse staff in the city's hospitals.[8]

I had entered a doctoral program in history with a commitment to documenting Filipino American experiences and specifically those of Filipino women. And I believed that further research on Filipino nurses would serve as an important window to view multiple historical phenomena, in particular the new highly educated, professional, and female Filipino immigration to the United States.[9] I situate my study at the intersections of Asian American, migration, labor, and women's studies. It participates in the project outlined by Asian American studies scholars Paul Ong, Edna Bonacich, and Lucie Cheng, who have argued that new immigration and labor trends, in particular the shift toward higher-educated, professional immigrants from Asia, needed to be explained.[10] In a 1992 article, Ong, Cheng, and Leslie Evans note that between 1961 and 1972, approximately 300,000 scientific, technical, and professional workers from "developing" countries migrated to Western nations and primarily to Australia, Canada, and the United States.[11] They observe that highly educated laborers from Asian countries played a significant role in this form of migration. The nearly thirty thousand Asians who settled in Canada during this time period constituted 52 percent of all third-world highly educated labor, while the sixty-five thousand Asians in the United States accounted for 72 percent.[12] While Ong, Cheng, and Evans include a number of Asian countries (India, South Korea, Philippines, China, Hong Kong, and Thailand) and occupations (math and computer scientists, natural scientists, social scientists, engineers, physicians, nurses, and postsecondary teachers) in their study, their statistics revealed that the migration of Filipino nurses merited closer attention. For example, in their table of immigration of highly educated Asians to the United States between 1972 and 1985, the number of Filipino nurses (20,482) surpassed those of other Asian (Indian, South Korean, Philippine, and Chinese) highly educated laborers in nine different occupations.[13]

My work also addresses one major area of feminist inquiry: the impact of work on women's lives and, specifically, the lives of professional *and* migrant women of color. The ways in which race, nationality, gender, and class have shaped the experiences of this unique group of women have been virtually ignored in both ethnic and women's studies.[14] The study of professional migrant women workers is often subsumed under the categories of highly educated laborers *or* migrant women workers in general. For example, while the Asian American and migration studies scholarship on Asian highly educated labor migration has included women, it has not paid close attention to gender as a useful category of analysis.[15] In other words, this scholarship has tended to focus on the historical, economic, and demographic commonalities of all Asian professional migrant workers regardless of gender. And while the feminist scholarship on migrant women workers takes gender seriously in its analysis, the unique educational and socioeconomic backgrounds of professional migrant women workers are often lumped together with those of domestic workers and prostitutes.[16] I am not arguing that there is little value in grouping professional women workers with highly educated male laborers or professional women workers with "unskilled" migrant women workers under specific circumstances. I am arguing that the experiences of professional migrant women workers need to be studied and understood on their own terms given the increasing significance of both highly educated and female migrations in the late twentieth century.

Since most of the scholarly literature on Filipino nurses is sociological and statistical in nature, one of my major objectives as I embarked on this study was to document a history that took seriously the personal as well as professional aspects of Filipino nurses' lives.[17] My mother had befriended many of the Filipino nurses in our apartment complex. Thus, I came to know these women in the context of my family's social relations and not solely as an occupational immigrant group.

The stereotype of the Filipino-woman-as-nurse problematized this study. In the July 1969 issue of *Gidra*, an Asian American publication, a comic strip titled "Stereotypes" featured several "controlling images" of Filipinos in America.[18] The first panel read, "One Filipino is a Ram quarterback," referring to former Los Angeles Ram Roman Gabriel. In the second panel, the strip continued, "Two Filipinos is a nurses' shift." The accompanying illustration depicted two smiling Filipino women in white nurses' caps and uniforms.

Seeing this controlling image of the Filipino nurse as subservient, nurturing, exotic, and sensual made me reconsider my own study on Filipino nurses, as I feared that more attention to this racialized and gendered occupational group would only reinscribe a stereotype. I had personally encountered this stereotype of the Filipino woman as nurse several times during the course of this project. For example, at a friend's wedding in New York, a woman whom I had just met asked me if I was a nurse. I unconsciously responded, "Oh, you must be thinking about my dissertation project on Filipino nurses," but then realized that she knew nothing about my project and that she had made an assumption about my occupation based on my gender and ethnicity.[19]

From personal conversations, I learned that other Filipino American women had similar experiences. They expressed anger, frustration, and resentment at the conflation of their ethnic, gendered, and occupational identities. These conversations compelled me to question if this project on Filipino nurses would only compound this controlling image, especially given the dearth of historical studies about Filipino American women.[20] However, I was reminded that there are multiple ways to challenge stereotypes.[21] One way is to focus on alternative images. Another way is to confront these controlling images directly.

(Re)Viewing the Literature from an American Shore

My academic training in the United States as a U.S. historian and Asian American studies specialist led me first to review the American literature on Filipino nurse migrants in the United States. On a practical level, the Philippine literature on this topic was not as accessible. More important, contemporary academic training is still very much divided by the borders of modern nation-states. For example, Rudolph J. Vecoli notes, about immigration history, that "while the desirability—and indeed necessity—of multi-group, cross-national, and comparative studies of migration was extolled at [the 1986 international conference A Century of Trans-Atlantic Migration, 1830–1930], there were few examples of this genre on the program as there are in the literature. Most studies continue to be limited within a single country."[22] Partly as a result of such observations, Jane C. Desmond and Virginia R. Domínguez have recently called for "a concerted effort throughout the American studies scholarly community to embrace actively a paradigm of critical internationalism as we move into the next century."[23]

Similar concerns have emerged in the field of Asian American studies, where conferences and symposia at Harvard University, the University of Washington, and California State University have focused on "revisioning" Asian American studies. Until very recently, Asian American studies scholarship has privileged the experiences of Asian Americans within a U.S.-nation-bound context. While scholars have done this in part to make the important point that Asian Americans have lived in the United States for more than 150 years, contemporary demographics have compelled Asian American studies scholars to rethink their methodological approaches.[24]

Contemporary Asian migration to the United States has shaped a very different, diverse, and complex Asian America. In the late twentieth century, Asian America has grown considerably from the influx of immigrants and refugees from Southeast and South Asia. By the late 1980s, the Philippines, Vietnam, and India were among the top ten nations sending immigrants to the United States. A majority of the contemporary Asian American population is foreign born. A significant percentage of this new immigration is highly educated and female. Contemporary Asian American communities have been established beyond the West Coast, in New York, Massachusetts, Illinois, Minnesota, Texas, Virginia, and Georgia. However, despite these dramatic changes, most histories of the Filipino American experience focus on the early-twentieth-century Filipino bachelor societies composed of cannery, service, and agricultural male workers in Hawaii, California, and the Pacific Northwest.[25]

Filipino nurse immigrants first appeared in American scholarly literature in the 1970s as part of a new wave of professional immigrants utilizing the newly established occupational immigrant visas of the Immigration Act of 1965.[26] These pioneering studies laid the groundwork for the conceptualization of Filipino nurse migration to the United States as a post-1965 phenomenon, a chronological as well as thematic framework that has been adopted by Asian American historians. In the two major surveys of Asian American history, Ronald Takaki's *Strangers from a Different Shore* and Sucheng Chan's *Asian Americans: An Interpretative History*, Filipino nurses emerge in the post-1965 chapters as a notable Filipino-American and professional subgroup.[27]

While this framework is useful in Asian American studies (I myself have developed a course, Post-1965 Asian America, that I teach at the University of Minnesota), it also has a blinding effect for some Asian American historians. Yes, we believe that contemporary migration needs to be understood in a historical context. But we sometimes assume that post-1965 topics and themes are devoid of an earlier history and that such research belongs in the disciplinary realm of sociology. On two separate occasions, I have had conversations with Filipino American historians who have quickly characterized my work as a post-1965 project and expressed surprise when I told them that the first part of my study focused on the American colonial period in the Philippines.

I had previously made the same assumptions about my own study. These assumptions shaped my initial conceptualization of my methodology and, specifically, the oral interviews I planned to do with Filipino nurses in New York City. I had originally tried to limit my interview pool by interviewing only those Filipino nurses who had immigrated through the occupational preferences of the Immigration Act of 1965 because the academic literature on Filipino nurses often emphasizes the connection between the increase of professional immigrants and these preferences. However, as I tried to create a pool of interviewees, I quickly learned that Filipino nurses had entered the United States through a variety of avenues: tourism, family reunification preferences, and exchange programs. Furthermore, I learned that a Filipino nurse could (and often did) use multiple avenues to enter, reenter, and/or remain in the United States. For example, when I interviewed Epifania Mercado, I asked her when she immigrated to the United States and she responded that she had arrived in 1971.[28] When I proceeded to ask her about her expectations about nursing in the United States, she then explained to me that she was *already* accustomed to working in this country. Epi (as she prefers to be called) first came to the United States in 1961 as an exchange nurse through the U.S. Exchange Visitor Program.[29]

Studies by Tomoji Ishi, Paul Ong, and Tania Azores have contributed to a more complex understanding of the macro-dimensions of Filipino nurse migration abroad.[30] Their findings helped me reconceptualize the spatial and chronological breadth of my project. These studies discussed several transnational links that facilitated this form of labor migration between the United States and the Philippines throughout the twentieth century: colonial nursing education in the early twentieth century, U.S. exchange programs in the 1940s and 1950s, and occupational immigrant preferences and temporary work programs in the 1960s and 1970s.

While Ishi, Ong, and Azores acknowledge the significance of the relationship among American colonialism, Philippine professional nursing training, and Filipino nurse international migration, their claim that Filipino nurse mass migration abroad was inextricably linked to an American and Philippine colonial past is undeveloped. In fairness to these authors, their article-length studies permit only an overview of the unequal political and economic relationship between the United States and the Philippines. However, their discussions of these transnational links between Philippine and American nursing inspired me to go beyond the unidirectional "Filipino nurse migration to and incorporation in the United States" approach, which I had been pursuing in my research thus far, and to begin researching and conceptualizing Filipino nurse migration in an international and transnational context.

This different approach led me to other bodies of literature on the international dynamics of physician and nurse migration in general. After reading this literature, I emphasized an international context in my study because the migration of Filipino nurses is a phenomenon of global significance and the United States is only one of their international destinations. For example, in 1979, the authors of a World Health Organization (WHO) report observed that the geographic distribution of the international migration of nurses was highly imbalanced.[31] Of an estimated 15,000 nurses moving each year, more than 90 percent went to eight countries—mainly to the United States, the United Kingdom, and Canada. Among the "nurse-sending" countries, the largest outflow of nurses by far was from the Philippines. The authors noted with interest that, with the exception of the Philippines, five of the first six nurse-sending countries were "developed" countries. These puzzling WHO report findings led me to raise one of the major questions of my project: Why has the "developing" country of the Philippines emerged in the late twentieth century to provide professional nursing care for "developed" countries such as the United States?

I had begun legitimizing my research project with the premise that Filipino nurse migrants had made a significant impact on the nursing profession in the United States, but the knowledge that the Philippines was the *world*'s leading exporter of nurses pushed me in different scholarly directions. For example, this important point led me to read the literature on the Philippine's export-oriented economy and to rethink this project with the Philippines (and not the United States) at the center of this study. Beginning in the early 1970s, the Philippine government, under the dictatorship of Ferdinand Marcos, institutionalized an export-oriented economy that included the export of female and male laborers as well as goods.[32]

The U.S.-based studies that focused on Filipino nurse migration to the United States emphasized the role of United States immigration and labor policies in facilitating this migration, and often marginalized was the equally important role of the Philippines' export-oriented economy and the nation's commodification of its own workers abroad. It seemed to me that, in order to answer the question I had posed above, engagement with both sides of this international story was necessary.

Transnational Spaces, Disciplinary Crossings

Although I approached my research as an historian, my work did not fall neatly into a traditional immigration historiography. Rather, my study has gained essential insights from the growing multidisciplinary body of scholarship on transnational frameworks and methodologies in migration, labor, ethnic, women's, and cultural studies. The work of Saskia Sassen was one of the primary influences on my study. In her 1988 *The Mobility of Labor and Capital*, Sassen explores the relationships among the transnational space for the circulation of capital, the formation of labor migrations, and the commodification of migrant laborers.[33] Although her work analyzes both male and female labor migrations within and across various countries, Sassen observed the large-scale migration of women and the commodification of migrant women's work. Particularly influential to my work was Sassen's analysis of the ways in which the presence of international/transnational institutions in certain countries—such as world market factories and plants in export processing zones (EPZs) in the Philippines—was linked to domestic, and eventually, international migrations of women workers. Sassen argues that these domestic migrations of Filipino women workers overflow into international migrations given the widespread practice of firing these women after a few years of work. Sassen's work inspired my inquiries about the transnational space that enabled the production, recruitment, and export of Filipino nurses abroad. However, unlike chief executive officers who can transfer garment and microelectronics factories in EPZs, U.S. hospital administrators cannot relocate hospitals to the Philippines; they must recruit Filipino nurses to work in American hospitals. This type of transnational recruitment then shapes new social as well as spatial relationships between Filipino nurses overseas and their families and friends still in the Philippines.

Roger Rouse's analysis of Mexican migration to the United States and the ways in which Mexican migrants have reshaped (as opposed to uprooted or transplanted) their ties with family and friends in Mexico informed my conceptualization of Filipino and Filipino American communities in this study.[34] In the late twentieth century, access to airplane travel and long-distance phone calls created what Rouse has called a geographically expansive "social space" that transcends national boundaries. These new social spaces have compelled researchers of contemporary urban, suburban, and rural Asian American communities to reconsider the ties that bind them together. They have challenged scholars to go beyond geographically marked borders, such as ethnic enclaves, in their study of communities. Hsiang-Shui Chen has responded to this challenge in his study of Taiwanese immigrants in contemporary New York, *Chinatown No More*.[35] Valerie Matsumoto has confronted the newness and complexity of these social relations in her study of the Cortez Colony, a Japanese-American rural community in California, noting, "Previously unconnected lives are linked with stunning rapidity …. Shared meanings and relations may now span vast distances."[36]

As Joseph Jinn has observed about one part of the Chinese-American community in Southern California, "'Taiwan is so close. From Los Angeles to Taiwan, it's 15 hours …. A lot of people still have family in Taiwan, they still have businesses in Taiwan. They buy and sell stocks in Taiwan, get rich and come to the United States and buy a house here and stay here, and then fly back to Taiwan and make some money and come back. It's a common practice …. In recent years the Chinese American community has become more complex than ever before.'"[37]

The work of Pierrette Hondagneu-Sotelo and Inderpal Grewal compelled me to take gender seriously as a category of analysis in transnational studies. Their work emphasizes that the experiences of women were central to understanding contemporary forms of immigration and travel respectively. Hondagneu-Sotelo's 1994 *Gendered Transitions: Mexican Experiences of Immigration* focuses on Mexican undocumented women and men who eventually settled in Northern California in the 1980s[38]; Grewal's 1996 *Home and Harem: Nation, Gender, Empire, and the Cultures of Travel* analyzes the impact of the nineteenth-century–European culture of travel on social divisions in England and India.[39] While these studies have focused on different groups of women, time periods, and locations and employed different methodological approaches (Hondagneu-Sotelo engages in ethnographic research and conducted oral interviews; Grewal analyzes English and Indian women's travel narratives), they both effectively highlighted the theme of multiple-gendered, racialized, and class-based subjectivities. Hondagneu-Sotelo's study features the voices of Mexican immigrant husbands who migrated without their wives, the Mexican wives who stayed behind, and Mexican husbands and wives who immigrated together, among others. Grewal compares and contrasts the writings of English women who traveled to India and Indian women and men who traveled to England and the United States. In my study I have tried to emulate the ways in which both works moved back and forth among broad political, ideological, and economic forces and individual perspectives, as well as within and across national boundaries. As Nina Glick Schiller, Linda Basch, and Cristina Blanc-Szanton have astutely noted in their conceptualization of transnationalism, "transmigrants deal with and confront a number of hegemonic contexts, both global and national."[40]

Locating and analyzing Asian immigrant women's work in the context of global economies and cultures is a contemporary Asian American studies project. In her essay "Work, Immigration, and Gender: Asian 'American' Women," Lisa Lowe challenges readers to imagine and rearticulate new forms of political subjectivity, collectivity, and practice when interpreting forms of Asian immigrant women's cultural production such as oral testimony.[41] I have attempted to respond to Lowe's challenges of imagination and rearticulation by crossing the disciplinary boundaries of history, anthropology, and sociology and the geographic boundaries of ethnic enclaves and nations. A study that illuminates the personal and professional significance of Filipino nurse migrants demands these intellectual and national crossings.

A Two-Shores Approach

The methodology of this project presented me with the greatest challenges and frustrations as well as rewards. The major source of difficulty stemmed from the absence of a central archive of materials about Filipino nurses. As a result, I was compelled to cast a wide net in my research, to find any materials I could about Filipino nurses, and to engage in multidisciplinary methods: archival research, oral interviews, and participant observation. I felt very much like historian Kristin Hoganson who writes in her book about American masculinity and the Spanish-American and Philippine-American Wars that she "sometimes had the sense of being in a kind of interdisciplinary no-man's-land, far from familiar landmarks."[42]

My research required significant travel within the United States to mine the American Nurses Association archives at Boston University, the Filipino American National History Society archives in Seattle, the National Archives in Chicago, and the newspaper collections of the University of California–Los Angeles's Asian American Studies Reading Room. While the materials I found in these places were eventually important in shaping my findings, during the research stage they only provided clues to the questions I was asking.

I built my own Filipino nurse archive primarily through ethnographic research, in particular the oral interviews. I conducted forty-three oral interviews; forty of these interviews took place in New York City, the remaining three in New Jersey and Washington state. My observations during two months of volunteer work at Bellevue Hospital in New York City, attendance at a Philippine Nurses Association of Southern California meeting in Fullerton, California, and a Philippine Nurses Association of America conference in Las Vegas, as well as my reading, informed my interview questions.

Although I had collected a significant amount of materials in the United States, I believed that a study that took seriously the transnational dynamics of Filipino nurse migration required a two-shores approach. My methodology included ethnographic and archival research in the Philippines as well as in the United States. Being physically in the Philippines as well as reading Philippine studies literature was invaluable to the reconceptualization of my study as a transnational project.

During a five-month research trip to the Philippines, I talked with nursing deans, faculty members, and students at several Philippine colleges and schools of nursing in Manila; directors of nursing and staff nurses at private and government hospitals in Manila; the current president and several members of the Philippine Nurses Association; government employees working in overseas-related agencies; and workers in nongovernmental organizations focusing on the welfare of migrant and women workers. My participant-observation included observing a beginning nursing class at St. Luke's College of Nursing in Quezon City, metro Manila (one of the oldest nursing schools in the country), participating in their community health projects and medical missions, and attending nursing and migration conferences.

I also conducted research in the libraries of Philippine government institutions, nongovernmental institutions, the Philippine Nurses Association, colleges of nursing, and migration and women's studies centers. While these libraries contained a variety of materials about Filipino nurse international migration, among the most interesting were the advertisements in the *Philippine Journal of Nursing,* the official publication of the Philippine Nurses Association, which recruited Filipino nurses to work in the United States.

These advertisements illustrated the complex transnational dynamics of Filipino nurse recruitment. For example, by the late 1960s, individual U.S. hospitals actively recruited their Filipino exchange nurses, who had returned to the Philippines, to come back to them for permanent employment. One summer 1969 advertisement from a Chicago hospital featured the faces of Filipino nurses encircling the caption "There's a Job Waiting for You at Michael Reese Hospital, Chicago, Illinois, U.S.A." The advertisement targeted Filipino nurses who were former exchange visitors at Michael Reese Hospital and publicized bonuses such as: "interest-free loans for travel expenses, continuous in-service education program, and tuition assistance at any recognized university." Furthermore, it highlighted the hospital's "beginning salaries for Philippine nurses with previous Reese experience."[43] They would earn $660 per month for day-shift work, $726 per month for nights, and $770 per month for evenings.

Being physically in the Philippines allowed me to observe the interconnectedness as well as the inequality between the Philippine and U.S. economies in powerful ways that are difficult to translate in academic scholarship. For example, I ran into a St. Luke's nursing student at a McDonald's that was located a few blocks away from the school one afternoon. We were having a very pleasant conversation about my research; she told me that she really wanted to go to the United States but that the waiting period for an immigrant visa was long and travel costs were expensive. At that time, the Christmas holiday was soon approaching and I was thinking that it would be difficult for me to be away from my immediate family that holiday season. But then this nursing student proceeded to tell me that her immediate family members were in different parts of the United States and that it had been several years since they were able to celebrate Christmas all together.

As I reflected on this experience, I thought about how I might incorporate our conversation in my academic work. On one level, our presence in this McDonald's (that served Philippine-style spaghetti and rice as well as the usual Big Mac fare), the student's wait for a U.S. immigrant visa, the prohibitive Philippine-to-U.S. travel costs, and the presence of her family members in different areas abroad exemplified the intersection of the global, transnational, national, and individual forces that I hoped to document. On a personal level, this experience struck me because it caused me to reflect more seriously about the social and economic privileges that I have as a U.S.-based Filipino American scholar who is able to compete for lucrative grant money, travel to various places within the United States as well as to the Philippines for a limited research period, and then return to reunite with family and friends. I wondered how I would go about writing these intersections of imperial domination and individual agency.

An Internationally Dynamic History

After I had conducted research in the Philippines, I analyzed the ways in which the creation, expansion, and export of a Filipino nursing labor force had been transnational processes involving the collaboration of both Philippine and American nurses, professional nursing organizations, government officials, and hospital administrators. I emphasized the *transnational* nature of this phenomenon to highlight the significance of movements—of persons, capital, goods, images, and ideas—across U.S. and Philippine national boundaries. I wrote that these movements were multidirectional and interdependent. I emphasized this notion of multidirectionality because American immigration studies tend to focus on the unidirectional movement of immigrants from the sending country to the United States.

I also focused on the "collaboration" of Philippine and American nurses, nursing organizations, and governments to highlight the complex interaction between, and the historical agency of, the Filipino *and* American participants in this history.[44] For example, during the American colonial period in the Philippines, the agitation of elite Filipino women *and* American educators combined with the labor of American nurses *and* the first Filipino nurse trainees to make the development and growth of professional nursing training in the Philippines possible. In the second half of the twentieth century, the labor demands of U.S. hospital administrators intersected with the social and economic desires of Filipino nurses and nursing students to culminate in the mass migration of Filipino nurses to the United States.

Throughout my study, I have resisted subsuming Filipino nurses under the homogeneous and powerless category of "third-world women." As Chandra Talpade Mohanty has observed, this homogeneity and powerlessness are the effects of Western scholarship, which—whether intentionally or inadvertently—stereotypes and silences women in the third world.[45] The creation of an international labor force of Filipino nurses is not the simple outcome of American conquest involving an almighty force of Americans controlling the minds and bodies of Filipinos. Rather, it is an internationally dynamic history that involves the interactions of numerous participants including the Filipino nurses themselves over time, across national borders, and in the context of unequal social, economic, and political forces.

Final Reflections

June 1999. I have often commented among friends that, after I had entered graduate school, I lost every creative bone in my body. In high school and college, I wrote poetry and short stories and studied modern dance and choreography. And now it is so difficult for me to write without severely editing my thoughts. But the future of Asian American history demands our imagination and creativity. We will have to research, reflect, and write in different ways, to conceptualize alternative historiographies and to build new archives as we study unchartered territory in history as it is currently written.

Can we imagine the United States as an extension of the Philippines? Such a picture might be fruitful for understanding Filipino migration overseas. In the late 1980s, the Philippines became the second-highest country for emigration to the United States, behind Mexico. However, even in the contemporary academic literature on U.S. immigration, the scholarship on Filipino immigrants is minimal. At the 1998 Conference of Social Science Research Council (SSRC) International Migration Fellows, sociologist Rubén Rumbaut shared his findings of an SSRC survey on immigration scholars and their areas of study. He observed that, despite the dramatic numerical significance of Filipino immigrants in the United States in the late twentieth century, very few immigration scholars chose to focus on Filipinos in their work. At that moment, I painfully realized that I was the only Filipino American studies scholar in the room.

However, I'm not going to end on a note of pessimism here because, although change is slow, Asian American historians and our students are changing the academic landscape. I recently developed and taught a seminar on Asian Americans and the politics of labor at the University of Minnesota and, as a result of my research, I was able to talk about professional Filipino nurse migration in more depth using the Michael Reese Hospital advertisement as a pedagogical handout. In my first year of teaching at the university, several students who have taken my Asian American studies courses have approached me to mentor them as they have decided to embark on pioneering Asian American studies research of their own. For example, this summer I am mentoring May yer Ly, who is interviewing Hmong-American students about their undergraduate experiences, and Jennifer Nordin, who is analyzing the creative writing of Korean adoptees in the United States. I look forward to working with them. I look forward to reading the results of their research. I look forward to the future.

Notes

1. Jesse Ventura, *I Ain't Got Time to Bleed: Reworking the Body Politic from the Bottom Up* (New York: Villard, 1999), 78.
2. Ibid., 4.
3. George J. Sanchez, "Race, Nation, and Culture in Recent Immigration Studies," paper presented at the 116th annual meeting of the American Historical Association, Seattle, January 8–11, 1998.
4. William Appleman Williams, "The Frontier Thesis and American Foreign Policy," *Pacific Historical Review*, no. 24 (1955): 379–95.
5. Catherine Ceniza Choy, "The Usual Subjects: Medicine, Nursing, and American Colonialism in the Philippines," *Critical Mass: A Journal of Asian American Cultural Criticism*, no. 5 (1998): 2.
6. Paul Ong and Tania Azores, "The Migration and Incorporation of Filipino Nurses," in *The New Asian Immigration in Los Angeles and Global Restructuring*, ed. Paul Ong, Edna Bonacich, and Lucie Cheng (Philadelphia: Temple University Press, 1994), 164.
7. Ibid., 165.
8. Ibid., 182.

9. Not all Filipino nurses are women. However, the vast majority of them are. I agree with historian Barbara Melosh, who, in her important work on the history of American nursing, writes that "because most nurses have been women ... I use 'nurse' as a feminine generic .... As a feminist I eschew such usage in everyday life. But as a feminist historian I have chosen these markers to emphasize the sex-segregation of the work force in medicine and nursing and to underscore my arguments about the relationship of gender and work"; see Melosh, *"The Physician's Hand": Work Culture and Conflict in American Nursing* (Philadelphia: Temple University Press, 1982), 12.

10. Paul Ong, Edna Bonacich, and Lucie Cheng, "The Political Economy of Capitalist Restructuring and the New Asian Immigration," in Ong, Bonacich, and Cheng, eds., *The New Asian Immigration*, 4.

11. Paul M. Ong, Lucie Cheng, and Leslie Evans, "Migration of Highly Educated Asians and Global Dynamics," *Asian and Pacific Migration Journal 1*, nos. 3–4 (1992): 543.

12. Ibid., 543–44.

13. Ibid., 545.

14. One notable exception is Agnes Calliste's article on the immigration of Caribbean nurses to Canada; see Calliste, "Women of 'Exceptional Merit': Immigration of Caribbean Nurses to Canada," *Canadian Journal of Women and the Law 6*, no. 1 (1993): 85–102.

15. Ong and Azores,"The Migration and Incorporation of Filipino Nurses," is a good example of this observation; see also Amara Bachu, "Indian Nurses in the United States," *International Nursing Review 20*, no. 4 (1973): 114–16, 122.

16. Grace Chang, "The Global Trade in Filipina Workers," in *Dragon Ladies: Asian American Feminists Breathe Fire*, ed. Sonia Shah (Boston: South End Press, 1997), 132–52.

17. Only a few published oral history collections of Filipino Americans and hospital employees provided first-person accounts of Filipino nurses' lives in the Philippines and their work experiences in the United States. See Luz Latus, "My Dream Is to Be Able to Give Something Back to My Country and My People," in *Filipino American Lives*, ed. Yen Le Espiritu (Philadelphia: Temple University Press, 1995), 81–91; the interview with Esther Villanueva in *Hospital: An Oral History of Cook County Hospital*, ed. Sydney Lewis (New York: New Press, 1994), 288–90; and interviews with Connie Chun, Maria Guerrero Llapitan, Perla Rabor Rigor, Irene Salugsugan, and Elizabeth Pucay Bagcal in *Caridad Concepcion Vallangca, The Second Wave: Pinay Pinoy* (San Francisco: Strawberry Hill, 1987), 86–91, 156–158.

18. See "Stereotypes," *Gidra*, July 1969, 2; for an analysis of "controlling images" and their relationship to the economic exploitation and social oppression of subordinate groups, see also Patricia Hill Collins, *Black Feminist Thought: Knowledge, Consciousness, and the Politics of Empowerment* (Boston: Unwin Hyman, 1990). For a comprehensive overview of "controlling images" of Asian Americans on television, see Darrell Y. Hamamoto, *Monitored Peril: Asian Americans and the Politics of TV Representation* (Minneapolis: University of Minnesota Press, 1994).

19. Catherine Ceniza Choy, "The Export of Womanpower: A Transnational History of Filipino Nurse Migration to the United States," Ph.D. diss., University of California–Los Angeles, 1998.

20. In Shirley Hune's bibliographic essay on teaching Asian American women's history, she writes under the heading of "Filipino American Women" that "Filipino Americans are an understudied community"; see Hune, *Teaching Asian American Women's History* (Washington, D.C.: American Historical Association, 1997), 47–48. She cites Fred Cordova's 1983 pictorial essay "Filipinos: Forgotten Asian Americans" (Dubuque, Iowa: Kendall/Hunt Pub. Co., 1983) and such articles as Dorothy Cordova, "Voices from the Past," 42–49; Barbara M. Posadas, "Mestiza Girlhood: Interracial Families in Chicago's Filipino American Community since 1925," 273–81; and Rebecca Villones, "Women in the Silicon Valley," 172–75, all in Asian Women United of California, ed., *Making Waves: An Anthology of Writings by and about Asian American Women* (Boston: Beacon, 1989) as among the very few published studies about Filipino American women's history.

21. Historian Michael Salman reminded me of this significant point.

22. Rudolph J. Vecoli, "From The Uprooted To The Transplanted: The Writing of American Immigration History, 1951–1989," in *From Melting Pot to Multiculturalism: The Evolution of Ethnic Relations in the United States and Canada*, ed. Valerie Gennaro Lerda (Genova: Bulzoni, 1992), 35.

23. Jane C. Desmond and Virginia R. Domínguez, "Resituating American studies in a Critical Internationalism," *American Quarterly 48*, no. 3 (1996): 475.
24. For a critical analysis of these changes in the field of Asian American studies, see Sau-Ling Wong, "Denationalization Reconsidered: Asian American Cultural Criticism at a Theoretical Crossroads," *Amerasia Journal 21*, nos. 1–2 (1995): 1–27.
25. The classic account of these Filipino male migrant workers' experiences is Carlos Bulosan, *America Is in the Heart* (New York: Harcourt, Brace, 1946). For a history of Asian American laborers in the Northwest canneries, see Chris Friday, *Organizing Asian American Labor: The Pacific Coast Canned-Salmon Industry, 1870–1942* (Philadelphia: Temple University Press, 1994); chapter 6 focuses on Filipino cannery workers. For a history of Asian American laborers, including Filipino laborers, in Hawaiian plantations, see Ronald Takaki, *Pau Hana: Plantation Life and Labor in Hawaii* (Honolulu: University of Hawaii Press, 1983).
26. See James P. Allen, "Recent Immigration from the Philippines and Filipino Communities in the United States," *Geographical Review 67*, no. 2 (1977): 195–208; Monica Boyd, "The Changing Nature of Central and Southeast Asian Immigration to the United States: 1961–1972," *International Migration Review 8*, no. 4 (1974): 507–19; Charles B. Keely, "Philippine Migration: International Movement and Immigration to the United States," *International Migration Review 7*, no. 2 (1973): 177–87; and Peter Smith, "The Social Demography of Filipino Migrations Abroad," *International Migration Review 10*, no. 3 (1976): 307–53.
27. Ronald Takaki, *Strangers from a Different Shore: A History of Asian Americans* (New York: Little, Brown, 1989); Sucheng Chan, *Asian Americans: An Interpretive History* (Boston: Twayne, 1991).
28. Epifania O. Mercado, interview with the author, February 3, 1995, New York City.
29. In 1948, the American government, through the U.S. Information and Educational Act, established the Exchange Visitor Program (EVP). Exchange participants from abroad engaged in both work and study in their sponsoring American institutions, for which they would receive a monthly stipend. Several thousand U.S. agencies and institutions were able to sponsor EVP participants, including the American Nurses Association and individual hospitals. The American government issued EVP visas for a maximum stay of two years. Upon the completion of the program, the American and the sending countries' governments expected the EVP participants to return to their countries of origin.
30. See Tomoji Ishi, "Class Conflict, the State, and Linkage: The International Migration of Nurses from the Philippines," *Berkeley Journal of Sociology*, no. 32 (1987): 281–95; and Ong and Azores, "The Migration and Incorporation of Filipino Nurses."
31. Alfonso Mejía, Helena Pizorki, and Erica Royston, *Physician and Nurse Migration: Analysis and Policy Implications* (Geneva: World Health Organization, 1979), 43–45.
32. See Manolo J. Abella, *Export of Filipino Manpower* (Manila: Institute of Labor and Manpower Studies, 1979).
33. Saskia Sassen, *The Mobility of Labor and Capital: A Study in International Investment and Labor Flow* (Cambridge: Cambridge University Press, 1988).
34. Roger Rouse, "Mexican Migration and the Social Space of Postmodernism," *Diaspora*, no. 1 (1991): 8–23.
35. Hsiang-Shui Chen, *Chinatown No More: Taiwanese Immigrants in Contemporary New York* (Ithaca, N.Y.: Cornell University Press, 1992).
36. Valerie J. Matsumoto, *Farming the Home Place: A Japanese American Community in California, 1919–1982* (Ithaca, N.Y.: Cornell University Press, 1993), 4.
37. Joseph Jinn, quoted in Robert Scheer, "They Don't Think They Need to Change," *Los Angeles Times*, February 14, 1994.
38. Pierrette Hondagneu-Sotelo, *Gendered Transitions: Mexican Experiences of Immigration* (Berkeley and Los Angeles: University of California Press, 1994).
39. Inderpal Grewal, *Home and Harem: Nation, Gender, Empire, and the Cultures of Travel* (Durham, N.C.: Duke University Press, 1996).
40. Nina Glick Schiller, Linda Basch, and Cristina Blanc-Szanton, "Transnationalism: A New Analytic Framework for Understanding Migration," in *Towards a Transnational Perspective on Migration: Race, Class, Ethnicity, and Nationalism Reconsidered*, ed. Nina Glick Schiller, Linda Basch, and Cristina Blanc-Szanton (New York: New York Academy of Science, 1992), 5.
41. Lisa Lowe, "Work, Immigration, and Gender: Asian 'American' Women," in *Immigrant Acts: on Asian American Cultural Politics* (Durham, N.C.: Duke University Press, 1996), 154–73.

42. Kristin L. Hoganson, *Fighting for American Manhood: How Gender Politics Provoked the Spanish-American and Philippine-American Wars* (New Haven, Conn.: Yale University Press, 1998), x.

43. Michael Reese Hospital and Medical Center, advertisement, *Philippine Journal of Nursing*, no. 38 (1969): 3.

44. The theme of collaboration in Philippine historiography has been used to refer to the political collaboration among American and Japanese colonial officials and ambitious Philippines political elites. See Michael Cullinane, "Playing the Game: The Rise of Sergio Osmeña, 1898–1907," 70–113, and Alfred W. McCoy, "Quezon's Commonwealth: The Emergence of Philippine Authoritarianism," 114–60, in *Philippine Colonial Democracy*, ed. Ruby R. Paredes (New Haven, Conn.: Yale University, Southeast Asia Studies, 1988).

45. See Chandra Talpade Mohanty, "Under Western Eyes: Feminist Scholarship and Colonial Discourses," in *Third World Women and the Politics of Feminism*, ed. Chandra Talpade Mohanty, Ann Russo, and Lourdes Torres (Bloomington: Indiana University Press, 1991), 51–80.

6

Migrant Filipina Domestic Workers and the International Division of Reproductive Labor

RHACEL SALAZAR PARREÑAS*

Migrant Filipina women are employed as domestic workers in more than 130 countries.[1] They constitute a substantial proportion of labor migrants in various nations in Europe and Asia as well as Canada.[2] To a lesser extent, they are also employed as domestic workers in the United States.[3] Even though Filipina migration is often assumed to be a middle-class professional stream (e.g., of nurses), two-thirds of female labor migrants from the Philippines are, in fact, domestic workers.[4] Only in the United States do Filipina migrant nurses outnumber domestic workers.[5]

Looking at the migration and entrance of Filipina women into domestic work, this article documents the creation of a division of reproductive labor in the global economy. This particular division of labor occurs among working-women and arises out of the demand for low-wage service workers in postindustrial nations. By *reproductive labor*, I refer to the labor needed to sustain the productive labor force.

Such work includes household chores; care of the elderly, adults, and youth; socialization of children; and the maintenance of socialites in the family.[6] Relegated to women more so than men, reproductive labor has long been a commodity purchased by class-privileged women. As Evelyn Nakano Glenn has observed, white class-privileged women in the United States have historically freed themselves of reproductive labor by purchasing the low-wage services of women of color. In doing so they maintain a "racial division of reproductive labor," which establishes a two-tier hierarchy among women.[7]

Two analytical goals motivate my query into the structural relationship between the politics of reproductive labor and the flow of Filipina domestic worker migration. First, I return to the discussion of the commodification of

---

*This essay has been edited from its original version which appeared in *Gender and Society* 14, no. 4 (2000): 560–80.

reproductive labor initiated by Nakano Glenn to extend her discussion to an international terrain.[8] In this way, my analysis of the division of reproductive labor considers issues of globalization and the feminization of wage labor.[9] Second, I extend discussions of the international division of labor in globalization from a sole consideration of productive labor to include analyses of reproductive labor. By analyzing the structural relationship between reproductive labor and the feminization of the migrant labor force, I show another dimension by which gender shapes the economic divisions of labor in migration.

The globalization of the market economy has extended the politics of reproductive labor into an international level. As I show in this article, the migration and entrance into domestic work of Filipino women constitute an international division of reproductive labor. This division of labor, which I call the *international transfer of caretaking*, refers to the three-tier transfer of reproductive labor among women in sending and receiving countries of migration. While class-privileged women purchase the low-wage services of migrant Filipina domestic workers, migrant Filipina domestic workers simultaneously purchase the even lower-wage services of poorer women left behind in the Philippines. In other words, migrant Filipina domestic workers hire poorer women in the Philippines to perform the reproductive labor that they are performing for wealthier women in receiving nations.

The international transfer of caretaking links two important but separate discourses on the status of women—Nakano Glenn's discussion of the "racial division of reproductive labor" and Saskia Sassen's discussion of the "international division of labor."[10] It demonstrates that these important formulations need to be expanded to take into account transnational issues of reproduction.

Reproductive Labor and Paid Domestic Work

My discussion of reproductive labor builds from research on domestic work and female migration. As I have noted, it is grounded in Nakano Glenn's important formulation of the "racial division of reproductive labor."[11] Although reproductive labor has historically been relegated to women, Nakano Glenn argues that there is a hierarchical and interdependent relationship, one that interlocks the race and class status of women, in its distribution in the formal and informal labor market. According to Nakano Glenn, class-privileged women free themselves of the "mental, emotional, and manual labor" needed for "the creation and recreation of people as cultural and social, as well as physical beings" by hiring low-paid women of color.[12] This form of low-wage labor encompasses a wide array of jobs including food-service production, hotel housekeeping, and nursing aid. In the commodification of reproductive labor, women are linked by gender and differentiated by race and class. Moreover, in its commodification, the worth of reproductive labor declines in society. As Barbara Katz Rothman poignantly notes, "When performed by mothers, we call this mothering ... when performed by hired hands, we call it unskilled."[13]

Various case studies on domestic work establish that women often use their class privilege to buy themselves out of their gender subordination.[14] As Mary Romero notes, "The never-ending job described by housewives is transferred to workers employed by women who treat domestic service as an opportunity to 'hire a wife.'"[15] From discussions of the spatial segregation of paid domestic workers to the documentation of the script of "deference and maternalism" in the workplace,[16] numerous studies have also shown that the race and class inequalities that structure this division of labor are aggravated in the daily practices of paid household work.[17]

While scholarship on domestic work establishes the unequal relations between domestics and their employers, it has yet to interrogate substantially the consequences of paid domestic work for the families of domestic workers themselves. An exception to this is Romero's research on the children of domestic workers.[18] One of the questions that needs to be addressed further is: Who cares for the domestics' family? In their article on transnational mothering, Pierrette Hondagneu-Sotelo and Ernistine Avila ask a similar question: "Who is taking care of the nanny's children?"[19] They found that transnational Latina mothers, many of whom are domestic workers, frequently rely on other female relatives as well as paid domestic workers for the care of their children left in the sending country. The observation of Hondagneu-Sotelo and Avila raises questions about the new forms of structural inequalities and social consequences that are engendered by the extension of commodified reproductive labor to an international terrain. To address international relations of inequality in reproductive labor, I now situate my discussion of the politics of reproductive labor in literature of female migration and the globalization of the market economy.

Women and Migration

Contemporary labor migration is situated in the globalization of the market economy. As Sassen has further indicated, globalization has sparked the feminization of migrant labor. Contributing an insightful theoretical framework on the position of women in the global economy, Sassen establishes that globalization simultaneously demands the low-wage labor of third world women in export processing zones of developing countries and in secondary tiers of manufacturing and service sectors in advanced, capitalist countries.[20] The case of women in the Philippines provides an exemplary illustration. While Filipina women constituted 74 percent of the labor force in export processing zones by the early 1980s,[21] they constituted more than half of international migrants (55 percent) by the early 1990s.[22]

In globalization, the penetration of manufacturing production in developing countries creates a demand for women to migrate to advanced-capitalist countries. First of all, the manufacturing production (e.g., of garments, electronics, and furniture) that remains in the latter set of countries must compete with low production costs in developing countries. This result is the decentralization and deregulation of manufacturing production (i.e., subcontracting or homework). Second, multinational corporations with production facilities across the globe, by and large, maintain central operations in new economic centers, or what Sassen refers to as "global cities,"[23] where specialized professional services (e.g., legal, financial, accounting, and consulting tasks) are concentrated. For the most part, global cities require low-wage service labor such as domestic work to maintain the lifestyles of their professional inhabitants. Notably, many of the low-paying jobs created in advanced, capitalist countries are considered traditional women's work. As a result, many of the immigrants that respond to the increasing demand for low-wage workers in advanced, capitalist countries are women.

Independent female migration has correspondingly increased with the feminization of wage labor in the global economy. In the case of the Philippines, the independent nature of female migration is shown by the different destinations of male and female labor migrants in the diaspora. As male and female migrants fill different niches in the global economy, migration from the Philippines results in gendered flows, with women initiating migration to countries with a greater demand for female workers and men migrating to countries with a greater demand for male workers.[24] In fact, the gender composition of many Filipino migrant communities is skewed. Women constitute more than 70 percent of migrant Filipinos in Asian and European cities, where labor markets have a greater demand for low-wage service workers.[25] In contrast, men constitute the majority of Filipino labor migrants in the Middle East, where there are more jobs available in construction and oil industries.[26]

On one hand, the case of Filipina domestic workers fits Sassen's theoretical formulation. As low-wage service workers, they meet the rising demand for cheap labor in the global cities of Asia and Europe and, to a lesser extent, the United States. On the other hand, this theoretical formulation only concentrates on relations of production in globalization. The structural relationship between work and family is not examined in macrolevel accounts of the demand for migrant laborers. In contrast, literature on female migration has turned to the institutional-level perspective to pay closer attention to the analytical principle of gender in the family. By analyzing social relations of men and women in the family, feminist scholars of migration have shown that gender organizes, shapes, and distinguishes the immigration patterns and experiences of men and women.[27]

Situating migrant Filipina domestic workers in the transnational politics of reproductive labor extends Sassen's formulation by stressing the fact that participants in the new international division of labor—from the low-wage migrant worker to the professionals whom they serve—have families.

Accounting for these families allows us to give greater consideration to gender in discussions of divisions of labor in globalization and enables us to more fully describe the labor processes of migration.

Methods

This article is based primarily on open-ended interviews that I collected with forty-six female domestic workers in Rome and twenty-six in Los Angeles. I tape-recorded and fully transcribed each of my interviews, which were mostly conducted in Tagalog and then translated into English.

I chose the field research sites of Rome and Los Angeles because Italy and the United States have the largest populations of Filipino migrants to Western countries.[28] Both destinations also have particular colonial ties to the Philippines. While the United States maintains economic dominance in relation to the Philippines, Italy enjoys cultural dominance indirectly through the institution of the Roman Catholic Church. As a consequence of these macro-historical links, Filipinos have come to represent one of the largest migrant groups in both Italy and the United States.[29] By 1990, the flow of legal migration from the Philippines was the third largest, next to Morocco and Tunisia, in Italy and the second largest, next to Mexico, in the United States.[30]

The interviews in Italy ranged from one and one-half to three hours in length. I also conducted tape-recorded interviews with various community leaders (e.g., elected officers of community associations). I collected an unsystematic sample of research participants by using chain and snowball referrals and began soliciting research participants by visiting numerous community sites such as churches, parks, and plazas. In Los Angeles, I collected a smaller sample of in-depth interviews with Filipina domestic workers, also ranging from one and one-half to three hours in length. My U.S. sample is smaller because, unlike their counterparts in Rome, Filipina migrants in Los Angeles or in the United States in general are not concentrated in the informal service sector. Instead, they occupy a wider range of occupational sectors. Another factor contributing to the smaller sample in Los Angeles is the small representation of Filipinas among domestic workers. Filipinas are but a minority among the larger group of Latina domestics. However according to the community-based organization Filipino Worker's Center, Filipinas dominate elderly care services in Los Angeles.

In the field research site of Los Angeles, tapping into the community began with the network of my mother's friends and relatives. To diversify my sample, I posted flyers in various ethnic-enclave businesses. Two women responded to the flyers. Using networks of domestic workers, the samples of interviewees were collected unsystematically through a snowball method, as had been the case in Italy. Participant observation provided a gateway to the community as I attended meetings of Filipino labor groups, the occasional Filipino town fiestas, and the more frequent Filipino family parties, and I spent time with domestic workers at their own and their employers' homes.

Characteristics of the Sample

My sample of domestic workers in Rome and Los Angeles reveals women who are mostly mothers with a fairly high level of educational attainment. Contrary to the popular belief that Filipina domestic workers are usually young and single,[31] my study shows a larger number of married women. In Los Angeles, only five of twenty-six interviewees were never-married single women, while in Rome, fewer than half of the women I interviewed (nineteen) were never married. Women with children living in the Philippines constitute the majority of my sample in both Rome and Los Angeles: twenty-five of forty-six in Rome and fourteen of twenty-six in Los Angeles.

Because they perform jobs that are considered unskilled, domestic workers are often assumed to lack the training needed for higher-status jobs in the labor market. In the case of Filipina domestics in Italy and the United States, the prestige level of their current work does not in any way reveal their level of educational training. Most of my interviewees had acquired some years of postsecondary training in the Philippines. In Rome, my interviewees include twenty-three women with college degrees, twelve with some years of college or postsecondary vocational training, and seven who completed high school. In Los Angeles, my interviewees include eleven women with college diplomas, eight with some years of college or postsecondary vocational training, and five with high school degrees. Even with a high level of educational attainment, Filipina women migrate and enter the domestic workplace because they still earn higher wages as domestic workers in postindustrial nations than as professional workers in the Philippines. In Rome, part-time workers—as day workers are called in the Filipino migrant community—receive an average monthly wage of 1,844,000 lira (US$1,229), live-in workers 1,083,000 lira (US$722), and elderly care givers 1,167,000 lira (US$778).[32] After taking into account the additional cost of living for part-time workers, there is just a slight difference in salary between the three types of domestic workers. In Los Angeles, Filipina domestic workers are not concentrated in day work as are other immigrant women. Instead, they are mostly live-in workers. In contrast to women in Rome, they receive a weekly instead of a monthly salary, which is an arrangement that they prefer as it results in higher earnings. Caretakers for the elderly receive on average a salary of US$425 per week and live-in housekeepers and child-care givers receive on average US$350 per week. Wages of domestic workers in Rome and Los Angeles are significantly higher than those that they had received in the Philippines. Among my interviewees, the average monthly salary of women who had worked in the Philippines during the 1990s was only US$179.

Reproductive Labor in Sending and Receiving Nations

Migrant Filipina domestic workers depart from a system of gender stratification in the Philippines only to enter another one in the advanced capitalist and industrialized countries of the United States and Italy. In both sending and receiving nations, they confront societies with similar gender ideologies concerning the division of labor in the family; that is, reproductive labor is relegated to women. However, in the receiving nation of Italy or the United States, racial, class, and citizenship inequalities aggravate the position of migrant Filipinas as women.[33] In this section, I discuss the politics of reproductive labor at both ends of the migration spectrum.

In the Philippines, men are expected to sustain the family and women to reproduce family life. In fact, ideological constructs of feminine identity are molded from "mothering and caring roles in the domestic arena."[34] The ideology of women as caretakers constrains the productive labor activities of women in many ways, including sex segregating them into jobs resembling wife-and-mother roles, such as household work on plantations and professional work in nursing and teaching.[35] Because women are expected only to subsidize the primary income of men, women's jobs are often less valued and far less lucrative than comparable men's work (e.g., fieldwork as opposed to household work in plantations).[36] Despite these constraints, women do participate in the productive labor force,[37] and in 1992, the female share of total employment in the Philippines reached 37.7 percent.[38] Considering that only 2 percent of all households in the Philippines can afford to hire domestic help, these working women are plagued by the double day.[39]

In the United States, women represented 46.5 percent of gainfully employed workers in 1992, a considerable increase over 32.1 percent in 1960.[40] In Italy, the downward trend in the labor force participation of women from 1959 to 1972 has since reversed.[41] In fact, Italy has witnessed an increasing number of married women in the labor force but a surprising decline among younger single women.[42] It has been argued that Italian women are turning away from starting families and concentrating on their advancement in the labor market.[43] Italy, although known to be "the traditional 'bambini' country," has the lowest birth rate in the world at only 9.6 per thousand inhabitants.[44]

According to Arlie Hochschild, at least in the United States, the majority of men do less housework than do their gainfully employed partners and men that earned less than their wives were even less likely to share housework.[45] And so today, a significantly larger number of women have to cope with the double day. Similarly in Italy, *doppiolavoro* (literally, *double work*) has been a recurring theme in the Italian feminist movement since the early 1970s.[46]

Notably, the amount of household work expected of women has increased with advances in technology.[47] While a higher income does not guarantee a more gender egalitarian distribution of housework, it does give families the flexibility to afford the services of other women. To ease the double day, many overwhelmed women in the United States have turned to day care centers and family day care providers, nursing homes, after-school baby-sitters, and privately hired domestic workers.[48] In Italy, this same trend is reflected in the concentration of women from the Philippines, Cape Verde, and Peruvian domestic services as well as the estimated 36.4 percent of illegal workers who are doing domestic work.[49] Notably, Italian women have turned to new tactics to minimize their reproductive labor; it can be said that Italian women have since taken to refusing to reproduce the family altogether.[50] Without doubt, this is a unique means by which many Italian women minimize their reproductive labor directly.

The labor market incorporation of migrant Filipina domestic workers into the United States and Italy fits into Nakano Glenn's schema. In both countries, they join the ranks of other groups of subordinated women who have historically performed the reproductive labor of more privileged women. In the Filipino migrant community, it is known that recent migrants frequently turn to domestic work.[51]

Reflecting the observations of Nakano Glenn, Jaqueline Andall associates the entrance of migrant women into Italy—as they are concentrated in domestic work—with the entrance of Italian women into the labor force. She writes, "The migration of women into Italy began at the same time as a number of changes were taking place in the role and position of Italian women within society … in the 1970s, an increased number of Italian women began to assert themselves outside the domestic sphere. This change in Italian women's activity became a pull factor in the migration of women from developing countries."[52]

Nakano Glenn's racial-division formulation of reproductive labor suggests that the demand for low-wage service workers, particularly domestic workers, arises not solely from the concentration of highly specialized professional services in global cities, as Sassen has argued (correctly), but also from persisting gender inequalities in the families of these professionals.[53] To fully consider the politics of reproductive labor in the migration of Filipina domestic workers, I now expand and reformulate the concept of the racial division of reproductive labor by placing it in a transnational setting. In doing so, I situate the increasing demand for paid reproductive labor in receiving nations in the context of the globalization of the market economy.

The International Division of Reproductive Labor

Globalization has triggered the formation of a singular market economy. As such, production activities in one area can no longer be understood solely from a local perspective. With the feminization of wage labor, global capitalism is forging the creation of links among distinct systems of gender inequality. Moreover, the migration of women connects systems of gender inequality in both sending and receiving nations to global capitalism. All of these processes occur in the formation of the international division of reproductive labor.

This division of labor places Nakano Glenn's "racial division of reproductive labor" in an international context under the auspices of Sassen's discussion of the incorporation of women from developing countries into the global economy.[54] It is a transnational division of labor that is shaped simultaneously by global capitalism, gender inequality in the sending country, and gender inequality in the receiving country. This division of labor determines the migration and entrance into domestic service of women from the Philippines. The international transfer of caretaking is a distinct form of the international division of labor in which Filipina domestic workers perform the reproductive labor or the private sphere responsibilities of class-privileged women in industrialized countries as they leave other women in the Philippines to perform their own. This international division of labor refers to a three-tier transfer of reproductive labor among women in two nation-states. These groups of women are (1) middle-class women in receiving countries, (2) migrant Filipina domestic workers, and (3) Filipina domestic workers in the Philippines who are too poor to emigrate.

Under the international transfer of caretaking, women's migration from the Philippines is embedded in the process of global capitalism. At the same time, gender is also a central factor of their migration. The process of migration for women involves escaping their gender roles in the Philippines, easing the gender constraints of the women who employ them in industrialized countries, and finally relegating their gender roles to women left in the Philippines.[55] The international transfer of caretaking refers to social, political, and economic relationships among women in the global labor market. This division of labor is a structural relationship based on the class, race, gender, and (nation-based) citizenship of women. In the international transfer of caretaking, Filipina domestic workers not only ease the entrance of other women into the paid labor force but also assist in the economic growth of receiving countries. In the article "Economy Menders," Linda Layosa, the editor of the transnational monthly magazine *Tinig Filipino*, describes the international transfer of caretaking, noting, "Indeed, our women have partially been liberated from the anguish of their day-to-day existence with their families and from economic problems, only to be enslaved again in the confines of another home, most of the time trampling their rights as human beings ... we have to face the reality that many of our women will be compelled to leave the confines of their own tidy bedrooms and their spotless kitchens only to clean another household, to mend others' torn clothes and at the same time mend our tattered economy."[56]

In her description, she falls short of mentioning who takes up the household work that migrant Filipina domestic workers abandon upon migration; most likely it is other female relatives, but it is also less privileged Filipina women, women unable to afford the high costs of seeking employment outside of the Philippines. Thus, migrant Filipina domestic workers are in the middle of the three-tier hierarchy of the international transfer of caretaking.

The case of Carmen Ronquillo provides a good illustration of the international transfer of caretaking.[57] Carmen is simultaneously a domestic worker of a professional woman in Rome and an employer of a domestic worker in the Philippines. Carmen describes her relationship to each of these two women:

> When coming here, I mentally surrendered myself and forced my pride away from me to prepare myself. But I lost a lot of weight. I was not used to the work. You see, I had maids in the Philippines. I have a maid in the Philippines that has worked for me since my daughter was born twenty-four years ago. She is still with me. I paid her three hundred pesos before and now I pay her one thousand pesos.[58] I am a little bit luckier than others because I run the entire household. My employer is a divorced woman who is an architect. She does not have time to run her household so I do all the shopping. I am the one budgeting. I am the one cooking. [*Laughs.*] And I am the one cleaning, too. She has a twenty-four and twenty-six-year-old. The older one graduated already and is an electrical engineer. The other one is taking up philosophy. They still live with her .... She has been my only employer. I stayed with her because I feel at home with her. She never commands. She never orders me to do this and to do that.

The hierarchical and interdependent relationship among Carmen, her employer in Italy, and her domestic worker in the Philippines forms from the unequal development of industrialized and developing countries in transnational capitalism, class differences in the Philippines, and the relegation of reproductive labor to women. Carmen's case clearly exemplifies how three distinct groups of women participate in the international transfer of caretaking. While Carmen frees her employer (the architect) of domestic responsibilities, a lower-paid domestic worker does the household work for Carmen and her family.

The Overlooked Participants: Children and Women in the Philippines

The private world remains devalued, as poor people become the wives and mothers of the world, cleaning the toilets and raising the children. The devaluing of certain work, of nurturance, of private domestic work, remains: child rearing is roughly on a par—certainly in terms of salary—with cleaning the toilet.[59] While the devaluation of child rearing could be lamented as a tragedy for children, the experiences of the different groups of children (and elderly) in the international transfer of caretaking should be distinguished between those who remain cared for and those who are not, and those who regularly see their parents/children and those who cannot. The fact that child rearing is considered on a par with toilet cleaning means that migrant Filipina domestic workers usually cannot afford the higher costs of maintaining a family in industrialized countries due to their meager wages. In the United States, where people of color have traditionally been caretakers and domestic workers for white families, mothering is diverted away from people of color families. Sau-ling Wong defines *diverted mothering* to be a process in which the "time and energy available for mothering are diverted from those who, by kinship or communal ties, are their more rightful recipients."[60] In an international context, the same pattern of diverted mothering could be described for Filipina, Latina, and Caribbean domestic workers as many are forced to leave their children behind in the country of origin.[61] The question then is: Who cares for these "other" children?

In the Philippines, it is unusual for fathers to nurture and care for their children, but, considering that not all migrant Filipina domestic workers hire domestic workers, some are forced to give in to the renegotiations of household division of labor brought on by the migration of their wives. Other female relatives often take over the household work of migrant Filipinas. In these cases, nonegalitarian relations among family members should be acknowledged, considering that for female family members left in the Philippines, "the mobility they might achieve through migration is severely curtailed."[62] However, hired domestic workers—a live-in housekeeper or *labandera* (laundry woman that hand washes clothes)—also free migrant Filipina domestics of their household labor. Almost all of my interviewees in both Rome and Los Angeles had hired domestic workers in the Philippines. This should not be surprising, considering that the average wage of domestics in the Philippines is considerably less than the average wage of migrant domestics.

Because migrant Filipina domestic workers are usually in the middle of the hierarchical chain of caretaking, they maintain unequal relations with less privileged women in the Philippines. Under the international transfer of caretaking, the unequal economic standing of nation-states and discrepancies in monetary currencies are prominent factors that distinguish the position of female low-wage workers in advanced, capitalist, and developing countries. They differentiate, for example, the position of domestic workers in the United States and Italy from domestic workers in the Philippines. Migrant Filipina domestic workers surely take advantage of these differences in wages and maintain a direct, hierarchical relationship with the domestic workers they hire in the Philippines. In the international transfer of caretaking, domestic workers (e.g., housekeepers and laundry women) hired by families of domestic workers abroad are the truly subaltern women.

The Social Consequences of Being in the Middle

The formation of the international division of reproductive labor results in particular social consequences that are embodied in the lived experience of its being in the middle. The process in which reproductive labor is transferred to migrant Filipinas is not as smooth as it sounds. For many, the process involves multiple contradictions in their positions in the family and the labor market.

To illuminate the consequences of being in the middle, I return to the story of Carmen Ronquillo. Before migrating to Rome, Carmen, who is in her mid-forties, had worked for fifteen years as a project manager of the military food services at the Clark Air Force Base. With the closure of this U.S. military base in 1992, Carmen thought that she could not find a job that offered a comparably lucrative income in the Philippines. Therefore, Carmen decided to follow her sister to Rome, where she could earn much more as a domestic worker than as a professional in the Philippines. Seeking employment in Italy was a huge investment for her family. Carmen paid an agency US$5,000 to enter Italy without a visa. The high costs of migration from the Philippines suggest that this option usually is limited to those with financial means. Consequently, labor migration for Carmen and the many other middle-class women that can afford to leave the Philippines usually entails the emotional strains brought on by a downward mobility toward the lower-status job of domestic work. As Carmen explains,

> My life is difficult here. Would you believe that here I am a "physical laborer"? When I was working in the Philippines, I was the one supervising the supervisors. [*Laughs.*] So, when I came here, especially when I cleaned the bathrooms, I would talk to myself. [*Laughs hysterically.*] I would commend and praise myself, telling myself, "Oh, you clean the corners very well." [*Laughs.*] You see, in my old job, I would always check the corners first, that was how I checked if my workers had cleaned the place well. So, sometimes I would just cry. I felt like I was slapped in the face. I resent the fact that we cannot use our skills, especially because most of us Filipinos here are professionals. We should be able to do other kinds of work because if you only do housework, your brain deteriorates. Your knowledge deteriorates. Your whole being is that of a maid.

As reflected in the bitter attitude of Carmen toward domestic work, a central contradiction of being in the middle of the international transfer of caretaking is the experience of *conflicting class mobility*. For migrant Filipinas, domestic work simultaneously involves an increase and decrease in class status. They earn more than they ever would have if they had stayed as professional women in the Philippines, yet at the same time they experience a sharp decline in occupational status and face a discrepancy between their current occupation and actual training. For the women in the middle, this discrepancy highlights the low status of domestic work.

According to Linda Basch, Nina Glick Schiller, and Christina Szanton Blanc, this decline in social status in migration generally pushes migrants to build "deterritorialized national identities."[63] They cope with their marginal status in the receiving country by basing their identities on the increase in their class status in the country of origin. In the same vein, migrant Filipina domestic workers resolve their conflicting class mobility by stressing their higher social and class status in the Philippines.

They do just that by hiring their very own domestic workers or perceiving themselves as rightful beneficiaries of servitude. In this way, they are able to mitigate their loss of status in migration. As Joy Manlapit of Los Angeles tells me, "When I go back, I want to experience being able to be my own boss in the house. I want to be able to order someone to make me coffee, to serve me food. That is good. That is how you can take back all the hardships you experienced before. That is something you struggled for."

Gloria Yogore, a Filipina in Rome, finds similar comfort in the knowledge of the higher social status she occupies and will occupy once she returns to the Philippines: "In the Philippines, I have maids. When I came here, I kept on thinking that in the Philippines, I have maids and here I am one. I thought to myself that once I go back to the Philippines, I will not lift my finger and I will be the *signora*. [*Laughs.*] My hands will be rested and manicured and I will wake up at 12 o'clock noon." Ironically, migrant Filipina domestic workers find comfort from the contradiction of the simultaneous decline and increase in their class background by stressing the greater privilege that they have and will have in relation to poorer women in the Philippines.

Another consequence of being in the middle is the experience of the pain of family separation. Being in the middle is contingent on being part of a transnational household, meaning a household whose members are located in two or more nation-states. Among my interviewees, forty-one of forty-six women in Rome and twenty of twenty-six women in Los Angeles maintain such households. I placed my interviewees categorically under this type of household structure on the basis that their remittances sustain the day-to-day living expenses of their immediate and extended families in the Philippines. Almost all of the never-married single women without children in my sample (fourteen in Rome and six in Los Angeles) are, in fact, part of transnational households. Notably, only one single woman does not send remittances to the Philippines regularly.

Emotional strains of transnational family life include feelings of loss, guilt, and loneliness for the mothers and daughters working as domestics in other countries. Plagued by the pain of family separation, women like Carmen struggle with the emotional strains of family separation in their daily lives.

"My son," she notes, "whenever he writes me, always draws the head of Fido the dog with tears on the eyes. Whenever he goes to mass on Sundays, he tells me that he misses me more because he sees his friends with their mothers. Then, he comes home and cries. He says that he does not want his father to see him crying so he locks himself in his room. When I think of them [her children] is when I feel worst about being here. I was very very close to my two children.... Whenever I think of my children, I am struck with this terrible loneliness." Being in the middle of the international division of reproductive labor entails geographic distance in families and consequently emotional strains for lonely migrant mothers and miserable children in the Philippines.

Another contradiction of being in the middle of the international division of reproductive labor or the international transfer of caretaking is the fact that women in the middle must care for someone else's grandchildren, children, or parents while they are unable to care for their own. In contrast to the two other social consequences that I have previously described, this is not unique to the transnational situation of migrant domestic workers. However, it does reflect one of the structural constraints faced by Filipina domestic workers in the process of globalization: The choice of maximizing their earnings as transnational low-wage workers denies them the intimacy of the family. Thus, caretaking is made a more painful experience. As Christina Manansala, a domestic worker in Rome since 1990, states, "Of course it is hard to take care of other children. Why should I be taking care of other children when I cannot take care of my own child myself?"

The pain of caretaking leads to another contradiction, and that is the experience of *displaced mothering*—or, more generally, *displaced caretaking*, which is also a social consequence that is not unique to the international division of reproductive labor. Unable to take care of their own families, migrant Filipina domestic workers, like the nonmigrant domestics forced into "diverted mothering" in the United States, find themselves needing to "pour [their] love" into their wards. As Vicky Diaz, a mother in Los Angeles who left five children between the ages of two and ten years old in the Philippines ten years ago, describes her relationship to her ward: "The only thing you can do is give all your love to the child. In my absence from my children, the most I could do with my situation is give all my love to that child." Trinidad Borromeo of Rome finds similar comfort from giving her love to her elderly ward: "When I take care of an elderly woman, I treat her like she is my own mother." Notably, some women develop an aversion to caretaking, like Ruby Mercado of Rome, who states, "I do not like taking care of children when I cannot take care of my own children. It hurts too much." However, most of my interviewees do indeed feel less guilt for leaving behind their families in the Philippines when caring for and pouring their love into another family. Ironically, as mothering is transferred to domestic workers, those without children, such as Jerrisa Lim of Los Angeles, begin to feel that they know what it is like to mother: "After doing child care, I feel like I experienced what it is like to be a mother. It is hard to have children. There are pleasures that go with it. That is true. But it is hard." The idea that domestic work involves the act of "pouring love" suggests that a certain degree of emotional bonds to dependents in the family, including children and elderly persons, is passed down in the transfer of caretaking. By operating in the realm of emotion, the commodification of caretaking is further heightened in globalization.

Conclusion

The hierarchy of womanhood—based on race, class, and nation—establishes a work transfer system of reproductive labor among women—the international transfer of caretaking. It is a distinct form of transnational division of labor that links women in an interdependent relationship. Filipina domestic workers perform the reproductive labor of more privileged women in industrialized countries as they relegate their reproductive labor to poorer women left in the Philippines. The international division of reproductive labor shows us that production is not the sole means by which international divisions of labor operate in the global economy. In globalization, the transfer of reproductive labor moves beyond territorial borders to connect separate nation-states. The extension of reproductive labor to a transnational terrain is embedded in the operation of transnational families and the constant flow of resources from migrant domestic workers to the families that they continue to support in the Philippines. While acting as the primary income earners of their families, migrant Filipina domestic workers hire poorer domestic workers to perform the household duties that are traditionally relegated to them as women. In this way, they continue to remain responsible for the reproductive labor in their families but at the same time, as migrant workers, take on the responsibility of productive labor.

The formulation of the international division of reproductive labor treats gender as a central analytical lens for understanding the migration of Filipina domestic workers. It shows that the movement of these workers is embedded in a gendered system of transnational capitalism. While forces of global capitalism spur the labor migration of Filipina domestic workers, the demand for their labor also results from gender inequities in receiving nations, specifically the relegation of reproductive labor to women. This transfer of labor strongly suggests that despite their increasing rate of labor market participation, women continue to remain responsible for reproductive labor in both sending and receiving countries. At both ends of the migratory stream, they have not been able to negotiate directly with male counterparts for a fairer division of household work but, instead, have had to rely on their race and/or class privilege by participating in the transnational transfer of gender constraints to less privileged women.

Ironically, women in industrialized (Western) countries often are assumed to be more liberated than women are in developing countries. However, many women are able to pursue careers as their male counterparts do because disadvantaged migrant women and other women of color are stepping into their old shoes and doing their household work for them. As women transfer their reproductive labor to less and less privileged women, we can see that the traditional division of labor in the patriarchal nuclear household has not been significantly renegotiated in various countries in the world. This is one of the central reasons why there is a need for Filipina domestic workers in more than one hundred countries today.

Acknowledgments

I wish to thank Evelyn Nakano Glenn, Arlie Hochschild, Raka Ray, Michael Omi, Pierrette Hondagneu-Sotelo, Jennifer Lee, and an anonymous reviewer for their helpful comments on earlier versions of this article and Christine Bose for her editorial suggestions. The University of California Office of the President and Babilonia Wilner Foundation provided support during the writing of this essay. Finally, I thank Thuc Nguyen for her editorial assistance.

Notes

1. James Tyner, "The Global Context of Gendered Labor Migration from the Philippines to the United States," *American Behavioral Scientist* 42, no. 4 (1999): 671–89.
2. See Abigail Bakan and Daiva Stasiulis, "Foreign Domestic Worker Policy in Canada and the Social Boundaries of Modern Citizenship," in *Not One of the Family: Foreign Domestic Workers in Canada*, ed. Abigail Bakan and Daiva Stasiulis (Toronto: University of Toronto Press, 1997); Catholic Institute for International Relations, *The Labour Trade: Filipino Migrant Workers around the Globe* (London: Catholic Institute for International Relations, 1987); Nicole Constable, *Maid to Order in Hong Kong: Stories of Filipina Workers* (Ithaca, N.Y.: Cornell University Press, 1997).
3. Chris Hogeland and Karen Rosen, *Dreams Lost Dreams Found: Undocumented Women in the Land of Opportunity* (San Francisco: Coalition for Immigrant Rights and Services, 1990).
4. Roland Tolentino, "Bodies, Letters, Catalogs: Filipinas in Transnational Spaces," *Social Text* 48, no. 3 (1996): 49–76.
5. Tyner, "The Global Context of Gendered Labor Migration." Responding to the shortage of medical personnel in the U.S. labor market, Filipina nurses entered the United States through the third preference category of the Immigration and Nationality Act of 1965 with the assistance of recruitment agencies in both the Philippines and the United States. See Paul Ong and Tania Azores, "The Migration and Incorporation of Filipino Nurses," in *The New Asian Immigration in Los Angeles and Global Restructuring*, ed. Paul Ong, Edna Bonacich, and Lucie Cheng (Philadelphia: Temple University Press, 1994) for an extensive discussion of the migration of Filipina nurses.
6. See Johanna Brenner and Barbara Laslett, "Gender, Social Reproduction and Women's Self-Organization: Considering the U.S. Welfare State," *Gender and Society* 5, no. 3 (1991): 311–33.
7. Evelyn Nakano Glenn, "From Servitude to Service Work: The Historical Continuities of Women's Paid and Unpaid Reproductive Labor," *Signs: Journal of Women in Culture and Society* 18, no. 1 (1992): 1–44.
8. Ibid., 1–44.
9. See Saskia Sassen, "Notes on the Incorporation of Third World Women into Wage Labor through Immigration and Off-Shore Production," *International Migration Review* 18, no. 4 (1984): 1144–67, and *The Mobility of Labor and Capital: A Study in International Investment and Labor* (New York: Cambridge University Press, 1988).

10. Nakano Glenn, "From Servitude to Service Work"; Sassen, "Notes on the Incorporation of Third World Women."
11. Nakano Glenn, "From Servitude to Service Work."
12. Ibid., 30.
13. Barbara Katz Rothman, *Recreating Motherhood: Ideology and Technology in a Patriarchal Society* (New York: W. W. Norton, 1989), 43.
14. Phyllis Palmer, *Domesticity and Dirt: House Wives and Domestic Servants in the United States, 1920–1945* (Philadelphia: Temple University Press, 1989); Mary Romero, *Maid in the U.S.A.* (New York: Routledge, 1992); Bonnie Thornton Dill, *Across the Boundaries of Race and Class: An Exploration of Work and Family among Black Domestic Servants* (New York: Garland, 1994).
15. Romero, *Maid in the U.S.A.*, 129–30.
16. Judith Rollins, *Between Women: Domestics and their Employers* (Philadelphia: Temple University Press, 1985).
17. Romero, *Maid in the U.S.A.*; Dill, *Across the Boundaries of Race and Class*, 1994.
18. Mary Romero, "Life as the Maid's Daughter: An Exploration of the Every Day Boundaries of Race, Class, and Gender," in *Challenging Fronteras: Structuring Latina and Latino Lives in the U.S.*, ed. Mary Romero, Pierrette Hondagneu-Sotelo, and Vilma Ortiz (New York: Routledge, 1997).
19. Pierrette Hondagneu-Sotelo and Ernistine Avila, "'I'm Here, but I'm There': The Meanings of Latina Transnational Motherhood," *Gender and Society* 11, no. 5 (1997): 548–71.
20. See Sassen, "Notes on the Incorporation of Third World Women" and *The Mobility of Labor and Capital.*
21. Ninotchka Rosca, "The Philippines' Shameful Export," *Nation* 260, no. 15 (1995): 522–27.
22. Maruja M. B. Asis, "The Overseas Employment Program Policy," in *Philippine Labor Migration: Impact and Policy*, ed. Graziano Battistella and Anthony Paganoni (Quezon City, Philippines: Scalabrini Migration Center, 1992).
23. Saskia Sassen, *Cities in a World Economy* (Thousand Oaks, Calif.: Pine Forge, 1994).
24. James Tyner, "The Social Construction of Gendered Migration from the Philippines," *Asian and Pacific Migration Journal* 3, no. 4 (1994): 589–615.
25. Constable, *Maid to Order in Hong Kong*; Rhacel Salazar Parreñas, "The Global Servants: Migrant Filipina Domestic Workers in Rome and Los Angeles," Ph.D. diss., University of California–Berkeley, 1998.
26. Tyner, "The Social Construction of Gendered Migration," 1994.
27. Sherri Grasmuck and Patricia Pessar, *Between Two Islands: Dominican International Migration* (Berkeley and Los Angeles: University of California Press, 1991); Pierrette Hondagneu-Sotelo, *Gendered Transitions: Mexican Experiences of Migration* (Berkeley and Los Angeles: University of California Press, 1994).
28. Jonathan Karp, "A New Kind of Hero," *Far Eastern Economic Review*, no. 158 (1995): 42–45.
29. Caritas di Roma, *Immigrazione: Dossier Statistic '95* (Rome: Anterem Edizioni Ricerca, 1995); Alejandro Portes and Rubén Rumbaut, *Immigrant America: A Portrait*, 2d ed. (Berkeley and Los Angeles: University of California Press, 1996).
30. Giovanna Campani, "Immigration and Racism in Southern Europe: The Italian Case," *Ethnic and Racial Studies* 16, no. 3 (1993): 507–35; Portes and Rumbaut, *Immigrant America*, 1996.
31. Catholic Institute for International Relations, *The Labour Trade*, 1987.
32. Approximately fifteen hundred lira equal one U.S. dollar.
33. Jaqueline Andall, "Women Migrant Workers in Italy," *Women's Studies International Forum* 15, no. 1 (1992): 41–48; Nakano Glenn, "From Servitude to Service Work," 1992.
34. Carolyn Israel-Sobritchea, "The Ideology of Female Domesticity: Its Impact on the Status of Filipino Women," *Review of Women's Studies* 1, no. 1 (1990): 26–41.
35. Sylvia Chant and Cathy McIlwaine, *Women of a Lesser Cost: Female Labour, Foreign Exchange and Philippine Development* (London: Pluto, 1995); Elizabeth Uy Eviota, *The Political Economy of Gender: Women and the Sexual Division of Labour in the Philippines* (London: Zed, 1992).
36. Eviota, *The Political Economy of Gender.*
37. Delia Aguilar, *The Feminist Challenge: Initial Working Principles toward Reconceptualizing the Feminist Movement in the Philippines* (Manila: Asian Social Institute, 1988).
38. Sylvia Chant, *Women-headed Households: Diversity and Dynamics in the Developing World* (New York: St. Martin's, 1997).
39. Aguilar, *The Feminist Challenge.*

40. Barbara Reskin and Irene Padavic, *Women and Men at Work* (Thousand Oaks, Calif.: Pine Forge, 1994), 24–25.
41. Donald Meyer, *The Rise of Women in America, Russia, Sweden, and Italy* (Middletown, Conn.: Wesleyan University Press, 1987).
42. Victoria A. Goddard, *Gender, Family and Work in Naples* (Oxford: Berg, 1996).
43. Michael Specter, "The Baby Bust," *New York Times*, July 10, 1998.
44. Ulrich Beck and Elisabeth Beck-Gernsheim, *The Normal Chaos of Love* (Cambridge, Mass.: Polity, 1995), 102.
45. Arlie Hochschild, *The Second Shift* (New York: Avon, 1989).
46. Lucia Chiavola Birnbaum, *Liberazione della Donne* (Middletown, Conn.: Wesleyan University Press, 1986).
47. Nona Glazer, *Women's Paid and Unpaid Labor: The Work Transfer in Health Care and Retailing* (Philadelphia: Temple University Press, 1993).
48. Ibid.; Rothman, *Recreating Motherhood*; Nakano Glenn, "From Servitude to Service Work"; Margaret K. Nelson, "Mothering Other's Children: The Experiences of Family Day Care Providers," in *Circles of Care: Work and Identity in Women's Lives*, ed. Emily K. Abel and Margaret K. Nelson (Albany: State University of New York Press, 1990); Reskin and Padavic, *Women and Men at Work*.
49. Kitty Calavita, "Italy and the New Immigration," in *Controlling Immigration: A Global Perspective*, ed. Wayne Cornelius, Philip Martin, and James Hollifield (Stanford, Calif.: Stanford University Press, 1994).
50. Birnbaum, *Liberazione della Donne*, 135.
51. This is caused by a combination of their undocumented status, inability to use their training and work experience from the Philippines, and/or the ethnic niche in caregiving that has developed in the Filipino migrant community. In a study of undocumented women in the United States, Hogeland and Rosen, *Dreams Lost Dreams Found*, 43, found that 64 percent of 57 survey participants from the Philippines are employed as domestic workers.
52. Andall, "Women Migrant Workers in Italy," 43.
53. Nakano Glenn, "From Servitude to Service Work."
54. Ibid.
55. Notably, in the Philippines, older (female) children, not fathers, are more likely to look after younger siblings while their mothers work; see Chant and McIlwaine, *Women of a Lesser Cost*. In addition, daughters are traditionally expected to care for aging parents.
56. Linda Layosa, "Economy Menders," *Tinig Filipino*, June 7, 1995, p. 7.
57. I use pseudonyms to protect the anonymity of my interviewees.
58. Approximately one thousand pesos equals US$40.
59. Rothman, *Recreating Motherhood*, 252.
60. Sau-ling Wong, "Diverted Mothering: Representations of Care Givers of Color in the Age of 'Multiculturalism,'" in *Mothering: Ideology, Experience, and Agency*, ed. Evelynn Nakano Glenn, Grace Chang, and Linda Forcey (New York: Routledge, 1994), 69.
61. Shellee Colen, "'Like a Mother to Them': Stratified Reproduction and West Indian Child Care Workers and Employers in New York," in *Conceiving the New World Order: The Global Politics of Reproduction*, ed. Faye D. Ginsburg and Reyna Rapp (Berkeley and Los Angeles: University of California Press, 1995); Hondagneu-Sotelo and Avila, "I'm Here, but I'm There." In most other receiving nations, migrant Filipinos are deterred from family migration by their relegation to the status of temporary migrants or their ineligibility for family reunification; see Constable, *Maid to Order in Hong Kong*.
62. Linda Basch, Nina Glick Schiller, and Christina Szanton Blanc, *Nations Unbound: Transnational Projects, Postcolonial Predicaments, and Deterritorialized Nation-States* (Langhorne, Penn.: Gordon and Breach, 1994), 241.
63. Ibid., 234.

7

Beauty Queens, Bomber Pilots, and Basketball Players: Second-Generation Filipina Americans in Stockton, California, 1930s to 1950s

When Anastacio Bantillo asked his teenage daughter Angelina to run for the 1942 queen contest of his Filipino fraternal group, she was adamantly opposed to the idea. Anastacio, a Filipino immigrant who arrived in San Francisco before the 1906 earthquake, was an esteemed Filipina/o American community leader in Stockton, California, the center of the Filipino population on the West Coast. As a member of the Stockton chapter of the popular Filipino fraternal order Caballeros de Dimas Alang, it was important to Anastacio that his daughter represent the family to the community by running for queen.[1] Angelina resisted because she did not want to have to campaign relentlessly within the Little Manila neighborhood in Stockton and in the surrounding areas. However, she was overruled, as she put it, because "my father's word was an order in our family."[2]

Most Filipina/o organizations in California during the first half of the century held queen contests and dances as important fundraisers. As Angelina Bantillo knew well, young Pinays worked intensely to run a campaign.[3] The queen contest circuit required that girls take publicity photos for distribution to potential ticket buyers and then attend several social functions dressed in traditional Philippine dress. Candidates sold tickets by soliciting donations and votes from community members in the San Joaquin Valley agricultural camps where most Filipina/os toiled. As a way to express her resistance, Angelina wore an austere, knee-length black dress to the vote tabulation dance while other young daughters of prominent Filipino community leaders wore elaborate, shimmering, floor-length gowns either imported from the Philippines or painstakingly sewn and embroidered by their mothers. "I felt like I was in mourning and that was my expression of my resistance," Angelina remembers.[4]

When a photographer came to the family home to take the publicity photos for the queen contest campaign, Anastacio ordered his daughter to change into her traditional Filipina dress. "I was an obedient daughter, and I kept my mouth shut and I changed to my Filipina dress and I was all set for the photographer," she recalls. "Just before I was supposed to go and pose for the photographer, I suddenly broke out and just cried and sobbed and I couldn't stop crying."[5] Incensed at her husband's insensitivity, Angelina's mother Virginia intervened and allowed her to bow out of the contest.

Angelina was one of approximately two hundred second-generation Pinays in Little Manila and in the nearby area. Angelina was typical of other Pinays of her age group in Stockton. Born into a large family, she worked downtown at a soda shop in Little Manila and in the potato fields in the summertime to contribute to the family economy. She was a founding member of the Daughters of the Philippines, a social network of young second-generation Pinays in Stockton dedicated to community work and leisure activities. She enjoyed spending time with her friends—also the sons and daughters of Filipina/o immigrants—at the local Filipino-owned soda fountain. She played piano, liked to dance, and liked stylish new clothes.

Angelina's strict upbringing and her yearning to resist the confines of an ethnic culture that prescribed rigid gender roles for women illustrate the kinds of pressures, negotiations, and responses experienced by young Pinays in the Filipina/o American community in Stockton as the second generation came of age from the 1930s to the 1950s. Because of their scarcity and their roles as symbols of homeland, family, and culture to the mostly bachelor community on the West Coast, women were prized in Little Manila, home to the largest Filipino American community outside Manila through most of the twentieth century. The lives of young Pinays in Little Manila illustrate vividly how the forces of Americanization and acculturation were expressed in the experiences of racial ethnic young women in California.

This essay builds on historian Fred Cordova's understandings of this generation and expands his analysis by examining the roles of young women in Little Manila and the ways that the sex-ratio imbalance, patriarchy, power, and popular culture intersected in their lives. These women engaged in high school rituals and shared experiences with other young women of color of the period. They drank ice cream sodas with their friends during leisurely afternoons, wore bobby socks, jitterbugged, sighed over movie actor Tyrone Power, crooned with Bing Crosby, sang jazz solos, and wore the latest fashions. The same women contributed to the family economy through farm labor and service work, sang traditional Filipino songs at ethnic community gatherings, and worked hard selling tickets for uniquely Filipina/o American beauty queen contests. How did the extreme gender imbalance influence the ways Pinays constructed new identities for themselves? Furthermore, how did young Pinays negotiate the multiple pressures of their parents and families, ethnic community, homeland culture, and American popular culture?

In this essay, I argue that during the pre- and postwar decades, young Pinays such as Angelina Bantillo negotiated ethnic and gender roles, carved out new spaces for themselves, and created new conceptions of Filipina womanhood in the ethnic community through peer networks, community organizing, social events, and their labor as well as leisure activities. The extreme sex-ratio imbalance in the Stockton and larger Filipina/o community in California and the influence of popular culture and ethnic culture brought multiple models of Filipina American identity for young Pinays to draw from, negotiate, resist, and transform.

These young women belonged to a large cohort of Filipina/o Americans born to immigrants who arrived in Hawaii or the United States prior to World War II. Cordova calls this cohort *the bridge generation* because these Filipina/o Americans "bridged" the early immigrants with later generations of Filipinos who immigrated after 1965.[6] Those born before the war, according to Cordova's analysis, functioned within the ethnic community as bridges both between their immigrant parents and American culture and between early and more recent Filipina/o immigrants. This generation, according to Cordova, himself a member of this group, "had their own special way of dressing, dancing, speaking, eating and surviving" that differed from their immigrant parents and from other teenagers in Stockton and on the West Coast.[7]

Historians focusing on youth and popular culture in the twentieth century call attention to the ways that the category of *teenager* became a relevant marketing and social category during the 1930s, just as the second generation of Filipina/o boys and girls came of age.[8] These scholars remind us that the category of teenager is as historically contingent as the categories of race, class, gender, and sexuality.

Several historians have studied adolescence among racial ethnic young women—among them Karen Anderson, Valerie Matsumoto, Vicki Ruiz, George Sanchez, and Judy Yung. Their research takes studies of the family, ethnicity, race, gender, class, citizenship, identity, and culture in new directions. These historians view race, ethnicity, and class as gendered categories that are as historical and dynamic, and their work restores agency to racial/ ethnic families. The women and the families in their work creatively resist Americanization and capitalist oppression, appropriate those cultural forms that they find useful and helpful, and, above all, maintain and continue to shape a strong ethnic identity in the face of overwhelming odds. Their work also utilizes creative methodologies through their uses of oral history and community documents, which makes their work increasingly complex and rich.[9]

However, there has been little research on Filipina/o American youth during the 1930s, 1940s, and 1950s. Additionally, most of the scholarship that has emerged from the field of Filipina/o American history and Chinese American history has focused on the bachelor culture of the mostly single, male immigrant population, resulting in an absence of scholarship on Filipina women, gender, family, and culture.[10] This research is an attempt to study notions of womanhood in American history by exploring ideas about gender and women in Asian American communities. It contributes to a nuanced and complex understanding of the constructions of womanhood in Asian American communities as well as the hopes, dreams, and experiences of racial ethnic young women in the United States in the early half of the century.

Filipina/o Americans and the Politics of Gender

The Filipina population in Little Manila was miniscule in comparison to the number of male immigrants in the decades before World War II. The lives of immigrant and American-born Filipinas were transformed by changing perceptions of women's roles in the Philippines, the gender imbalance, the lack of elders who would uphold traditional views and enforce social control, and the entry of Filipinas into the wage-labor market. These women challenged and transformed constructs of gender and femininity in the Filipina/o American community. Second-generation Filipinas, along with their mothers, were held in the highest esteem by Filipino men as symbols of the wives, mothers, sweethearts, daughters, aunts, and sisters left behind in the Philippines.[11] As symbols of Filipina womanhood in America, second-generation Pinays negotiated their changing conceptions of womanhood and femininity with the static and restrictive constructions idealized by Filipino men and encouraged by their mothers, who were themselves in a period of rapid gender-role transformation. The vast majority of all Filipinos in California were engaged in farm labor or service work, and most women worked in the fields and in Filipino-owned shops in Little Manila. Filipina American women also found their identities tied to their work roles in the fields and in service jobs as waitresses and pool hall girls.

Young Pinays worked alongside men in order to help feed their parents, brothers, and sisters and buy school clothes and other necessities. Women worked under a blistering sun under horrific conditions, and wages were substandard, with women earning generally less than the average of ten cents an hour to about forty cents an hour for Filipino Americans during World War II. "Sorting potatoes in the nearby islands during the summer was a job any young person would want since there were no other jobs," remembers Angelina Bantillo Magdael.[12] She sorted potatoes for ten hours a day in the blistering heat of California's Central Valley every summer of her adolescence during the Depression. Hawaii-born Mary Inosanto, who as a young girl traveled to Stockton from Hawaii with her family, remembers one grueling summer picking tomatoes in order to earn enough money for school clothes. "Visions of sweaters, skirts, shoes encouraged me to bend and grab the first ripe tomato," she remembers. "It was so hot that perspiration was pouring down and I had to stop and wipe my face. This was a delay, and a vision of only one sweater was my goal for the day ...."[13]

Young Pinays and Filipina American Ethnic Culture

Second-generation women in particular forged a distinct Filipina/o American ethnic culture that bridged the differences among Filipina/os from different regions and language groups. All-women's organizations helped second-generation women forge bonds of sisterhood and unity. A lively Filipina/o American press covered their community, family, and personal activities. Moreover, an active ethnic press created and maintained a network of Filipina/os in Stockton, Seattle, Los Angeles, Salinas, San Diego, and San Francisco. In Stockton, various short-lived newspapers and magazines such as *Three Stars*, the *Commonwealth Times*, the *Philippine Journal*, the *Philippine Yearbook*, and the *Philippine Record* were published periodically from the 1920s to the 1950s. In Salinas, the *Philippines Mail*, Delfin Cruz's popular weekly, reported on Northern California Filipina/o American community news. The ethnic press served a variety of functions. Newspapers offered Filipina/os a glimpse of what other communities were doing in terms of community organizing and reported on Philippine homeland politics. Stockton-based political newspapers such as the *Philippine Journal*, the official organ of the Filipino Agricultural Laborers Association, and the *Commonwealth Times*, edited by radical labor and political leaders Carlos Bulosan and Claro Candelario, advocated for Philippine independence, Filipina/o American citizenship, fair wages, and better working conditions for Filipina/o American laborers.

In addition to serving as community voice, the ethnic press devoted pages of ink to the social activities of the small population of Filipina immigrants and their daughters and created an environment in which immigrant and second-generation Filipinas were carefully surveilled. Reporters for the ethnic press published articles on such noteworthy activities as the graduations, eighteenth-birthday "coming out" parties (also called "debuts"), engagements, and weddings of young Pinays. Newspapers even published reports on the mundane and everyday, such as young girls' birthday parties, their colds, and even their bouts of pneumonia. Filipina/o American newspapers placed Pinays on pedestals for the community to admire.

Filipino men placed intense pressure on young Filipinas to uphold traditional, Philippine-based gender roles and ideals. Young Filipinas were watched from the moment of birth until middle age—surrounded by what I term a *culture of surveillance* in which the tiniest details of their lives were scrutinized, discussed, and critiqued by those in Little Manila and in the larger Filipina/o American community on the West Coast. The intense scrutiny with which community elders watched young Pinays through the ethnic press certainly added pressure and high expectations for young Pinays. Through articles and photos in the ethnic press, journalists and community leaders (mostly men in their twenties, thirties, and forties) instructed young women to uphold ideologies of gender brought over from the Philippines, even while those ideologies were under critique in the homeland.

In the 1940s and 1950s, the Filipina/o American press continued their coverage of social boxes* and queen contests, and community groups continued to rely on these events as lucrative moneymakers. Almost every weekend from the Depression into the 1950s, Filipina/o families from as far as Watsonville and San Francisco converged on the civic auditorium in downtown Stockton, several blocks from Little Manila. The social calendar for June–July of 1942, printed in the *Philippines Mail,* counted nine dances in the cities of San Francisco, Watsonville, and Salinas alone.[14] Queen contests and social boxes continued to commodify Pinays, control Pinay bodies, and construct static and repressive ideas about Filipina womanhood and standards of beauty.

Filipina bodies were used as frequently as a foil to raise funds for the Filipina/o American community. Few Filipinas protested, in part because queen contests were serious business. They had the potential to raise thousands of dollars for the organizations they would benefit. The funds from queen contests were a godsend to struggling Depression- and wartime-era Filipina/o ethnic organizations. Some organizations used the contests as their sole moneymaker. In May of 1948, the San Francisco Filipino community needed to pay their balance of $9,500 for their community center at 2970 California Street. Four high school students—Corazon Balcita, Nancy Agustin, Betty Basconcillo, and Esther Pinaroc—competed against one another for the title of queen of the San Francisco Filipino Community by selling tickets to other Filipina/os. "It is the desire of the Community Officers to pay off this balance in order to concentrate on (the building's) improvements," wrote the *Philippines Mail.* The queen contest was so successful that as the final tabulation date approached, the organization had raised more than $7,000.[15]

For community-wide contests, such as Miss Philippines, "large amounts of money were spent for the candidates," remembers Terri Jamero, who was born in Little Manila. "Basically, one group would get together to back one girl and at the social box dance they would sometimes open their candidates' box at $1,000, and of course, during the dance all their *kababayans* [town mates] would take a turn at $20 to $100 a turn."[16] Such large amounts of money invested in young girls created some difficult situations. Leatrice Bantillo Perez, Angelina's younger sister, remembers some unfortunate Pinays whose queen contest campaign managers interpreted their investment as a promise of marriage. Because contests often involved thousands of dollars, parents felt obligations had to be met and consented to marriages.[17]

---

*At dances called *social boxes,* men placed money in boxes held on the girls' laps in order to dance with them. At the end of the night, the proceeds from each box were split between the sponsoring organization and the girl's family.

The contests promoted intense competition among Pinays and within the Filipina/o American community in general. Different ethnic organizations, labor camps, and regions in California would endorse candidates monetarily. A family's integrity and popularity would be measured through the number of tickets they sold, and victory assured a rise in a family's status. Invaluable support came from prominent labor unions, fraternal organizations, and Filipino American community groups. "Money was an important factor in getting one elected as queen," recalls Mary Inosanto. "One had to have friends or sponsors who were willing to gamble or risk large sums of money. Sometimes lodges or associations can make the difference in sponsoring a candidate."[18] Men considered influential, rich, and/or powerful in the ethnic community managed the campaigns. These men built coalitions among Filipinos that were factionalized by language, class, hometown, fraternal order, religion, leisure activities, and membership in different regional Filipina/o American communities statewide. Old regional conflicts would arise, recalls Flora Mata. "(Queen contests became) contests between Ilocanos against Visayan candidates," she remembers. "Some contests became bitter rivalries among Ilocanos, Visayans, and Tagalogs."[19] Results of ongoing contests, which could last for months, were printed alongside hard news stories of U.S.–Philippines relations and battle stories from World War II.

Filipina/o American newspapers compared Pinays running against one another in various queen campaigns, often unfavorably, and upheld rigid standards of beauty, femininity, and ethnic identity that were difficult, if not impossible, for many young women to emulate. The local press dubbed 1939 Golden Gate Exposition queen candidate, *mestiza* Flora Enero, as "Vallejo's sweetheart."[20] A profile of her in the *Filipino Pioneer* noted that the high school student enjoyed music and literature. "When asked what her ambition is," the reporter wrote, "she blushed, and with an innocent twinkle of her pretty eyes she said she would rather be a good housewife. 'To a woman,' she added, 'there is no career more lofty.'" Flora's favorite singer was Bing Crosby, and her favorite movie actor was Tyrone Power. Her "natural beauty" and her "evident Oriental demureness" made her a good choice for queen, the reporter wrote.[21]

Despite large numbers of participants and the endurance of the practice (queen contests continue to figure prominently in Filipina/o American communities), many Pinays would rather have refused the crowns bought, given, and forced upon them had they a choice. Angelina Bantillo Magdael's story of her initial resistance to running for queen of the Caballeros Dimas Alang reveals a great deal about the pressures put upon young Pinays by their families and communities. Angelina had little choice in her participation but managed to resist in minor but significant ways, making important statements about control of her body by refusing to wear traditional dress. "Some parents objected to having their daughters in the contest because it was like selling merchandise," recalls Flora Mata. "The contestant had to dance with everyone who bought a ticket from her."[22] Terri Jamero refused to run in any queen contests. "The girls who ran would do it for family or the organization, but most often if they had a choice, they wouldn't have run," she remembers.[23]

Immigrant parents, Filipina/o ethnic institutions, and fraternal orders developed a distinct Filipina/o American ethnic culture through its world of queen contests and social boxes in the 1920s to the 1950s. As the second generation came of age in the late 1930s, Filipina Americans began to form their own organizations and networks, which combined Filipina/o American priorities with influences from mass culture in the late 1930s, reflecting larger patterns among Depression-era youth.[24] But exclusion from the mainstream culture, like the young Nisei women in urban enclaves like Little Tokyo that Matsumoto describes, pushed Filipina teens to create their own networks and a distinct American ethnic culture of their own.

Though their parents and the ethnic community still surveilled them heavily, parents were less likely to restrict their daughters if their peer networks were the sons and daughters of their own adult peers. Additionally, Filipina youth, who were excluded from the leisure activities of white youth in Stockton, San Francisco, Salinas, and other West Coast cities, sought to create their own social world of dances, fundraising for the community and World War II war bonds, cultural events, and sports tournaments.

Trinedad Godinez, who spent her childhood and adolescence in Little Manila, was a serious and intellectual high school student who eschewed the whirl of social boxes and popularity and queen contests. She wanted Filipinas to organize social events centered on the activities, issues, and concerns that mattered to second-generation Filipinas, like cultural identity. She organized her friends into the Daughters of the Philippines in the late 1930s, a club specifically for second-generation Filipinas. As a reflection of the new ways these girls were thinking of their roles in the community at large, they changed the name to the Modern Girls Club but soon finally settled on the more ethnic-specific Filipina Society of America. The members ranged in age from preteen to age 18, and the peer group was widely respected in Stockton for its dedication to community work, recalled former members and sisters Angelina Bantillo Magdael and Leatrice Bantillo Perez.[25]

The young women in the Filipina Society of America dedicated themselves to organizing serious community advocacy work as well as not-so-serious social events. Trinedad, while still a high school student, garnered nationwide Filipina/o community support when she spearheaded an exhibit in 1938 on Philippine art and culture at the Haggin Museum in Stockton, the region's main art and history museum. The exhibit was the first of its kind in the United States. Previous exhibits on Filipinos in the United States included the racist and exploitative 1904 St. Louis World's Fair exhibition of "native" Filipinos. "Here is an opportunity to show to the American people that our nation is possessed of a distinct culture," wrote the editors of the *Filipino Pioneer* about the Haggin Museum exhibition. "The low regard other people have on us is partly due to the ignorance of the true measure of our culture .... If only to correct the mistaken notion the Americans have about us, the project deserves the wholehearted support of every Filipino."[26]

The activities, organizing flair, popularity, and fashion exhibited by the members of the Daughters of the Philippines/Modern Girls/Filipina Society of America demonstrate the different ways young women in Little Manila were negotiating parental boundaries, American mass culture, and ethnic identity. Photographs of the young girls bring forth striking differences in the fashions they chose, demonstrating the ways they negotiated tricky boundaries between Filipino ethnic culture and mainstream culture. During social events and in their free time and at school, young women wore fashions popular among most girls in the late 1930s and early 1940s. At a Filipina Society Easter egg hunt, Trinedad Godinez's brother noted cheekily in his column in the *Filipino Pioneer* that they had the audacity to wear shorts.[27]

However, when representing their generation to the rest of the community, they wore heavy, intricate Filipino gowns to dances and community events and sang traditional Tagalog, Visayan, and Ilocano songs to homesick audiences. At one social, the *Filipino Pioneer* reported that the members sang jazz songs, reflecting the jazz craze that had come over most young Americans during the 1920s and 1930s.[28] But more "traditional" ethnic culture still held sway among the generation: Several second-generation Pinays participated in the first annual Filipino Carnival in Stockton in July of 1937, which premiered Filipina immigrant playwright Lucia F. Cordova's Tagalog play *Walang Kamatayang Pagibig* (Love Eternal), lauded as the first Filipina/o American stage production. Other young women took Tagalog classes with Mrs. Cordova in Stockton.[29]

After the bombing of Pearl Harbor and Manila on December 7 and 8, 1941, the Filipina/o American community sprung into action to defend their twin allegiance to the United States and the Philippines. The men and women left behind in California Filipina/o communities contributed to the war effort with war bond rallies, where young Pinays provided the main entertainment. Like teenagers across America, young Pinays threw themselves into war work.[30] The presence of women was a draw that brought thousands of Filipino men to events in Stockton. The role of second-generation Filipinas in raising thousands of dollars for the war effort was laudable, but the ways in which their bodies were used as symbols of homeland was problematic.

In 1943, several Filipina/o groups in Stockton organized the Great War Bond Drive, with a goal of selling enough war bonds to buy a fighter plane for the war effort. A portable stage and booth was set up in the heart of Little Manila at El Dorado and Lafayette Streets in Stockton. Over several weekends that summer in the booth and on stage, young Pinays sang traditional Filipino songs for a musical program broadcast over the local radio station, KGDM. After the program, they invited people to buy war bonds and helped them to fill out bond applications. Angelina Bantillo's younger sister, Norma, led the effort and participants included young daughters of prominent members of the Filipina/o immigrant community. The women, who wore traditional Filipina dresses and sang patriotic Filipino songs, were such a draw that the community ended up buying *two* planes.[31]

During the war, young women's bodies symbolized the Philippine nation for Filipina/o Americans. At community events, socials, war bond rallies, and dances across California, young Pinays were the featured entertainment, singing traditional Tagalog, Ilocano, and Visayan love songs; Filipino patriotic songs; and American standards. Among the most popular singers was Pacita Todtod, lauded as the "glamour girl" of the second-generation set by the *Philippines Mail* and other Filipino newspapers.[32] Pacita became one of the first Filipina American movie stars when she starred in *They Were Expendable* and signed a contract with MGM in 1945.[33] Young Pinay singers and the Filipino songs they performed became so popular that an enterprising Filipino American radio programmer, Francisco Lomongo, published a collection of traditional and patriotic song lyrics along with photos of California's most popular young Pinay singers in 1943.[34]

The Postwar Pinay

As the second-generation population grew in the 1940s and 1950s, the networks that seemed to draw immigrant and second-generation Filipinos together began to unravel after the war. Young people in America had a new role: they were "teenagers," a new identity created by the media, marketing, and young people themselves. According to historian Grace Palladino, adolescents flush with postwar prosperity embraced their own styles of dress, dance, music, and money.[35] Their important roles in war bond rallies and in military service inspired a new confidence among young Pinays and Pinoys. In the postwar period, Filipino youths began to demarcate the line between the "old" and "new" communities, going so far as to criticize the relevance of older ethnic institutions to younger Filipina/os.

Filipina/o youth asked that immigrant community leaders respond to their requests for recreation centers and more youth-centered activities. When elders summarily ignored a youth representative to a 1946 statewide Filipina/o conference in San Jose, Filipina/o youths in Stockton wrote an angry open letter to the community in the *Philippines Star Press*. "They apparently think the youth hasn't the facilities to express his own opinion so consequently we were ignored," the youths wrote. "Yet the main topic of discussion of the 'Filipino Adults' is the 'Scandalous Youth.' It's a shame that we youth are always talked down by our own nationality."[36]

When adults failed to provide "something worthwhile," Filipina/o youth turned to their own generation. Queen contests and social boxes still brought out crowds of families and single immigrant men, but young people wanted to socialize exclusively with their own peers, reflecting a larger trend in American youth culture of the 1940s and 1950s. The Filipina Society of America, the pioneering organization of the late 1930s and early 1940s, and the sisterhoods forged during the war bond era, paved the way for coed youth organizations that sponsored their own dances, rituals, sports, and clothing that were specific to postwar Filipina/o American youth. A new Filipino-American Youth Association was organized in Stockton in 1944.[37] Adults were invited to their events, and their support and approval was requested, but elders did not set the agenda for these Pinays and Pinoys who traveled between Stockton and Watsonville, Los Angeles, and Salinas to be with other second-generation brothers and sisters to play basketball and dance the jitterbug.

Interest in athletics spurred by high school activities and mainstream culture inspired area-wide sports tournaments organized with other Pinays and Pinoys in California cities, creating a peer network that extended into the 1950s. The rise of Filipina/o American athletic youth clubs in the 1940s, 1950s, and 1960s helped young Filipina/o Americans gain a sense of place and identity, within the ethnic community and in American society. "Our parents belonged to clubs, regional or fraternal, that brought their generation together," notes Terri Jamero in the Filipino American Athletic Youth Clubs reunion program. "They supported each other in whatever family crisis, need, or discrimination they encountered. We, in turn, did that for each other."[38]

Almost every California community with a handful of Filipina/o families boasted a youth athletic club by the mid-1940s. The San Jose Agenda played the Salinas Filipino Youth Council, and the San Francisco Mangoes and Man-goettes battled the Livingston Dragons and the Sacramento Static Six. The United Filipino Youth of Stockton, an athletic club organized in 1955, held an annual dance that drew hundreds of Pinoys and Pinays from all over California to Stockton each year. The San Francisco Filipino Youth League held an Autumn Rendezvous dance that drew several hundred second-generation Pinoys and Pinays to the Fairmont Hotel in November of 1948. Sports teams also created networks with other Asian American youth who were excluded from mainstream sports teams. Unlike their parents, whose relationships with Chinese and Japanese immigrants were at worst antagonistic and at best polite, the younger Filipina/os mingled freely with Chinese and Japanese American youth. National "All Oriental" invitational tournaments pitted the San Francisco Chinese Saints and the San Jose Nisei Zebras against such teams as the Vallejo Val-Phi.[39]

Within the tight-knit network of second-generation Filipina/os in the sports tournaments, Pinays found a source of support and sisterhood. In the newly organized Filipino Youth Association of Stockton, formed in the mid-1940s, the younger sisters of the original Filipina Society of America formed the Filipina Athletic Club. Their studio portrait, which was printed in various Filipina/o American publications, shows more than a dozen Pinays wearing pigtails and shorts, surrounded by tennis rackets, baseball bats, and basketballs. Second-generation Pinays played softball, volleyball, and tennis, participating wholeheartedly in organizing area-wide tournaments with other second-generation women in California communities such as San Francisco and Los Angeles.

The burgeoning Filipina/o youth culture, and the new identities emerging from these peer networks, began to irk immigrant parents in the same ways that other American teenagers seemed "alien" to their parents in the 1940s and 1950s. The late 1930s and early 1940s found parents and teachers obsessed with fears of "juvenile delinquency," as evidenced by films like *Reefer Madness* and such radio programs as *Young America in Crisis*.[40] Wartime delinquency, defined as disrespect and insolence, was creating a crisis, according to adults. The "new" Pinay of the late 1940s and 1950s—educated, confident, independent, athletic—may have alarmed some older Filipina/os, and elders reacted quickly to remind young Filipinas of the standards they were expected to uphold. An editor of the *Philippines Mail,* in a front-page declaration to the community written in 1951, reminded Filipina girls that they were pushing the boundaries of acceptable behavior. In "The Ideal Filipino Girl," young Pinays were reminded that "the ideal Filipino girl is not necessarily pretty of face and figure, but pretty within." He wrote,

> The Ideal Filipino Girl is self-possessed, intelligent. She talks sense, may talk nonsense too. She loves literature, endeavors to know things by extensive readings …. The Ideal Filipino Girl is industrious. If not sewing or cooking, she is writing or playing the piano. She loves music and children. When her hands are not busy, her mind is—with grand noble thoughts. The ideal Filipino girl is virtuous, not prudish: religious, not fanatical …. She dresses well. She is for sports, society, parties, but knows the limit …. She is alive and living, so much so that her face beams and a glow shines in her face, revealing a woman's soul.[41]

The paper did not print responses from young women, but as evidenced by their participation in popular youth culture such as sports tournaments, jitterbugs, and swing dances, many Pinays resisted these "old-fashioned" expectations. Elopements and forbidden romances between second-generation teenagers are further evidence that young Pinays did not always accommodate their elders' wishes.

Courtship and Marriage

While Pinays may have been enjoying the leisure activities of other American youth at the time (dances, sports, high school club activities, and the latest fashions), they certainly did not "date" like other white, working-class adolescents of the 1930s and teenagers of the 1940s and 1950s.[42] The experiences of Pinays were similar to those of the youth Ruiz and Matsumoto have described. Like their Nisei and Mexican American counterparts, second-generation Filipinas yearned for the romance and love popularized in movies, magazines, and music of mainstream culture but were often constrained by the expectations of their parents and traditional ethnic culture and religion.[43] They did have the extreme gender imbalance in their favor, which radically changed how Filipina/o men and women marry and create families: young women had more choice, and the balance of power shifted toward women in deciding their fate in terms of marriage and family.

The extreme sexual imbalance rendered complicated courtship rituals from the Philippines fairly obsolete but no less arduous. As Roman Catholics (though a few families in Stockton, such as the Arcas and the Bantillos, were members of the prominent Filipino Presbyterian Church), and influenced by a restrictive Spanish-Filipino immigrant culture, the experiences of second-generation women were also similar to the Mexican American women of the same time period. Filipina Americans, like their Mexican American sisters, were engaged in contentious battle with their parents over men, courtship, and marriage. Perhaps a product of Spanish colonial Catholic morality, the practice of chaperonage among Filipina/o American and Mexican American families was common. Ruiz describes chaperonage as "a manifestation of familial oligarchy whereby elders attempted to dictate the activities of youth for the sake of family honor."[44] Chaperonage, Ruiz argues, was a way in which families could exhibit social control over their daughters.

It was rare to see second-generation girls at community events, movie dates, and dances without their Filipina immigrant mothers or other relatives such as brothers, sisters, or cousins as chaperones. The Bantillo sisters, Leatrice and Angelina, remember that when boys wanted to ask them to the movies, their beaus instead asked their mother if *she* was free. When she agreed, they would all—mother, daughter, and "date"—proceed to the Fox Theater in downtown Stockton. At community socials and dances, the entire family was usually in attendance, and sons and daughters socialized and danced under the watchful eyes of their parents.

Whereas Filipino men (immigrant and American-born) went to great lengths to marry Filipinas, immigrant parents exhibited the same resolute insistence on protecting their daughters from men that they did not approve of. Stockton Pinay Susanna Caballero Mangrobang recalls that her father was adamantly against her marriage to another second-generation Filipino simply because he was from a different province in the Visayan region of the Philippines. To prevent the union, her father locked her in a room. It was several days before her older brother entreated her father to let her out so that she could get married.[45]

Most Filipinas acquiesced to the wishes of their parents and families and married men who were agreeable to their parents. But like Mexican American young women chafing under the control of their families, a few Filipinas evading the strict control of parents often eloped.[46] The popular Eleanor Galvez, lauded by the Filipina/o American press as the "lone rose of Roseville" and the daughter of one of the Filipina/o community's oldest families, scandalized her elders by eloping with Filipino immigrant Eddie Olamit in Reno in 1942.[47] Her elopement made front-page news in the *Philippines Mail,* the same newspaper that three years earlier had called her "the most beautiful and most typical Filipina on the coast."[48] According to Eleanor Olamit, her mother refused to bless the union because her fiancé was a member of the Legionarios del Trabajo fraternal order, and Galvezes were members of the rival Caballeros de Dimas Alang. She recalled that her mother didn't speak to her for a number of years.[49]

As more second-generation youth matured, courtship and dating became easier for Pinays. By the late 1940s and 1950s, the advent of Filipina/o sports tournaments had spawned a tight-knit network of Filipina/o American teenagers, and many young Pinays picked their spouses from this network. Not all working parents could chaperone their daughters to every sports event.[50]

Conclusion

The extreme gender imbalance of fourteen Filipino men to each woman had a profound influence on Pinay experiences in the ethnic community. Because of the scarcity of women, Pinays were subjected to intense scrutiny and male attention. Ideas about Filipina womanhood and "authentic" and "traditional" homeland culture were projected onto the bodies of young Pinays, even while those gender roles were undergoing scrutiny in the Philippines, with high expectations for their enthusiastic representation of all that would be pure, womanly, and authentically Filipina. A Filipino nationalist project—which in the 1930s advocated Philippine independence and in the 1940s victory over the Japanese during World War II—often used Pinay bodies as easily exploited symbols. The tight control the ethnic community exerted over their young women and the resistance young Filipinas exhibited illustrate a tension between women's ideas about their own lives and identities.

However, Pinays found ways to resist the strict confines of ethnic culture and create their own ideas of Filipina American identity. Pinays became pilots in the Aero Club and basketball players on the sports-tournament circuit, danced a sweaty jitterbug, and, when asked, sang traditional Filipino songs in itchy, uncomfortable Filipina dresses to aid the war effort. These young women took in multiple influences: mass culture in the form of music, food, and clothing and homeland Filipino and regional culture brought by their parents to create a distinctly Filipina/o American ethnic identity in Stockton, which reflected American experiences and priorities.

In many ways, Americanization of Filipina/o culture occurred for their parents in the colonized Philippines, complicating discussions of the ways in which Americanization affects second-generation children of other immigrant groups. Filipinas in Little Manila coming of age during the Great Depression, World War II, and the Cold War created a new ethnic and gender consciousness within the Filipina/o American community and engaged in constant negotiation with mass culture, forces of Americanization, and their immigrant parents over gender roles, labor, leisure, courtship, and their roles as second-generation Pinays in the ethnic community.

Acknowledgments

I would like to acknowledge the assistance, suggestions, advice, and critique offered by Al Camarillo, Gordon Chang, Fred and Dorothy Cordova, Joan May Cordova, George Fredrickson, Valerie Matsumoto, Allyson Tintiangco-Cubales, the Stockton chapter of the Filipino American National Historical Society, and my former colleagues in the graduate program in history at Stanford University: Marisela Chavez, Shelley Lee, Cecilia Tsu, and Kim Warren. A great debt goes to all of the women who agreed to be interviewed for this research project, including Anita Bautista, Camila Carido, Eleanor Galvez, Angelina Bantillo Magdael, Leatrice Perez, and Teofila Sarmiento. *Maraming, maraming salamat sa inyong lahat.* Thank you all very much.

Notes

1. The Caballeros de Dimas Alang was founded in San Francisco in 1920 and the Legionarios del Trabajo was founded in Manila in 1919 and brought to the United States by early immigrants. Both fraternal orders, which are still active, are based on Masonic ritual and on the secret, revolutionary Masonic organization that overthrew Spanish rule in 1898. The fraternal lodges functioned as mutual aid organizations for the ethnic community. For a more detailed description of the histories of the lodges, see Steffi San Buenaventura, "Filipino Folk Spirituality and Immigration: From Mutual Aid to Religion," *Amerasia Journal* 22, no. 1 (1996): 27.
2. Angelina Bantillo Magdael with Cheryl Magdael, interview with the author, Filipino Oral History Project, Inc., Stockton, Calif., 1981.
3. *Pinay* is the Tagalog term for a Filipina; *Pinoy* is the term for a Filipino boy or man.
4. Magdael interview.
5. Ibid.
6. Fred Cordova, *Filipinos: Forgotten Asian Americans* (Dubuque, Iowa: Kendall/Hall, 1983), 155. According to the 2000 U.S. census, Filipino Americans are the second-largest Asian American group, second only to Chinese Americans; see Melany de la Cruz and Pauline Agbayani-Siewert, "Filipinos," in *The New Face of Asian Pacific America: Numbers, Diversity and Change in the Twenty-First Century*, ed. Eric Lai and Dennis Arguelles (Los Angeles: *AsianWeek* Magazine/UCLA Asian American Studies Center Press, 2003), 45. Only Mexico has sent more immigrants to the United States since formerly racist and discriminatory immigration laws were changed in the Immigration Act of 1965.
7. Cordova, *Filipinos*, 165.

8. The pioneering work on the history of adolescence is Joseph F. Kett, *Rites of Passage: Adolescence in America, 1790 to the Present* (New York: Basic, 1977). Grace Palladino, *Teenagers* (New York: Basic Books, 1996)—a synthesis of the social and cultural history of adolescence—brings together Kett's work with a range of more recent historiography on the development of the social and cultural category of *teenager* during the 1930s, 1940s, and 1950s.

9. Matsumoto, Ruiz, Sanchez, and Yung, in Chicana and Asian American women's history, have described the ways in which young women of color have drawn from a variety of sources to create new ethnic and gender identities.

   Vicki L. Ruiz, "Star Struck: Acculturation, Adolescence and the Mexican American Woman, 1920–1950," in *Building with Our Hands: New Directions in Chicana Studies*, ed. Adela de la Torre and Beatríz M. Pesquera (Berkeley and Los Angeles: University of California Press, 1993), 109–29, and *From out of the Shadows: Mexican Women in Twentieth Century America* (New York: Oxford University Press, 1998) describe how a generation of young Chicanas in Los Angeles experienced acculturation and U.S. pop culture. Ruiz calls attention to the ways in which "immigrants and their children pick, borrow, retain and create distinctive cultural forms," and reminds us of the importance of the ways in which racism and patriarchy "constrain aspirations, expectations and decision making" (*From Out of the Shadows*, xvi).

   Valerie Matsumoto, "Japanese American Women and the Creation of Urban Nisei Culture in the 1930s," in *Over the Edge: Remapping the American West*, ed. Valerie Matsumoto and Blake Allmendigger (Berkeley and Los Angeles: University of California Press, 1999) and "Japanese American Girls Clubs in Los Angeles during the 1920s and 1930s," in *Asian/Pacific Islander Women: A Historical Anthology*, ed. Shirley Hune and Gail M. Nomura (New York: New York University Press, 2003) also focus on Los Angeles and the peer networks forged among Japanese American youth in the area. Matsumoto focuses on work, recreation, courtship, and activities within the ethnic community, showing how Nisei women dealt with multiple roles and pressures to create a distinctly Japanese American urban youth culture and identity.

   See also Karen Anderson, *Changing Woman: A History of Racial Ethnic Women in Modern America* (New York: Oxford University Press, 1996); Valerie J. Matsumoto, *Farming the Home Place: A Japanese American Community in California* (Ithaca, N.Y.: Cornell University Press, 1993), "Desperately Seeking Deirdre: Gender Roles, Multicultural Relations, and Nisei Women Writers of the 1930s," *Frontiers* 12, no. 1 (1991): 19–32, and "Redefining Expectations: Nisei Women in the 1930s," *California History* (Spring 1994): 44–53, 88; George Sanchez, *Becoming Mexican American: Ethnicity, Culture and Identity in Chicano Los Angeles, 1900–1945* (New York: Oxford University Press); and Judy Yung, *Unbound Feet: A Social History of Chinese Women in San Francisco* (Berkeley and Los Angeles: University of California Press, 1995).

10. Studies on early Filipino immigrants have focused largely on bachelor culture and adverse social conditions immigrants faced, including restrictive immigration and citizenship laws, deportation, and exclusion. Carlos Bulosan's ethnobiography *America Is in the Heart* (Seattle: University of Washington Press, 1977) has been key in shaping our understanding of early Filipino immigrants, and Ronald Takaki's descriptions of early Filipino American life is drawn largely from Bulosan's narrative. Other pioneering work in Filipino American history include H. Brett Melendy, *Asians in America: Filipinos, Koreans and East Indians* (Boston: Twayne, 1977); Howard DeWitt's work on Filipino labor struggles in California during the 1930s, *Violence in the Fields: California Filipino Farm Labor Unionization during the Great Depression* (Saratoga, Calif.: Century Twenty-One, 1980); and Cordova, *Filipinos*, a pictorial history of Filipino immigration from the Manila galleon trade and eighteenth-century settlement in Louisiana to postwar experiences. Women immigrants have been studied by Dorothy Cordova in "Voices from the Past: Why They Came," in *Making Waves: Writings by and about Asian American Women*, ed. Asian Women United of California (Boston: Beacon, 1989), which discusses experience of Filipina immigrant women but does not delve into the lives of their daughters.

11. Cordova, *Filipinos*, 153.

12. Magdael interview.

13. See Journals of Mary Inosanto, in Demonstration Project for Asian Americans, Filipino Women in America Project, journals, comp. Joan May Cordova; Filipino American National Historical Society National Archives, Seattle, 1985.

14. *Philippines Mail* (Salinas, Calif.), May 31, 1942.
15. *Philippines Mail,* May 31, 1948.
16. Terri Jamero, in Cordova, comp., Demonstration Project journals.
17. Leatrice Bantillo Perez, interview with the author, November 1999.
18. Inosanto, journals.
19. Flora Mata, in Cordova, comp., Demonstration Project journals.
20. *Mestiza* is a Spanish-language term for a woman of mixed race. Some second-generation women were daughters of white women and their Filipino husbands, but such unions were rarer in California than Mexican–Filipino unions.
21. *Filipino Pioneer* (Stockton, Calif.), August 5, 1938.
22. Mata, journals.
23. Jamero, journals.
24. American youth began engaging in a commercial culture that included swing music, radio, dancing, and fun as the nation underwent economic recovery in the late 1930s. With more than 80 percent of the nation's adolescents in high school, the group, notes Palladino in *Teenagers,* "demonstrated strong and identifiable tastes in music, clothes, and recreation, and they regularly displayed 'typical' teenage behavior that skirted the boundaries of respectable life" (45–51).
25. Angelina Bantillo Magdael and Leatrice Bantillo Perez, interviews with the author, November 1999.
26. *Filipino Pioneer* (Stockton, Calif.), March 14, 1938.
27. *Filipino Pioneer,* May 16, 1938.
28. *Filipino Pioneer,* July 1, 1938.
29. *Filipino Pioneer,* July 1, 1938.
30. Young people raised millions of dollars in war bond campaigns, collected salvage, worked in agriculture, and cultivated victory gardens during the war; see Palladino, *Teenagers,* 72.
31. Frank Perez and Leatrice Bantillo Perez, "The Long Struggle for Acceptance: Filipinos in San Joaquin County," *San Joaquin Historian,* no. 8 (1994): 16 (special issue on Filipino American history.)
32. *Philippines Mail* and *Filipino Pioneer,* various issues, 1938–44.
33. *Philippines Mail,* April 1945.
34. Angelina Bantillo Magdael, *Philippines Song Review* (Stockton, Clif., 1943).
35. Palladino, *Teenagers,* 93.
36. Philippines Star Press (Stockton, Calif.), May 18, 1946.
37. *Philippines Mail,* July 31, 1944.
38. Filipino American Athletic Youth Clubs, "Grand Reunion of Filipino American Athletic Youth Clubs, 1940s–1970s," souvenir program, collection of the Haggin Museum, Stockton, California, 1991.
39. Ibid.
40. Palladino, *Teenagers,* 82.
41. *Philippines Mail,* June 1952.
42. Palladino, *Teenagers,* 7–8.
43. Matsumoto, "Japanese American Women," 296.
44. Ruiz, "Star Struck," 52.
45. Susanna Caballero Mangrobang, interview with the author, August 1999.
46. Ruiz, "Star Struck," 60–61.
47. *Philippines Mail,* May 31, 1942.
48. *Philippines Mail,* May 27, 1939.
49. Eleanor Galvez Olamit, interview with the author, 1996.
50. Filipino American Athletic Youth Clubs, "Grand Reunion."

III
Peminist (Dis)Engagements
with Feminism

8
Pinayism

ALLYSON GOCE TINTIANGCO-CUBALES

What is Pinayism? I have tape recorder in hand, armed with participant–observer research methodologies and theories of feminist standpoint epistemology, postcolonial-womanist deconstruction and difference, and bell hooksian ideas of radical possibility floating around in my mind. I head out to the New Park Mall in Newark, California to find out what local Pinays think of Pinay womanism and/or feminism. I thought if I went into this field site—the mall that can be called "the bastion of Pinays and Pinoys" and a place that was basically my teenage hangout nearly ten years ago—I would be able to approach Pinays and inquire about their opinions.

I got a swift kick in my researcher/Ph.D.-candidate ass—or perhaps I should I say that being a researcher or Ph.D. candidate doesn't save me from looking like a teenager perpetrating, nor does it save me from getting my ass kicked. All I wanted to ask these Pinays was: "What do you think it means to be Pinay?" But I felt that the real question was: "To dog or not to dog?"

Three strikes and I was out. Opportunity number 1: As I approach the entrance of the mall, I notice a group of Filipinos, four teenage girls and a boy, hanging outside. I think to myself how cool an opportunity it is to talk to this *barkada* (group of folks who hang out with each other) about Pinayism. Keep in mind: I'm dressed just like a South Bay Pinay, from my baby tee with my bootleg-cut jeans down to my platform Steve Maddens. (Part of being a participant observer is to camouflage yourself so that you'll blend into the population of the field in study.) I begin walking toward them, with my tape recorder in full view, with a huge grin on my face as I make eye contact with one of the Pinays. She looks me up and down, checkin' out my gear, and it looks like she's about to say something to me. I am about ten steps away and her look of inquiry turns into a straight-up dog, with mad attitude. I'm still smiling, probably looking like a nerd by now. She stops looking at me, turns to her friends and starts cracking up. They all stare at me. I feel like I am fifteen again, except now I am the victim of humiliation that my own barkada (back in the day) would have chastised. I decide to walk away and find other subjects for my research.

Opportunity number 2: I head over to Contempo Casuals, where many Pinays worked and shopped when I was younger. Things have not really changed. I kind of browse, playing like I am shopping, even pick out a few pairs of pants to try on. I help myself to the dressing rooms and try on these tight blue, plaid bell-bottoms. I open the door of my stall to check them out in the long mirrors outside and I see another Pinay (about eighteen years old) trying on the same pants. I smile at her and find this to be a great opportunity to start a conversation with her. I catch her eye in the mirror as I smile and comment, "Cute pants, huh?" She responds, "They may be cute on you, but they make me look fucking fat!" She goes back into her stall and slams the door. Again, I decide to walk away and find other subjects for my research.

Opportunity number 3: I go to Wet Seal, for a change of pace. I begin to look through the clearance racks where finding Pinays is inevitable. I notice a Pinay salesclerk, and I assume that this would be a perfect opportunity to talk to her since she gets paid to be nice to customers like myself. She is straightening up the clothes that have been thrown around by other shoppers. I watch her as she proceeds to collect empty hangers and she acknowledges my gaze. I approach her and say, "Excuse me …." She responds abruptly, "What do you want?" I am a bit astonished at her question but I continue to explain my purpose and objective. I explain to her that I am researching ideas on what Pinays think of feminism and womanism. Then I ask her if I could ask her a few questions. She pauses with an irritated look and questions, "Are you going to buy something? I don't have much to say about your questions. I really don't know what you mean." I begin to explain the ideas I have about Pinayism and she says, "You should probably go talk to some other girls, I told you I don't have anything to say." She walks away and I decide to stop looking for other subjects for my research.

I leave the mall after this last strike with a sick feeling in my stomach. Have I failed as a researcher? What kind of threats have I had to my internal validity? Were all my theories thrown out the door? Has academia sheltered my ability to understand reality? Does this mean my construction of Pinayism is part of a fantasized vocabulary that lacks true empirical data? What do I do now that I have to write this article for *Maganda* magazine? Should I forget it? Should I hide my insecurities? Should I mask the problems and complexities that could alter my theory of Pinayism?

In the process of writing this article, I found myself in check, forced to be in a constant mode of rearticulation. Writing, talking, and theorizing about Pinay womanism/feminism were my initial and only objectives for this piece. But these objectives decidedly had to change after having conversations with Pinay activists about "what's really going on with us." In creating the concept of Pinayism, I knew that I could not do it alone. I sought out the help of other Pinays, whom I have personally known as "activists." Informally, I interviewed twelve Pinays.[1] These women were service providers, academics, political organizers, cultural workers, writers, artists, students, and teachers. Each of the women contributed greatly to my development of Pinayism. Their words and ideas are referenced throughout this article to provide a collective statement on Pinayism.

The process of reformulating the objectives for this article began in a conversation with Claudine del Rosario, counselor for Filipinos and Asians with substance abuse issues at the Outpatient Drug and Alcohol Service for Asians and former editor in chief of *Maganda*. She questioned my optimism and positivist attitude toward finding a place for Pinays on the continuum of white feminism and black womanism. She suggested that instead of trying to fit ourselves somewhere in between black and white, we need to create a place for ourselves outside the continuum. She and other Pinay activists helped me formulate challenges that we need to deal with before and while we create a space for Pinayism. These are: (1) How should we define what do we mean by the terms Pinay and Pinayism? (2) How should we deal with sexism and negative stereotypes that are imposed by external structures? Who should we ally ourselves with in the fight to rid these social ills? (3) How should we deal with internal complexities such as competition between Pinays and how do we renegotiate our standards of downness?

I have broken down this article according to these three main challenges. The first section will attempt to present possible definitions of Pinayism. I will then address the basic issues of sexism through a discussion on making allegiances. Third, I will deal with the hardest challenge of discussing the relationships and interactions between Pinays. In this third section, I will return to my mall experience by using the mall as a metaphor for the sites and areas where Pinays interact. This metaphor includes the "Mall of A's" (academe, the art scene, and activism) and the "Mall of Downness." After addressing these three challenges, I will end with a proposal of Pinayism as praxis, a place where theory transforms into practice.

Pinay + ism: Pain + Growth

It is a painful process to define Pinayism. But pain implicates growth. Although this article aims to be accessible in terms of language, it will not resort to simplistic notions and facile explanations. In creating a concept or coining a term to represent the ideas of multiple subjectivities, one must take into consideration the possibility of contradiction and opposition.

First and foremost, here are some claims of what Pinayism is not. Pinayism is not about one single epistemology (i.e., an explanation of how you know what you know), nor does it have a set definition or rendition. Pinayism is not meant to divide Pinays from Pinoys, but Pinayism will not ignore abuse from Pinoys. Pinayism is not just a Filipino version of feminism or womanism; Pinayism draws from a potpourri of theories and philosophies, including those that have been silenced and/or suppressed.

Pinay + ism: Pinay is a woman of Filipino descent, a Filipina in America and/or a Filipina American. Dawn Mabalon, a Ph.D. student in Stanford University's history department and community activist, identifies the terms Pinay and Pinoy as having roots in Filipino American history as far back as the 1920s and 1930s. Choosing to use Pinay + ism symbolically challenges traditional debates about *P* versus *F* (Pilipino versus Filipino).[2] Moving beyond identity politics and linguistic arguments surrounding the "correct" word to use in identifying ourselves, it is important for us to explore and create new forms and mechanisms to understand the Pinay/Pinoy experience in the United States. Pinayism is localized in the United States, although it tries to provide a forum to make connections to the issues of Filipinas and Filipinos in diaspora. In the Oxford American Dictionary we read this definition: "-ism: *suffix* used to form nouns meaning action, as in baptism; condition or conduct, as in heroism; a system or belief, as in conservatism; a peculiarity of language, anarchism; or a pathological condition, Parkinsonism."[3]

Playing with the conventional designations of *-ism* as a suffix, we can look at Pinayism in these ways: Pinayism is a revolutionary action. Pinayism is a self-affirming condition or conduct. Pinayism is a self-determining system or belief. A traditional dictionary can see Pinayism as a peculiarity of language, like anarchism. And by the opposition, colonizers, and by the colonized, Pinayism can be viewed as a pathological condition.

The main purpose of defining Pinayism in these somewhat audacious extremities is to emphasize its endless possibilities and also look at the multiplicity of what it means to be Pinay and a Pinayist. In defining and creating this space, we must also acknowledge the obstacles and strategies of Pinayism as a fluid concept, having an inherent ability to be changed and also being an impetus for change.

How to Make Allies in the Fight against Sexism

The importance of rethinking allegiances can be a book in and of itself. This section is a collection of thoughts and questions reviving old issues such as tradition, sexism, and negative stereotypes. In particular, this section will address how these social ills have inhibited the Pinay's ability to coalesce with others—specifically, womanists and feminists, Pinoys, and Pinays in diaspora.

Womanists and Feminists

Is Pinayism just a Pinay form of feminism and/or womanism? It is presumed that feminism has been dominated by white, middle-class, liberal women and that womanism has originated in black feminist thought. In submitting to the widely recognized framework of feminism, the issues of Pinays may get buried under more dominant and accepted voices.

As black critical theorist bell hooks points out, "Feminism in the United States has never emerged from the women who are most victimized by sexist oppression …. White women who dominate feminist discourse, who for the most part make and articulate feminist theory, have little or no understanding of white supremacy as a racial politic, of the psychological impact of class, of their political status within a racist, sexist, capitalist state."[4] Womanism, on the other hand, has been designated as women of color's reaction to feminism's negligence. Has womanism been able to encompass the issues of all women of color, including Pinays? In a conversation I had with Lalalee Vicedo, community Pinay activist and New College (San Francisco) student, she stated, "I even view womanism as not dealing with internationalism, not looking at the class structure that we live in, the system that we live in; I think that it is very absent in womanism and feminism …. I think that it is something we have to establish especially with that word [Pinayism] …. And I think that it is a really cool word to use."

The critique of both feminism and womanism is mandatory in creating space for Pinayism. However, it should not stop Pinayists from engaging in the feminist and/or womanist dialogue and creating allies. Pinayism is not just a Pinay form of feminism and/or womanism. Pinayism is beyond looking at gender politics as the major focus. Pinayism aims to look at the complexity of the intersections where race/ethnicity, class, gender, sexuality, spirituality/religion, educational status, age, place of birth, Diasporic migration, citizenship, and love cross.

Pinoys

Speaking of love, where do Pinoys fit in the conversation on Pinayism? Feminism and womanism have made it very easy to accept that Pinays suffer from sexism at the hands of American men. Filipino academics and activists have found one explanation rooted in American military involvement at Subic Bay. But we find difficulty in saying that the actions of Pinoys can be sexist. The blatant issues of domestic violence and unwanted pregnancy are not easily digested, especially when they are inflicted by Pinoys upon Pinays. And in many cases, covert issues of the underestimation of Pinays by Pinoys are even harder to discuss. In my conversations with some of the Pinay activists, one of the major challenges was the difficulty in including Pinoys in a Pinay struggle. For many Pinoys, this "gender-based" struggle can be alienating and viewed as separatism. Pinoys may feel a lack of ownership in Pinayism. When issues of domestic violence and unwanted pregnancy are voiced by Pinays, they are seen as troublemakers.

How should Pinays create Pinayism while continuing to serve the Filipino/Filipino American community as a whole? If Pinays speak out on Pinoy sexism, they are accused by members of the Filipino community of dividing the community or even buying into white feminism. How can Pinays be dividing a community that has yet to unify? Can we truly find unification at the expense of Pinay dignity and self-determination? How can Pinays buy into a white feminism that does not address the issues of Pinays? In dealing with Pinayism as a concept that is self-determining, where do Pinoys fit? This poses difficult challenges that cannot be ignored.

Rejecting white feminism, where women fight with men for equality, Pinayists must take steps to include Pinoys in the fight against sexism by making connections to issues such as classism and neocolonialism. Similar to sexism—the system of discriminatory beliefs and behaviors based on one's gender—classism is also a system of discriminatory beliefs and behaviors based on social and economic class as well as the imbalanced allocation of resources. Along with sexism and classism, neocolonialism is a system that maintains unequal relations of power on economic, political, and ideological levels in a postcolonial period.[5] Profound relationships exist among sexism, classism, and neocolonialism. Discrimination on the levels of classism and neocolonialism that has disempowered Pinoys can severely affect how they exercise sexism upon Pinays. Pinoy sexism can be attributed to their discontent with their class status and political power, combined with the internalization of the colonized ideology that women are inferior. It is important to take a critical look at the connection among the issues of Pinoy sexism, classism, and neocolonialism because the -isms do not stand alone. They work with each other to continue to maintain unequal relations of power.

Pinoys must learn to engage in the conversation on Pinayism so that they may better understand a more complete rendition of the struggle of "Filipinos in America." Pinayism does not just serve the needs of Pinays. It also serves the Pinay/Pinoy community as a whole, because domestic violence, unwanted pregnancy, and mental abuse by Pinoys on Pinays are not just "Pinay" issues. Rather, they are community issues.

Pinays in Diaspora. What about Pinays outside the United States? *Community* is a term used to imply a location and/or a sense of connection. The issues that affect Pinays and Filipinos as a community go beyond borders and are connected directly. Domestic violence, unwanted pregnancy, and mental abuse do not just affect Pinays who are in the United States; they also affect those in diaspora. *Diaspora*, as a notion, can be an abstract and complicated term to describe Filipinos in migration. However, diaspora also holds the idea of "interconnectedness." This means that Pinays who live in the United States are affected by the situations of Pinays in the Philippines, Australia, Canada, Kuwait, Japan, and around the world.

Although Pinayism is localized as a U.S. concept, this does not mean that the issues of Pinays in diaspora are not part of the Pinayism conversation. There is a failure to recognize the interconnectedness between the problems of Pinays in and outside the United States. For example, treatment of Pinays in the United States is based on negative stereotypes. Some of the stereotypical statements that Pinays in the United States encounter describe Pinays as submissive, mail-order brides, prostitutes, and maids or domestic workers. On the outside, these stereotypes seem clearly wrong, and on the surface they must be dealt and done with. In many ways these issues are more convoluted than expected. Pinays must begin to become more critical of the issues that they face. In the fight to eliminate these stereotypes, Pinays are tempted to neglect the issues of those women who *are* submissive, who *are* mail-order brides, who *are* prostitutes, who *are* maids—and their issues. Pinayists should also try to make connections with how classism, neocolonialism, and sexism have pushed many of those women to those positions. Although Pinayism is localized in the United States, the effects of colonization, internationalism, globalization, and the transplantation of Pinays in diaspora must be part of the conversation.

It has been easy to acknowledge issues that have been the center of feminist debate, such as sexism and negative stereotypes, but dealing with them must come from a critical Pinayist standpoint. It is time for Pinayists to check themselves and how they wish to seek out and keep allegiances with allies, including each other.

Love/Hate Relationships with Pinays at Malls: Heartbreaks in Romanticizing Sistahood and Solidarity

Personal epistemology: I have romanticized the vision of an all-inclusive "sistahood" throughout my political life. I have been challenged by this endeavor to develop this thing called Pinayism. And I look to reevaluate my ideals and search for explanations from the mall situations in our (Pinays') lives. In this section, the mall will be used as a metaphor for sites where Pinays interact.

The Mall

My personal attempts to do research at the shopping mall brought out areas in Pinayism that I did not want to deal with, such as the negative interactions between Pinays. As Dr. Pauline Agbayani-Siewert, University of California–Los Angeles Professor in Asian American studies and social welfare, points out, "You are dealing with something that we are not willing to talk about, but we need to deal with." In talking with other Pinay activists, I found out that there is a universal understanding of issues at the mall. Glenda Macatangay, a sixteen-year-old student at American High School in Fremont, California, and president of *Kapatid*, the Filipino student group at her high school, says of her mall experience, "There is a lot of like dogging and everything whenever we go there …. We just go to the mall and there is a whole bunch of other [Pinay] girls and they all just dog a lot …. Especially if I'm with a lot of guys, they totally, like mug it."

The acknowledgment of the "dogging," in terms of competition and downness (the act of being "down" with radical/leftist-community politics), would make it seem like we cannot get along and that Pinayism would not be possible. Whether it is at a shopping mall, at a college/university, in art circles, or in activist groups, Pinays find a way to "dog" each other. How do we explain this phenomenon? And how do we deal with it?

Competition and Downness. The coin of competition has two sides. It can be a tool for individual advancement, but it can also be a tool for divisiveness. I will be focusing on the latter side, the negative side. Competition has been part of our existence since many of us Pinays were born. Because our parents pushed us to be the prettiest, the smartest, the most virginal, the fairest skinned, and the most accomplished, we have internalized their ideals as reasons to compete.

I also wonder if there are differences in the competition we face among Pinays versus the competition we face with others outside our community. Is Pinay competition any different than competition among black women, among Chicanas, among whites, among Asians, among Native Americans, among Pinoys? There is no tool to measure the differences in competition but, according to a Pinay artist and activist who chooses to remain anonymous,

> I can't really say that others don't face the effects of competition in their own circles and communities but I swear to you there is something to say about the competition I feel when another Pinay walks into the room. I feel a cross between being thankful and being threatened .... It don't even matter if I'm the only other Pilipina in the room or if I'm in a room full of Pilipinos .... I hate being tested if I'm down or not. Other Pinays look at my work and what I choose to write about, what I wanna wear, or who I talk to ... and sometimes I think they don't really think I'm down .... But I know I'm guilty, too. I can't help to judge others, especially Pinays, by my own standards ... sucks, I know, but that's how it is.

This dichotomy of love and hate propagates confusion, but it also conveys the complexities of Pinays' relationships with each other. Many of us have taken the competition with other Pinays to levels and areas of our lives that our parents have never even dreamed.

The Malls of Academe, the Art Scene, and Activism. The "Mall of A's" is what I call it, and it is made up of the malls of academe, the art scene, and activism: these three places are where my interviewees and I interact the most with Pinays. *Academe* refers to the circle of Pinays who are students, teachers, and professors. The *art scene* consists of certain people centered on art events (such as poetry readings, art exhibitions, and performances). *Activism* is an area of practice that can include providing services, protesting, organizing, and membership in political and cultural groups. These three malls, in the collective "Mall of A's," are sometimes separate from each other, but in most cases the membership in the three can overlap.

Making reference to Pinays in academia, the Filipino art scene, and Pinay community activists, Dawn Mabalon questions, "Who's gonna be the next Jessica [Hagedorn]? … Because there can only be one Jessica, because there can be only one beauty queen …. Because there was only one Maria Clara." This is funny coming from Mabalon, who is hailed as "the bomb poet," a "Pinay critical theorist," and "a hard-ass Pinay." She raises questions that may seem outrageous and controversial around what she refers to as the "beauty queen syndrome," but she lends us an analysis that somewhat resembles that of classism. She goes on to say,

> Growing up, some of the worst enemies I felt that I've had, my own personal demons, have been other Filipino women …. I think I couldn't be like them, even though my family wanted me to be like them and I couldn't be like them or there has been antagonism between us over a man, over resources, over titles … over being the queen again …. And it has been interesting looking at my little sister's life and the things she's had to deal with, as an adolescent, as a preteen, that some of the people in her life that have given her the most grief, the most pain, have not been white men, has not been the system—but of course those all play into it, just invisible hands—but have been other Filipino women.

Mabalon and several of the other women that I interviewed pointed out Pinays' competition within structures of hierarchies. Whether the issue is class, education, beauty, or skin color, these areas are all part of a hegemonic system that does promote competition among Pinays, where "invisible hands" are often the most powerful. These hands have created room for only one Jessica Hagedorn, one Pauline Agbayani-Siewert, one beauty queen, one Maria Clara.

The Mall of Downness: Challenging a Neohierarchy/Neocanon. A neocanon is formed from judgments about whether one is worthy of being included. Within the malls or neocanons of academia, the art scene, and activism, another mall exists—that of downness. In terms of downness, another Pinay community activist admitted, "I go to poetry readings and they [the art circle] don't really acknowledge me. They don't know me …. I don't really feel welcomed." This occurs even though she is a writer and she has been very active in the Filipino community. She goes on to share her feelings of sadness toward how the art circle must view her.

Meg Mateo, a recent University of California–Los Angeles graduate and student activist with Samahang Pilipino Education and Retention, articulates the mall of downness as another place where Pinays participate in "dogging" each other. She criticizes some Pinay feminists and their standards of downness by stating:

> It is really dividing as far as when you're trying to uphold Pinay issues but the people you're trying to be there for are just not seeing you .... You separate yourself but you're still trying to help .... [With] that kind of mentality ... how are you supposed to bridge [between Pinays]? ... As far as bridging people ... we're definitely not .... One thing that always happens is when I hear other people [Pinay feminists] ... they start dogging on other people for some ignorant comment that they have made. And I don't think that's right to start talking about people in that way ... like, "She doesn't even know what she's talking about." ... They may not have been educated in that [feminist] manner growing up, or even exposed in that manner .... We have to understand where people are coming from and that's the only way.

Within this mall of downness, a neohierarchy of standards has been created, privileging those who have been educated or exposed to feminist ideas. The importance of multiple epistemologies comes into replay. We do "have to understand where people are coming from; that's the only way" to create Pinayism.

Along with renegotiating standards of downness, Pinays must reevaluate the standards of what it means to be Pinay. What makes one "more Pinay" than another is just as destructive as the neohierarchy of downness. As Rowena Ona, a student at University of California–Berkeley and student activist with the Pilipino American Alliance and Pilipino American Student Services, has distinguished, "Pinay would mean empowerment .... I consider myself Pinay in some aspects but sometimes I don't think I am .... I guess part of being Pinay is knowledge, history .... I don't think I'm aware of my history, my culture, the history of my culture ... so I consider myself Pinay most of the time but I don't think I would be the poster child."

Who is the poster child who symbolizes what it means to be Pinay? Ona brings out a point that is unexplored by Pinayists. Barbara Reyes, community activist, poet/writer, and former editor in chief of *Maganda*, says of her identity as a Pinay, "I do [identify as Pinay] ... if you want to talk about just earning the right to a name ... it's not because I served as editor-and-chief of *Maganda* and people know me because of my tattoos or because of my poems ... because we all deserve to be called by any name we want to be called."

Once again, the importance of multiple epistemologies comes into replay. Standards for being Pinay intertwine with downness but they also intertwine with other issues such image, queerness, and skin color. Christine Balance, University of California–Berkeley student, community activist, and past editor in chief of *Maganda,* notes, "Back to the mall situation, a lot of people assume, or a lot of times in dominant Filipino American ideology—like shit they spout at youth conferences—if you have lighter skin you kind of have this assumed privilege like all across the board …. So sometimes I feel like when I go into a Filipino American space then all of a sudden it's like, 'Since you get all this privilege outside of this space we're gonna give you shit while you're inside.'"

These notions—of what a Pinay should be and look like and how she should act—have been internalized by many Pinays, even activists. From competition to downness, to rearticulating our beliefs and standards for what it means to be Pinay, Pinayists need to remember that pain implicates growth. For Pinayism to grow, we need to participate in the painful process of checking ourselves before checking others.

Pinayism as Praxis

Praxis is where theory and practice merge. Pinayism is where the theories of rethinking allegiances and critically looking at competition and downness merge with truly redeveloping a sistahood. Although this article emphasizes areas that induce great discomfort, Pinayism is about pain and growth. And growth has happened. Claudine del Rosario reevaluates her relationships with Pinays and states, "Sure, my worst enemies have been Pinays, but they've also been my best friends … my sister and my mom."

Remember that Pinayism is only at the beginning stages of creation, but that does not mean that the dialogue must be basic. Pinays and Pinoys should not be afraid to be uncomfortable, unsure, and unaware. These feelings can become catalysts to achieving transformative discourse and transgressive praxis.

Let the operative word be ownership. Pinayism should belong to Pinays and Pinoys who are willing to engage in the complexity of the intersections where race/ethnicity, class, gender, sexuality, spirituality/religion, educational status, age, place of birth, diasporic migration, citizenship, and love cross. It is time to return to the malls in our lives, to resist the question "To dog or not to dog?" and to begin to engage in a discussion that should be a repetitive process of reevaluation, reconstruction, retransformation, re-transgression, and, especially, relove for one another.

Beyond the Malls

Virna Tintiangco, the founder of the Filipina Women's Network in California's Bay Area, describes the organization as "the best thing I have ever done that is sustainable, that has brought so many types of women together." Despite the mall syndrome, organizations have managed to emerge where the issues of Pinays can be addressed, such as Pinays at UCLA, the General Assembly Binding Women for Reform, Integrity, Equality, Leadership, and Action (GABRIELA) and its GABRIELA Network, or GABNet. And organizers and community activists—like Jeannie

Celestial with Filipinos for Affirmative Action's young girls program; Wilma Consul and Rona Fernandez with Youth Radio; and Rachel Paras, Janet Co, and Trina Villanueva with Project Pull—have taken it upon themselves to work with young Pinays and Pinoys.

Pinay historians like Dorothy Cordova, Liz Megino, Meg Thornton, and Emily Lawsin from Filipino American National Historical Society have archived our experiences. The academic and creative work of V. Kay Dumlao, Teresa Ejanda, Anna Alves, Darlene Rodrigues, and Rhacel and Celine Parreñas around Pinay issues here in the United States and in diaspora has paved a critical path toward realizing the dreams of Pinayism. From the poetry written and sung by Anita, Olivia, Trina, and Ella from the Lapu Lapu Crew; to Los Angeles's Pinay spoken-word artists like Irene Suico Soriano, Myra Dumapias, and Faith Santilla; to the dances performed by Pinays like Amihan and Claudine; and from Barangay to DJ Symphony to the clothing of Haydee Vicedo (Pinay T-shirts) to the voices of Pinay (previously known as the Pinay Divas) to Pinay professors/community activists like Angel Shaw, Pauline Agbayani-Siewert, and Steffi San Buenaventura; to writers like Jessica Hagedorn; to the women in *Maganda*, to all the *manangs*—so many Pinays have contributed to and inspired Pinayism. Special thanks to my mom Inay and my sister Adrienne for making me Pinay.

Notes

1. Interviewed for this article were: Dr. Pauline Agbayani-Siewert, Ph.D.; Christine Balance; Gwen Cabrera; Dawn Mabalon; Glenda Macatangay; Meg Mateo; Marlo Rabuy; Barbara Reyes; Claudine del Rosario; Rachel Sancho; Virna Tintiangco; and Lalalee Vicedo.
2. Someday, someone might want to explore the root of the term *versus*, and how it has symbolically divided our community.
3. *Oxford American Dictionary*, Heald Colleges ed. (New York: Oxford University Press, 1979), 471.
4. bell hooks, *Feminist Theory: From Margin to Center* (Boston: South End, 1984), 3–4.
5. Currently, Filipinos and Filipino Americans live in a postcolonial period. This period refers to the era after the Philippines was colonized by the Spanish and the Americans. The Philippines suffered from colonialism, the system by which Spain and America imperialized the Philippines as a foreign colony particularly for economic exploitation. Both Filipinos and Filipino Americans are a neocolonized people because they continue to uphold doctrines and opinions learned in the period of colonization.

9

Filipino American Men: Comrades in the Filipina/o American Feminism Movement

FRANK L. SAMSON

Pinay is a woman of Pilipino descent, a Pilipina in America, and/or a Pilipina American.

—Allyson Goce Tintiangco-Cubales, "Pinayism"

While Filipina American women have resisted sexism and patriarchy for decades, Filipina American feminist theories have been lacking until fairly recently. Since the first publication of Allyson Tintiangco-Cubales's essay "Pinayism,"[1] Filipina American women have continued to construct and elaborate Filipina American feminist theories. As she recounts in her essay, Tintiangco-Cubales found it very difficult to develop a theory distinct from both traditional feminisms and the emerging theoretical work done by African American women. She believes that traditional feminisms are dominated by white, middle-class women's voices, while black feminism did not adequately address the unique issues and circumstances of Filipina American women. In addition, Tintiangco-Cubales writes, "Pinoys must learn to engage in the conversation on Pinayism so that they may better understand a more complete rendition of the struggle of 'Pilipinos in America'" (9). Responding to Tintiangco-Cubales's invitation to enter into the dialogue, I reflect upon the subject of Filipina American feminisms and my role as a Filipino America male, a Pinoy, in the feminist movement.

My entry into the conversation is not without its limitations. I am aware of the difficulties involved when those who occupy a privileged location attempt to speak about and against that privilege. The dangers in such an act include omission, exclusion, or silencing of marginalized voices, in a gesture that reinscribes the authority of the oppressive subject. In a patriarchal society, constant vigilance must be taken when men attempt to enter feminist conversation and struggle lest our actions, despite good intentions, unwittingly appropriate and sabotage feminist critique and transformation. Aware of the contradictions and limitations that might arise from my intervention, I nevertheless offer my reflections and potential contributions to the theoretical and practical construction of Filipina American feminism, hoping that something can be learned and gained from this critical engagement.

How can Filipino American men participate in the Filipina/o American feminist movement? Using Tintiangco-Cubales's article as a springboard, this essay will begin with a general overview of the origins of Pinayism as an entry point into Filipina/o American feminism, speculating on actual and potential dialogical partners among other strands of feminist theory and, finally, exploring more specifically the role of Filipino American men, or Pinoys, as comrades in the struggle.

Constructing Pinayism

Because Filipina/o American feminisms must be varied and flexible enough to speak to a wide range of issues, individuals, and locations, the theories must necessarily be open-ended and constantly open to critical rearticulation. Acknowledging this, Tintiangco-Cubales explores the construction of the word *Pinayism* and what it might represent (6). She begins by grounding Pinayism in a revolutionary praxis—that is, it must actively work to transform institutions. Given the ways in which patriarchy devalues women, Pinayism is a means of self-affirmation and self-determination. Envisioning a relationship different from the status quo, Pinayism is subversive, threatening those in power and, therefore, judged deviant from the oppressors' norms. Rather than abiding by the dominant norms that mark deviance as degeneracy, Pinayism inhabits a marginal space that resonates with the subversive power articulated by bell hooks in her essay "Choosing the Margin as a Space of Radical Openness." In reclaiming the space of marginality, hooks writes:

> Marginality [is] much more than a site of deprivation ... it is also the site of radical possibility, a space of resistance. It was this marginality that I was naming as a central location for the production of a counter-hegemonic discourse that is not just found in words but in habits of being and the way one lives. As such, I was not speaking of a marginality one wishes to lose—to give up or surrender as part of moving into the center—but rather of a site one stays in, clings to even, because it nourishes one's capacity to resist. It offers to one the possibility of radical perspective from which to see and create, to imagine alternatives, new worlds.[2]

This marginality provides Pinayism with the vantage point and location from which to critique the oppressive realities that Filipina American women experience the "sexism and negative stereotypes ... imposed by external structures" as well as the "internal complexities such as competition between Pinays" (4).

While Filipina American feminisms should definitely address the patriarchy, sexism, and misogyny that exist within society and our communities, unlike earlier forms of white bourgeois feminisms, Pinayism resists essentialist categories that would lump together all women against all men. As Tintiangco-Cubales explains, "Pinayism is beyond looking at gender politics as the major focus. Pinayism aims to look at the complexity of the intersections where race/ethnicity, class, gender, sexuality, spirituality/religion, educational status, age, place of birth, diasporic migration, citizenship, and love cross" (7). In other words, Filipina Americans inhabit distinct social locations that mediate their experiences of oppression and also inform their modes of resistance.

Because of the diversity of relational networks, providing access to various resources and allies, Filipina American feminisms must necessarily speak to the different situations Pinays find themselves in. Acknowledging the embeddedness of Filipina American women in complex social relations provides a step toward developing the sophisticated social analytical tools to aid in their liberation, yet also recognizing the different "selves" that constitute the Filipina American can be a vigorous source of energy to fuel action.

Given the need to develop Filipina American feminisms that appropriate the insights of multiple sources of already existing feminisms, Pinayism must be a constructive project. In her early attempts to find out what young Pinays think about feminism, Tintiangco-Cubales encountered difficulties in approaching and engaging her potential sources. Reflecting on these complications, juxtaposed with the immediate need to find a responsive audience, Tintiangco-Cubales instead drew upon the activists in the community to provide initial reflections that later informed the initial working principles of Pinayism. One of these activists "questioned my optimism and positivist attitude towards finding a place for Pinays on the continuum of white feminism and Black womanism" (4).

Tintiangco-Cubales realized that trying to map a Filipina American feminism on a continuum between white feminism and black womanism would be problematic at best, even if such a continuum could exist given the wide range of feminisms (lesbian, existentialist, poststructuralist, postcolonial, to name a few) that would immediately shatter such a continuum. She recognized that a Filipina American feminism would need to carve out its own space, critically transforming various insights from preexisting theories to suit its own ends and excavating the sites of memory and margins to draw upon those riches not readily available to the "malestream" intellectual or mainstream feminist discourses. In other words, "Pinayism is not just a Pilipino version of feminism or womanism; Pinayism draws from a potpourri of theories and philosophies, including those that have been silenced and/or suppressed" (5).

Given the status of Pinays as nonwhite in a white-supremacist society, African American feminisms provide an initial and accessible dialogical encounter. Referred to by some as *womanism*, a derivation of the term *womanist* defined by

Alice Walker,[3] Tintiangco-Cubales asserts, "Womanism ... has been designated as the Women of Color reaction to feminism's negligence" (7). African American feminist and womanist theories challenged the prevailing notions of feminism, which were dominated by the perspective of white, middle-class women. White feminists did not acknowledge the strong bonds of unity and community forged between black men and women through antiracist struggle against a white supremacist society that devalued, degraded, and dehumanized them. Since Pinoys and Pinays share the same struggle against white racism in the United States, it is not surprising that Tintiangco-Cubales looks to African American feminisms to begin her theoretical invention.

While the importance of bonds of cooperation between Pinoys and Pinays against white supremacy should not be dismissed, neither should the emphasis on solidarity and community between Filipino American men and women be used to silence, undermine, or discredit feminist challenges to Pinoy patriarchy, sexism, and misogyny. Tintiangco-Cubales points out, "We find difficulty in saying that the actions of Pinoys and Pilipino men can be sexist. The blatant issues of domestic violence and unwanted pregnancy are not easily digested, especially when they are inflicted by Pinoys upon Pinays. Additionally, in many cases covert issues of the underestimation of Pinays by Pinoys is even harder to discuss .... When issues of domestic violence and unwanted pregnancy are voiced by Pinays they are seen as troublemakers" (8).

Communities of color face difficulties in critiquing sexism and patriarchy within their communities due to the legacies of white supremacy and imperialism. Western imperialist discourse and colonialization developed and deployed patriarchal constructions of manhood imbued with notions of male sexual dominance and terrorism. As bell hooks writes in "Reflections on Race and Sex":

> Sexuality has always provided gendered metaphors for colonization. Free countries equated with free men, domination with castration, the loss of manhood, and rape—the terrorist act re-enacting the drama of conquest, as men of the dominating group sexually violate the bodies of women who are among the dominated. The intent of this act was to continually remind dominated men of their loss of power; rape was a gesture of symbolic castration. Dominated men are made powerless (i.e., impotent) over and over again as the women they would have had the right to possess, to control, to assert power over, to dominate, to fuck, are fucked and fucked over by the dominating victorious male group.[4]

Colonialization socialized men of all colors into these patriarchal and misogynist conceptions of manhood, measured vis-à-vis the level of domination (physical, mental, emotional, and sexual) asserted over women. While this understanding does not excuse black men, or any man for that matter, from their sexism and misogyny, hooks is aware that for a man who feels powerless, "[w]hen he beats or rapes women, he is not exercising privilege or reaping positive rewards; he may feel satisfied in exercising the only form of domination allowed him."[5]

The same holds true for Filipino American men, who may feel powerless within the white supremacist United States. Again, this does not excuse Pinoys from their sexist treatment of women, domestic violence, and other misogynist behaviors, but it does shed light upon the operations of masculinist socialization. Such powerlessness also motivates the silencing of feminist critiques raised by Pinays—critiques that threaten to undermine the patriarchal relations that all Pinoys may exploit to reaffirm their ill-defined sense of security and masculinity. However, as Gale Yee astutely reminds us, we must guard against the "injunctions to women to protect the 'fragile male ego,'" a pitfall that can arise when the problematization of masculinity results in the reinscription of patriarchal relations that subordinate women to service the needs of masculinity-in-crisis. As Yee suggests, "Men have to become accountable for their violent actions toward women and their privilege under sexism," a personal accountability that does not reproduce patriarchal hierarchy.[6]

The silencing of critique and labeling Filipina feminists as "troublemakers" is also rooted in the Filipina/o people's history of colonization. Tintiangco-Cubales observes, "If Pinays speak out on Pinoy sexism they are accused by members of the Filipino community of dividing the community or even buying into white feminism" (8). By drawing from the insight of postcolonial feminisms, a Filipina American feminist can learn to interpret these remarks as symptomatic of conservative, traditionalist, and dogmatic anticolonial nationalism. The pejorative "buying into white feminism" used to silence Filipina American feminists is glaringly similar to the use of "Westernization" as the "negative epithet of choice" deployed by anticolonial nationalists against postcolonial third-world feminists.[7] The need to unpack the legacies of the "colonized mentality" remains another project tied to the elaboration of Filipina American feminism.

The dialogue with postcolonial and third world feminisms brings to the forefront other useful resources for the theoretical expansion of Filipina American feminisms beyond the encounters with African American feminist or womanist theories. This connection to a global perspective becomes essential to the development of Filipina American feminisms, because Filipina/o Americans shape and are shaped by the historical legacies and continued cultural, political, and economic links to the people of the Philippines. In recognition of this fact, Tintiangco-Cubales writes, "[Pinayism] tries to provide a forum to make connections to the issues of Pilipinas and Pilipinos in diaspora" (6).

Philippine feminist theories can provide a nascent Pinayism with reflections on colonial and neocolonial legacies and a vitally important grounding in political economy. The dedicated and critical contemplation of Philippine women's issues in the developing Philippines—legatee of Spanish and American colonialism, embedded within the unequal structuring of power, wealth, and resources that constitute hierarchical north/south, core/periphery nation-state relationships   provides Philippine feminist theories with indispensable insights. Philippine feminist theories offer crucial theoretical analytical tools to Filipina American feminism by equipping Pinay feminists with the historical and materialist approaches to unpack what Tintiangco-Cubales asserts is common knowledge among Pinays: "Pinays suffer from sexism at the hands of American men. Pilipino academics and activists have found one explanation rooted in American military involvement at Subic Bay" (8). Acknowledging and moving beyond the U.S. military presence at their former naval base in the Philippines, Philippine feminisms provide the larger historical context, revealing the U.S. empire's expansionist goals in taking over and building upon the Spanish colonizing apparatus. Critical investigations of the pioneering work of Philippine feminist theorists Sr. Mary John Mananzan, Delia D. Aguilar, and Elizabeth Uy Eviota provide essential and nuanced explanations for the stereotypes applied toward Pinays. Tintiangco-Cubales keenly points out that these stereotypes of women—as "mail-order brides," "prostitutes," "maids or domestic workers," and "submissive"—reflect the "interconnectedness between the problems of Pinays in and outside the United States" (10).

One of the earliest, and still central, figures in Philippine feminist writings and feminist theology is Sr. Mary John Mananzan, OSB.[8] Her essay "Sexual Exploitation in a Third World Setting" describes the growth of prostitution in the context of the limited opportunities that exist in the Philippines, due to its export-oriented economy and reliance on foreign investment.[9] She documents the boom in prostitution that grew alongside tourism and the U.S. military presence in the Philippines. Addressing the lack of research and writing that focused specifically on Filipina women, Sr. Mananzan's *Essays on Women* brought together a collection of compositions spanning such topics as the women's movements in the Philippines, Filipina images in the media, and women's spirituality.[10] Her next edited book, *Women and Religion*, concentrated on issues of theology and spirituality, offering a few systematic elaborations of feminist liberation theology, some situated in Philippine women's religious experiences.[11] Pinayism, or any other articulation of Filipina American feminisms that wish to delve into spirituality and religion, would do well to begin its theological musings by exploring Sr. Mananzan's rich and extensive corpus of work.

Another advocate for Philippine feminism, Delia D. Aguilar, in her 1988 book *The Feminist Challenge*, draws links between the legacy of Spanish and U.S. colonialism, the rise of capitalism, and their roles in the formation of a political economy that continues to exploit Philippine women today.[12] This chronicle of the development of the Philippines' third world economy contextualizes the ongoing abuses and suffering of Philippine women, and the poor masses as a whole, without silencing their past and ongoing resistance. Beholden to the structural adjustment programs of the International Monetary Fund (IMF) and World Bank, abetted by a *comprador* elite government that caters to foreign capital, the Philippines developed a "warm body export" of female migrant, domestic, and sexual labor. She also analyzes the Philippines' industrialization and development processes that funneled women into low-paying, export-oriented manufacture. Other essays in this collection include a reflection on Marxism and Marxist feminism and demythologizing the social construction of the Filipina. In later essays, Aguilar discusses the tensions and miscommunication that can arise between first world and third world feminists.[13] Class-reductionism, patriarchy, and ghettoization of women's issues in the national liberation movement in the Philippines, plus persistent colonial mentalities, pose new challenges and opportunities for the renewal of a Philippine nationalist feminism.[14] In *Toward a Nationalist Feminism*, Aguilar revisits some of these same threads and recontextualizes them within the latest developments in feminism as well as the effects of global restructuring in the Philippines that continue to service the juggernaut of late capitalism.[15]

In a more in-depth historical exploration of the relationships between capitalist-development expansion and women's oppression in the Philippines, Elizabeth Uy Eviota charts the transformation of the sexual division of labor in the Philippines. She links this transformation to changes in the political economy—from pre-Hispanic, through the first and second halves of Spanish colonialism, U.S. colonialism, and the postcolonial era spanning the period after nominal Philippine independence was granted by the United States in 1946.[16] With various industries emerging and the cultivation of various agricultural products, Eviota maps the ways in which the sexual division of labor was shaped by these forces. As housework and production were altered to meet the needs of the growing markets, women were pushed into segregated and limited occupations. Bringing her analysis up to date, she incorporates the rise of the sex trade and gendered contract labor, all within the neocolonial context of international economic relations polarized along the North/South axis and dominated by international lending agencies such as the IMF and World Bank. Taking on the task of producing instructional materials for "gender-awareness" training in the Philippines, Eviota edited an anthology of materials written by Philippine feminists who discuss such topics as "(i) sex and gender, (ii) ideology and cultural practice, (iii) the social construction of sexuality, (iv) the family household, (v) the sexual division of labor, and (vi) strategies toward gender equality."[17] Eviota's important contributions to

Philippine feminisms span not only insightful political and economic analyses but also popular educational and programmatic curriculum.

Engaging with a large and diverse selection of feminist theories could enrich Filipina American feminisms. Pinayism, a Filipina American feminism initially theorized by Tintiangco-Cubales, drew initial insights from African American feminists. However, the immigrant and colonial histories of Filipina/o Americans in the United States necessitated broader outlooks, ones that are provided by third world, global-feminist standpoints. Philippine feminisms provide needed interventions, drawing from Marxist and socialist traditions pointing out the complex interrelations among white supremacy, imperialism, and patriarchy without downplaying the last in light of the other two. It remains open and exciting to see how Pinayism (and other versions of Filipina American feminisms) can continue to evolve and be transformed by other dialogical partners—ecofeminism, queer feminism, and feminist liberation theologies, to name a few—yet still remain grounded in the concrete material experiences of Pinays in the United States.

The Role of Filipino American Men: Theories and Praxis

The Responsibility of Intellectuals

As an intellectual, I can contribute to Filipina American feminisms by participating in their theoretical evolution. The interlocking systems of race, class, gender, sexuality, and empire are just a few of the many forces that combine to create an oppressive social environment against Filipina American women. The competition and hierarchies that arise between Pinays, or as Tintiangco-Cubales states it, "to dog or not to dog" (1), can be explored as a result of the convergence of market values, consumer identities, and colonized mentalities that racialize and gender the identities of Pinays in a white supremacist, heterosexist, imperialist patriarchy. It is perhaps not coincidental that the field site and metaphor chosen by Tintiangco-Cubales is that of the mall, one of today's exemplary models of privatized, commodified spaces where market forces and values shape the desires and identities of young Pinays and Pinoys. The unmasking of these ideological forces and the dismantling of these hierarchical, constraining structures and political economies become necessary and crucial tasks in the theoretical, cultural, and material practice of Filipina American feminism.

In an academic setting such as the university, my role as an intellectual can also be in the recovery and promotion of previously silenced Filipina American "herstories." Researching and documenting the contributions of Pinays of the past has often been a task left to today's Filipina American women intellectuals to complete. Pinoy intellectuals should also take responsibility in furthering this research and writing, either by pursuing such historical inquiry as part of one's own academic project or encouraging and supporting the efforts of colleagues and students who show interest in this aspect of the Pinayist struggle. The recovery of agency is not limited solely to excavating herstory but is also found within creative cultural and artistic work. As intellectuals, Filipino American men can also play a substantive role as cultural producers, through song, music, dance, spoken word, poetry, theater, and the like.

In addition, as educators we can design and implement curriculum that substantively incorporates women's perspectives and encourages the development of feminist tools of analyses. For instance, in an Asian American experience course that I have taught, I assigned required readings that documented the different experiences women had with immigration to the United States and important events in Asian American history (e.g., World War II). I also asked students to reflect and write about how women's stories might differ from non-female-centered accounts of Asian American history.

The opportunities for male intellectuals to engage in theoretical contributions to Filipina American feminism are many. Beyond theory construction, male intellectuals can also actively introduce and highlight feminist issues in classroom settings. However, the most substantive role Filipino-American men can play may lie not in the intellectual or academic arena, but outside such privileged spaces, simply—or perhaps not so simply—as men engaged in praxis.

Praxis: From Individual …

For those "Pinoys [who] may feel a lack of ownership in Pinayism" (8), the first step to engaging in the women's liberation struggle and experiencing a sense of ownership is for Pinoys to develop a Pinayist consciousness. For Filipino American men who have access to such educational resources, this consciousness-raising can involve taking courses on women and gender studies. Others can look to feminist community activists who are engaged in women's issues, as Tintiangco-Cubales had done for her research. Some Filipino American men can turn to self-disciplined study, reading incessantly on various theories, topics, and issues in feminist studies. Others can engage in dialogue with the Pinays in the community—their mothers, sisters, aunts, cousins, friends, partners, coworkers—listening to and carefully reflecting upon their stories and how their lives are shaped by and resist patriarchy and sexism.

For heterosexual Filipino American men, the development of a Filipino American feminist consciousness is a long, solitary, and painful process. In our patriarchal society, masculinist identities are constantly reproduced through social interactions and reinforced by popular culture. The solitary process of relinquishing patriarchal privilege can involve periods of isolation and alienation. Having experienced this alienation myself, I can attest to the existential loneliness and internal turmoil that develops when I have vocally challenged the sexist actions and words of my male peers—whether they be family, roommates, classmates, or friends. In the past, my critique and intolerance of such sexist behavior among my male compadres have resulted in the severance of longstanding and deep friendships. In retrospect, I am confronted with the realization that such severance was an inadequate and reactionary response to the problems of patriarchy. The "politics of conversion,"[18] grounded in "the love ethic," challenges me to rethink the role of commitment in the midst of the struggle to love, especially among those we disagree with.[19] If I cannot commit myself to transforming the relationships of those closest to me, how can I expect to subvert the interrelational and structural dimensions of patriarchy?

Negotiating that space between accepting an individual for who she is—without enforcing my own judgments on her person—and the moral commitment to a feminist consciousness that is critical of patriarchal or dehumanizing behavior toward my Pinay sisters (and women in general) has been a constant battle in my life, one that takes the form of the proverbial two steps forward, one step back. For, to be a feminist man in a patriarchal society is to situate oneself in the periphery, risking the safety of conformity for the possible loneliness of being an exception to the norm. However, just as the margins for bell hooks became a site of radical possibility, the position of outcast can be a source of inspiration.

However, the bouts of loneliness and isolation, as potentially empowering as they can be, must inevitably end because political transformation requires collective struggle and healthy, meaningful interpersonal relations. This entails the creation of communities based on the dialogue of communion and the act of loving. Seeking out and surrounding oneself by those Pinayist women and men and their allies who are deeply committed to the fostering of loving friendships is an integral part of building oppositional communities of love, a radical response to the lovelessness pervasive throughout modern heterosexist, imperialist, white-supremacist patriarchal culture.

For Filipino American men, the difficult choice to remain dedicated to the development of a Pinayist self-consciousness and active in the political liberation of Filipina Americans and all women requires an ethical and moral commitment to justice. In a society that equates heterosexist patriarchal norms with masculinity, publicly opposing patriarchy invites external perceptions that one is either "queer" or "not man enough." Resisting the judgmental perceptions that seek to silence critique through the questioning of male sexuality and gender, heterosexual men who make a feminist commitment must confront their homophobia and the denigration of women-as-other in order to incapacitate these silencing tactics. Drawing insight from the works of John Stoltenberg, bell hooks commented in a 1999 public lecture that the male struggle against patriarchy and sexism at some point comes down to an individual commitment to either "manhood" or "justice."[20] This decision to develop a feminist consciousness is an individual and personal choice and entails self-disciplined commitment, but as individuals living in community.

From this individual commitment, Filipino American men must employ their Pinayist consciousness in their interpersonal relations with Pinays, other women, and other men. Prior to forming actual relationships, the constant challenge, deconstruction, and dismantling of sexist stereotypes, patriarchal thinking, and misogynist strains within masculinist thought must be developed into an ongoing habit. This includes vigilance against thoughts that objectify women, perceive them as incapable of self-determination without male intervention and, as Tintiangco-Cubales, in chapter 8, has pointed out, the "underestimation of Pinays by Pinoys." Stereotypes such as the submissive woman, or Pinay, spring from these patriarchal-mental images that not only are grounded in male domination and the will to power but have also been reproduced in Philippine culture as a legacy of Spanish colonial relations—the Maria Clara archetype—and a patriarchal Christian icon: the Madonna figure.

This abusive will to power must also be connected and understood, but never excused, as a reaction to life experiences that have caused a sense of powerlessness, emotional/psychological pain, or lack of self-esteem and self-confidence in Filipino men. Moreover, the will to power should be interrogated from the standpoint of the construction of masculine identity vis-à-vis the domination and control of women. This necessarily entails reconstructing our notions of self, masculinity, and relationships. Unless Pinayist men undertake the painful process of building self-love independent of the presence or domination of women, healthy, nonsexist interpersonal relationships are vulnerable from the start, already sabotaged by the patriarchal male mind before thought can manifest into words or action.

Alongside the commitment to an independent love of self must lie the commitment to free masculinity from controlling impulses. Jealousy, as a masculine reaction based on the desire to control a woman's choice of whom she loves and cares for, is one emotional impulse that requires serious confrontation, reflection, and honest dialogue. Discomfort and/or jealousy, in the face of women's open expression of the people they have chosen to love, signals the need to revisit our masculine identities and liberate them from the lack of self-love and the pernicious will to control. It is also imperative to reconstruct our ideas about relationships and love, creating examples of loving friendships and forms of communion that do not devolve into mass media–propagated and commodified notions of romantic attachment. We should not allow romance to get in the way of love.

… To Interpersonal …

The responsibilities of Filipino American feminist men must then move from challenging individual thoughts and the development of a Pinayist consciousness to Pinayism as a way of life, a way of being in the world. This affects relationships with mothers, sisters, grandmothers, aunts, cousins, nieces, partners, and friends: all women with which one interacts. This means treating our mothers and family members with respect and not taking them for granted or assuming they are there to cook, clean, or run errands for the male family member. Communication, thoughtful listening, and deep respect are important in interpersonal relations. Often men expect women to be there to listen to them talk but do not reciprocate by being emotionally and mentally available or attentive to Pinays who voice their concerns or aspirations. Filipino American feminist men must also be on guard against allowing white supremacist or colonized standards of beauty bias interactions and relationships. Dismissing, ignoring, or marginalizing women who do not conform to Western norms of beauty while approaching, privileging, or elevating only women who are deemed "attractive" amounts to alternative forms of objectification or dehumanization.

Domestic violence in the Filipina/o American community is a serious problem that both Pinoys and Pinays must learn to address. Pinoys must not only check themselves but also check others who are perpetuating verbal, physical, and sexual assault against Pinays and other women. Unplanned and teenage pregnancies as well as single-mother households are other manifestations of sexual objectification and evasion of responsibility by Filipino American men.

In our daily interactions, Filipino American men must refrain from sexist jokes, comments, or behaviors that would constitute sexual harassment, whether that be in the workplace, in the classroom, social gatherings, or wherever we interact with women. Patriarchal male bonding often takes the form of conquest storytelling and/or sexual innuendos that dehumanize, degrade, or sexually objectify women. Pinayist men must be critical of participating in such male-bonding forms and must be assertive in challenging vocally those behaviors among peers, whether or not women are present. Pinayist men must also resist "perpetrating," "fronting," or otherwise engaging in feminist critique only when women are present, performing a political role as a way of impressing women for patriarchal ulterior motives. These are some of the ways Filipino American men can resist the effects of patriarchy and sexist socialization that condition interpersonal relations.

… To Institutional

One of the biggest areas of institutional interventions by men is in regards to the sexual objectification of women. In a market society that puts a high premium on stimulation and titillation, the proliferation of sexually suggestive images of women is pervasive. In the Filipino American community, images of Pinays (usually those deemed beautiful by bourgeois, white-supremacist aesthetics) are used on party fliers to promote dances, imported car shows, and other social events, or to sell magazines and calendars. These fliers and images decorate the walls of many of today's young Filipino American men's homes and/or workplaces.

The consumption of soft-core and hard-core pornography is also widespread. Filipino American men have yet to take a moral stand against pornography as a patriarchal institution. Many of these videos promote dehumanizing and misogynist depictions of women that tailor to the patriarchal male imaginary. The development of the Internet has transformed the distribution and easy accessibility of pornographic material in profoundly troubling ways. Patronage of strippers at private gatherings—birthdays, bachelor parties, and so forth—as well as at bars and strip clubs are other forms of sexual objectification in which many Filipino-American men participate. Disturbingly, heterosexual Filipino American men are not the only consumers of strippers and strip clubs; heterosexual Pinays as well as gay men and lesbians in the community also uncritically utilize strippers. Men, as well as women, should not be sexually objectified.

Whether or not the female being objectified or commodified is Filipina or Filipina American, Pinoys must take a stand against sexual objectification as a dehumanizing act of violence against all women. Forms of resistance include speaking out against the exploitation of Pinay images and boycotting events and products that utilize such images. Choosing not to purchase, rent, or in any way patronize the pornography, exotic dancing, and stripping industries is another way of utilizing consumer economic power for political and moral purposes. Individually choosing to resist all these but also challenging peers to do the same is equally important in creating collective resistance to male-owned and -dominated institutions that profit from the sexual objectification of Pinays and women in general.

As mentioned earlier, the Internet not only has transformed the deployment of pornographic images and materials but has also facilitated the expansion of the mail-order bride industry, which has become the subject of a few articles and essays.[21] Some websites, rife with descriptions and pictures of Filipinas (many of them twelve to eighteen years old), covertly disguise these transactions as pen pal services; others are less "discreet" and blatantly reveal their objective in selling women as brides to single and willing men, providing secure online credit card purchases. Other websites offer sex tours, package vacations inviting men to travel to the "exotic islands" where local hosts will introduce them to the local "entertainment" spots. Less technologically proficient agencies still use brochures and catalogs to offer the same services. These abuses against women in the Philippines have become so much a part of the mainstream culture that media figures such as Howard Stern and sitcoms such as *Fraser* brazenly believe they can use these stereotypes without serious public outcry. Filipino American men must play a role in pursuing legal and political action against these celebrities, mail-order bride companies, and sex tourism agencies. Participating in demonstrations, programs, and other actions organized by various women's organizations and networks against sex trafficking is another way Pinoys can aid in the Filipina American feminist struggle. At the same time, we should act to change political economic relations that foreclose opportunities for Filipina women, thereby limiting their options to attain economic security.

Another institutional form of oppression affecting Pinays is female labor exploitation. Whether that exploitation takes place in the domestic sphere or extends out into the public labor force, Filipino American men must take a stand against such unjust practices against Filipina American women. The "underestimation of Pinays by Pinoys" is a prevalent sexist norm that extends from interpersonal relationships into the workplace. Pinays, like other women, have access to limited occupational opportunities in a patriarchal society and, as women of color or even newly immigrated women of color, the opportunities available to Pinays are even more severely constrained. Filipina American women often find themselves in underpaid, overworked clerical positions or working for domestic or physical care services, and sometimes assembly line or sweatshop labor, not to mention the "global trade in Filipina workers" made possible by the socioeconomic dependency of the Philippines.[22] Filipino American men must challenge the lack of employment opportunities through legal and political action and resist the undervaluing of Pinays, both of which contribute to the exploitation of Filipina American workers. Pinoys can also play a role in organizing and protecting the rights of Filipina overseas contract workers.

Filipino American men committed to the Filipina American feminist struggle must also begin to challenge and transform the patriarchal family. The patriarchal family is built around the sexist and gendered division of labor that includes domestic work as well as parenting responsibilities. The sexist and gendered division of housework must be abolished, and men must take more responsibility in sharing the day-to-day tasks of maintaining a residence and household. There must also be a reevaluation of the parenting responsibilities. Many psychoanalytic feminists attribute sexist behavior, in part, to this unequal distribution of parenting time and energy that puts mothers at the child-rearing forefront. Psychoanalytic feminists often claim that the omnipresence of mothers in early childhood development can result in blaming mothers and, by association, all women for the troubles that men face. Whether or not one gives validity to this psychoanalytic reading of the institution of motherhood, Pinayist men should seriously take responsibility and invest more time and energy into fathering or parenting. This includes the increasingly more common situations in which the male partner is not the biological father, due to irresponsible abandonment or behavior of the biological father, as well as same-sex households that involve child rearing. As many feminists rightly suggest, the patriarchal notion of the family, and its sexist and gendered division of labor, must be challenged and transformed as part of a women's liberation movement. Experimenting with new forms of family life are ways of prefiguring possible social and household associations that can result in more equitable, just, and mutually beneficial relationships.

Sexist and patriarchal thinking can also infect relationships and behaviors in organizational settings. Recently, I found myself guilty of perpetuating such thinking and behaviors during a conference hosted by an organization with which I am involved. In this particular situation, I chose not to help with some of the nitty-gritty details leading up to the start of the conference. In retrospect, I realized critically that I could always have done more, especially with regard to the more mundane chores. Meanwhile, I conveniently overlooked the fact that my female colleagues and friends in the organization also had busy schedules, if not busier than my own, but were still willing to put in the extra effort, time, and sacrifices to make the event a success. In Filipina/o American communities, where several organizations—political, community service, religious, business, educational, and so on—attempt to address the various needs of our populations, we as men should be especially vigilant against such sexist and patriarchal thinking that disproportionately places the organizational and programmatic burden on women's time, effort, and energy. Even though an organization may be Pinay led and run, patriarchal and sexist thinking and behaviors could still be enacted when male members refuse to share equally in the responsibilities of maintaining the organization or conducting activities, particularly the small, tedious, behind-the-scenes work that is indispensable, if not always recognized or glorified.

As this section hopes to communicate, the role of Filipino American men in the Filipina American feminist or Pinayist movement is essential to its success. As comrades in the struggle, Pinoys must make a commitment to revolution at the individual, interpersonal, and institutional levels. As expressed earlier in my theoretical reflections, the success of a Pinayist movement would inevitably fall short without linking itself to the materialist transformation of global capitalism. Insofar as Filipina and Filipina American women's oppression, and constructions of sex and gender, are irrevocably linked to imperialism and political economy, committed Pinayists should ally themselves with organizations and coalitions that challenge the predatory and parasitic power of multinational corporations and transnational capital. However, it is equally important to never lose sight of the necessity of love, spirituality, and communication as the foundation for our personal and interpersonal relationships as well as the sustaining ethic for our social movements.

Presented here are just a few initial suggestions that can guide further reflection and praxis on the role of men in Pinayism. While not meant to be a comprehensive list, my hope is to provide a springboard for further dialogue, reflection, theorization, and, most important, the practice of advancing the Filipina American feminist movement and identifying the role that Filipino American men, like myself, can play in the struggle.

Reflections

I have titled this section "Reflections" rather than "Conclusion" because the Pinayist movement has only just begun. We are at a point in time as a community where more and more Filipina/o American women and men are developing a feminist consciousness. The opportunities for further theorization and dialogue on Pinayism will continue to unfold as Filipina/o American communities evolve to meet the new challenges and social contexts that constantly change and arise. Nevertheless, as agents making herstory, inheriting the resources and lessons of feminist movements around the globe, we have the potential to create positive changes while vigilantly anticipating and minimizing unforeseen negative consequences. Because of the pioneering work of Allyson Tintiangco-Cubales and other theorists of Filipina/o American feminisms, as well as the rich Philippine, feminist-theoretical elaborations of Delia D. Aguilar, Elizabeth Uy Eviota, Sr. Mary John Mananzan, and others, new feminist-freedom lovers can draw on a wide array of theoretical and analytical tools to push the ideological, cultural, spiritual, and material struggle forward. Putting forth a call for men and women to join in this feminist struggle, I hope to have shared some insight as to how a Filipino American male can contribute to the struggle for women's liberation.

Postscript (2003)

I wrote the bulk of this essay in 1999, as a master's student at Harvard University enrolled in a graduate seminar, Feminist Theories and Theologizing, taught by Gale Yee at the Episcopal Divinity School in Cambridge, Massachusetts. This essay was meant to be an initial and general introduction to the subject matter.

Since then, however, I have recognized that a number of improvements and new directions are possible. These include and are not limited to:

- the consideration and incorporation of a variety of feminist theories, in addition to new works
- reconsidering perspectives laid out in this reflection paper, in light of criticism and growth
- adding to the variety of interventions that men can make in the feminist movement
- elaborating on the specificity of Pinays' roles, images, and assumptions, through in-depth historical, cultural, and political analyses, including the impact of patriarchal religious teachings and institutions on gender and sex role socialization
- describing in great detail the specific mechanisms involved in the construction and reproduction of Filipino American masculinity and patriarchal and sexist thinking and behaviors

In a future essay, I plan to revisit some of these themes and explore new directions, hopefully in partnership with Pinayist men and women willing to tread these difficult waters with courage, comradeship, and commitment to subverting patriarchy and realizing loving and egalitarian relationships.

Acknowledgments

Portions of this paper were written or revised while under the support of a National Science Foundation Graduate Research Fellowship. Any opinions, findings, conclusions, or recommendations expressed in this publication are those of the author and do not necessarily reflect the views of the National Science Foundation.

I would like to thank Professor Gale Yee for providing the intellectual space and instruction to begin these initial reflections. I would also like to thank bell hooks for her textual and in-person encouragement of my undertaking anti-patriarchal struggle, and Joan May Cordova for her faith in the value of my voice and writings. I would like to recognize the strength and example of my family members, especially my mother and sister, whose support make my work so much easier to do. Last but not least, I would like to thank Christine G. Cordero for her "revolutionary love." I am deeply indebted and inspired by all of these remarkable people for their spiritual wisdom, fierce examples, and unrelenting commitment to the practice of loving.

Notes

1. Allyson Goce Tintiangco, "Pinayism," *Maganda*, no. 10 (1996): 5; hereafter, page numbers will be cited parenthetically in the text. This essay is reprinted in the present volume, in slightly different form.
2. bell hooks, *Yearning: Race, Gender, and Cultural Politics* (Boston: South End, 1990), 149–50.
3. Alice Walker, *In Search of Our Mothers' Gardens* (New York: Harcourt Brace Jovanovich, 1983).
4. hooks, *Yearning*, 57.
5. bell hooks, *Feminist Theory: From Margin to Center* (Boston: South End, 1984), 73.
6. Gale Yee, personal comments to the author on earlier paper draft, 1999.
7. Uma Narayan, *Dislocating Cultures: Identities, Traditions, and Third World Feminism* (New York: Routledge, 1997), 14.
8. An interesting note: Sr. Mananzan is chairperson of the General Assembly Binding Women for Reform, Integrity, Equality, Leadership, and Action (GABRIELA), one of several women's organizations working toward women's liberation in the Philippines. Given the splits in the Philippine Left, it would be interesting to analyze if and/or how progressive women's organizations cooperate across political, ideological, and strategic differences. It also would be interesting to engage in feminist analyses of various strategies for bringing about Filipina women's liberation, ranging from reform-oriented measures to the armed struggle advocated by a variety of Filipina/o activists and organizations.
9. Sr. Mary John Mananzan, "Sexual Exploitation in a Third World Setting," in *Women in Asia: Status and Image,* ed. Sr. Mary John Mananzan (Singapore: Christian Conference of Asia, 1979).
10. Sr. Mary John Mananzan, ed., *Essays on Women* (Manila: Women's Studies Program, St. Scholastica's College, 1987).
11. Sr. Mary John Mananzan, ed., *Women and Religion* (Manila: Institute of Women's Studies, St. Scholastica's College, 1988).

12. Delia D. Aguilar, *The Feminist Challenge: Initial Working Principles toward Reconceptualizing the Feminist Movement in the Philippines* (Manila: Asian Social Institute, 1988).
13. Delia D. Aguilar, "Lost in Translation: Western Feminism and Asian Women," in *Dragon Ladies: Asian American Feminists Breathe Fire*, ed. Sonia Shah (Boston: South End, 1997), 153–65.
14. Delia D. Aguilar, "Gender, Nation, Colonialism: Lessons from the Philippines," in *The Women, Gender and Development Reader*, ed. Nalini Visvanathan, Lynne Duggan, and Lau Nisonoff (Atlantic Highlands, N.J.: Zed, 1995), 309–16.
15. Delia D. Aguilar, *Toward a Nationalist Feminism* (Quezon City, Philippines: Giraffe, 1998).
16. Elizabeth Uy Eviota, *The Political Economy of Gender: Women and the Sexual Division of Labour in the Philippines* (Atlantic Highlands, N.J.: Zed Books, 1992).
17. Elizabeth Uy Eviota, *Sex and Gender in Philippine Society: A Discussion of Issues on the Relations between Women and Men* (Manila: National Commission on the Role of Filipino Women, 1994), iii–iv.
18. Cornel West, *Race Matters* (Boston: Beacon, 1993).
19. bell hooks, *All About Love: New Visions* (New York: William Morrow, 2000).
20. bell hooks, "Remembering Rapture: The Writer at Work," Author series lecture at Boston Public Library, January 21, 1999.
21. See Venny Villapondo, "The Business of Selling Mail-order Brides," in *Making Waves: An Anthology of Writings By and About Asian American Women*, ed. Asian Women United of California (Boston: Beacon, 1989), 318–26; Raquel Z. Ordoñez, "Mail-Order Brides: An Emerging Community," in *Filipino Americans: Transformation and Identity*, ed. Maria P. P. Root (Thousand Oaks, Calif.: Sage, 1997), 121–42.
22. Grace Chang, "The Global Trade in Filipina Workers," in Sonia Shah, ed., *Dragon Ladies*, 132–52.

10

Feminism across Our Generations

DELIA D. AGUILAR AND KARIN AGUILAR-SAN JUAN

Preface

We are a Filipino mother and Filipino American daughter whose perspectives on feminism—as a theory and as a political practice—have been formed over years of study, discussion, debate, and struggle in the Philippines and in the United States. In this essay we offer our reflections as food for thought. We offer them because, despite the inevitably personal markings of the experiences we recount, they are in reality reflections of specific historical moments and of ongoing sociopolitical changes to which others, Filipino or not, might in some ways relate. We believe that our individual stories are ultimately all tied up with a broader and more enduring collective narrative about gender, race, colonialism, and national liberation.

Who are we? Delia was a professor of women's studies and comparative American cultures at Washington State University and at Bowling Green State University in Ohio. She now teaches women's studies courses at the University of Connecticut. She has written several books published in the Philippines: *The Feminist Challenge, Filipino Housewives Speak*, and *Toward a Nationalist Feminism*. Her most recent book, an anthology titled *Women and Globalization* and coedited with Anne Lacsamana, addresses her latest concern.[1] She was born in Capiz in 1938 and has lived in the United States since 1961. Karin, the older of Delia's two children, was born in Boston, Massachusetts, in 1962. Karin is a former editor for *Dollars and Sense* magazine, a progressive monthly for noneconomists, and a former member of the South End Press publishing collective. Ten years ago, she edited and introduced an anthology, *The State of Asian America: Activism and Resistance in the 1990s*.[2] Since 1999, she has been a tenure-track faculty member in the American Studies Department at Macalester College in St. Paul, Minnesota. Her courses focus on racism and racial inequality, urban sociology, and Asian American studies. She likes to refer to living in Minnesota as being "stranded in the Great White North."

In place of a coauthored formal essay on feminism, we decided to engage in a "dialogue" where we would draw out each other's ideas by responding to a set of questions that we could answer in writing and exchange via e-mail.

Our first question, "How did you become a feminist?" led naturally to the second question, "Did/does feminism help to frame your politics? Or does/did your politics frame your engagement with feminism/feminists?" The third and last question, "What do you see as the concerns of young Filipino American women today, and how would you address them?" came as an effort to connect our thoughts about the past to the present and to establish some generational links in our own experiences that we hope would interest not only Filipinos and Filipino Americans but also those whose feminism has an international reach.

Question 1: How did you become a feminist?

Karin Aguilar-San Juan

I feel that the "how" in this question must first bring in the "when," and then the "why," and, finally, the "with what consequences." I would say that I became a feminist *in utero*. How could I not with a powerhouse for a mother? But that answer would as easily implicate my mother—who will speak for herself here—as it would take me off the hook, as if biology could provide any kind of answer to this ultimately political topic.

If I was not a feminist by birth, at least I was born a girl into a world that does not see girls as having the same potential as boys. Maybe that was not always true in my family, but it was true in school, with my friends, and in the town in which I grew up. I was encouraged to read and write and practice spelling, not to play soccer or basketball as I would often have preferred. Sometimes I cannot separate the moments in which I was treated as "a girl" from the moments I was treated as "not American." In fact, being racialized—treated like a foreigner because of my physical appearance and assumed cultural traits—during childhood is a much more vivid memory for me than being gendered. So actually, I do separate the gender and the racial process as I look back on my past. Perhaps that is also because I probably fit into many of the expectations of girlhood, much more than I fit into the expectations for being "an American."

My mother taught me to fight for my rights. I began practicing these lessons in the backyard. I remember wrestling little Bobby Tate to the ground for borrowing my bicycle without my permission—stealing it, really. I think Mom watched from the kitchen window; she might have cheered me on. Later, I had to confront the white boys (always boys) in high school who would taunt me with racial slurs. Armed at home with nasty rejoinders by my mother, I would walk up to these pathetic individuals and say, "Do you know that in my country we *eat* white monkeys like you?" I don't remember any response from them—just mild shock. Sometimes I would have to confront my high school teachers for their narrowness of mind, particularly regarding the politics of the time. I learned to use polite language and references to ideas and books in my comments. It was the late 1970s and there was plenty to debate in the classroom: the justness of the war in Vietnam, police brutality against antiwar protesters, whether radical activism is an American tradition, and the role of labor unions in improving society. Then there is, of course, my favorite topic: the role of the U.S. government in propping up the dictatorship of Ferdinand Marcos in the Philippines. I gave my teachers all of my mind in those years and I could only do so because I thought I deserved to be heard. I think that made me a feminist of some kind—at least in the eyes of those I harassed.

In college I began to take on feminism as a political cause. I remember writing an essay for the newsletter of the women's center on Raya Dunayevskaya and her idea of humanism. Early on, then, I wrote about social change as a feminist, from a feminist perspective. Instinctively I knew that the women's center was providing one of the only venues I would ever have for developing and articulating my views about the world. Feminism became one place, one theoretical platform, from which to interpret and criticize the world. I remember that in a seminar on Karl Marx and social theory, my classmates and I had a mutiny when our professor declared that feminists had nothing to say about Marxism or social theory. After that session, we took over and taught the class to ourselves. I worked hard on a paper about Juliet Mitchell, one of the first Marxist feminists I encountered, as if I were planning to convince our professor about the relevance of feminist theory. It was good for me, but I don't think he ever changed his view about feminists.

When I came out as a lesbian in my last year of college, "feminism" finally made sense to me as a theory and as a way of life. It just felt like all the pieces fit together and I got a clue about who I was and who I might become. Looking back, I would say that feminists made a place for me to take control of my own future; without an idea of personal independence (which is a very loaded, biased, and historically constructed idea), I could not have pushed on to new things. As far as I was concerned, feminism allowed me to deal with my inner world on my own terms. In a way, feminism allowed me to move "past" gender, to disregard people's expectations of me as a young woman who should eventually marry a man and produce his children and live in his—and their—shadows.

In the end, I was not as interested in feminism as I was in other social issues or causes. My main issues back then were Central America and the Philippines. I was mostly interested in fighting U.S.-based multinational corporations and their death grip on the third world. Of course, the people who cared what I thought were usually feminists or people who were influenced and informed by feminism. I don't think I made much of an impact on big, old, white corporate men or women. When I began to work as an educator and organizer in Boston in the mid-1980s, I did so in an environment that accepted and encouraged women to be strong people in their own right. So that had to involve feminism in some way. As a young lesbian, I also had to find my way in a local movement that did not always know what to do with me. Within a week of moving to Boston, I had a semitraumatic encounter with the hard-core leftists in Chinatown who told me I would have to "subordinate my cause" (meaning: homosexuality) to the cause of socialism. They actually used those words, too. It was semitraumatic because I had the same attitude toward them that I had toward the boys who taunted me in high school. I was just enraged and annoyed at their stupidity. I could not believe people could be so idiotic as to draw such simple lines in the sand and believe in them heart and soul.

My eleven years as an activist in Boston are in many ways foundational to my thinking now about feminism. I don't attend to being a feminist; I mean, I don't label myself that way, nor do I spend much energy in feminist organizations. I gave $25 to Planned Parenthood and I walked miles and miles to help find a cure for breast cancer, and that is what many people—especially rich, white, suburban housewives—mean by "feminism." But those gestures are simple, not profound or radical. I did those things because they don't hurt anyone and maybe they help a tiny little bit. But I think I do other things with much more gusto, attention, and belief. I attend to other ways of creating political and social change in the world.

When I think about whether or not I am a feminist, I remember what Sonia Shah wrote in her introduction to *Dragon Ladies: Asian American Feminists Breathe Fire.* She said that Asian American women have to deal with Asian American issues because no other feminists will do that for them.[3] It's not like we can expect white or black women to take up our Asian issues. In the same way, I cannot pretend that I don't care about feminism, because there is hardly any other venue in which my work and my vision—and more generally, the fate of women like me—will be entertained as worthwhile. If I were to walk away from feminism as a cause, I think I could not expect to be treated seriously by nonfeminists, antifeminists, homophobes, or racists. In the end, I am forced to embrace feminism and to make feminism matter to me, because the world is otherwise not going to have a place for someone who thinks, and acts, like I do.

Delia D. Aguilar

This question would have been easier to answer ten or fifteen years ago. It isn't that I would have had a different response then; it's simply that feminism means so many different things now, partly as a result of the success of the women's movement of the 1960s and 1970s. Now institutionalized and integrated into the mainstream, feminism has become domesticated, losing its critical edge. So it just isn't possible for me to speak with the same excitement or urgency. But perhaps I can talk about this later.

I came to feminism, I suppose, the way that many others during my time did—through political struggles of a broader nature. I was politically awakened, to use the jargon of liberation movements of that period, by events transpiring in the homeland. The declaration of martial rule by Ferdinand Marcos was met with fierce opposition by large masses of people, many of whom were placed on the wanted list of the regime and forced to join the revolutionary underground. In the United States, a group of young Filipino progressives who had fled the repression began to organize in support of the anti-imperialist, national-democratic movement, urging attention to the U.S. government's complicity in giving military and economic aid to the dictatorship. It was through participation in this movement that I came to grips with what leftist circles called "the woman question." Put more plainly, it was in the process of organizing—at rallies, picket lines, house meetings, and, more crucially, in closed meetings where the "political line" was set forth and discussed—that I was struck by the incongruity of it all. Here we were, talking about fighting for a more humane society, one in which class differences would eventually be eliminated and where women would gain equality with men. However, I saw that the way we were conducting ourselves contrasted sharply with these stated goals. Without question, men consistently took leadership positions in the most important activities (those requiring the use of the mind), while women were relegated to traditional support roles.

I think it is important to emphasize that my awareness of women's subordination by no means came automatically. I happened at this time to be attending meetings on my campus of a group called the Women's Radical Union. We read socialist literature, discussed the Marxist analysis of capitalism, and talked about the emancipation of women. While many of the women in this group were graduate students who were acutely sensitive to macho behavior among their male peers and professors, their feminism was tempered by their socialism. In this way they differed markedly from liberal or radical feminists whose feminism was confrontational and direct but narrowly confined to gender relations. The latter never had any appeal for me because, of course, I was deeply conscious of my third world status. It was also at this time that I first began to teach women's studies, courses in marriage and family, and gender-roles socialization. Because textbooks on these topics broached from a women's perspective were not to see print until several years later, in the beginning years of my teaching I used pamphlets from the *New England Free Press* and other underground publications, all of which stressed the overthrow of patriarchy as well as capitalism. Interestingly enough, despite these activities, I did not refer to myself as a "feminist." Feminism in revolutionary third world struggles was then anathema. It was considered bourgeois, individualist, and divisive. I understood well that MAKIBAKA, the revolutionary underground women's organization founded in 1970, stood for the liberation of women, not feminism.

Though I was not a feminist, I was determined to engage "the woman question" among my revolutionary comrades because, by this point, the limitations of the national democratic platform's stance on women had become apparent to me. The fights I had were angry, fierce, and heated and were not confined to men. I questioned what I saw then as the productivist orientation of the movement and its instrumental reckoning of women's participation in it. I wanted conventional gender relations addressed and changed. I was told in not so many words that women in the Philippines were already liberated because they controlled the purse strings in the family, because they were respected members of society, and because they were strong. Weren't women guerrilla fighters proof of this? That's what I received in response to my mailed queries to the Philippines—underground photos of red women fighters! And aren't women, by merely joining the movement, already beginning to cast off old norms that require them to stay home? I remember addressing an audience of mostly women in the Philippines in the early 1980s, where one very articulate woman stood up and told me exactly that, using this very language. (A mere two years later, she was to become an outspoken feminist and head of a women's nongovernmental organization.) Those were extremely frustrating times for me, so frustrating that I decided to turn to academic work to find empirical support for my stand. I set to work on an examination of the gender division of household labor in the Philippines, an issue I considered vital to my argument, by conducting interviews with women across class (women who were mothers) and letting them speak for themselves. I decided to write about this as I could not find a receptive ear and felt that our debates had reached an impasse.

At about this time, I was invited to join an ongoing Marxist/feminist study group that had been in existence since the early 1970s. My involvement here also proved to be another significant source of tension, for if I was waging a battle against sexism among my Filipino comrades, with these women I would be raising doubts about their specific version of Marxism, or of Marxist feminism. Within this group, however, I found support in the few women of color who had been invited to join along with me. They, too, were active in national liberation solidarity struggles and had reservations about these Marxist/feminist women that were identical to mine. What was "Marxist" about these women when their vocabulary was circumscribed by patriarchal issues and the politics of gender? Holding our own separate meetings, we women of color explored the ways in which we could effectively bring our anti-imperialist concerns to the main group. We were particularly taken aback and appalled by the reaction of one white woman after we had given individual presentations on national liberation in Puerto Rico and the Philippines. Turning to the other white women, she casually dismissed our very presence by asking, "Should we support national liberation struggles that are patriarchal?" I would say that the tensions I encountered in this and other arenas of conflict were often quite unsettling, but they were useful in goading me to study Marxist feminism on my own.

In the meantime, feminist stirrings could be discerned at the margins of the national democratic movement back home. In groping for answers to my questions, I was put in touch with a group of women in the Philippines who, themselves no longer satisfied with the old line on women, were starting to hold forums about organizing an autonomous women's movement. Many of them had earned their place in the movement as cultural workers; several had undergone incarceration as political prisoners. I am certain that it was their immersion in the movement that gave them the confidence to express dissent without feeling vulnerable to the facile charge of "divisiveness." I still recall the excitement of those small gatherings. While these activists called upon me to provide the theoretical frame within which their discomfiture as women could be articulated, the now-gendered stories that they shared with me gave me the foundation, in practice, upon which to base my critique. I was also much encouraged and energized in knowing that there were several such aggrupations of women, not just the one I was meeting with. Not long after this, Ninoy Aquino was assassinated. The event drew the ire of the middle class, who took to the streets, as it had not before. The ensuing opening up of what is now referred to as a "democratic space" led to the mobilization of a wide variety of "sectors" constituting Philippine society. Shortly afterward, a semiautonomous women's movement developed and flourished, easily becoming the most vibrant of the sectoral organizations. The National Federation of Women's Organizations, GABRIELA, was founded and, with its establishment, women came out in the open declaring themselves feminists.[4] It must be remarked that when they did, they made sure to explain that they were appropriating the term for themselves and imbuing it with their own nationalist content. It was not until this moment that I, too, could give myself this label.

Question 2: Did/does feminism help to frame your politics? Or does/did your politics frame your engagement with feminism/feminists?

Delia D. Aguilar

Although it may seem circuitous, I think that I can best answer this question by continuing my narrative. In 1987, we (Karin's father, brother, and I) spent the year in the Philippines. That was a very, very stimulating period. Politics was in the air and the atmosphere was, quite simply, electric. The women's movement, a feminist one now, was the most alive and visible among the progressive associations. I set up a small study group of women who met weekly to read and study feminism. It was very different from any group in which I had participated in the United States. For one thing, these women had a wealth of experience in revolutionary activity and so every little paragraph that we read (representing theory) was incessantly interrupted by a discussion of multiple examples of lived realities (representing practice). For another, many of our weekly meetings had to be shelved because there were urgent actions constantly taking place, some of them on behalf of a person or persons arrested or tortured, while others entailed joining massive demonstrations. But now that the democratic space allowed travel and an easy flow of ideas from the West, I perceived an understanding of race and racism to be an important subject for us Filipino feminists to grapple with. That was not a topic that was readily grasped in our study group. But it bothered me no end that U.S. feminists would come and lecture to Filipino women about how, for example, we should "not keep blaming colonialism for [our] problems as women." The message: move on, already; you just don't know it, but it's your men who are the problem. It also bothered me that Filipino feminists could mindlessly quote something that, say, Betty Friedan wrote and apply that directly to our situation as Filipino women. As a result, I found myself waging a wholly new educational struggle. I began reading feminist theory in a different way—and now feminist presses and feminist-theory making in the United States were burgeoning—and I started thinking and writing about how feminist theoretical production in the industrial West could adversely affect third world women's movements.

When we returned to the United States, the growing dominance of the "cultural turn" was becoming evident in the academy. Having just arrived from the Philippines where, despite a lively women's organization, the progressive movement as a whole had retained its economist character, I welcomed this trend as an antidote. Postmodernism seemed to give room for conversations around race and gender in addition to class in its insistence on recognizing "difference." I initially experienced this trend as freeing, both from the restrictions of a rigid class-bound perspective embraced by national liberation and from the racism and narrowness of middle-class, white feminism. By this time, too, the neoconservatism inaugurated by the administrations of Ronald Reagan and George H. W. Bush had taken hold and progressive organizations in the United States had all but disappeared. What was left of organizing became local and specific, having lost any overarching or unifying metanarrative. In fact, thinking back, I realize that it was as early as 1982 that feminists in the United States started asking one another, Where's the women's movement? Connected as I was to the struggle in the Philippines, I wasn't troubled by this, knowing full well that it was very much alive in the Philippines and in other third world countries.

Today feminism is confined to the academy in the United States. There has not been a women's movement to speak of for sometime, although its absence is something feminists themselves seem fearful of examining seriously. Progressive politics in the academy has been enacted mainly in the discursive, cultural terrain, with a profound disconnect from the real world, even when it employs leftist rhetoric. Its language is elitist, its jargon incomprehensible except to initiates, and its progressive claim highly questionable. To be expected of a third world neocolonial formation, the academy in the Philippines has not been free of this influence. But as always, rapid changes in the global political economy—more specifically, the devastation and immiseration that neo-liberalism has brought about—have spawned a worldwide antiglobalization movement that is now difficult to ignore. The "Battle of Seattle" at the meeting of the World Trade Organization in 1999 and the numerous international gatherings in its wake signal a new, altogether different type of movement. In contrast to academics, feminists included, whose unspoken mantra has been Margaret Thatcher's TINA (There Is No Alternative), anti-globalization activists speak of a new world that is possible. Perhaps some among them imagine a "new world" in which capitalism might be humanized, but one hopes that others will come to envision a totally different society. This has to happen, because following the catastrophe of September 11, 2001, the George W. Bush administration's "war on terror," and the invasion of Iraq, it is an understatement to assert that we live in perilous times.

Of course, I continue my interest in Filipino women and in political struggle. The unprecedented diaspora of Filipino migrant workers is currently a topic that is being researched by feminists in the United States. This is all very good, but only if these studies do not fail to critique the predations of globalized capitalism. So far, unfortunately, little is happening along these lines. For this reason, feminist politics as it exists right now is hardly relevant to me. You might say that my tenure as a "feminist" has been very short lived.

Karin Aguilar-San Juan

I think for me, because of when and how I grew up, feminism and politics were all the same thing. I mean that "feminism" was one small, mostly unspoken part of what I understood as "politics." It was all just woven together into one cloth: the idea that girls/women are human and the idea that all humans deserve to live in a just and fair society. As I remember my childhood, feminism hardly ever needed to be spoken out loud. I was the oldest child and I do not remember being treated differently from my younger brother. I saw my mother as her own person, not a shadow of my father, as was the case for some of my friends' parents. Politics writ large shaped my memories of school and growing up as a political person, and included discussions with my parents, homework assignments, and arguments with my teachers about the evils of capitalism, colonialism, and U.S. imperialism.

From the kitchen table, I could see a poster my parents had taped to the dark wood paneling. It was a black mask on an orange background that read *Kung hindi ngayon, kailan pa?* (If not now, then when?). I always interpreted that to mean that one day there would be a people's revolution and, on that day, the people would be free. It was a hopeful message but also a call to action and political consciousness—warning about the dangers that would come if one did *not* act or become aware.

From when I was in fifth grade in 1972 until 1984, when I graduated from college, the main issue—really the defining issue—that shaped my political life was the U.S.–Marcos dictatorship in the Philippines. This was the issue that shaped my parents' vexed relationship to their homeland and, therefore, it also shaped my sense of connection to a place and a history beyond my parents. Looking back, I know this is so because at my tenth high school reunion in 1990, a white American woman whom I liked but barely knew greeted me with a fist in the air. "*Makibaka!*" she shouted, flashing me a big grin. She was referring, of course, to the revolutionary slogan of the anti-imperialist movement that I taught all my classmates (and everyone in the entire school, evidently) and also wore plastered in orange letters on my favorite brown sweatshirt for our class picture that year. I stood in the middle of the front row, so the slogan is plainly visible to this day to anyone who still has the picture!

I don't think I ever thought of myself as anything other than Filipina until after college in the mid- to late 1980s. Feminism was an assumed category; it could be so for me because my parents did not place any obvious expectations upon me to fulfill my "womanly" role as someone else's wife, and I was never instructed to marry a doctor, lawyer, or some such professional *man.* Instead, I was very clearly expected to become that person *myself.* In addition, I also received the message that my professional independence should be the highest—maybe *only*—goal above and beyond any kind of personal or family relationship. I wonder if other women of my generation got a similarly strong message from their 1970s activist parents.

And the role models I had for being a politically engaged Filipina were not only, maybe hardly ever, men. For example, I remember Sister Caridad and Father Gigi, crazy-acting radical clergy who gave themselves wholeheartedly to fighting martial law in the Philippines. I remember my parents' friends who were hippie artists or writers or students or teachers. I remember that hardly anyone my parents knew and liked got married in a traditional ceremony, and certainly none of the women went so far as to change their last names. In contrast to these activist friends, "regular" (white, mainstream, heterosexual) people in town, such as the town doctor and dentist, had "all-American" families with wives who didn't even have their own first names and children who were actually allowed to go out on dates and drive the family car.

Feminism became an identifiable political agenda unto itself for me in college. Having professional, academic parents boosted me into an elite world in which I was able to find myself and define myself in personal, social, and political terms. As it turns out, many of my female peers were raised in horribly patriarchal families where ancestral lineage mattered because generations of accumulated wealth were passed down through men. Many of my smartest women friends were never expected to do much more than graduate with a shiny degree from our fancy college, only to find a man of the same, or better, social status. They were rebelling against the weight of all of that, something I didn't know anything about. My best friend in college came from a similar background as I with a powerful, highly educated mother and clearly articulated expectation that she be her own person. We got along because of an assumed belief in our own capabilities as human—which, since we are women, could be called "feminism."

Today I would say that feminism gives me political voice. I mean that without feminism as an agenda that demands attention for marginalized groups, my views and my ideas would never be included in any political forum. But at the same time, feminism does not necessarily guide me in determining the terms of my political engagement. Now as a person with job stability in academia, I look for ways to build and support movements for social justice. I am less interested in feminism as a theory—say, coming out of women's studies—than I am in feminism as form of engagement among theorists and practitioners of social change. I was never very attracted to women's studies or to the professionalization of feminism in academia. At the same time, as a person now seeking tenure at a liberal arts college, I am very grateful to the feminists in academia who included me in their circles even before I had earned the "proper" credentials because they recognized my writings and organizing work as contributions to their field.

While feminism and feminists have helped me to find myself, I think I would have to say that as a political agenda for broad-based structural change, feminism has never appealed to me. And, as feminists have moved into academia and turned common-sense ideas about women and gender oppression into high theory, I have been even less compelled to keep up with what is going on there. Similarly, I have not followed developments in lesbian/gay/ bisexual/transgendered studies, or queer studies, because I have not found them interesting, or engaged, with the realities that I understand deeply and care about. In some ways that has been my loss, as I have been unable to participate in sophisticated ways in conversations happening across academia. Recently, a queer Latino scholar visited our campus and I was invited to join an informal conversation with him over dinner. Considered a "rising star" in his field, this person is immersed in academic culture, its norms and its values are embedded in his every gesture, yet he is also committed to theorizing for social change. I admired his dedication to his work; I even got excited about some of the ideas he proposed about "queer" as a stance of political rebellion, for instance. But I do admit that the job of high theorizing does not appeal to me much—which is what most of the feminists and queers around me are doing these days when they are not going shopping.

So if feminism does not shape my politics, what does? I think I have created my own framework for social justice out of an eclectic, and perhaps somewhat strange, collection of life and work experiences. In this, of course, I demonstrate my many privileges: my view of what is wrong in the world—and how it should be changed—is not based in a position of stark oppression or economic subordination and I do not keep an organic connection to a neighborhood, a social group, a political party, or a nation. In this, I suppose I am very "American," very individualist, middle-class, and just plain petite-bourgeois. This is my background and I don't think I can or need to do anything to change it. On the other hand, one of the points of these essays is to suggest that our views about feminism have been shaped by the particular contexts in which we developed into politically conscious adults. I have been exposed throughout my life to a variety of people and struggles from which I have learned that human suffering is not natural or inevitable and that many changes are both possible and necessary.

Now, as a person who is paid to teach and write about that world—even though I am deeply ambivalent about being ensconced in an ivory tower and being stranded, as I often tell people, in the Great White North—I would say that you cannot claim to "know" anything if you do not understand who you are and where you came from. That may not be a question of feminism, but it is definitely a question of community.

Question 3: What do you see as the concerns of young Filipino American women today, and how would you address them?

Karin Aguilar-San Juan

I see this question as a gesture toward the issues I'd like young Filipino American women to think about and understand more fully. Maybe I'll break this question down into two parts. The first part is about my relationship to young Filipino American women today. I ask myself, do you even know what the concerns of young Fil-Am women are today? How do you know? What, if any, do you think are your obligations to them? And the second part is about feminism as it relates to young Filipino American women. I ask, does the feminism that mattered to you as you were growing up still matter to young women today? In other words, how has the world changed for Filipino American women since the 1970s and 1980s when you were "young?"

For the first question, I will have to assess my relationship to young Filipino American women frankly—indeed, to young women of any nationality, race, or ethnicity—as sociological rather than direct, as a theoretical matter of shared experience mostly imagined, not based on everyday occurrences. Sometimes, I think this is sad; it is a tribute to my assimilation both as a "hyphenated American" and as a second-generation academic. I have moved away from anything that looks like "roots." But I think it is important to be honest, to reflect, and to acknowledge my "flotation" position in this regard, because there is always someone out there who wants me to "represent" a category I may not fully understand or relate to. I think we all know too well what it means to be tokenized and sometimes I have no choice but to play the role I have been given by dominant society. In being frank and transparent, I hope I raise some questions about what it means to be "authentic."

The easiest way for me to find out something about Filipino American women, given my estranged and alienated relationship to almost any kind of Filipino American group, is to "Google" them. But what do I discover by typing "Filipino women" into an Internet search? The same thing you'll find. There will be lots and lots of sites for sex and marriage: single women seeking foreign men, pen pals, pornography featuring "cherry blossoms," and mail-order brides. Sick to my stomach, I scroll down hoping to find something more empowering, political, community oriented, or, at the very least, just plain angry. The first informational site I see is a 1995 article about Filipino women campaigning against sex tourism in Australia; the second, a scientific article about breast cancer among Filipino American women; and the third, a United Nations document about trafficking of Filipino women to Japan. So far, that is not uplifting.

A few more pages of scrolling and I find the Filipino Women's Network, based in the Philippines, and learn about a conference to discuss, among other things, what the Filipino American community will look like in 2013 (a good marketing idea for this book, right?). Another site reminds me of the anthology of writings by Filipino and Filipino American women—but these are not young people or youth. Eventually I find newfilipina.com and *Botika Babae* (www.babaegear.com), where I learn about Urduja, a legendary tribal warrior princess. Of course, it is not long before I find the site for the Filipino American Women's Network (FAWN), an organization dedicated to Filipino American women that is based in Minnesota—so close to me that it is in the same zip code! (I am friendly with at least one member of FAWN; I don't have any principled reason for being out of touch with them.) Several hours later, I discover myself bleary-eyed from web surfing, having visited everything from a Filipino youth group to Jim Zwick's online anti-imperialist history lesson and bookstore.

There are other ways that give me a sense of what is going on for my younger counterparts. I teach Asian American studies and I have met Filipino American students on many campuses and in many different communities. A few years ago, I was asked to deliver the keynote address for an organization representing Filipino Americans in the Midwest. I got a feeling then for some of the things young Filipino American women care about. Recently through my action/research projects, I have gotten to know teenage activists of color in Detroit and Mineapolis–St. Paul. They are not Filipinos, and some of them are boys, but they are all youth who are becoming politically aware and engaged in social-movement building. Through them I am learning about the world through young eyes and getting in touch with a new generation of leaders for social change.

What do I think I know about today's Fil-Am women? I know that some things have not changed since I was younger. They are bombarded with contradictory messages about their beauty and desirability (from the perspective of white European men), their exotic culture (eminently salable in the form of jewelry, clothing, and music, but somehow not distinct enough to merit recognition in mainstream U.S. venues), their history of resistance to colonization in the Philippines, their struggle for survival as migrant workers throughout the Filipino diaspora. Certain things have definitely changed for the better since I was young: professional narratives about our history and current-day experience as Filipino Americans are more comprehensive and complex than they were thirty years ago. I believe this is largely the result of decades of grassroots activism among students and faculty who demanded that education at public universities serve the needs of the surrounding communities. Out of these struggles for ethnic studies, and Filipino American studies in particular, has emerged a population of Filipino American scholars and teachers who help us all to articulate our own sociological condition.

Although these past few years seem to promise troubled times in the future, the possibilities for radical social change are all very exciting. This is not to downplay the very horrible conditions that face many young Filipino and Filipino American women (particularly the domestic workers in the United States, Canada, and around the globe) who are so far from home and family, trapped in lives of virtual slavery. Their voices—among others—are what remind me that oppression is real, that for many people "being a Filipino woman" is not an imaginary state of existence but a completely real and tangible state of struggle for survival and connection to home and family.

I see great hope, but not so much in my (or my mother's) ability to make these conceptual connections between our lived realities and the collective history of the Filipino people. After all, the point is not simply to liberate ourselves as individuals, to feel good about where we have been and who we have become. I would say that Mom and I have done a lot of "cognitive liberation" for ourselves. Besides, if all I expected from feminism was my own personal freedom, I might as well have become a right-wing Christian fundamentalist. At least then I would feel more victorious at this particular historical moment—a moment, I believe, that must soon pass.

I see hope, instead, in the possibility that the younger generation, Filipino American women included, will create a new synthesis of radical thought and action that draws constructive lessons from the 1960s, 1970s, 1980s, and onward. Perhaps in the twenty-first century, Pinay feminism will have a role in these changes.

So what can be done to improve the condition of Filipino American women? Educate! Organize! The same work that must be done to free all humanity from the deadening cycles of mass consumption: the food that we eat is deadly, the news that we read is censored, the taxes that we pay go to fund war, the schools that our children attend teach them compliance, the homes that we live in tie us into lifetime contracts of debt. All of this we justify by striving toward an "American Dream" of fitting in, of being accepted, of having "equal access" (to consumer goods and services), of preserving our cultural icons (in their most innocuous forms). These are not issues that only Filipino American women face, of course, but they are ultimately the issues that we *all* face.

Delia D. Aguilar

I would like to begin by saying that I came to the United States at age twenty-two, more or less already a fully formed adult. My sense of myself as a Filipino was firm; there was nothing about it to be either doubted or confirmed. Consequently, in bringing up my children, all I could teach them was what I knew, which was how to be a Filipino in the United States. It was much later, when they had developed their own separate selves, that I gleaned from them what it meant to have this other identity, Filipino American. Now I cannot say how my insistence on "Filipinoness" inoculated them against the warping effects of U.S. consumerist culture (which was my hope), or whether this insistence constrained their development in ways I did not wish. In any event, one always is relieved when things turn out just fine in the end in spite of one's worst failings. And when your offspring surpass and exceed your wildest dreams and expectations, what can you do except bless your stars?

Having admitted my shortcomings, let me now try to answer the question. I suspect that Filipino American youth are forced to confront their identity as "other" by the racism that they encounter. From what I've observed, those whose parents are immigrants may not find much help because many immigrant Filipinos tend to negate or deny their racialized experiences, attributing these, instead, to their own insufficient enculturation or their individual failures. Filipino American women may experience racialization not as outright derogation of their person, but in terms of being exotified. On the other hand, for better or for worse, there are now many more Filipinos in the United States than thirty years ago, and we live more closely to one other and in large enough numbers to establish a distinct community. It is possible now to produce movies about Filipino American life, for example, and to have an audience for these. As a result, racism, and the alienation it gives rise to, may be mitigated by living in the presence of an organized community.

I think that there are two general topics that young Filipino Americans should educate themselves about, whether or not they ever visit the Philippines with their parents. They should study the history of the United States and learn about what's called internal colonies. In doing so, they will be able to locate themselves alongside other racialized "minorities" whose labor in cities and in farms has been appropriated to build this country and to create wealth that they have no access to. Today no one—certainly not Filipinos—can afford to remain ignorant about the nature of the society we live in. They should study the history of the Philippines, in particular accounts written by Renato Constantino,[5] and learn about how our history is tightly bound up with that of the United States. It is through educating themselves about these matters that they can begin to comprehend the current diaspora of Filipinos, more than 70 percent of whom are women, in more than 162 different countries—as mail-order brides, overseas contract workers, and entertainers. Whether they like it or not, it is this diaspora that sustains the public perception of Filipino women as patient, docile, well equipped to please men, and with those other qualities that "liberated" white women are presumed to have forsworn. They need to understand why the country of their parents has been declared as "the second front of the war against terrorism" and what implications this has for them.

If there is an opportunity to visit the Philippines, young Filipino Americans should seize it, less to frolic in megamalls and to be impressed by the luxurious accommodations offered by local tourist spots than to learn how the majority of Filipinos actually live and how they organize for change. For instance, I have sent three students (alas, they were not Filipinos) to study in the intensive women's studies "intercultural program" of St. Scholastica's College in Manila. Although it is commonplace to say that students' lives get turned around by practically any study-abroad stint, I can say that this experience is singular. Another student (a Latina, this time) attended the Philippine Forum–sponsored Philippine studies summer program and she, too, underwent a profound political transformation. I think what these young people acquired from their visits is a kind of awareness that has been out of fashion in this country for a while now. Egyptian feminist Nawal El Saadawi has expressed that feminists in her country today are "unaware of the connection between the liberation of women on the one hand and of the economy and country on the other. Many consider only patriarchy as their enemy and ignore corporate capitalism."[6]

This lack of political awareness has led to a return to essentialism, notwithstanding postmodern endeavors to eradicate it, as shown by the popularity on campuses worldwide of Eve Ensler's V-Day. In the Philippines, the ban on *The Vagina Monologues* at Ateneo University was met with vigorous protests by both faculty and students, all in the name of artistic freedom and freedom of expression. No one thought to question the patently upper-middle-class, "made-in-USA" stamp of the play nor its condescending gaze on the third world female populations it is determined to "save." No one even thought to consider the ramifications of the landing in the Southern Philippines, at that very same time, of U.S. Navy Seals and Green Berets and to connect these concurrent events.

If I speak with what might appear like a curious presumption that Filipino American youth could actually have an interest in these weighty issues, it is because I've been at conferences set up by young people (yes, Filipino

Americans) where these have been the main themes. A couple of decades back, there were too few young Filipino Americans in universities to make such conferences possible. Moreover, a decade ago the political quiescence of U.S. society as a whole lent itself easily only to cultural events accentuated by *adobo* and *pancit* (popular native dishes), and *tinikling* (popular native dance)-type offerings in a bid for "ethnics" to assimilate and to celebrate their "diversity" simultaneously. But events are fast transpiring—the recent summary deportations of Filipinos, among them—that force a recognition of a radically different geopolitics. That young Filipino Americans are holding conferences of the kind that I attended is very encouraging. I have no doubt that gatherings like this will soon become more widespread. Also full of promise is the fact that, unlike in the 1970s, Filipino Americans now have become a fairly visible contingent in mass mobilizations like antiwar and anti-globalization rallies. All of these are hopeful signs of a coming to political cognizance of a new generation of Filipino Americans.

Notes

1. Delia D. Aguilar, *The Feminist Challenge: Initial Working Principles toward Reconceptualizing the Feminist Movement in the Philippines* (Manila: Asian Social Institute in cooperation with the World Association for Christian Communication, 1988); Delia D. Aguilar, *Filipino Housewives Speak* (Manila: Institute of Women's Studies/St. Scholastica's College, 1991); Delia D. Aguilar, *Toward a Nationalist Feminism* (Quezon City, Philippines: Giraffe, 1998); eds. Delia D. Aguilar and Anne Lacsamana, *Women and Globalization* (Amherst, N.Y.: Prometheus, 2004).
2. Karin Aguilar-San Juan, ed., *The State of Asian America: Activism and Resistance in the 1990s* (Boston: South End, 1994).
3. Sonia Shah, introduction to *Dragon Ladies: Asian American Feminists Breathe Fire,* ed. Sonia Shah (Boston: South End, 1998), xix.
4. GABRIELA has established solidarity networks outside the country; more information is available online at http://www.gabnet.org.
5. Renato Constantino, *A History of the Philippines* (New York: Monthly Review, 1975); Renato Constantino, *Neoclassical Identity and Counter-Consciousness* (New York: M. E. Sharpe, Inc., 1978).
6. Nawal El Saadawi, "Egypt's Leading Feminist Unveils Her Thoughts," interview with Ahmed Nassef, *Women's eNews,* February 25, 2004; online at http://www.womensenews.org/article.cfm/dyn/aid/1726/context/ourdailylives.

IV

Theorizing Desire:
Sexuality, Community, and Activism

11
Tomboy, Dyke, Lezzie, and Bi: Filipina Lesbian and Bisexual Women Speak Out

CHRISTINE T. LIPAT, TRINITY A. ORDONA, CIANNA PAMINTUAN
STEWART, AND MARY ANN UBALDO

This chapter is excerpted from a two-hour telephone roundtable conducted in July 1996 among Filipina lesbian and bisexual women organizers in New York (Christine Lipat, Ann Ubaldo) and San Francisco (Trinity Ordona, Cianna Pamintuan Stewart). Invited to submit an article on Filipina lesbians for Maria P. P. Root's *Filipino Americans: Transformation and Identity*,[1] Trinity instead gathered three other women to share their experiences as Pinays (Filipino women), lesbians, and queer organizers. Their lives and opinions represent a range of different geographic, cultural, social, and political locations in the United States and the Philippines and reflect some of the diversity among Filipino lesbian and bisexual women.

Christine, twenty-five years old and born and raised in New Jersey, is the eldest daughter of two medical professional immigrants from the Philippines. She is an activist in the Asian American arts, women's, and lesbian communities and is currently a board member of the Astraea National Lesbian Action Foundation and the acting executive director of the Asian American Arts Alliance in New York City. Ann, forty-four years old, from a middle-class–professional family, was born and raised in Manila and graduated from the University of the Philippines. She emigrated to New York City in 1985, where she lives as an artist, musician, photographer, and self-employed jeweler, creating her designs in Filipino motifs using the *alibata* script. Christine and Ann are cofounders of Kilawin Kolektibo, a Pinay lesbian collective based in New York. Cianna, twenty-nine years old, is a mestiza Filipina who lived in Davao City until she was six, when her family returned to the United States following Ferdinand Marcos's declaration of martial law. Cianna studied theater and divides her time between theater directing and organizing around Asian/Pacific Islander sexual and gender diversity through the Visibility Campaign, Living Well Project: Asian and Pacific Islander AIDS Services in San

Francisco. Trinity, forty-five years old, was born and raised in San Diego, California, in a post–World War II immigrant family of thirteen children. She has participated in the Filipino, Asian American, women's, and gay liberation movements over the past twenty-five years; she is a community organizer and graduate student in the history of consciousness at the University of California–Santa Cruz, conducting research on the social history of the Asian/Pacific lesbian and bisexual women's movement in the United States.

Coming Out—Finding Self, Finding Others

Coming out—accepting one's homosexual/bisexual identity—is a lifelong process of revelation and disclosure. Sharing one's "coming out" story is a familiar ritual in the queer community and often establishes a common bond among people across race, nationality, age, class, and cultural differences. Christine and Ann knew each other through building Kilawin, a Pinay lesbian collective in New York City. Trinity and Cianna worked together in San Francisco in the Asian/Pacific Islander Parents and Friends of Lesbians and Gays Family Project to provide support to families of Asian/Pacific Islander (A/PI) gay people. To build a friendship bridge between them, they first shared their "coming out" stories with each other.

Trinity: In the 1970s, I got involved in the Filipino movement and radical politics in the San Francisco Bay Area. I was editor of radical Filipino newspaper *Ang Katipunan* and blacklisted by the Marcos government. I also fell in love with a woman in the seventies, but I could not come out in the Filipino movement. Open homosexuality was not acceptable in the community or movement. In 1986, I attended a lesbians of color conference. Soon, I sought out other Asian lesbians and organized the first A/PI lesbian retreat in 1987. I have been here in the Asian and Pacific Islander lesbian and bisexual women's (APLB) community ever since. Organizing Asian lesbians has been the easiest political work I have ever done. It is fulfilling and it fits me. And it helps that I am married. (*Everyone laughs.*) My mother likes Desiree and we had a big wedding ceremony in 1988. Now we are planning to have a baby next year. I do not feel very radical anymore. (*More laughter.*)

Ann: Domesticated!

Trinity: I know. I feel very settled down.

Ann: It is about time, Trinity.

Christine: You do not have that edge anymore! [*Laughter.*]

Trinity: I am glad that I met Desiree when I did; I was ready. A year later, marriage came up when we decided to have children. Suddenly, the Filipino voice inside me said, "Des, we have to get married." When I tell this story to other Filipinos, they know what I am talking about. Do you?

Cianna: Yes, definitely. And when you get married, you stay married. You are not supposed to break away from that marriage.

Ann: Back home, we do not have divorce, so marriage is "forever." My parents never forced me to get married; it was never an issue. My mom asked me, "Do you have a boyfriend?" I said no. "It is okay," Mom said. Then I said to her, "Mom, I have a girlfriend."

Trinity: So you told your parents?

Ann: I told my parents and they did not approve. They said I did not have a future. They care for me but do not think a long-term relationship will work with a woman.

Trinity: What about you, Christine? What is your story?

Christine: Let us see. I have been attracted to women since I was a kid. In junior high, I had dreams, but I knew it was not something to be talked about. In college, I finally came out, but it was not easy.

Trinity: What do you mean?

Christine: Oberlin College [in Ohio] was a liberal place where students wore pink ribbons (as symbols of gay pride) on their backpacks. It was okay to talk about sexuality, but finding people I could personally relate to was difficult. Finally, in my junior year, I heard of a people of color lesbian/gay/bisexual group and I went to one of their meetings. Because I had a steady boyfriend then, they said, "Oh my gosh, Christine! What are you doing here?" [*Everyone laughs.*] So I met all these cool women and was able to come out. My first girlfriend was in that group. After graduation in 1992, I returned to New Jersey and started looking around, hoping for an Asian lesbian group. I had just returned from San Francisco for my first pride march.[2] I was in Chinatown, New York City, wearing my San Francisco gay pride T-shirt, when two Asian women came up, gave me an ALOEC [Asian Lesbians of the East Coast] business card. One of them said, "I think you need this." "Great, I have been looking for you," I replied. "Come on, come to a meeting," they said. [*Everyone laughs.*]

Cianna: That is great!

Christine: I also met people from the Asian American Writers Workshop. They had a coffeehouse and I told myself, "This is a place where I feel comfortable in New York City." Then I joined Youth for Philippine Action,[3] and they told me about Kambal sa Lusog, the Filipino lesbian and gay group in New York City.[4] I had seen Kambal march in the New York City Philippine Independence Day parade, which was the only way I knew about them. It was through networking, though, that I met some Kambal people.

Trinity: What about you, Ann?

Ann: Well, I will tell you my love story with the girls. [*Laughs.*] When I first transferred to this new school in Manila, I knew there were girls looking. I was a guitarist and a player at that time.

Trinity: Wait a minute. You were a *player*?

Ann: Yes, a softball player.

Trinity: Oh, I see. I thought you were a different kind of player. (*Everyone laughs.*)

Ann: I was eleven years old, grade 5, and a softball player when I learned there were some girls who had crushes on me. "Oh my God," I said. I did not do anything until college, but I just felt it. I met this classmate of mine twenty-five years later in the States, and she said, "I knew you were a 'boy' when you went to our school." Even all my classmates said they knew I was one. My first girlfriend was when I was nineteen in college. After that, I never left the women. Twenty-five years later, I have *furthered my résumé*. I have been pretty adventurous! [*Laughs.*]

Trinity: You came out as a lesbian in college in the Philippines, then came to the United States?

Ann: My girlfriend wanted to try it out in the States, so I said, "Yeah, I want to." So I wrapped up my business in the Philippines and told her to look for a place for me in New York and I will be there. And I did. I came. But it did not work out with that girlfriend I followed. After two months, she married a guy.

Trinity: Oh.

Ann: So I hung out with a few lesbian friends from back home. I was a lost soul for a while. I only met the Kilawin girls after one year here in New York, after searching and searching for these beautiful Filipina dykes.

Trinity: Let us talk about Kilawin.[5] It is the first Pinay lesbian group in the United States. How did it get started?

Christine: Everybody was involved in different movements and learning different skills. Then we met each other and created our own informal friendships. Some of us were involved in Kambal sa Lusog, but by 1993 its membership was waning. Then a few of us started going to GABRIELA Network meetings.[6] They opened the door for us and invited us to participate.

Ann: What helped convince us to organize ourselves was meeting many of the other Filipina lesbians who were organizing in San Francisco, Toronto, and the Philippines during the Stonewall March in New York City in 1995. During the next six months, about fifteen of us met and created Kilawin Kolektibo, a sociopolitical collective working to create a cultural space for Filipina lesbians.

Christine: Our first political action, via letter and e-mail, protested the degrading, stereotypical portrayal of a Filipina mail-order bride in the Australian drag queen road movie, *The Adventures of Priscilla, Queen of the Desert*.[7] Our unique cultural viewpoint—as women, lesbians, and Filipinos—gave us the vantage point to critique this mainstream crossover movie.

Ann: But we were the lone voice of protest in the gay community! Many just did not "see" the problem, while others wanted to overlook it, saying, "The rest of it was so good." This is a good example of the gay community "advancing" at the expense of people of color!

Christine: After the *Priscilla* protest came the Philippine Independence Day march, the gay pride march, Asian American student conferences and community forums, benefits, fundraisers, and potluck parties, and a visit to our Pinay sisters in Toronto. It is amazing that we did so much in so little time!

Ann: There are about thirty Pinays on our mailing list, with at least twelve or so coming to the monthly meetings. We try to blend our personal friendship with our politics, and it's been exciting to have Kilawin around.

Trinity: Cianna, what about you? How did you come out and find community?

Cianna: For me, it was bisexuality. I came out at Wesleyan University [in Connecticut], where I first met other lesbians. I went to the meeting of the Lesbian, Bisexual, and Questioning Women's Group. I walked in, and they all looked at me and said, "We have been waiting for you to show up. We knew you were coming." Then I said, "I am glad I am here. Finally I figured it out, I am bisexual, so that is why I came." They said that they would wait a little time longer.

Christine: You mean, until you turned lesbian?

Cianna: Yeah, until I turned lesbian. So I got really angry. I have been doing political activism since I was nine years old. I started out as an environmentalist, then became an antinuclear protester and abortion rights activist. When I went to college, it was queer activism. I started a campus bisexual group with another bi woman. Everybody who went to school received our flyer: "If you are bisexual and want to talk about it, come to a meeting on Thursday." Forty people showed up.

Everyone: Wow!

Cianna: And everybody had told us there were no other bisexuals! It was support group with a political tone. We wanted the campus gay, lesbian, and bisexual organization to acknowledge that "bisexual" meant something. After college, here in San Francisco, I was later involved at the national level with the bisexual community and ran the national Bisexual Network for two years.[8] In 1992, I got to know individuals in the community through my safer-sex work with the dykes in San Francisco. I was a founding member of the Safer Sex Slut Team,[9] so …

Christine: I heard about them! [*Laughs.*]

Cianna: Yep, yep. [*Laughs.*] I got pulled into the community through dating an Asian dyke. Then I got this job here at the Living Well Project and have been working with the Asian/Pacific Islander community for the last several years. My primary community, however, are gay and bisexual men. I also have a lot of dyke friends, including A/PI dykes.

Coming Out Queer—Youth, Family, and Community

In this section, the women share their knowledge and opinions about differences among Filipino queers in the United States, especially between older and younger generations of Filipina queers. The section ends with a discussion of gay men and lesbians in the Philippines, citing the greater social acknowledgment of gay men, counterposed by the invisibility of lesbian women in Philippine society.

Trinity: Cianna, tell us what you know about gay youth.

Cianna: Through my own interest, and just being here at this agency, I am familiar with one of two A/PI queer youth groups in the country. AQU[25]A—Asian and Pacific Islander Queer and Questioning under 25 Altogether—is really, really active. They have a combination of socials plus support, HIV/AIDS information, leadership training, and political activism. They lobbied in Sacramento, our state capital, to persuade state senators to include queer issues in the public school system during California Queer Youth Lobby Day. They use [the term] *queer* more than *gay*, *bi*, or *lesbian*. Some people actually refuse to use any other word but *queer*.

Christine: Why?

Cianna: They have a more fluid conception of sexuality. They are still figuring their identity, yet acknowledge there is no single identity, no fixed qualities. They also have a stronger conception of the movement as a cogendered movement/multigendered movement. I think that is why they have embraced the term *queer*. Sometimes people from the older gay and lesbian movement think of queer, lesbian, and gay as the same thing—and also eliminate the bisexual from their rubric. The youth, however, make a very clear, concerted effort to include bisexual and transgender folks. In fact, there is a member of AQU[25]A who is straight. She is kind of queer in that she does not align herself entirely with the straight, more homophobic straight community. She feels very comfortable in AQU²⁵A, and everyone feels very comfortable with her because she fits in. She feels it is a group she can socialize with, even though she is not there to get social support around her own "queerness" because she is straight. She is part of AQU²⁵A. Nobody has a problem with it.

Trinity: What about their parents? What do they think?

Cianna: Some of the youth are out, some of them are not. In AQU²⁵A, they learn ways to talk about their sexuality. They get support for coming out and share coming-out stories with each other. They are more prepared and have ways to support each other, regardless of the outcome of their coming out. There has been quite a range of reactions among their parents. Most parents have generally been okay—not openly excited or anything. Parents just say, "Do not talk about it." But no one has been kicked out of their house.

I have met more kids who have not come out and their fears are really intense—fear of getting disowned, fear of parents not supporting them. Some of them do not want to come out until they have finished high school. Up until you are eighteen or in college, you are so completely dependent on your parents. It is also hard to come out when you are living at home with your parents—[*everyone laughs*]—where you get monitored more closely.

Trinity: Have you noticed anything particular about the Filipino youth?

Cianna: Not specifically. Some Filipino families seem to have no real problem with it; other Filipino families have been very hostile. It does not really seem to matter whether they are immigrant or American born, or whether they self-identify very strongly as Catholic or not. There are both very devout Catholic parents who are really supportive, others do not really care, and some are really hostile. I have not seen anything that I can really put down as a truism.

Trinity: What about in Kilawin?

Ann: Are they accepted in the family? The parents of some of the younger ones are pretty cool. But the older ones—like my parents' age—are conservative and it's still not accepted. Don't ask, don't tell.[10] It is like that back home. But for the younger ones, I think it is more accepted.

Cianna: Younger parents or younger kids?

Ann: For parents who are in their forties, it's not such a problem. Marisol is eighteen years old and pretty new in our group; her dad joined us in the Independence Day parade. We all said, "I wish my dad was like yours!"

Trinity: He marched with your contingent!

Ann: Yes. It was really cool, you know. Most of them, it is really cool with their parents.

Cianna: I've also seen the story that Sasha Mobley tells in *Coming Out, Coming Home*.[11] It is something I've heard before—parents are afraid there's something really, really bad going on in their kid's life. They're worried that their kid is going to be thrown in jail or becoming a social dropout. When the kid finally says, "I am queer," the parents say, "Oh. That is not as bad as I had imagined." If anything, I have found it harder to generalize about the Filipinos than East Asians; it is that there is a wider range of reaction.

Ann: We have our Philippine Independence Day parade, but the Irish lesbians and gays cannot march [in the St. Patrick's Day parade].[12] But with the Filipinos, it is fine. I asked Ninotchka Rosca why.[13] She said that we have a very strong women's movement. When issues about gay/lesbian rights or children's rights or any other minority rights come up, the women hold up an umbrella. When lesbians are being discriminated [against], it is always the women that support us. That is how it is in the Filipino community here.

Christine: The first time we marched in the New York City Philippine Independence Day parade, the parade marshals kept delaying us. Both Kilawin and GABRIELA Network were moved from place to place to await our turn to march.

Ann: We had been waiting for two hours in the sun. We were the only all-female group in the parade, so there was instant discrimination. When Ninotchka finally said, "It is time for us to march," we started marching and the parade organizers did not say anything.

Trinity: So the women's group and the lesbian group marched together?

Ann: Yes. We always march together.

Cianna: Cool.

Trinity: Christine, when Kilawin marched in the Independence Day parade, what did it mean for you?

Christine: It was fun and for the small number of people who do see the parade—there are never that many people—they were pretty supportive. The Filipino radio show Radyo Pinoy interviewed us, too.

Ann: There was a good article on us in *Filipino Express*,[14] and we marched side by side with GABRIELA.

Christine: Not only because we support each other's causes but also so that the people in the closet could march with GABRIELA.

Trinity: That means that you are really "out" in the Filipino community?

Christine: Yes, a lot of people would say that it is a lot easier to march in the gay pride [parade] than in your own back yard! [*Laughs.*]

Trinity: That is for sure.

Ann: Half of us are GABRIELA members. It is not hush-hush. We can be up front. Gay men, however, are more accepted than gay women, but we are trying to deal with it.

Trinity: Are gay men more accepted in the Philippines?

Ann: Yes, in Philippine society, gay men are more accepted. It has always been like that. But now the gay women are coming out. We are making a stand and saying we are more than the stereotype. It has been improving for the last ten years.

Cianna: But it is a particular kind of gay men. The *bakla*.[15]

Christine: Yes, I was recently visiting Chicago and they had a videotape of some Filipino comedy shows. They always have the drag queen character.

Ann: It is very popular.

Christine: I know I have seen a sitcom or two with a lesbian, but somehow they always end up with men. [*Everyone laughs.*]

Cianna: When I went back to Davao three years ago, my family told me, "Oh, the bakla boys are having a volleyball game. You might want to go down there." We own a hotel and there is a disco in the hotel where a whole group of them hang out. One of my aunts is a clothing designer and many of her designer friends are bakla boys, too. They are always at the hotel or in the coffee shop—it was fine; [as for lesbians,] my aunt, whispering about a woman in this band, said, "I think she is a tomboy, so you'd better watch out."

Trinity: "Better watch out"—meaning what?

Cianna: Meaning, she might get "crushed out" on me. [*Laughs.*] She was cute, too. But it was a real contrast from the States. My family, a very public family in the Southern Philippines, has gay men all over our social engagements, everywhere.

Trinity: Openly gay?

Cianna: Yes, very open. You talk about it and you laugh about it in public, too. The bakla boys were flirting openly with my brother, who is straight. And the whole family was kidding him about it without being derogatory to the guys flirting with him. But when it comes to any visibility of lesbians, the first time I met a lesbian woman from Davao was at Stonewall in New York City.

Empowerment and Visibility

Citing a link between activism and the Filipino lesbian/bisexual women's community and organizing, this section probes the connections between gender and sexuality, oppression of women, and future prospects for organizing Filipina queer women in the United States and the Philippines.

Cianna: Is there a strong *Mars* and *Pars* presence in the Filipino women's community in New York?[16]

Ann: Yes; they are mostly *Fil-Fils*.[17] They stick together; many came from the same schools and have common friends. Whatever their situation back home was they bring to New York or wherever they go.

Trinity: But they are involved in the activist groups?

Ann: No, but with Kilawin coming out, as well as other Asian lesbian groups, I think it will make everyone's situation better. Visibility is very important.

Cianna: I also think it is better. Hopefully, people can come out without the stereotypes getting in the way.

Ann: And being political and making people more aware of what we are doing will really improve the situation; educating them, too.

Trinity: Why do you think there is this connection between activism and Filipina lesbianism? To be visible, we also need some political consciousness just to put ourselves out there. The bakla are already known and accepted in Philippine society—I do not know about accepted, but at least known. But lesbians are invisible. They do not exist.

Ann: I was also wondering why we must have politics to be visible. With the gay men, they are the hairstylists, the artists, and it is okay. It is harder for us.

Christine: People do not talk about Filipino lesbians or even say the word *lesbian*. You have to educate yourself, learn the words for what you are and what you are feeling, but they are not common, everyday words. Even then, it's hard to talk about it!

Cianna: There have always been some women who have been dressing and living as men, blending into mainstream society there. If you are a flamboyant cross-dressing male, it is hard to hide. At the same time, he is not threatening to the power structure because he is [perceived as] *downgrading* his status by acting more feminine: He is not a threat; he is a joke. But a lesbian woman is actually threatening to the power structure because she is taking her own power. This is political because it is a power struggle.

Trinity: We cannot overlook the gender issues underlying sexuality. For example, women going up the corporate ladder are often criticized for being bitchy and unladylike. In the same regard, when lesbians and bisexual women assert their sexuality preferences in their social and personal lives, then it, too, becomes threatening. The political edge to a lesbian or bisexual identity for Filipino women is a necessary path. Otherwise, we never get taken seriously.

Cianna: Yes. It becomes so completely tied into the role of women overall in society; we cannot escape that political correlation.

Trinity: It is one thing to put down a tomboy and say, "Oh, she is just trying to be a boy, but she does not have the equipment." But it is another thing to understand that also means that *she does not need men.* Women who live that way, however they dress, are much more threatening.

Cianna: A straight butch is never going to come under fire as much as a tomboy. That is just the way it has always been.

Trinity: Right.

Cianna: There are athletic or butch women who may get harassed on the street, but in their social circles where it is known that they are not queer, they do not face the harassment that we do.

Trinity: It is also good to mention the case of Beth and Vangie in the Philippines and the emergence of several activist-oriented lesbian groups in the Philippines. Beth and Vangie worked in a social service NGO [nongovernmental organization] when they fell in love. Once everybody found out, half of the office got homophobic about it.[18]

Christine: Especially the guys.

Trinity: The presence of gay liberation groups in the Philippines is an expression of a growing political consciousness among Filipino gays and lesbian and bisexual people. The Philippines is no longer a country that people left behind. That was my father's experience. Since the 1965 immigration wave began, Filipinos continue to go back and forth to the Philippines all the time. So, too, with the gay connection. Linking up with gay groups in the Philippines is very helpful to our own visibility and coming-out process here in the United States. It also proves that homosexuality is not just a white thing or an American thing. It happens in all countries.

Christine: Being out and visible also has its problems. When you first start, there is excitement from organizing around the issues—like the *Miss Saigon* protest with Kambal,[19] or joining the Stonewall march[20]—you meet a lot of people and get to know each other. But then division and factionalism start—breaking trust, breaking expectations. I think the real challenge is trying to get past those problems and find out our commonalties, what we are building for the future.

Ann: It is really hard to work together for a common cause. We have a common struggle and we should work together wherever we are, whether we are here or in the Philippines. That is the hard part. But if we keep trying and communicating, we can work on projects together.

Cianna: My concern for the future is to get past the problem that I have encountered, not only with a queer Filipino movement but through several different Filipino groups—who is really Filipino and who is really queer? Proving yourself has been something that I personally live as a mestiza and bi. I hope we are going to stop "proving ourselves" and "questioning each other" and focus instead on the work that has to be done.

Trinity: Let us remember that up until the overthrow of the Marcos government, the Philippines has been in a colonial relationship to the world and within itself. It has never really had the chance to be its own country. This has had colonizing effects on people's thinking and how the whole country has developed or, rather, underdeveloped. We would not be able to talk about this subject if Marcos was still alive and running the country.

Everyone: Right, right.

Trinity: We have to appreciate our progress as Filipino gays just in the last ten years.

Ann: The coming out of lesbianism in Philippine society is also part of the women's movement.

Cianna, Trinity: Yes.

Trinity: And lesbian rights were also advanced at the Beijing U.N. Women's Conference. It was a controversial issue among feminists in the international women's movement if lesbian issues would remain in the closet. Even though mention of lesbian rights and issues was eventually withheld from the official document, the struggle over its inclusion unfolded in front of the eyes and ears of the international women's movement. These were significant first steps. By the next decade's U.N. Women's Conference, our progress will be even greater.[21]

Conclusion

The lives of Filipina lesbian and bisexual women—as attested by the women's stories above—have changed radically over the past twenty years. For the two older lesbians, Ann and Trinity, family and community acceptance in the 1970s was minimal, if forthcoming at all. On the other hand, Cianna's and Christine's coming-out experiences in college in the 1990s were positive and supportive. Although both generations of Pinays faced the same difficulties—coming out, negative stereotypes, societal homophobia, and family rejection—new opportunities exist today for a greater degree of acceptance in the family, community, and overall society. Through the efforts of many gay liberationists before them, today's queers are surrounded by a community of friends and organizations and provide the context for this emergent Filipina queer empowerment and visibility movement. Filipina lesbian and bisexual women in the United States and the Philippines are part of a global Pan-Asian queer movement and have been both agents and beneficiaries of this international mass liberation movement for gay, lesbian, bisexual, and transgender rights for the past twenty-five years.

Notes

1. Maria P. P. Root, ed. *Filipino Americans: Transformation and Identity* (Thousand Oaks, Calif.: Sage, 1997).
2. The Stonewall Rebellion, a riot that took place on June 29, 1969, outside the Stonewall Inn, a gay bar in New York City, came about as a spontaneous response to regular police raids on the bar. The Rebellion launched the modern gay liberation movement and is commemorated yearly in June with gay pride marches in major gay, lesbian, bisexual, and transgender communities across the United States (and in some other countries). The New York and San Francisco parades gather at least 300,000 celebrants each annually.
3. Philippine Action was a Filipino American youth activist group in New York City, 1990–93.
4. Kambal sa Lusog, translated, means "Twins in Health," a name chosen to include both Filipino male and female homosexual and bisexual people. The organization was formed in 1992.
5. *Kilawin* is a hot and spicy Filipino dish; Kilawin Kolektibo, formed in 1995, is a "hot and spicy" Pinay lesbian collective based in New York City.
6. The GABRIELA (General Assembly Binding Women for Reform, Integrity, Equality, Leadership, and Action) Network, based in the United States, works with GABRIELA-Philippines to organize, educate, and network on issues that affect the women and children of the Philippines but that have their roots in decisions made in the United States.
7. In the film, a sex-starved, half-crazed, Tagalog-speaking Filipina wife of an older Australian white man in the outback performs a gross dance routine popping ping-pong balls from her anus (which is not shown onscreen). Besides Kilawin, Filipina women's groups in Australia and Manila lodged complaints about the movie.
8. BiNet (Bisexual Network), founded in 1989 in San Francisco, is a national coalition of bisexually-identified groups and individuals.
9. The Safer Sex Slut Team was a multiracial bisexual and lesbian health education outreach team that gave safer-sex demonstrations in lesbian bars in San Francisco, 1990–93; it was sponsored by Lyon-Martin Women's Health Services and organized by the prominent bisexual community organizer Lani Ka'ahumanu.
10. U.S. military policy, initiated under the administration of president Bill Clinton in 1992, permits homosexual soldiers to serve but not to engage in homosexual activities while in the service. "Don't ask, don't tell" has become a catch phrase for the policy, since senior military officers are not supposed to ask about a soldier's sexual orientation ("Don't ask") and soldiers are not supposed to volunteer the information ("Don't tell").
11. See Asian/Pacific Islander Parents and Friends of Lesbians and Gays (A/PI-PFLAG) Family Project, prod. and dir., *Coming Out, Coming Home* (Fremont, CA: A/PI-PFLAG Network, 1996, videocassette. This video contains interviews of four families of Asian lesbian and gay children. Filipina mestiza lesbian Sasha Mobley and her lover, brother, and mother share their experience with Sasha's "coming out" to the family.
12. In New York, where Ann lives, and also in Boston, Irish lesbian and gay contingents have been formally banned from participating in the annual St. Patrick's Day parades.
13. Ninotchka Rosca is a well-known journalist, feminist organizer, and leading member of the GABRIELA Network.
14. "New Filipina Lesbian Group Joins Philippine Independence Day Parade," *Filipino Express*, June 12–18, 1995, p. 13.

15. *Bakla* is a Tagalog slang term for a male homosexual, and it connotes a soft, "swishy" man; like the English term *faggot*, it can be positive or negative, depending on the context and intent.

16. *Mars* and *Pars* are Tagalog slang for *Kumadre* and *Kumpadre* (close friend, female and male) and are used among Filipina lesbian tomboy and fem couples.

17. *Fils* are Philippine nationals.

18. Beth Castronuevo and Vangie Lim were fired on September 6, 1994, from their jobs at Balay Rehabilitation Center after news of their lesbian relationship polarized the office. Balay is a nongovernmental organization dedicated to aiding families of Philippine political prisoners. Beth and Vangie's dismissal was met with public protests by lesbian and women's groups in Manila. A lawsuit is currently under litigation.

19. *Miss Saigon,* a musical update of *Madame Butterfly* by Alain Boublil and Claude-Michel Schonberg, opened in New York City in April 1991 after months of criticism for its sexist and racist content and casting practices. Lambda Legal Defense Fund, a leading national lesbian and gay organization, came under fire from Asian lesbian and gay groups for using *Miss Saigon* for its annual fundraiser. A highly publicized protest led by a coalition of Asian and gay groups disrupted the April 6 and 11 performances during opening week. For details, see Yoko Yoshikawa, "The Heat Is on 'Miss Saigon' Coalition: Organizing across Race and Sexuality," in *The State of Asian America: Activism and Resistance in the 1990s,* ed. Karin Aguilar-San Juan (Boston: South End, 1994), 275–94. Furthermore, according to Christine Lipat, the *Miss Saigon* controversy was the first activist campaign that brought Filipino gay men and women together, setting the stage for the later formation of Kambal sa Lusog, which in turn led to the formation of Kilawin Kolektibo.

20. Celebrating twenty-five years of struggle since the Stonewall Riots launched the gay liberation movement, more than 1.5 million gay, lesbian, bisexual, and transgender people (and their supporters) gathered for a weeklong celebration in New York City that culminated in a march and rally in Central Park on June 25, 1994.

21. The Fourth United Nations World Conference on Women in Beijing, August 30 to September 9, 1996, gathered more than 200,000 international delegates. Controversy over lesbianism emerged before the conference when China wanted to deny entry to lesbians, Tibetans, Taiwanese, Asian women's rights groups, and some organizations militantly opposed to abortion. In addition, the nongovernmental organizations forum, which preceded the UN gathering, was moved to Huairou, thirty miles outside the capital, making it nearly impossible for NGO groups to observe the Beijing event. At the conference, controversy focused on the specific inclusion of lesbian issues in the UN Platform for Action. Before Beijing, proleesbian recommendations were submitted by NGOs at the Latin American and Caribbean preparatory meeting. The Europe and North American Regional Platform for Action mentioned sexual orientation in its preamble and directed governments to include lesbian groups in the design, development, and implementation of strategies for change. This was the first time that a document adopted by UN member states had included any mention of sexual orientation.

12
Deflowering the Sampaguita

M. EVELINA GALANG

First Holy Communion

First. Like never before. Like when you know everyone but you is doing it. Teenage girls wearing hose instead of anklets, sitting at the back of the bus among the boys; your older cousins with flip-teased dos, painted toenails, false lashes, and padded bras; the neighborhood baby-sitter reeking of nicotine, bubble-gum lip gloss, and cheap eau de toilette; your beautiful auntie who flies from Russia to China to Norway to you, planting big red kisses all over your face, ripe and luscious as strawberries in late August; your mommy sleek and steady, smart and calm; and even your very old and shaky lola. They are doing it. Every week. Every Sunday. Some even every day. And up until now, on this, the first weekend in May, you have always been too young. Too innocent. Too irresponsible.

The priest has told you and an entire classroom of girls just like you: When you are old enough. When you have matured. When you are able to understand and appreciate, you will have your turn. A chance. An opportunity to receive the body. To hold the body. To feel its texture on the tip of the tongue where you will hold Him there, gently, carefully, making sure you don't bite down. You will someday bond with Him. The first time is always the most special, Father tells you, I still remember my First Holy Communion years and years ago, and you will, too.

Until today, you were not part of the club. You watched the women, older than you, more sophisticated than you, painted and coiffed and powdered like beautiful angels, floating down the aisle, arms held up in prayer, eyes lowered. For years, you have imagined yourself in line with them. Painted up. Cloaked in white. Until today, you were not worthy, and neither are they, but they have been given permission. At last, it's your turn.

For the last month, you have spent your Sunday mornings preparing yourself. Locked up in the safety of your girl bathroom, you practiced walking down the narrow aisle—you lined your toes up and marched down the skinny row of tiles between the bathtub and the sink and toilet. Hands folded, eyes lowered, you walked right up to the edge of the full-length mirror. Stared yourself down, brown eye to brown eye. Studied the dark flecks in the center of your pupil. Looked for the light. The mystery. The glow you knew you'd possess once you received. "Body of Christ," you imagined Father saying.

"Amen," you answered loudly, proudly. Because as young as you are, you know you believe. You know with all your heart because Mary, your Mother of God, the woman whose name you bear, would never lie to you. This first time, this moment, the First Holy Communion is something blessed and real and meant only for good girls. For women like the ones you dream of growing up to be and you will—Goddamn it—be one of them. You stuck out your tongue, pressed it to the cold, hard reflection in the glass, closed your eyes the way you'd seen Theresa, Carmen, and Tita Ana close their eyes—lashes fluttering—and you imagined some magic, some wave of holiness coursing through your body. Your soul, light and winged, soared to places you had never known. Took you up to heaven and back, to the outer limits of the universe, maybe as far away as Mars, or Saturn, or Jupiter. You left your body and, for a moment, you were one with God. You communed with Him and the saints and all the angels, tangible cherubs amid white gauze, luminous skies, and the clouds.

You know; today you will know this. This is what you've been told. Here is how we come to learn of Jesus, our Savior. Here is what they tell us. First Holy Communion. Like the first time you are with the man you love—but they don't say that part. Even though they dress you up in white lace and pearls and satin and white veils—like the bride you practice becoming. The nuns, the fathers, even your older brothers and sisters will tell you—First Holy Communion is just like that.

Such attention to detail. Such lessons. Such accuracy in the Divine. Such parallels to love and lovemaking. But no one ever tells you that part. Mothers never speak of it and, even when they suspect you know, you want, you do, there is silence. Silence, as if you are still too young, too innocent, too immature to understand this, the complexity of human relationships, the depth of desire, the transcending of spirit and the holiness of bodies. Love, desire, sex. Taboo.

As girls, we are taught the way. Given all the tools. The equipment. The desire. In our quest to be true, to have faith, to love, we seek love. Love of God and love of family and love, true love. But nobody ever tells you that part.

How You Learn about It

Slumber party. Sometime during fifth grade—the Michaels' basement. You don't even know what they told you. Who knows? All those seedy details cloaked in giggles and whispers:

"Uh-huh."
"No way"
"Gross."

What you remember is the damp of wet cement. The gray bricks, steel poles cold as ice in the bottom of a MacDonalds Coca-Cola. What you see is the pitch of midnight when all good ten-year-olds clustered together like moths wrapped tightly in their sleeping bag cocoons should be sleeping, should never know this hour of night, not even when they grow to be young women. Who knows what they said exactly, but that's when you first heard about it. And it was as true then as it is now. Yuck. Gross. No way my momma and daddy would ever do that. Why? It sounded so disgusting. And then the picture of it, the very image, awkward and misshapen—entirely inaccurate—of the two of them doing *that*. No way.

What for? To make a baby. To make you and Danny and Tony. Unbelievable. Disgusting.

No talk that night of love and desire. No connections among wanting, needing, giving. No understanding of the body and how it can be this gift like springtime in February, or recess all day long, or chocolate for breakfast, lunch, *and* dinner. It was just something grown-ups did to make a baby. You imagined they closed their eyes when they did it. You imagined they must have turned their faces away in embarrassment—like when someone has farted and you pretend not to notice or when your crazy cousin pretends she's a nun and blesses strangers on the street.

Shouldn't someone older than you, more knowledgeable and more caring, someone experienced in these matters and close to you—shouldn't someone like that have explained sex to you? Made connections for you? Told you, this is what happens, here is what to expect, here is what to do. Shouldn't you have been trained for this?

Of course, the one you kiss is the one who teaches you how to. Together, you explore, experiment, nudge your way around a lip, and slip the tongue just so, across a row of teeth, smooth and white as a chorus line of shiny pearls. Together you learn when to swallow, when to breathe, when to open your eyes. Together, you learn about dancing your body around his, how to slide an arm, a leg, a finger just so. You learn to alter breath, to initiate a whisper and make it grow, loud like a cry that fills you up so full it bursts. You learn about timing, how it is everything. It is when you are out in that proverbial field that you learn the difference between love, lust, and the thing both share—desire.

But who tells you what it means? Why you do it? How come when the breathing falls and rises and rises and falls, your hands want to move around? A kiss becomes a fondle, the fondle initiates the undressing. The hook unhooked makes zippers slide, buttons snap right off. Why is it when he rolls his hips over yours, dances his way into you, teasing you like this, you ache, grow full? Something blossoms wild and uncontrollable, peals open petal on petal like morning dew into hot noonday sun. You can hardly stand it and you don't know why. And what about that moment—you know the one—the no-turning-back moment where it doesn't matter if you love him or know him? What do you do then? What happens that moment you let go?

And what has that to do with love? When one body slides over another, and he slips part of him into you, and you find yourself floating to some distant planet—is that love? Does it have anything at all to do with companionship or friendship—and why is it more fun with some than others and is it about making babies after all?

Your mother should tell you. But your mother is silent. Babies are a gift from God, she says (not a lie at all), she and your father love each other (also true), and they had to fuck each other to make you (no word on this).

So what's a girl to do? What's she to think? How's she to find a life partner, the right one, without guidance?

Figure out sex on your own. Search and practice and watch. You may or may not, may never make the connections on your own. You may even come to think there are no ties between love, lust, and baby making.

Silence

With silence comes disapproval. What is not spoken of is not happening. Not to men and women, not to married couples, and never to single ones. And don't even dare think a boy and girl would ever—not even when no one's watching, not even when their parents have discreetly left the lesson out of all their never-ending lectures.

From littlehood, you have been taught how to speak, how to listen, how to behave in every circumstance imaginable—to your lolas and lolos, to the uncles and aunties you are not related to, to your teachers, priests, nuns, and even to the strangers in the grocery store. You've gone over this ground with Mommy and Daddy and you will always come out gracious and elegant. Polite. You know how to make mano, offer anyone in a five-mile radius of your house something to drink, something to eat, a place to take a nap. Even now you hear your Tito Boy saying to the plumber whose car has broken down, "Wanna eat? Want some rice? How 'bout a beer?" You know how to behave at baptisms, weddings, and even you, at five or six, have been briefed on the etiquette of funeral masses. You have been taught to respect people and their feelings, to be giving—so what's this? Why hasn't your mother, your father, your Tita Baby, Tito Butch, your ates and kuyas—why hasn't anyone told you how to act around him?

When the two of you are sitting so close that you feel him breathing, soft and low; when the whisper of his breath into your ear and the heat of him, the tiny wind that soars from the words he speaks, "I think of you always," spirals through you like some kind of strange monsoon, runs rampant round your ribs, circles the heart, flushes whatever it is you ate for lunch right out of you—BOOM, BOOM, BOOM—you are at a loss. Suddenly you feel faint, your body melting like mozzarella on pepperoni and black olives—and what you want and how you act and what you say conflict with everything Father, Son, and Holy Ghost have not said, scream out to all your mother refuses to acknowledge, your father will not see. Your body has taken a turn—and from the way your family acts, you believe it might be for the worst.

At night, you shift the shade from your lamp; cast a giant shadow of your body across the naked wall of your teenage bedroom. You lift your arms up and with your eyes you trace your body—outline your breasts, tiny shells, cupped like oyster beds. Circle the space in your chest where you imagine a heart. Slide your fingers down the length of you—zing—in and out where the hips, not yet planted, not yet settled, but hopeful and anxious, will someday be. Brush the soft hairs, growing, silky like milkweed, hiding what? Covering who? Protecting some buried treasure, or is it a curse? Is something wrong with your body? Why is it you like him so and still, you don't know how to say it and how to act when the heat of his body affects your skin, your muscles, you, like this.

Once your mother stood up high against the windowpane of the living room and watched you sitting on a tree stump, hand and hand with the boy next door. When he leaned into you, put his arm around you, she pounded on the glass. She shook her head at you. Later, she forbade you to see him, speak to him. Hung the phone up on him when he called. Your father took to ignoring him, looked right through him when he stood on the threshold of the door, called him some other boy's name, referred to him as "that guy." They never told you why.

What your mother didn't know is that while you sat there with him, listening to your transistor radio blurt, "All you need is love," you were conducting a storm inside your belly. A hurricane spun in the hut of your chest. A host of discrepancies inhabited your body like demons taking possession of your soul. You wanted to kiss him. You didn't. You liked him, but you knew you shouldn't. You wanted nothing more than to lie with him, naked, wrapped only in his flesh, his embrace. You felt guilty thinking this was not a dirty image at all—it was beautiful. You didn't know why. And before your mother knocked on that glass, before you ever heard her, you were pushing him away from you, slapping him for touching you. Today because he did, tomorrow because he wouldn't.

Years later, you and your college boyfriend, home for the weekend, fall asleep on the couch, watching *The Way We Were*. Your parents, coming home from a Saturday night of poker and mah-jongg, suspect there must be something amiss when they enter a dark house at midnight, his car out in the driveway.

BOOM. Your father's voice calls your name, your mother bangs the den door wide open, and streaks of light reveal their silhouettes, large, luminous, and angry. Their bodies merge, one gigantic torso. There are two heads. Arms flail in the night like giant birds swooping down on the two of you. "How could you do this to us?" your mother cries. "How could you?"

How could you do what? They never tell you. They never bring it up again. After your boyfriend leaves, the only thing your daddy says is "Behave."

Here, the silence, unbearable, tense, and fraught with disapproval, leaves you confused. So you stop watching old movies. Refrain from references to Robert Redford, Barbra Streisand, and that ridiculous song. You stop holding your boyfriend's hand in public. Pull away from him when your mother calls you. Move out of his embrace at the very mention of your family. Stop speaking all together. Behave.

Say prayers instead. Read books. Go to theaters where it is impossible to fall asleep. Years later, avoid those questions, the ones aunties and uncles throw at you. "So when are you going to get married?" and "Do you have a boyfriend yet?" Don't tell them, "Of course I do, have, will, but you will never know." Keep your love life to yourself. Like them, remain silent. Pretend your silence is tantamount to abstinence, virginity, and holiness.

Deflowering the Sampaguita

With a group of your best Pinay friends, and their boyfriends, pile into a van and take over a local dance club. Dance less than a breath apart.

Crowd the floor like a cluster of rich red grapes, threaded together by a single vine. You have colored your mouth burgundy, teased your hair, and decorated your neck, your ears, your skinny brown arms with gold and copper bangles. You have stretched a cotton shirt, scoop necked and slightly swollen at the breast, around your body. Your pants hang low, slide across your hips, just about reveal your belly. You and your friends are beautiful flowers, fragrant, sweet, ripe. You draw your boyfriends close. They hover just above you. Gaze into your eyes. Run their strong hands along your waist, torso, and thigh. Dance holding hands. Move together. To the beat. Closer and closer. Close your eyes and he wraps his arms around you. Taken.

It is as though you move to that drum, that tribal gong. Your hips and legs move and sway, knees bend and pose, like a mountain princess crossing the river—head up, eye to eye. The drumming brings you closer; the bells chiming in the distance dispel reality. It is the Kulintang, dense rhythmic drumming. And even though you were never a Mindanao Princess, even if you never took a folk-dance lesson in your life, the pressure of the heels, down on the linoleum floor; the way you hold your back up straight, tall, and proud; the way you cast your spell, hypnotic and full as the golden moon; the way you float right out of consciousness is something that comes easily, part of your blood, indeed, part of your human condition.

Amid the confusion of what to say, to think, to feel, you lose yourself someplace in the middle of a kiss. Feel stars bursting inside you, oceans washing up against your hips, water welling and brimming just below your pelvis, and before you can swim your way back to your senses, he is deep inside you. You not only let him in, you invite him. "Right this way," you whisper. Become part of this wave, this delightful tumult. Know nothing, only that you hope this feeling never stops. This is right. This is natural. This is your intuitive self, honest and true. You let go.

In the aftermath gloom sets in, chaos begins. Picture your mother and father, sitting in a pew before God and all the heavens. Think, better to die than ever let them know. Better to keep things a secret. Wonder how something this beautiful can be that wicked? Are you going to hell?

The very first time, when you knew little of love, when hormones controlled the sky and moon, he came and you said to yourself, "Is that all?" Like a tailor with a needle, he slipped in and out and in and out of you and you thought, *So?* And still, you couldn't help yourself, you opened up. Again and again. For years, you switched boys, lovers, men. You learned about give and take and generosity. Sewing turned into surfing, riding a wave high, wild, free, and dangerous. Instead of "Is that all," you thought, "Please, let's don't ever stop." You learned the difference between fucking and making love. You preferred the latter and saved your body for men you loved. The act became a gift you shared with lovers.

And when a baby grows, ripe and free, fills your baby fat belly with baby, you confess. Are sent away. You have a baby. You do one of two things: You give her away, like a door prize on Philippine Independence Day, or you bring her home and she becomes your baby sister. Your baby is not your baby. Your mommy no longer looks at you as if she were your mommy. Your daddy stops speaking. Be grateful, they tell you; you are lucky this is all.

Other girls from your First Holy Communion didn't get this far. Never got to see their babies. Sleeping was easier for them, dying was less disgraceful than bearing a child. There was no stopping the chaos in their bodies, no one to talk to, and there the fight died. And who could blame them, really? All that confusion bottled up inside, all that and a child smaller than each teenage girl, just as sweet and innocent as the child mother, in search of someone to love, to talk to, to cry to—all that bursting out of their still boy-like bodies. Who could blame them for silencing the conflict of their hearts?

Or maybe you are one of the many who marry after all. Three months pregnant, twenty years young, loving your high school sweetheart. Nobody knows, just you and your boyfriend, your parents and his. No one tells. You bear your child, you bear many, and nobody is wiser. Not a word spoken. When your daughter and son grow, when their bodies change and their voices drift away from childhood, you begin the practice of silent disapproval; you continue the cycle. You insist on impossible chastity. You attempt to keep the Sampaguita in bloom, fresh, young, never acknowledging the nature of things.

You live your life like a spy. Secret agent 99, complete with double life. Another you. The doctor daughter, the lawyer daughter, the wife daughter, and the well-behaved and decent daughter. You cook, you serve, you lead the family prayers. And when you leave your parents, you slow your walk. You sway. Smile out of the corner of your eye. Whisper. Charmer you, you seduce unknowingly. Walk into your cousin's office and kiss her boss on top of his balding head. Do it without thinking twice. Do it because you are young and you know that everyone will think it's cute. Do it because you know this and a thousand other traditionally unacceptable gestures are things you and only you can get away with. When your *ate* tells you to stop it, cut it out, and "Don't go kissing my boss on the crest of his balding head," say, "But he's so delicious." Your mother, who knows you better than you think, who secretly knows, maybe even remembers what it's like to be this young, this beautiful, this brimming with sex appeal and truly powerful, says, "You've got to learn to control yourself, *hija*, even if he is delicious."

Sex stimulates you like a drug, empowers you in new ways. Teaches you about walking around slinky and smooth, as if in constant dance, constant seduction. Teaches you that men want to do your bidding when you smile just so, or look away just when. Sex and being sexy charms you, and you like it. You can't help it. And when you try, when you let your two selves battle out right and wrong, marry love and lust, there is nothing but turmoil, and your lover wonders why he can never do anything right. "You are a walking contradiction," he tells you.

Because there is the family. Think. What if they found out. This prospect haunts you like ghosts in an old hotel. Pops up when you least expect, in the breath you take just after you've been together. Taps you on the shoulder as you answer the telephone. Think if on top of defiling your body, you made a baby, too. Run away, first choice. Suicide, second. No, suicide first, run away after the failed suicide. You would rather die. You would rather float away in a stream, clear and fresh and cold. Take me away, you think. Take me far away, where Mom and Dad will never have to see me. Never have to be embarrassed because of me. Ultimately, you worry their worry is what others will say, will think.

Wild and fresh, little white star with fragrant petals, once planted, once in bloom, you are left clinging to the vine that is the family you were born to. Face up to the sun, stretching out, reaching, but never breaking free, you are tangled in two worlds—wanting and not wanting. Speaking and silent at once. Filipina girl, American born and of two cultures, Western like MTV, tropical as the Sampaguita, you are left alone to figure out the rest. Because no one dares to tell you that when you make love to your lover, your husband, your boyfriend; when you date one another and flirt; and when he leans over for that first kiss, first moment of intimacy, sinking into you long and slow, it is your first holy communion all over again. Spirit floating high in the sky and then, for an instant, for one breath, you are one.

Author's Note

The "you" in this creative nonfiction essay represents the collective "you." The experience in this essay is neither biographical nor autobiographical to any particular woman but is a conglomeration of various anonymous interviews with young women from New York, Illinois, Wisconsin, Ohio, and Virginia. Yes, these are your daughters speaking.

13
The Long Road Ahead

TRINITY A. ORDONA

Foreword: March 1, 2004

This article, originally written in October 1997, was published in *Tibok: Heart Beat of the Filipino Lesbian*, the first lesbian anthology in the Philippines.[1] I wrote it as Filipino American lesbian-community activist with three decades of organizing experience in the antiracist, international solidarity, Asian American and gay/lesbian liberation movements in the United States. I was especially motivated to share my story with my Pinay (Filipina) sisters in the Philippines. My community activism, which began in 1968 with the civil rights movement, was deeply personalized on September 22, 1972, when President Ferdinand Marcos placed the Philippines under martial law. My subsequent involvement in the antidictatorship movement during those crucial years (1972–86) catapulted me into Philippine history, politics, and culture and new levels of international solidarity and political activism. Much of the liberatory vision and organizing skill I now bring to the gay and lesbian community developed in those heady "David versus Goliath" days of the movement.

In updating this article, now for a Filipino American audience, I still want to share my experiences living in the "liberated zone" of San Francisco, where gays and lesbians have successfully struggled for a relatively open life. Those reflections are now, however, historically relevant. On February 12, 2004, San Francisco city officials issued gender-neutral marriage licenses and married same-sex couples. The city's support of same-sex commitment blossomed overnight into a mass celebration of love chronicled in newspaper headline stories and television broadcasts across the country. In reaction, the conservative opposition viciously condemned the same-sex marriage movement. Now gay marriage is a political football in the 2004 U.S. Presidential Campaign, with President George W. Bush calling for a national constitutional amendment enshrining marriage as a heterosexual-only institution.

Since that landmark day, several thousand same-sex couples, including my partner Desiree and I, have been married at city hall. Whatever the outcome of the legal and political struggle over same-sex marriage in the time ahead, this will be an account of love, marriage, family, and coming out together by a Filipino American lesbian on the front line.

Love and Marriage

These are words and rituals that resonate throughout all societies, yet they have a particular historical significance at this time for lesbian, gay, bisexual, and transgender people. We are boldly reaffirming, redefining, and reconstructing the very meaning of these concepts to resonate our lifestyles.

On June 25, 1988—fifteen years before today's heated national controversy over legalizing same-sex marriage—my lover and I were married in a big wedding witnessed by more than a hundred family members, friends, and coworkers. We wore floor-length wedding gowns made by my mother and our "best butches" wore tuxedos as they walked us down the aisle. Our good friend and matchmaker from Honolulu officiated, blessing us with a Hawaiian wedding chant. Friends flew in from Hawaii to play the wedding music and brought gorgeous flowers and leis for the ceremony. We had flower girls, a three-tiered wedding cake, diamond wedding rings, gifts, a thousand gold paper cranes, and two garter belts tossed by the two brides to two lucky women (who have since gotten married), and a big dance party led my brother's Top 40 band.

It started in 1987, when Desiree and I attended a seminar series called "Lesbians Choosing Children." The seminar was a springboard for discussion, and we found ourselves in agreement about having children. Suddenly I said, "First we have to get married." It just came out of my mouth that way. I tell everyone that it was the Filipino in me. Whenever I say that, all the Filipinos in the room agree and chime in, "Yes, and marriage is for life, too!"

Gay marriage was not legal and I had no expectations that it would change in the near future. But marriage is, first of all, an act of personal choice and commitment between two people. Long before there were courts, laws, judges, and priests to perform "marriages," people were marrying each other, anyway. I wanted to ceremonialize our personal commitment with a big party; that's a wedding.

Desiree did not think the same as I, at first. She had majored in women's studies at the University of Hawaii and viewed marriage as a destructive institution sanctioning the oppression of women by men. But we soon came to agreement once we reflected on our tight-knit family experiences and the commitment of our parents to the children. Bringing children into the world (and for lesbians, it is a quite deliberate act) goes beyond oneself. If we wanted to bring another human life into a world full of homophobia and social ostracism, then we had to be committed to that future together. We wanted from each other the kind of commitment we had witnessed in our own families. In 1988, we created a ceremony that reflected this meaning.

We looked to the heart of marriage: the personal commitment promise. It is these mutual bonds of commitment between two persons that bind them to the other, whether an official pronounces the words or not. Thus, we were married in the eyes of each other and witnessed by family and friends in 1988. Getting married then was truly a liberating experience and being married has been an important part of our relationship.

Fifteen years later, on February 16, 2004, Desiree and I stood outside in the rain, waiting to get into San Francisco's city hall. We were joined by hundreds of other couples, many of whom had been together for many years—ten, on the average. Eight hours later, when we stood on the steps of the city hall and took our civil marriage vows before Supervisor Tom Ammiano, we cheered when he declared us "spouses for life!" Though legal recognition had been long delayed, the thrill and excitement of the moment was still there.

Up until last month, when anyone asked me "how to get married," I would tell them our story and happily said the "details" were completely up to them. Now I can add our story of obtaining a marriage license and standing for a civil ceremony in San Francisco. It all counts!

Importance of Family

I realized I was lesbian when I was twenty-two years old in 1974. Though I had crushes on girls in high school, I did not understand my feelings nor did I act on them. I came out as lesbian after I had already become a student activist at the University of California–Berkeley shortly after the Third World Strike for Ethnic Studies. As progressive as the movement was on racism, women's liberation, and international solidarity, it was backward on the gay question. Homosexuality was condemned as "bourgeois decadence," and the gay and lesbian movement was denigrated as petty and irrelevant; so gays and lesbians were not open in the movement. Fortunately, Filipino gays and lesbians found a home in Katipunan ng mga Demokratikong Pilipino (the Union of Democratic Filipinos). But afraid that homosexuality would be used to discredit our political work in the community, we were never open beyond the eyes of familiar faces.

Looking back, the constant political turmoil, excitement, and demands of the 1970s made it possible to distract the voice inside that wanted me to "come out, loud and proud." Ironically, I could bravely lead a rally to fight racist discrimination or confront prodictatorship forces but not face homophobia in the movement. I had internalized it within me. But my greatest fear was rejection from my family; I could not stand even the thought. I kept my lesbianism a secret. Hoping to keep the "truth" from slipping out, I kept my family at a distance and said nothing about my personal life—for years and years. Coming from a large and close family, it was hard not to say anything, to give any hint of my personal happiness—or sadness. Then the AIDS crisis forced homosexuality to the foreground of American society. By the late 1980s, as I saw the country grappled with the human dimensions of the pandemic, I took heart. Longing to be all of myself at the same time, all the time, I came out to my family, slowly, in edible bites. We Filipinos—and all Asians I believe—grow up with strong ties to family. I counted on those ties to open a space in the family for homosexual me. And it did—the Asian way. And it was traditional marriage that guided my path and lit the way back to my Filipino family.

Desiree and I met in Hawaii in 1985. A year later, we formed our relationship and she moved to San Francisco. Within months, she met my parents and all but one of my twelve brothers and sisters. We were meant to be. In December 1987, Desiree and I decided to have children and we got engaged. (As I explained earlier, we "had to get married!") I called my Mom in San Diego and told her the news of our upcoming marriage. My mother is a professional seamstress and with eight girls in the family—out of thirteen children—she always made her daughters' wedding dresses. Now it was my turn. I asked her to make my wedding dress.

Mom said, "Why are you doing that? She's just going to leave you anyway. Besides, you are too domineering." This was said without malice or anger. She just told me the truth of her feelings. I did not take offense and immediately understood her point of view. Yes, she had seen me with several different girlfriends over the years and these relationships had all ended in a breakup. Maybe gay relationships never last? Yes, I am headstrong and maybe I would drive Desiree away, like my mother thought I had the others; however, she did not disapprove. Then I asked her again about my wedding dress and told her I wanted a Filipino dress with Maria Clara sleeves. I was the first and only girl who had wanted a Filipino dress. Suddenly, Mom's tone changed. By the time we hung up, I knew my Mom's mind was not yet made up. There was still time to win her heart.

I knew Mom could make the wedding dress and still not come to my wedding. I really wanted her approval and wanted to know where she stood *before* the wedding. If she were not going to come, I would need some time to get over it. In my family, all the children—especially the girls—first ask permission of my parents before a wedding was announced and invitations sent. I felt I had to do the same thing. It was a Filipino tradition I wanted to follow, somehow. Usually, the "boy" asks the parents, but in this case, since there was no "boy," I did not know what to do.

In April 1988, we both went to San Diego to fit my dress. Mom draped me in the *pina* cloth (a special material made from pineapple leaves). She took my measurements and settled on the design. With Desiree standing next to me, I then asked Mom to take her measurements so we could send them to Honolulu for a special Hawaiian formal dress (*holokuu*) to be made. We showed a picture of Desiree attired in a holokuu at her high school graduation from Kamehameha School for Hawaiian Children. Mom studied the photo carefully. After a few moments, she said, "I can make Desiree's dress, too." It was something I never expected but it was her way of saying yes, of granting approval. That weekend, Mom made both our wedding dresses and from that day on, she has been with us all the way.

Ever since Desiree and I were married, my parents, brothers, and sisters treat us like any married couple. Desiree, now daughter-in-law, attends all my family functions, and we do so openly as a lesbian couple. This was tested immediately, too! My brother Bernie married a few months after we did. During the traditional picture taken after the ceremony, Desiree took her place next to me in the family photograph. (This was the last full family photograph—with parents and all thirteen children and their spouses—before my father died a year later.) Later, at the wedding reception, my brother played the piano to our wedding song and his wife Remy and her sister Mary sang the lyrics. Knowing they did this on purpose just for us, we danced together in front of their two hundred Filipino guests! As long as Desiree and I were okay with my family, then we had to be okay with my sister-in-law's side of the family. We were a family fact.

Desiree's brother and sister-in-law also have been very supportive of us. Ed, Desiree's brother, and his wife have twins and they give us regular "auntie" updates on their exploits and growing-up pains. Back in 1988, Ed volunteered to talk to the parents and invite them to the wedding. But it was a double whammy: the invitation was also Desiree's coming out to her parents. It was too much at the same time, so they did not attend the wedding. Her parents—her father is Chinese-Hawaiian and her mother is third-generation Japanese—needed time to adjust. After the wedding, Desiree returned to Hawaii for a family visit, and the next time I came along. While it has taken some time, they treat us as a couple and I do not have to pretend that we are roommates. We just *are*.

This is helped by the fact that there are other gay people in Desiree's family and on both sides of the family, too. Once, during a visit to Hawaii with her parents, aunt, and uncle in Kona, her aunt talked about her youngest daughter who "drove a truck and coached the local volleyball team." When they commented that she "never wore dresses," Desiree's mother matter-of-factly added, "We've got one, too"—referring, of course, to Desiree. Then, on another dinner occasion with Desiree, myself, and her gay cousin, his mother chided the three of us for "not getting married." We all, except her cousin's mother, rolled our eyes and wanted to burst out laughing. Auntie had no idea what the joke was—and still doesn't. It seems that gays and lesbians are just part of family life. On our most recent Christmas visit to Hawaii, a local Japanese *hapa* lesbian friend told me that the defeat of same-sex marriage in Hawaii had not really stopped anyone from getting married. As testament, she explained that while she herself was not explicitly "out" in her family (though everyone knows), her mother and father had just attended the wedding of her gay Japanese cousin and his partner!

The acceptance that Desiree and I found in our families after our marriage has opened up my mind and heart entirely. In hindsight, our behaviors—of both the gay and lesbian children and their parents—make perfectly logical sense when viewed from an Asian/Pacific family perspective. My own experience and talks with many other Asian Pacific Islander (A/PI) lesbians here has convinced me of the different ways that we come out to our families and the different cultural difficulties they face when we come out to them. Don't get me wrong: I think coming out is an essential part of our liberation process. One must break free of the fear and live one's own life. My own experience with getting married and coming out in a big way finally put an end to concealing ourselves to others outside our circle of lesbian friends. But it is a lifelong process for us as gay people *and* for the people in our lives.

I came out to myself as a lesbian when I was twenty-two. I was twenty-eight when I first told my mom and thirty-six when I got married. Now I am fifty-three years old. During the thirty years in between, I followed my instincts and told my family about me—gradually—when I was ready and in a way they could understand. By now, my mother has attended a few lesbian events with us. In 1996, at an award ceremony where I was honored as a "lesbian of achievement, vision, and activism," she sat at the head table with my sisters and stood proudly for an ovation when I introduced her. Later that year, Mom spoke with me on a panel on culture and sexual orientation at the Filipino American Women's Network National Conference in Minneapolis. In 1998, when I received a University of California–San Francisco Outstanding Service Award for my community-organizing work, Mom stood up with me—without any discussion or coaching—and we walked together to receive the award from the chancellor. Each time that Mom took a step forward, it was one she could handle. As I said, mine is a "family coming out together" story—the Asian way.

Coming Out—In Our Own Way

One of the cornerstones of American-style gay liberation is coming out. Current available psychology literature defines it as an outcome of a successful process of gay, lesbian, and bisexual identity development. The most popular models describe it as a linear process that comes in stages: feeling different, acknowledging one's homosexuality, disclosure to others, acceptance of homosexual identity, exploration and experimentation, and intimacy. The underlying assumption is that being out is a desired state in and of itself; in fact, some leaders frame coming out as a political strategy for gay liberation and a litmus test of one's commitment to gay rights. However, notions about gay identity and coming out have been largely based on predominantly white-identified people whose cultural values are individualism, independent identity, and separation from family of origin.[2] In Asian/Pacific cultures collectivism, group identity, interdependence, and family obligation are held in high regard. Therefore, other people—especially one's family—also are considered in our coming-out process.

Here in the United States, Asian and Pacific Islander (A/PI) gay people often take several years to come out fully, and family is one of the last groups to be informed. Unlike our white American counterparts, who are raised with a strong emphasis on individuality and independence, we grow up with a relational orientation whereby we see ourselves as part of a group, not separate from a group.[3] As family is our first and primary group, it is very important to us how our parents will take the news. We utilize a bicultural mode here in the United States, as very different cultural and familial norms inform our process than those practiced by most white gay Americans. While much attention in the literature has been given to gay people's fear of rejection in the coming-out process, for A/PIs, our fear is coupled with a consideration for our parents' feelings. How will they take it? Is it the right time? How can I help them understand? With relational orientation comes reciprocity, interdependence, and interrelatedness between child and parents.

How A/PI gay people come out to our families, if and when we do, is important. We learn that discussion of any difficult matter—whether it is a job or school failure, alcoholism, divorce, or homosexuality—often requires us to employ indirect, discreet, nonverbal, and nonconfrontational methods of communication. I cofounded a group, Asian and Pacific Islander Family Pride, to address the special cultural and language needs of families of lesbian, gay, bisexual, and transgender A/PI people. We provide peer support to families, utilizing a videotape interview of four Asian families with gay children (*Coming Out, Coming Home*) and a Chinese-English booklet of letters by parents and siblings of Chinese lesbians (*Beloved Daughter*).[4] As our culture relies on the family for self-sufficiency, we know our parents are generally disinclined to seek outside help. Therefore, most have little or no support to help them through the process when we come out to them. Many wrestle alone with their conflicts; some go deep into the closet, unable to discuss it at all. In the privacy of their homes, families learn about other Asian and Pacific Islander families with gay children. Through the videotape or booklet, they can see families like their own with homosexual children. The "in-your-face" confrontational politics advocated by the current generation of gay American activists may work well for street politics, but most A/PIs leave it at the front door when it comes to the family. It just does not work well for us. It does not mean we are more homophobic or less proud or lack self-esteem. It means that we come out in our own way.

Marriage is not the only institution under reconstruction. Gay people—as single parents, couples or a combination of the two—are becoming parents! What began fifteen years ago as a dribble has become a gushing faucet.

And here in San Francisco, there are about forty children of A/PI lesbian (mostly), bisexual, gay, and transgender people. This is another area where the A/PI culture plays a unique role in the process. Among the Asian lesbians I know who have become mothers, all have spent a long time and concerted effort to come out to their family and bring their parents along, especially. The parents who thought they would never have grandchildren from their gay child are completely and pleasantly turned around by the "gay-by boom." Once babies come into the picture, the closet comes tumbling down and they establish a new relationship with their gay child, now as grandparents concerned about the future, safety, and happiness of the next generation.

Gay liberation is a global movement of millions. In each movement, every person must take her place in the struggle. It is a long road ahead, but for Filipinos, we are not alone. Most of us have three to four generations of immediate family to consider: our grandparents, our parents, our siblings, and our children, nieces, and nephews. This could be a group of anywhere from three to thirty or more! Bringing our family along our journey is a long and difficult task, but it an ultimately rewarding one. In the end, we know that when we stand in the struggle, we do *not* stand alone.

Notes

1. Anna Leah Sarabia, ed., *Tibok: Heart Beat of the Filipino Lesbian* (Manila: Anvil, 1998).
2. Althea Smith, "Cultural Diversity and the Coming Out Process: Implications for Clinical Practice," in *Ethnic and Cultural Diversity among Lesbians and Gay Men*, ed. Beverly Greene (Thousand Oaks, Calif.: Sage, 1997), 279–81.
3. David Yau-Fai Ho, "Relational Orientation in Asian Social Psychology," in *Indigenous Psychologies: Research and Experience in Cultural Context*, ed. Uichol Kim and John W. Berry (Newbury Park, Calif.: Sage, 1993), 240–59.
4. The video and booklet are available from Asian and Pacific Islander Family Pride, P.O. Box 473, Fremont, CA 94537; phone (510) 818-0887, or online at www.apifamilypride.org.

V

Talking Back:
Peminist Interventions in Cyberspace and the Academy

14

Creating NewFilipina.com and the Rise of CyberPinays

PERLA PAREDES DALY

BagongPinay not only hopes to help redefine the identity of Filipinas on the Internet and in the world, but to also redefine it in Philippine society and Filipino communities ... it hopes that it can help open up doors to ideas and options for Filipinas so that they can create their own identity and better decide who they can be for themselves. What Is NewFilipina.com?

—"What is NewFilipina.com?"
www.newfilipina.com/whois/whynew.html

The combination of my being a Filipina, my feelings about peddled images of Filipinas on the Internet, and my becoming a web designer set the stage for the 1998 creation of *BagongPinay*. It is a website that would initiate a strong cyberPinay presence countering the pervasive Filipina stereotypes marketed by Internet entrepreneurs.[1] This article describes how my work in cyberspace has been part of several journeys: an advocacy for Filipinas online, a soul journey, and an exploration of the connection between feminism and Filipino identity.

Discovering the Cybermyth of Filipinas

I began using the Internet in 1991. In 1995, having lived away from the Philippines for a while, I began to check out the web and to use it to reconnect with my roots. This is when I found www.filipina.com, a web site whose homepage title was "mail-order–brides from the Philippines." I was stunned and upset. This site spoke only for a small percentage of Filipinas.[2] Hoping to find better websites than this one, I did a *Yahoo!* search for the word *Filipina* but became disheartened when I found numerous site results that were just the same thing—Filipinas looking for foreign pen pals, friends, and husbands.[3] My dismay grew into horror when I also found many explicit websites about Philippine bar girls, sex tours, and pornography. I was miserable at how these sites used *Filipina* within their domain names.[4]

I researched online and found that many of these sites were owned and operated by men; some matchmaking sites were owned and operated by married couples. These sites' customers were men from the United States, Germany, Australia, the United Kingdom, and some from Japan. According to Robert Scholes, many Asian women who use these services expect to find a better economic life for themselves when they marry foreign men, and many of them think Western men will be husbands who are more faithful than Asian husbands. Foreign men who use these services expect to find an "old-fashioned" woman who defers to the man's authority and does not believe in divorce.[5]

Within these sites I see marketed two icons of men's idealized femininity, the *domestic goddess* and the *sex goddess*. Beyond promulgating sexist stereotypes, these sites are disturbing for the following reasons: they exploit Filipina beauty and femininity for online profit; they idealize Filipinas through commodification, commercialism, and chauvinism; they further exploit women who are already economically and socially disadvantaged[6]; and many market underaged women.[7]

In 1995, I knew the Internet was a powerful medium by which people connected with people, goods, and services, as well as with knowledge and ideas. And so, when I found these sites, I understood that their presence on the web was establishing an unfair generalization of Filipina behavior and thus was creating an Internet stereotype of Filipina women—a Filipina *cybermyth*. I began hoping that I could visit the Internet later and find better websites for Filipinas. It didn't occur to me when I began to learn web design that I would make a web site for and by Filipinas that could advocate for a better cyberspace identity.

Women Launching into Cyberspace

In 1995, I was already in the field of multimedia graphics, creating art production for interactive CD-ROMs. Web design was the next field I wanted to get into, so by 1996 I learned the Macintosh HTML software called *Adobe PageMill*. My first web project was a set of personal pages that included a scrapbook of photographs of the 1986 "People Power" events[8] and a journal of my experiences of that time.[9] I searched for other Filipinos online and invited them to share their experiences as well. Few responded. But I did connect with other Filipino "Netizens" around the world, including old college friends. I also realized that I was one of the first Filipinos establishing Filipino presence, along with Ria Roncales-Goodwin and Ken Ilio.[10]

Before I would start a Filipina site, I was to first experience cybercommunity with some pioneering American women online. By 1996, I was an online member at *Amazon City*,[11] created by Stephanie Brail, whose homepage logo was a silhouette of a strong and sexy super heroine. By 1997, I became part of

Cybergrrls and *Webgrrls*,[12] started by Aliza Sherman. The first *Cybergrrl* webpage offered information on software and links to other female-oriented sites. When Sherman realized that women in Internet businesses needed their own support groups, she organized *Webgrrls* meetings and created a website. I joined the newly forming Connecticut chapter of *Webgrrls* in 1997. One of the reasons why I and other women joined *Webgrrls* for a support system within information technology was because men dominated the field. Thus, it was affirming to discuss with other smart and talented women topics like cyberspace challenges, content creation, and web function and design. It was also exciting to be involved in a cutting-edge field with other women. By the end of 1997, it finally dawned on me that I myself had both the resources and interest to begin creating a site for Filipinas.

New Media for the New Filipina

A fervent desire for a totally new Filipina web representation came over me when I decided to start a website in defiance of Filipina stereotyping online. As a fresh start from Filipina.com, I bought the domain of NewFilipina.com in January 1998. Later I decided to name the site *BagongPinay*, as it was the Filipino translation of "new Filipina." That is when I got an epiphany: NewFilipina.com would not only be a "new" web representation of Filipinas but would also mean evolving the identity of Filipinas.

I designed a draft of the *BagongPinay* homepage, starting with a photograph of a casual, hip-looking young *morena* woman wearing a white T-shirt, jeans, and red sneakers.[13] In the background I layered an antique photograph of one of my great-grandmothers wearing traditional formal dress. I wanted the collage to honor both my ancestors and the modern attitudes of Filipinas today because I wanted *BagongPinay* to stand for the best Filipina traditions and values, old and new, that today's Filipinas integrate within themselves.

I uploaded this draft in February 1998 and then sent out an e-mail to more than two hundred Filipinos, as many as I could find in a short time. I announced brainstorming *BagongPinay* and briefly explained the state of Filipina representation online. I gave the link of the draft page and asked for any forms of help, especially in writing content. Also, I requested that people forward the announcement to any other Filipinos online. Two key Manila Netizens sent encouraging, eye-opening responses. Jesse Liwag, Editor of *i-Site*, wrote in with farsightedness,

> If for Pinays only, the image or identity cannot be left to be determined by those selling sex tours in the Philippines or mail-order brides. The Filipino woman is much, much more than that—but she has to know this, believe in this, and fight for this. The Net is one great place to do it. You can have a hundred online magazines and websites in no time. You can create a worldwide network to support this so that in the end, when

someone would search for "pinay" or "Filipina" in Yahoo! these sites would top the list.

Additionally, Mila D. Aguilar, a Philippine video documentary producer who was working at the *Manila Standard* and the Institute for Filipino Cinema, set me afire with urgency in a message that noted that

> ... computers and the Internet are some of the tools that will finally liberate both women and Asians from bondage. You see, women in general, and Asians as a set of countries and races, could never have come to the fore in the Industrial Age of Steel and big machines. These were meant for the big men of brawn ...
>
> [T]he tools of production shifted from iron and steel machines to electronics, computers and the Internet, which are small, handy, fine, cheap, and require more mind than brawn to operate. What are more necessary now are fine hands and minds, both of which are amply available among women and Asians.

Encouragement came from dozens of other Filipinos. But actual offers to help create the site were few and slow to come. And so, I turned to a friend nearby—Elke Aspillera, a college friend from the University of the Philippines–Diliman, who lived and worked in New York City. At once we brainstormed in a spirit that harked back to our student protest days—a fiery outlook of anger and indignation ignited us against what we perceived to be patriarchal exploitation of the Filipina image on the Internet. "*Makibaka!*" became our slogan once again, as it had been in college.[14] I drafted a site introduction, a hard-lined, blistery discourse on the historical double standards and inequality that Filipino women had to experience at the hands of men in their homeland, in the world, and now in cyberspace. Then, Leticia Perez, a friend of a friend, offered to help write for the site. Tish read the introduction and discussed it with a handful of friends. She got back to me with great advice, for which I am grateful. She and her friends, all recently arrived from Manila, plainly believed that the site should not be full of scorching gripes and rants about problems. They thought the site would be refreshing and inspiring if it offered positive ideas and solutions. Consequently, this was the approach *BagongPinay* took.

We decided that we should immediately publicize the site while developing it, so *BagongPinay* would have: (1) a first stage: a teaser campaign, (2) a second stage: an online discussion, and (3) a grand opening. For the teaser, we wanted thought-provoking digital art. Elke and I each created a Photoshop collage inspired by quotes from progressive feminists. I uploaded the digital art for the April 1998 prelaunch and then e-mailed an announcement. Meanwhile, we worked on the sections of the site and then in May we launched the second stage: a discussion titled, "Who is the new Filipina?" Tish again contributed her talent by giving us a thoughtful introduction for the discussion. Her searching words set the tone not just for the discussion but also for *BagongPinay's* beginnings.

> Who Is the New Filipina?
> You may not know me.
> Truth is I am still getting to know my new self.
> The last time I looked, I was bound by my fears.
> I felt that I had no one. I thought I had no choice.
> I know now that is not true.
> I have a choice. I can be who I want to be.
> I can go where I want to go. I am proud of myself.
> I am the New Filipina.
> Are You?

I rendered her words into another digital art piece. With the discussion in place we again e-mailed an announcement and we waited. The discussion took place through e-mails, since I still had to learn how to create message boards. Here are some highlights:

Maida: A New Filipina embraces and celebrates being a Filipina … here is a great beginning to change the way Filipinas think about ourselves, and, in turn, empower us all to change the way the world thinks about us ….

Bamboo Girl: To be a New Pinay means to identify with how oneself wants to identify, in religion, in sexual orientation, in ethnic background, among many other factors. There are many sides to the strong Pinays today …

Mae: I inherit a lot of attitude from my women ancestors.

Betty Jose: I am glad we have Filipino-made Web sites about Filipinas.

Elke: If a Filipina by birth and a non-conformist by nature is an oxymoron, then you can call me that …. I never understood the secondary roles women played in our society.

Dyketra Santos: Yeah!!! Womyn rule! … I have no inferiority complex!

Sockie: I feel like a completely different woman …. So many opportunities to explore, so many goals to attain and not enough excuses to not go for it!

There were about seventy posts when I closed the discussion. *BagongPinay's* first visitors were mostly Filipinas, but there were also some men. There were hot exchanges when discussing stereotypes, and when one man wrote in as a self-proclaimed chauvinist. Overall, the initial discussion was a great beginning for the site. We had brought together the thoughts, opinions, and views of Filipinas of different backgrounds through an interactive event that began to create an icon of the "new Filipina."[15]

CyberPinays Making Cyperspaces

In June 1998, during the centennial celebration of Philippine independence,[16] *BagongPinay* became the first online community for Filipinas. At the domain of NewFilipina.com there was now a homepage, an editorial, and links to various sections. These sections were intended to bring about an ongoing, composite representation of a multidimensional Filipina image as opposed to the one-dimensional, Filipina cybermyth. It was a site for and by Filipinas where we could share and uphold our struggles, triumphs, intelligence, wisdom, creativity, strengths, and energy—finally, a place online to enable the rise of a strong cyberPinay presence.

From its launch, *BagongPinay* has called for Filipinas from different generations, social and educational backgrounds, and walks of life, to come forward and share their wide range of opinions and lifestyles. In the first two years, we mostly got Filipina visitors from the United States, but as time progressed, more came from the Philippines and around the world.[17] We have also a small male audience, a global mix of Filipinos and foreign men who are related, married, dating, or interested in meeting Filipinas. We even got input from some women who met their husbands through matchmaking services.[18] Thus, a wide range of topics has been discussed at *BagongPinay's* multiple message boards. Moreover, a dozen or so contributors have given their works of poetry, art, and essays to be published at the website.[19] Also, *BagongPinay* promotes and supports the projects and organizations of Filipinas around the world with free press releases, links, articles, homepage features, banner space, ad sponsorship, and event announcements.

BagongPinay has grown to become an established online presence and it continues to represent and link Filipinas throughout the world. In 2004, after six years online, *BagongPinay* finally found its way to top results in *Google* and *Yahoo!* searches for "Filipina." Traffic to the site has increased steadily, too. When we started in 1998, we were getting just over a thousand visitors a month. By 2004, the site was getting more than sixty thousand visitors a month.

I am gratified by *BagongPinay's* impression on visitors; here are a few responses:

Alpha, Q.C. Philippines: Whoa! Finally a site that is a sight for sore eyes on the internet about Filipinas ....

Pam, Cavite City, Philippines: Discovering that we have a web page like this uplifts my spirit as a filipina because I'm very much disappointed [at] the negative perception that net users of different nationalities have about us filipinas. I really hope that a lot of people, not only net users, have a clear perception of what a true filipina is.

Fig. 14.1 Screenshot of NewFilipina.com by Perla Daly. (Reprinted with permission of the artist.)

Clarice: I'm of Hungarian/Czech background, but I love your site. It is for all women! I have it on my favorites list for inspiration.

Elin, Lanao del Sur: Am I glad that there's a website for Filipina women! The kind of women that I want to be associated with … we Filipina women have more then meets the eye. But I believe that we Muslim women in the Philippines suffer more because of the double cross we are bearing. First as Filipina women and secondly as Muslim women … we Muslims are also negatively portrayed.

Eddy: I've seen your site and it's not just feminist territory. I can visit, too. Thanks!

These posts (among many others) tell me that *BagongPinay* is reaching a wide audience in positive ways.

Another small yet important triumph must be mentioned. Due to the generosity of Adrian Gonzalez of *Icestorm Services,* the domain of pinay.com has been on loan to *BagongPinay.* He bought the domain to save it from what he called "the wolves of the Internet" and then later he loaned pinay.com to *BagongPinay* in exchange for my patronage of *Icestorm's* hosting services. From 1998, I used pinay.com as a linking page to *BagongPinay.* In 2003, I made it a portal page that linked to *BagongPinay* plus other "quality Filipina sites."[20]

Nevertheless, *BagongPinay* and other quality sites still vie with the matchmaking and sex services for the top ten in *Google* and *Yahoo!* searches. Most, if not all, of these quality sites still don't appear in even the top fifty "Filipina" search results,[21] as they are outnumbered and outranked by matchmaking and sex sites. Why is this? I think that there are both simple, technical reasons and also complicated causes that relate to the underlying effects of colonization and the philosophies of imperialism.

Colonization, Nationalism, and Search Engines

To begin an answer, I must mention that the Philippines has experienced three colonizing imperial forces: Spain during the sixteenth to nineteenth centuries, Japan during World War II, and the United States from 1898 to the present.[22] One of the cultural consequences of U.S. colonization in the Philippines today is the widespread use of English as a second language: thus, the majority of Philippine citizens speak English in schools and in the workplace, hear English on television and radio, read English in newspapers and magazines, watch foreign movies in English, dress like Americans, and buy American-branded products as part of their daily life. The Philippines is also the only predominantly Christian country in Asia, a legacy from the Roman Catholic Spanish and Protestant American colonizers.

There is also the unseen psychological effect of colonial rule called *colonial mentality.* Leny Mendoza Strobel describes it as a Filipino's lack of ethnic pride and inability to articulate or manifest a strong sense of ethnic identity.[23] Renato Constantino calls it, in his nationalist essay of 1966, the "Miseducation of the Filipino."[24] While I cannot discuss all the identity challenges that Filipinos face due to more than four hundred years of colonial rule, I can briefly discuss how colonial rule and imperialism may have affected a challenge for Filipinas' ethnic and gender identity within cyberspace.

Earlier I mentioned that a cybermyth of Filipinas exists because of stereotyping commercial services marketing Western men's idealizations of Filipinas. I briefly mentioned that the reality of Philippine economic hardship is an important influence.[25] What I would like to add is that the early dominance of Western men on the Internet has also influenced the initial way Filipina identity was shaped on the web. Additionally, Internet technology has enabled an explosive growth of mail-order bride and pornographic industries.[26] Thus, a strong, multidimensional cyberPinay presence is still up against powerful, global, commercially viable industries that profit from the trafficking of women and sexist images. There is a continual prevalence of these sites in search engines and in traffic ranking over quality Filipina sites.[27]

I can share some of the technical reasons why this is so. From a programming standpoint, web producers of quality Filipina sites may have (1) failed to use the word *Filipina* as a keyword in their meta tags;[28] (2) failed to use the term *Filipina* frequently or at all in their homepage and subpages; and (3) failed to create rich interlinkages with other Filipina sites. These technical points are ways that *Google* and *Yahoo!*, the top search engines, rank sites in searches using the term *Filipina*.[29]

Moreover, I believe that there is a remarkable lack of use of the term *Filipina* within many quality Filipina sites and that this is also related to colonial heritage. First of all, *Filipina* is a term brought about by Spanish colonial rule.[30] Also, due to colonial rule by the United States, the Philippine-educated classes and mainstream media most frequently refer to Filipinas by the English terms of "women" or as "females" and less frequently as "Filipinas." There may also be the circumstance of using *Filipina* more frequently in an international or diasporic context when and where ethnicity and nationality are issues. What's more, foreigners may use the term *Filipina* in their websites more often then Filipinos themselves do, while Filipinas in the diaspora refer to themselves as "Filipino women," "Philippine women," "women of the Philippines," and "Pinay" more so than they do "Filipina" in their websites. Clearly, the usage of the term *Filipina* in cyberspace deserves further study. However, because of the way *Google* and *Yahoo!* work, we know that many quality Filipina sites are not applying technical elements that would enable their higher rankings in online searches and that, because of their higher and more frequent rankings, commercial matchmaking and pornography websites are, in fact, applying these technical advantages. What's more, commercially viable service sites (matchmaking and penpal) buy highly visible advertising space at search engines.

Additionally, I believe that most other quality Filipina sites have not attempted to respond to the cybermyth for reasons ranging from lack of technical know-how and resources, to lack of intent. The creators of the F.I.L.I.P.I.N.A webring have mentioned Filipina stereotyping online in their webpages. Thus far, *BagongPinay* and the F.I.L.I.P.I.N.A webring are the only quality Filipina sites ranked in the top ten of a query for "Filipina" at *Yahoo!* and *Google* (unfortunately, *BagongPinay* and most quality Filipina sites are not yet found in the top ten in most search engines other than *Yahoo!* and *Google*).

Regarding the Filipina cyberspace myth as being affected by colonial rule and even an imperialistic worldview,[31] I can only give abstract glimpses by conveying some parallels between the phenomena of the Filipina cybermyth and colonization. The dynamics of hierarchal status, power, and privilege are intertwined within these parallels:

- The racialized and non-egalitarian matchmaking sites and sex sites, owned and operated mainly by men in Western and developed countries, have created a damaging and stereotypical Filipina cyberidentity. This is synonymous with how Western colonial powers in the Philippines have had a debilitating effect on the racial and ethnic identity of Filipinos.
- The racist and sexist roles that we observe between women and men within nonegalitarian matchmaking sites or "mail-order bride" sites can be summarized as "the Western man is a source of financial security and the dominant, controlling partner" and "the Filipina is an obedient, dependent wife and submissive partner." These beliefs are analogous to Western conquerors' philosophy of the "White Man's Burden" that justifies their domination and control as the racially, economically, and culturally "advanced and developed" colonizer over the colonized "the little brown brother."[32] The colonized people are taught that they are backward and underdeveloped and learn to justify their dependence on and submission to their colonizer.
- Marriages of economic and social convenience brought about by mail-order bride services are tantamount to a form of marital "benevolent assimilation," whereby an economically and socially disadvantaged Filipina seeks to be assimilated into the foreign husband's country,[33] an "advanced" first world nation and world power (such as Australia, Germany, Japan, the United States, and the United Kingdom).
- The modern elements of racialized desire and sexual privilege that validate Asian fetish sex tours and porn sites are relative to historical, patriarchal perceptions of racialized superiority and economic privilege that

have validated U.S. military expansionism and corporate-market globalization within the Philippines.

Clearly the Western patriarchal worldview propagated by colonization and imperialism must be considered as we seek solutions to what has been, and still is, hurtful to Filipina identity online and to Philippine ethnic, cultural, and national identity. Before I end this essay, I will discuss an antithetical worldview.

There is a term that signifies the unlearning of colonial mentality and healing from colonization's negative effects: *decolonization*. Decolonization is described by Strobel as a holistic process by which one finds a progression of healing one's ethnic and personal identity. In *Coming Full Circle*, she writes that it is "a process of learning to love one's self again … of learning to face the truth and learning to tell the truth … learning to draw up the powers from the deep like before … going back to our roots."[34]

In my case, when creating *BagongPinay*, I consciously regarded it as a Filipina site because I was reclaiming Filipina identity online deliberately and defying a cybermyth. Although I did not consider *BagongPinay* a patriotic act in the beginning, I now recognize that there is indeed an element of nationalism inherent in its motivation and creation. Working on *BagongPinay* has effected a decolonizing, healing process for my very own ethnic and cultural identity. Additionally, *BagongPinay* is doing the same for others who participate at the site. Feedback from Filipino visitors shows that they are finding a measure of their own ethnic identity and pride, too. For example, Erlou Penado writes, "Opening the website always makes me feel good and proud of being a Filipina. Not only that it presents a positive image of us Filipinas but it tells more of who we are, what we think and what we have in our hearts. Thank you for keeping the site alive and constantly reaching out to other Filipinas."[35]

Nationalism—in the sense of love of being Filipino, of other Filipinos, of our ancestors' heritage, of *Inang Bayan*[36]—needs to be drawn upon to fight the cybermyth, to resist misrepresentations of who we are. Filipinas reclaiming and embracing their identity are experiencing a form of healing and decolonization. Moreover, when Filipinas consciously produce web content to reclaim their identity, they are expressing a form of Filipina feminism in cyberspace —a cyberPinay feminism.

Resistance and Empowerment, Cyberstyle

Today *BagongPinay* is an international community witnessing the different, and overlapping, issues and concerns that Filipinas face around the world: family, relationships, education, work, gender bias, sexual harassment, and domestic abuse. Issues like trafficking in women and children, corruption in leadership, brain drain, migrant labor, and poverty have become concerns for socially conscious Filipinos. No matter what country they have made their lives in, they are organizing together across oceans to take action and arrive at solutions. Clearly the Internet not only is a force that demonstrates to Filipinos how our experiences are similar and interrelated, but it is also a force we can harness to bring us together and mobilize us.

As founder, site director, impromptu editor, writer, artist, and discussion moderator at *BagongPinay*, I am witness to how NewFilipina.com develops and thrives from many Filipina voices in order to create an empowered and empowering online identity. Moreover, I have observed the excitement of hundreds of Filipinas evolving their own images. A year after *BagongPinay* came about, its mission and the overwhelming enthusiasm for it could not be contained within a single website and, thus, its *diwa*, or "ideals," also became an organization in February of 1999. It was named NewFilipina, Inc. (NFI) in honor of reclaiming our Filipina cyberidentity with the domain of NewFilipina.com.[37]

The organization relies on volunteers' giving of their time when they can and believing in NFI's goals: to broaden Filipinas' horizons and to help them discover and harness the power and strengths that they have within themselves; and to connect Filipinas to other Filipinas around the world, to ideas old and new, and to the means to take action for themselves and for others. The organization goals are not only Filipina empowerment but also upholding the identity of all Filipinos and, ultimately, Filipino community healing.

Many other creative efforts were born from *BagongPinay* and NFI's mission. In 1999, I set up an annual newsletter called *Tinig ng Pilipina sa Internet* (Voices of Filipinas on the Internet). We held informal Filipina networking nights in New York City. In 2001, I created a *BagongPinay* advice group—a big sisters' program with *ates* and *manangs*.[38] In Manila in April 2002, Valeria Tapalla and I debuted the first of many gatherings for women of different ages and backgrounds to celebrate feminine wisdom. We nicknamed these events *Wowee! Nights*.[39] In the summer of 2003, for an organization fundraiser, I created *BotikaBabae*,[40] an online store for *Babae*-Gear slogan T-shirts and books. With Mary Ann Ubaldo of *Urduja Jewelry*,[41] I designed a unique jewelry piece called the Babae Pendant as a special NFI fundraiser; for 2005, NFI is organizing the next Filipino American Women's Network conference in New York City.

Peminism and Pakikipagkapwa

After I began working on *BagongPinay*, I searched more deeply for my Filipino roots, and began exploring the background and meaning of feminism, because I wanted to clarify and deepen the meaning of the *BagongPinay's* and NFI's work.

My interaction with other Filipino organizations, leaders, and Filipina feminists grew as well. I began to encounter the Filipina feminism terms of *Pinay power, Pinayism* and *Peminism.* Just before I encountered Allyson Tintiangco-Cubales and her concept of Pinayism at the FAWN 2000 conference, I had written a *BagongPinay* editorial called "The Accidental Feminist." In it I related how I came to realize I was a feminist. In my own life, I had never taken up women's studies or read about the lives of feminists. I broke down my own previous hang-ups of "*what* a feminist was" by coming to know "*who* a feminist was" and *what* a feminist's work *was about.* Thus, by the time I heard about *Pinay power* and so forth, the varying terms' linguistic aspects did not concern me as much as their core meaning. To me, they all signify the Filipina faces of feminism, a sense of power within being Filipina, and a feminism that addresses the challenges facing Filipino women wherever they are in the world. I believe that all forms of resistance by Filipinas against exploitation fall under the category of Filipina feminism.

Today it should be requisite for the socially awakened Filipino to identify Filipina feminism and its forms, to discuss it and learn from it; however, it is also imperative that we not get caught up in separating it from various Filipina expressions of activism and advocacy. Nor should we set Filipina feminism against other contexts of feminism such as Western theory and practice. To prioritize expressions of feminism is to continue seeing things through a hierarchical perception that hinders progress by obsessing over superiority and resource competition. The Filipino consciousness of *pakikipagkapwa* enables us to see that the highest goals of different forms of feminism, and of all liberation and equality movements, are the same. *Pakikipagkapwa* is a worldview that within our deepest inner being *(loob)* all things are connected and united within Creation.

Patriarchal institutions and imperialism operate from a worldview based on a hierarchal order that establishes status and competition and justifies oppression and exploitation. This philosophy creates notions of superiority and privilege that underlie antagonism, colonization, racial discrimination, and male dominance. This philosophy is that of the Oppressors' and the Conquerors' of World History.[42] It is a philosophy based on external power and is, in fact, the exact opposite of what the deepest values of Filipino ancestry really are—that of *loob* and *kapwa* (connection and oneness with others).[43] Filipinos today must therefore realize that the antithesis of patriarchy's worldview is the Filipino consciousness of *pakikipagkapwa.* The philosophy is based on awareness of *lakas ng loob* (internal power) and spirit and how they give way to healing, compassion, and wholeness. Ultimately it can lead to widespread progress and unity among Filipinos and humanity. To recall this ancestral way of being enables Philippine people to embrace their identities and not look down upon themselves as inferior to their colonizers or to any other nationality, culture, or religion. Subscribing to the worldview of *pakikipagkapwa* and unsubscribing from the patriarchal worldview are inherent in decolonizing not only the colonized, but also the colonizer.

My journey with *BagongPinay* has given me first-hand experience and awareness of:

- Filipina Feminism, as an individual and collective experience.
- Pinay Power, existing within global Women Power.
- Pinay Power, interwoven with Filipino "People Power."
- Filipino People Power and Women Power, in turn, interwoven with the power of humankind.
- *Pakikipagkapwa* is an individual experience and a nationalistic experience. By other terms in the world,[44] I now know that *pakikipagkapwa* is universal wisdom expressed by Filipinos.

These new awarenesses have led me to feel the mysterious, spiritual aspect of feminism: the rise and awakening of women is a process in the healing of the ills of humanity. Within that concept, moreover, is interwoven the thread that Filipina feminism is also essential to the overall healing and wholeness of collective Filipino identity.

Whispers of Diwata

What really matters is that we do it with love.

—Marianne Williamson, *Woman's Worth*

The journey of *BagongPinay* has uncovered within me a deep connection to my ancestral home, the Philippines. *Diwa* is Tagalog for "idea," "concept," "essence," and "cause of inspiration and energy," so I believe that is exactly what *BagongPinay* manifests from—Philippine ancestral ideas, essence, energy, and inspiration. *Diwa* also means "spirit," "thread of thought," "consciousness," and "soul." Discovering all these meanings, I now find it compelling that the root word of *diwata* ("nature spirit," "enchantress," or "muse") is *diwa*.[45] Because *BagongPinay* has brought about such profound things for me, I think that there has been *diwata* guiding me as a Filipina—creating projects that explore and embrace the power of being a Filipina. This is important to me because as a Filipino American, the geographic dislocation of my identity from the Philippines has been reconciled by a spiritual connection.

BagongPinay, in the sense of its *diwa*, in turn, inspired a deepening journey of soul-searching so that I could deepen the meaning of Filipina feminism and keep true to its highest purpose. In this journey, I came to a conscious *pagbabalikloob*—return to the inner self, or self-discovery—and found the power of being Filipina and of my feminine strengths. I also found the spirituality of being a mother, wife, daughter, soul sister, woman, Filipina, and feminist.

I came to know personalized elements of Filipina empowerment as expressing *loob* in certain choices and actions:

- Reclaiming dignity and freedom for oneself.
- Expressing creativity and using one's talents and resources to serve others in finding their own dignity and freedom.
- Enhancing awareness and clarity through meditation, prayer, and spiritual practice.
- Believing in one's own feminine traits (intuition, compassion, and wisdom) and balancing it out with one's masculine traits (logic, control, and competitiveness) and being the best woman that one is capable of being.
- Believing one is here on Earth as a Filipina for a reason—owning one's identity as a Filipina and finding a way to contribute to Philippine-community healing and progress.

Because of the spiritual aspects of my journey, I have learned that at every moment, I must discern whether I am making a decision out of my ego or out of love. I am mindful now that one can make decisions based on the concept that one is separate from others (Western patriarchal worldview) or that one is connected to others (*pakikipagkapwa*). Empowerment is a state of finding *lakas ng loob* and inner power and, thus, finding more choices for oneself and making the most powerful choices that serve not only oneself but also the Greater Good.

Creating *BagongPinay* has helped me come to a perception that there is a sacred contract in being born a Filipino. This new consciousness has furthered the reaches of my creativity and expanded my interest in Filipino collective soul and explorations of what could be Filipinos' place in the "grand scheme of things." This mystical curiosity led me to create new explorations into *pagka-Pilipino* (being Filipino), such as the *Pagbabalikloob* online discussion group with Leny Strobel,[46] the esoteric concepts of archetypes and in artwork at babaylan.com,[47] and spiritual contemplations in The *Bahala Meditations*.[48] These works are born from the awakening experience of feminism and their beauty lies in their universality. They are relevant for people regardless of gender, race, nationality, or culture. These are further endeavors into deepening my journey into Filipino *loob* and *pakikipagkapwa*. Can the experience of Filipina feminism do the same for other women and men? I believe so. We are witnessing their stories unfolding even now.

Conclusion

I believe that many other Filipinas have become aware of what is happening on the Internet regarding limited representation of themselves and that, by becoming part of *BagongPinay* and/or through their own cyberworks, they have begun applying their own stories and their own resources to give dignity to Filipina identity on the Internet. In the process, other Filipinas have also gathered up or discovered self-love and even a sense of Filipino national identity. When we consciously produce Internet content this way, then we certainly bring about a form of Filipina feminism in cyberspace, a cyberPinayism.

Filipinas defying all gender and race stereotypes and myths—and taking an active part in creating and presenting their identity and transforming it for themselves, regardless of cyberspace—are part of the larger struggle of Filipino people reclaiming their identity. The deeper significance of Filipina feminism is that it is intrinsic to the process of Filipinos everywhere realizing themselves as a healthy, whole, and progressive nation.

Notes

1. *Pinay* is a Tagalog word for Filipina; thus, *cyberPinay* denotes a Filipina who uses cyberspace or the Internet.
2. According to GABRIELA Network's "A Primer on Sex Trafficking" (online at members.tripod.com/~gabriela_p/8-articles/990601_prose.html), from 1989 to 1998, 148,074 Filipino women left the country either as fiancées or wives of foreign nationals. The General Assembly Binding Women for Reform, Integrity, Equality, Leadership, and Action (GABRIELA) Network, or GABNet, is a Philippine–U.S. women's solidarity organization and works with GABRIELA-Philippines—the oldest and largest Philippine multi-sectoral alliance of more than two hundred women's organizations—against U.S. bases and local prostitution issues.
3. When the Philippine government enacted a law in 1990 outlawing mail-order bride businesses, many such businessess changed their description to offer "pen pal" services.
4. Dating, pen pal, and matchmaking service web sites with the domains that use the term *Filipina* include www.all-filipina.com, www.beautifulfilipina.com, www.filipina.ch, www.filipina.de, www.filipina-focus.com, www.filipina-ladies.com, www.filipina-ladies-personals.com, www.filipina-love.com, www.filipinabridesonline.com, www.filipinaconnection.net, www.filipinacupid.com, www.filipinafriends.com, www.filipinaheart.com, and www.filipinalady.com. There are numerous domains that contain *Filipina, Filipino woman* or *Filipino gal* that belong to porn sites. Even the domain that uses *babae* (Tagalog for "female") is also pornographic. The homepages of these sites contain prolific images.
5. Robert Scholes, Ph.D., with the assistance of Anchalee Phataraloaha, M.A. *The Mail-Order Bride Industry and Its Impact on Legislation* (Washington, D.C.: U.S. Immigration and Naturalization Service, 1999); full report available online at uscis.gov/graphics/aboutus/repsstudies/Mobappa.htm.
6. Venny Villapando notes, in "The Business of Selling Mail-Order Brides" in *Making Waves: An Anthology of Writings by and about Asian American Women,* ed. Asian Women United of California (Boston: Beacon, 1989), 322, that the business of promoting Filipinas as brides "takes advantage of the economic deprivation faced by women in underdeveloped Asian countries."
7. Scholes and Phataraloaha, *The Mail-Order Bride Industry,* notes that "20 percent are 16–20 years of age."
8. "People power" is the short name given to the historical events at which Filipinos demonstrated to the rest of the world that a peaceful means of change may be more effective than violent revolts. The "people power revolution" in 1986 made international headlines while over four days the vigilance of Filipinos by the millions, armed with nothing but prayers and flowers against military tanks and guns, helped cause the overthrow of Ferdinand Marcos's twenty-year dictatorial regime and restored democracy to the country.
9. The website for "We Remember People Power 1986, Philippines" is online at home.earthlink.net/~pdaly2/ppwrWe.html.
10. By 1994, Roncales-Goodwin was running a set of webpages called AKDA, a site on Philippine literature. She also created Picturesque Philippines, one of the first and best collections of Filipiniana on the web. With this site she also made a webpage for "various Filipina oriented links"; these webpages are no longer online. By 1998, Ilio was running the first web

directory of Filipino links, called Tanikalang Ginto, which is Tagalog for "golden links"; see www.filipinolinks.com.

11. Stephanie Brail created one of the first women's communities online; this service is no longer available.

12. Today, Webgrrls International's goal is to provide a forum for women in or interested in new media and technology to network, exchange job and business leads, form strategic alliances, mentor and teach, intern, and learn the skills to help them succeed in an increasingly technical workplace and world; see www.webgrrls.com.

13. *Morena* means "dark-featured," as in native Filipinos' black hair, black eyes, and brown skin.

14. *Makibaka* means "struggle" in Tagalog. As a slogan of student activists, it connotes perseverance and strength.

15. Read the "Who Is the New Filipina?" discussion at *BagongPinay*; available online at www.newfilipina.com/whois/index.html.

16. In 1998, the Philippines celebrated its centenary anniversary as an independent nation. June 12, 1898, is the date of the Philippine Declaration of Independence from Spain. See www.msc.edu.ph/centennial/independence.html.

17. In a video interview and through correspondence online between 1998 and 2004, Heinz Bulos, former editor of the Philippine-based *The Web* magazine and Internet consultant since 1998, has discussed with me the concept of Philippine Internet history and access, wireless technology and trends, and the "digital divide." He has explained that a good number of people get access to the Internet at work and school and that many people in the lower-income levels go to cybercafés, where people are charged by the hour to surf, chat, and play games online. Bulos is presently the editor of *Enterprise*, a business magazine published by ITNetCentral, which previously published *The Web*. Bulos, videotaped interview with the author, Manila, April 2002; e-mail correspondence, March 2002 and March 2004.

18. Visit the *BagongPinay* discussion on mail-order brides online at www.newfilipina.com/members/magsalita/98.12/SNM-MOB/forum.html.

19. In the United States and the Philippines, a handful of volunteers such as Joann N. Aquino, Lorial Crowder, Christina Dehaven, Bernadette Ellorin, Serina Fojas, M. Theresa Marino, Ronnie Miranda, Rushty Ramos, Olivia Maristela Rebanal, and Valeria Tapalla has helped promote and sustain the site with their time, energy, and talents.

20. For brevity's sake, I shall use the term *quality Filipina sites* to refer to sites and webpages that are by and for Filipinas and that add to a multidimensional image of Filipinas as opposed to the stereotypes of Filipinas as submissive wives and sex objects.

21. Search results mostly refer to searches performed on *Google* and *Yahoo!*.

22. Stanley Karnow, *In Our Image: America's Empire in the Philippines* (New York: Random House, 1989), 26–77, 288–322, 79.

23. Leny Mendoza Strobel, *Coming Full Circle: The Process of Decolonization among Post-1965 Filipino-Americans* (Manila: Giraffe, 2001), ix.

24. Renato Constantino, *Miseducation of the Filipino* (Quezon City, Philippines: Foundation for Nationalist Studies, 1966), 1982.

25. Mila Glodiva and Richard Onizuka, *Mail Order Brides: Women for Sale* (Fort Collins, Colo.: Alaken, 1994), 47, note that "the Third World [bride] sending countries often are mired in poverty, and they have deteriorating economic conditions and experience feelings of powerlessness."

26. Donna Hughes, "The Use of New Communications and Information Technologies for Sexual Exploitation of Women and Children," *Hastings Women's Law Journal* 13, no. 1 (2002): 129–48; available online at www.uri.edu/artsci/wms/hughes/new_tech.pdf.

27. Alexa.com, a subsidiary of Google, enables visitors to see the traffic ranking of web domains.

28. A meta tag is an HTML code that is found in the source code of a webpage; meta tags hold information about the webpage they are found in. Search engines use meta tags to categorize and sort webpages.

29. *BagongPinay* is not the only Filipina site that has applied these techniques and found a higher ranking at search engines. The F.I.L.I.P.I.N.A, a webring at filipina.happyclams.net, is another quality Filipina site that has managed to rank among the top ten. It is a compilation of links to online journals written by Filipinas. This particular webring has created a high frequency of interlinks with at least seventy-one other Filipina web journals.

30. The Philippine archipelago gets its name from King Philip II of Spain, the monarch in power when the Spanish first came to that country in the fifteenth century. Initially, the Spanish

did not refer to indigenous people in the Philippines as Filipinos but rather as *indios*. Spanish colonizers based in the Philippines were the first Filipinos. *Filipino* as a name for Philippine nationals of the republic is a relatively modern term.

31. Strobel, *Coming Full Circle*, 41–42.
32. Karnow, *In Our Image*, 167–95.
33. "Benevolent assimilation" is what the United States called their methods of colonizing the Philippines. The U.S. colonizers believed that they were to civilize Filipinos and make the colonized like the colonizer; see Karnow, *In Our Image*, 197–98. See also William McKinley, "Benevolent Assimilation Proclamation," December 21, 1898, at the website of author Jim Zwick, www.boondocksnet.com/centennial/sctexts/assimilation.html.
34. Strobel, *Coming Full Circle*, 50–51.
35. The feedback page at *BagongPinay* is www.bagongpinay.com/feedback/feedback.html.
36. *Inang Bayan* is Tagalog for "motherland."
37. NewFilipina, Inc.'s cofounders are Elke Aspillera, Serina Fojas, and Valerie Tapalla.
38. *Ate* and *manang* translate as "big sister" in the Tagalog and Visayan dialects, respectively.
39. *Wowee!* comes from the terms *women* and *wisdom* ("wo" from *women* and "wee" from w-i in *wisdom*) put together. *Wowee!* events also are described as "celebrating women's wisdom gatherings." More information is available online at http://wowee.org/
40. The store is found online at www.botikababae.com and www.babaegear.com.
41. *Baybayin* is an ancient Philippine indigenous writing system. Mary Ann Ubaldo of Urduja Jewelry crafts the Babae Pendant; information on her work is available online at www.urduja.com.
42. All of us, male and female, who have been raised in Western civilization or in these Judeo-Christian traditions have been socialized into this dream's way of perceiving the world—as a sacred order that ranks all diversity in relation to some preordained cosmic value. What we are dealing with is a chain of command that runs from what is up ("higher") to what is down ("lower"). It is assumed here that those above (adults, males, and ultimately God) give orders and create order, and those below (women, children, and the rest of nature) adjust and simply obey. Real "spirit"—that which has power and gives power and is valued, and is to be obeyed—dwells only in the top echelons of this pyramidal reality that characterizes dominion theology. From Augustine at the end of the Roman Empire through medieval times and the Reformation and on into the nineteenth century, this pyramidal view of reality was known as "the great chain of being." See Elizabeth Dodson Gray, "Nature as an Act of Imagination," in *The Goddess Re-awakening: The Feminine Principle Today*, ed. Shirley Nicholson (New York: Theosophical Publishing House, 1989), 272.
43. *Kapwa* is Tagalog for "both; fellow-being"; see Leonardo N. Mercado, *The Filipino Mind: Philippine Philosophical Studies II*, Cultural Heritage and Contemporary Change series vol. 3, Asia vol. 8 (Washington, D.C.: Council for Research in Values and Philosophy, 1994), 35.
44. Gray, "Nature as an Act of Imagination," 272, notes that "we are beginning to see ourselves living within the interconnected system of natural or biological reality on this planet, in a nonverbal companionship with the sky, the sea, the trees, the birds, the animals, the insects—a companionship in which diversity is valued and appreciated and never ranked."
45. The root of *Diwa* (proto-Austronesian) and *Diwata* (proto-Philippines) is *dyw* (proto-Indo-European) which means "divine" and "light."
46. Strobel calls this group Pagbabalikloob/Return to Home. Created in November 2001, the discussion group provides an online forum to discuss the body of works and the concepts of the process of decolonization for Filipinos (in the Philippines, in the United States, or in the diaspora). Available online at groups.yahoo.com/group/pagbabalikloob/. Discussion groups are mostly conducted through e-mail and should not be confused with discussion boards, which are conducted directly within posting forms on webpages.
47. *Baylan* is the Visayan term for "shaman." *Babaylan* is the term for a female shaman or priestess and for female leaders of Philippine villages and communities. Created in 2003, the website is www.babaylan.com.
48. *Bahala Meditations* are the contemplative writings of a personal Filipino spiritual practice. *Bahala* and *Bathala* translate to "great divine being" from Tagalog. Created in 2003, the transcript of *Bahala Meditations* can be found online at www.babaylan.com.

15

Ain't I a Filipino (Woman)?: An Analysis of Authorship/Authority through the Construction of Filipino/Filipina on the Net

EMILY NOELLE IGNACIO

Merging Computer-Mediated Communications and Postcolonial Studies

Both computer-mediated communication (CMC) and postcolonial scholars analyze the creation and re-creation of identity. However, these discourses have not intersected with each other because their reasons for studying identity transformation differ. Scholars who study CMC are generally concerned with how technology will affect traditional social units such as communities and the self.[1] Thus, they often document either the transcendence and/or erasure of traditional identities, and they express a concern that cultural identities will be homogenized because of the current U.S.-centric nature of the World Wide Web. These scholars show that the Internet can be an arena in which identity can be radically altered because it is constantly changing and transcends not only time zones but also traditional political boundaries. Most of the focus has been on gender identities as well as on the link between postmodern subjectivities and the Net;[2] however, none have shown how people online systematically and radically alter national cultures, race, and/or ethnicity.

Postcolonial theorists have been and still are focused on peeling away the "fixed shapes of historic ethnicity"; their studies often revolve around the fragmentation and (re-)creation of ethnic (as well as racial and gender) identities. Many seminal works on postcoloniality explore the development, maintenance, and possible decentering of national, cultural, racial, gender, and/or ethnic identities through archival research on a colonial period.[3] By studying the images of male and female colonizers/colonized, we learn how both patriarchy and ethnocentrism (and their intersection) were used to justify imperialism and colonialism. Deconstructing "embedded" stereotypes and grand narratives are two major goals of postcolonial writers.[4] Studies of construction in the present show us how racialized/gendered images of the colonizer and colonized continue to be maintained.[5] But they also show the importance of imagination and shared experience in possibly recreating images in such a way that they are antiracist, antisexist, and empower the colonized.

Still, postcolonial writers study the maintenance of racial, national, cultural, and/or gendered imagery outside cyberspace. This is not to say that postcolonial scholars have not written about the present impact of new global media on diasporic members. Arjun Appadurai, Paul Gilroy, Stuart Hall, and Rojagopalan Radhakrishnan are among many scholars who have traced cultural (re)productions across national boundaries.[6] However, postcolonial studies remain in the realm of "real life" and usually within the colonial period largely because most postcolonial scholars have been concerned with exposing the *origin* of the constructed images. I argue that Internet research can add to our understanding of postcoloniality (and postmodernity) in that it allows us to see the process of redefinition among self-defined members of diasporas. In addition, in cyberspace subjects are decentered; that is, there is the potential for more voices to be heard simultaneously.[7]

In this chapter, I show how participants in the Internet soc.culture.filipino newsgroup define membership in the Filipino community. I focus on their discussions about what constitutes a Filipina to show that "historic ethnicities" do travel into cyberspace. Specifically, their discussion of Filipinas reflects the participants' desire to differentiate their culture from the colonizers' (in this case, United States) culture that, some postcolonial theorists argue, many former colonies do to form a strong national and/or ethnic identity. Although participants did not explicitly talk about colonial history, anticolonial politics served as the backdrop of all discussions of identity. When gender was discussed, the category of Filipino woman was, in the words of Nira Yuval-Davis and Floya Anthias, a "gender marker" between nations.[8] In other words, essentialized images of Filipino versus (white) U.S. women were utilized to differentiate between the two cultures. As a result, in the discussion surrounding the stereotyping and commodification of Filipino women, the participants were not always concerned with Filipinas' rights as *women*. Rather, participants' postings reflected concerns with maintaining cultural integrity of an "authentic" Filipino community in that they firmly believed the idea that the maintenance of a race and culture is dependent upon controlling the women of that race and/or culture.

This strict dichotomizing between U.S. and Filipino culture marginalizes Filipino women (especially those raised in the United States) who do not fit the established mold of a "real Filipina." Because of participants' desire to redefine Filipino culture in opposition to U.S. culture, Filipino women who reject the sanctioned stereotypes of Filipinas are perceived as sellouts and often are ostracized. This caused at least one Filipino American to internalize the dichotomy and change her identity from a "Filipina" to a "woman [of Filipino heritage] born and raised in the United States."

These struggles shed light on the Internet's potential for giving voice to decentered subjects. While on this (and any other) newsgroup each poster is an authority in that anyone can post to the group and all voices have the potential to be heard, real-life hierarchies and inequalities continue to be perpetuated on the Net. This chapter will shed some light on how and why silencing and marginalizing continues in this new medium. With respect to political strategies, I show why a community of interest cannot use "simple identity politics" (e.g., a project to form distinctive identities) to fight oppression[9] but must try to use other tactics, such as what Bernice Reagon calls "coalition politics."[10] However, as we will see, defining the coalition is difficult, as members must negotiate the terms of membership that, in this case, are often outlined in reference to the U.S.–Philippines colonial relationship.

An Explanation of the Site and Methods

The soc.culture.filipino Community

The soc.culture.filipino newsgroup was established to "provide an open discussion on issues concerning the Philippines … [including the discussion of] Filipino culture."[11] This newsgroup may help others to understand "what our culture is really like and not what it is rumored to be." This newsgroup offers information about "real" Filipinos while simultaneously serving as a "virtual homeland"—a place where thousands of Filipinos can convene to exchange and discuss Filipino culture and society.

While the majority of those who post messages on soc.culture.filipino live in the United States, between 1995 and 1997, self-defined Filipinos have posted from the Philippines, Canada, Singapore, Australia, Austria, Sweden, and Greece. This newsgroup has allowed Filipinos to "go back home" and see what's happening there.

Filipinos in the United States cannot escape the computer revolution because we are constantly inundated with advertisements about global communication and the Internet. These promise global yet tight-knit communities on the web, herald the freedom of speech, and imply that the Internet world is egalitarian and without real-world structural barriers. The Net may appear to shrink the world, but many gaps have widened as well.

Sherry Turkle has described the communities she studied as "parallel worlds"; that is, they were separate from the "real world," and new communities and community practices emerged in these locations.[12] But many Internet communities are based on those within the real, nonvirtual world, including soc.culture Usenet groups. So even though the soc.culture newsgroups are located in a transnational virtual space, they are still based on traditional, boundaried spaces (usually nations). Thus, I argue, these particular transnational, virtual locations are "perpendicular worlds" that computer-mediated communication theorists have not yet systematically analyzed.

However, in a place that is supposed to liberate Filipinos from the sting, effects, constant reminders, and memories of colonialism to provide a virtual home for Filipinos who don't feel at home in their host countries and shift empowerment away from the center to the margin, Filipino women are silenced and rendered passive by the words of the largely male posters.[13] This silencing and stereotyping of Filipino women, which reflects patriarchy and sexism, are also closely tied to ideas of an authentic culture, nationalism, and anticolonialism.

Analyzing Newsgroup Conversations from a Cultural Studies Perspective

People constantly rearticulate their identity in nonvirtual locations. I witnessed this as I was growing up. Although these events were sporadic, I saw my aunts rearticulate their identities as relatives from the Philippines or third-generation Filipino Americans visited our home. On soc.culture.filipino I watched this articulation and rearticulation occur daily among people physically located in different places. By watching the debates unfold, I could see how members of the diaspora established what Filipino identity means to people back home and how people at home forged an identity with members of the diaspora, especially those in the old colonial country. Thus, despite many potential methodological problems with Internet research, this is an excellent way to study the transnational negotiation of ethnic identity formation.

I used the method of instances, used by conversation analysis researchers, to examine the features and structures of instances (in my case, posts and their related threads) on the newsgroup.[14] Mikhail Bakhtin has argued that, when studying conversations, scholars should study utterances and responses to utterances rather than structures of sentences.[15] As far as context is concerned, each utterance has its own context and is in itself a rejoinder to another utterance. The method of instances is based on the same premise: each instance (in my case, each thread and post) contains a context that members understand and to which they respond. I chose this method because I wanted to see what people debated, how the debates played out, and if and how they articulated Filipino identity during these debates.

Applying conversation analysis methods involved the process of (1) grouping the posts by thread, (2) analyzing each thread to find out what the major debates were about, (3) grouping the threads by debate (similar to grouping instances into collections), (4) reanalyzing each thread from a cultural studies perspective, and (5) choosing which threads to present in my study. My chosen threads facilitated an exploration of how Filipino identity is debated, reconfigured, and invalidated; what happened when members disagreed; and how debates were temporarily resolved. I aimed to present threads with topics frequently discussed from 1995 through 1997 so the reader could experience the kinds of debates that the participants engaged in during this time.

From 1995 to 1997 I logged onto the newsgroup at least once a week to see how the participants talked about, debated, and/or defined Filipino identity[16]; if anything within the post referred to Filipino identity, I saved and printed it. Most of the time I "lurked," simply reading the debates; however, if a person wrote anything that I felt needed clarification, I entered the discussion by posting a response to the whole newsgroup. As a participant-observer, my own stories and posts are included in the empirical material. If something within the discussions made me rethink my own identity, I either wrote it down in my notes or I posted a response to the newsgroup.

After analyzing and reanalyzing each thread in a collection, I separated them into two piles: "possibly present" and "don't present." The threads that immediately were placed in the "don't present" pile contained too many immature rejoinders and not enough substantive debate about the definition of "Filipino." Most threads ended up in this pile.

Of the two-hundred-plus threads I collected, roughly two-thirds of the discussions centered on Filipino women. These discussions often revolved around personal ads, but they also touched on issues such as the plight of mail-order brides and domestic workers. The common thread that linked all these posts is that they stereotyped Filipino women as "virtuous, traditional, yet sexually adept." To make things worse, mail-order bride catalogs and personal ad posts used these stereotypes literally to sell Filipino women. While many Filipino mail-order brides willingly entered such marriages,[17] the focus of the posts was not on their agency but on controlling the images of Filipino women. As we will see, this entailed the retention of stereotypical images of Filipino women, not their disposal.

In Whose Honor? Stereotypes of Filipino Women on the Newsgroup

> Where I come from (Norway) all we ever hear about is prostitution, child prostitution and poverty. In addition to that, "all" (most) Filipinas we see, are relatively young Filipinas that have come here to marry an old Norwegian man .... I think we just have to admit that Filipinas ... are viewed as "cheap."
>
> —From a white, male participant in Norway who wants to fight against the stereotyping of Filipino women

My friends' sordid stories and the numerous debates about Filipino women on soc.culture.filipino have made me suspicious of all men's intentions. Why are they paying attention to me? Is it because of me or because of the stereotypes of my race? Filipino women around the world have had to endure these stereotypes. But because of political and economic instability in the Philippines and the economic and political relationship between the Philippines and the United States, they have had to fight against another stereotype: that they are cunning women who would do anything to make money, including prostitute themselves or trap wealthy men into marriage.[18] This section briefly discusses prostitution in the Philippines and shows why Filipino women are stereotyped as prostitutes.

Cynthia Enloe argues that prostitution in the Philippines must be analyzed in relation to "nationalism, land reform, demilitarization and Filipino migration overseas."[19] Until the early 1990s, the United States operated several military bases to the Philippines. The three bases employing the most people were the Clark Air Base, Subic Bay Naval Base, and Wallace Air Base. Brothels around these bases were subsidized by both the United States and Philippine governments to provide soldiers with "necessary R and R."[20] When nationalists discuss prostitution in the Philippines, they usually point to the bases, arguing that militarized prostitution is not only a women's issue but also a threat to the integrity of the Philippines and Filipinos in general.[21] That is, they frame prostitution in anticolonialist, antimilitary terms.

However, Enloe shows that in the mid-1980s there were more brothels around tourist spots in the Philippines, such as Manila or Cebu City, than there were near the military bases.[22] During this decade, the government of Ferdinand Marcos developed the sex-tourist industry as a short-term strategy to bring in international currency and minimize the nation's deficit.[23] Marcos simultaneously capitalized on stereotypes of Asian women, stereotypes of "Eastern" and "Western" culture, and the growing feminist movements in Western countries to promote the sex-tourist industry. By pitting the images of exotic "beautiful Filipino girls" against "emancipated" Western (white) women, Marcos sold Filipino women as "natural resources" to foreign men who believed that "oriental" women were more available and subservient than women in their own countries.[24]

By 1991, one third of the tourists who visited Cebu, the second-largest city in the Philippines, were from foreign countries, including Australia, Canada, France, Germany, Italy, Japan, Switzerland, Taiwan, the United Kingdom, and the United States.[25] Although by 1992 the majority of the tourists came from East Asian countries such as Japan and Taiwan, Filipinos concerned about the sex-tourist industry tended to frame the issue in Western/Eastern and white/Asian terms.

Lisa Law has found that most women willingly enter the sex-tourism business.[26] However, she warns, we should not accept their stated motivation at face value, but instead look at their political and economic situation,[27] as well as the idyllic images of life in America and other Western countries that bombard Filipinos.[28] In fact, many scholars and Filipino feminist nationalists emphasize the structural factors that push Filipino women into the sex-tourist industry.[29] These Filipino women face high levels of unemployment and underemployment; thus, the high wages offered at "bikini bars" are attractive. Many of these

Filipino women are also drawn to the image of liberating, modern Western countries and often marry Western men in hopes of attaining that lifestyle.

Many Filipino nationalists draw attention to issues of prostitution, overseas workers, and the sex-tourist industry to expose the shortsightedness of the Philippine government's economic policies and the fact that Filipino women are treated as commodities.[30] Unfortunately, many people worldwide have conflated the commodification of Filipino women with the stereotype of Filipino women as prostitutes.[31] Thus, some people (including participants on the newsgroup) characterize all Filipino mail-order brides and entertainers as selfish gold diggers and dismiss the argument that some of these women were forced into these situations. In addition, many generalize this sexually adept, prostitute stereotype to Filipino women worldwide.

Lois West and others have shown that to combat this stereotype, yet another stereotype was constructed: that of the Maria Clara, or the proper, marriage-minded, Filipino Catholic woman with "good morals."[32] This has emerged simultaneously with the prostitute stereotype and parallels discussions of the Madonna/whore dichotomy prevalent in the discussion of other groups of women such as Latinas.[33] As stated before, many (but not all) Filipino feminist nationalists point to prostitution as a reflection of U.S. imperialism. This argument associates promiscuity and prostitution with Americanization and Western values. Filipino values, on the other hand, center on the family. Traditional patriarchy is not fought against, but embraced. In this way, the Spanish influence, despite being a colonial influence, is embraced, while the U.S. influence is rejected.

Despite these stereotypes' basis in U.S. military intervention throughout Asia, and despite the U.S. media's deployment of these stereotypes, participants on soc.culture.filipino nevertheless invoke these images. Various postings to the newsgroup indicate that such deployments complement the definition of an authentic, unadulterated, Filipino culture to dismantle the legacy of U.S. colonialism in the Philippines. References to this history of U.S. colonialism, which was never explicitly talked about, shaped the conversations about identity, including Filipina identity.[34] Because the stereotypes of Asian and white women have been consistently invoked to demarcate the difference between colonized and colonizer, it is particularly difficult for participants to isolate and challenge these stereotypes. Validated by their association with anticolonial politics, these stereotypes have become common currency on soc.culture.filipino.

These stereotypes of Filipino and Asian women are ubiquitous in the soc.culture.filipino newsgroup and on the web. The quote of the Norwegian participant indicates that the stereotypes are not just prevalent in the United States but have spread worldwide. With respect to the newsgroup, one particularly offensive thread called upon participants to list reasons "why Filipinas need to be loved." In this thread, respondents reinforced the stereotypes that Filipino women are hypersexual and are good (i.e., monogamous) wives. The fact that the initial poster's main concern was that "bad words" not be used shows that he considered these stereotypes of Filipino women as "normal," not degrading. This became particularly apparent when this participant stated that the contributions were meant to "honor Filipino women, not slander them":

> Please add your comment.
> Why are Filipina women great lover [sic]
> (please no bad words, remember your kids might read this)
> No. 10 She wash her flower everyday
> No. 9 She eats eggplant in the dark
> No. 8 She love lollipops
> No. 7 She loves to ride horsey-horsey
> No. 6 She is a mother, friend, and lover
> No. 5 She is monogamous
> No. 4 She always comes back (for more)
> No. 3 Her donut-hole is small

This post provides a variety of functions: first, it idealizes women who are both monogamous and sexually adept; second, it differentiates Filipino women from (white) U.S. women; third, it establishes a singular Filipina identity. Though this piece may seem like just a list of stereotypes, this particular definition of Filipino women was sanctioned because it was written by self-defined Filipinos who presented contributions as facts rather than as expressions of desire. And when stereotypes become "facts," they assume a certain legitimacy that is cited and deployed for diverse and sometimes conflicting arguments. For example, some respondents who seek Filipino empowerment embraced this thread because it differentiated Filipino women from (white) U.S. women. However, in embracing these characteristics, they (perhaps unwittingly) sanction the commodification of Filipinas.

The following is an example of how the stereotypes not only served as gender markers but also supported such commodification:

> I have a guy in Cebu City, Philippines. He's the father of a girl who married an American. This guy now makes his living by introducing visiting American guys to local girls. We are talking late-teen, young-20's virgins from (what over there passes for) lower-middle class families.

This post reflects the demand for Filipino women as wives and, like mail-order bride catalogs, panders to U.S. men. Its author, a frequent poster on the newsgroup, knew by the plethora of personal ads and ads for online mail-order bride catalogs that he had an audience.

This is not about getting laid. You most certainly can get laid any evening in Cebu for very little money (he can show you the ropes on that, as well). It's about getting one of those incredibly gorgeous girls in the dept stores or restaurants or wherever you saw her, to go out on a date with you ….

Here the participant acknowledges the common stereotypes of Filipino women as hypersexual yet "good" wives, as well as the image of rampant prostitution in the Philippines. Though there are prostitutes and "good wives" in any culture or nation, what makes this part of the post stand out is that this author puts all Filipino women up for sale. All Cebuanas are commodities, mere candy, at the disposal of pimps and their U.S. customers. The poster also assumes that all Filipino women desire the company of U.S. men. By rendering Filipino women commodities, desirable objects of exchange, he has completely stripped Filipino women of their agency.

Thus, even on a newsgroup created to discuss "what Filipino culture is and not what it is rumored to be," characterizations of Filipino women as hypersexualized commodities are rampant and are perpetuated by Filipino and non-Filipinos alike.

How the Anticolonialist Stance Reifies Colonialism: Reactions of Male Participants

Yuval-Davis and Anthias, among other scholars, have shown that nationalists often treat women as property, not as human beings with rights.[35] The phenomenon of Filipino women in relationships with non-Filipino men is often described as "losing our women" and therefore a threat to Filipino integrity. Responses to the above post parallel this argument. The first post below was from a Filipino man (Ray) in response to "the pimp," but, as we will see, he was angrier that Filipino men were left "out of the loop" than about the stereotype itself:

This guy is offering to connect whites (American guys) with Filipinas from Cebu. He wants to cut us Filipinos out of the loop and, frankly, I've had enough of this.

Another thing that makes this post stand out is that Ray (1) assumed that the "pimp" is "white" and (2) conflated "white" and "American." The normalization of American as white is not an uncommon move. However, as we will see in the next part of Ray's post, the conflation of white and American is utilized to highlight the twin evils of colonialism and racism:

If anyone is going to get a sexy, 19 yo. Cebuana to take out and have sex with—it damn better be me!

Taking our women and cutting us out of the picture, it's time for a real race war.

Scholars have shown that being able to control one's women is perceived as reflecting the strength of the nation and/or culture.[36] This is one of the major reasons that so many participants were angry about the stereotypes and commodification of Filipino women. Many of the participants were aware that many Filipino women were dating and marrying white (U.S.) men. In addition, many believed that white men posted the personal ads and web addresses for mail-order bride sites. Ray's wish to keep Filipino women "safe" from whites reflected his desire to preserve the cultural integrity of Filipinos and the race. Thus, the opposition to the commodification of Filipino women is not necessarily about *Filipinas'* rights, but about their rights *as Filipinos.*

Here is a quote from Bill, a frequent poster on the newsgroup, in response to the earlier post about buying brides. His arguments are similar to other posts leveled against mail-order bride recruiters and posters of personal ads:

SCF is NOT a Filipino news group as much as it is a magnet for Kanos with "yellow fever"—Kanos who's interest in the RP and Filipino culture is limited to "wanna have a Filipina."

This response and others like it all referred to the Kano/Filipino dichotomy, in which Americans are the "enemy" and Filipinos the "victim." *Kano* is technically short for "Amerikano" or "American." Often, Kano refers to whites, whether they are Americans or not, again reflecting the normalization of whites as Americans. In addition, when participants other than Ray used the terms *Kano* or *American*, race was often brought into the picture in that they assumed that all Kanos are white. This did not happen for just this thread; in all of the responses to these types of ads that I collected, only five (of about eight hundred) implicated nonwhite men. Again, the emphasis on white (American) men "taking our women" is related to the stereotyping of white men as virile and desirable and Asian women as hypersexual "good wives." And we will see that some of the participants attribute the fact that whites take Filipino women away from Filipinos to the fact that Filipino national identity is so weak. The feeling is that Filipino identity could be strengthened if Filipino women could be protected from white men.

Although it's true that Bill guessed the race of the pimp correctly, there is no evidence that only white U.S. men are involved in pimping/prostituting. In fact, many pen pal correspondence websites are maintained by white male/Filipino woman teams. U.S. men (especially white U.S. men) are held suspect because, although scholars have shown that many women have willingly entered mail-order bride relationships out of economic need or for personal reasons, these relationships have been historically linked to the continued economic and cultural colonization of the Philippines.[37] At the same time, Filipino women are seen as complicit in "selling out the race":

Since filipinos lack national identity and culture, I wonder if they are a liability to the asian race. filipinos have been raped by the spaniards, japanese, and americans. they don't have their own national identity and filipino women will marry anyone who is not asian ....

At first glance, this post may appear to be a debate only about the merit of interracial relationships. But the participant's frustration at the lack of national identity and culture shows that the arguments against interracial relationships are not just about race mixing; they are intertwined with the need to establish an authentic culture and independence from U.S. hegemony.

Unfortunately, in the struggle against the mail-order bride industry, pen pal services, and the prostitution and commodification of both Filipino and Asian women, all white male/Asian female relationships are questioned:

Everywhere I look, I see Asian women trying to sell themselves to any white man they can get and I also see Asian parents selling their daughters to any white men who will pay the most (about 3 dollars for white skin). Since the females are the most valuable asset a race can have, therefore Asians are losing out to the white race when it comes to the racial competition.

In this part of the post, a man named Jonathan alludes to the argument that forming a strong racial identity depends on maintaining gender boundaries around women. In the post, women who do not conform to the ideals of the group (e.g., Asian women who date outside their race) are labeled as traitors.

I also see Asian females bleaching their hair color, getting their eyes rounded, and trying to act white. Why are Asians so desperately seeking ***WHITE WASH*** treatment?

Jonathan equates women who actively try to change their physical features to look white with women who are in relationships with white men, yet these are two separate and not necessarily related acts. Although some women do alter their physical features and/or date white men because they are ashamed of their race, Jonathan leaves no room for Asian women in interracial relationships who are proud of their ethnicities and/or race.

Responses by Filipino Women: Does Decentering Give Rise to Multiple Voices?

The use of the Filipino woman as a gender marker between the United States and the Philippines discursively marginalized Filipino women participants who did not fit the criteria. This led to at least one person's redefining her identity. It is difficult to assess, numerically, how many and in what ways

Filipino women were affected because—as in other, nonvirtual communities—not many women joined the conversation. While it is apparent that most of the participants on soc.culture.filipino are male, this fact in and of itself does not explain why Filipino women did not participate in this particular conversation. I argue that the reason many women were silent is because of the threat of being known as a "race traitor."

With respect to interracial dating, Filipino women who stated that they are happy in interracial relationships (especially with white men) were derided mainly because of the belief that "yellow fever" runs through all Kanos. All participants in Asian women/white men relationships were criticized and stereotyped. One Filipino American woman in particular complained of the conflation of mail-order bride relationships with all interracial relationships. She began,

> I've always been opposed to [mail-order] brides. It gives relationships between Filipinas and American men a stereotype that basically disgusts me.

Then she tried to counter two stereotypes: (1) that all white men enter interracial relationships with Filipinas because of the stereotypes associated with Filipino women and (2) that Filipino women enter relationships for financial security:

> My beau fell in love with me not because I'm Filipina ... but because he could see me as an equal intellectually. At least that was the start. My parents are wealthy back home so there is no need to worry about offering financial help. Still, I hate getting stared at!!! I'm not sure whether it's because I'm tall [she's 5' 10", which is unusual for Filipino women] or because my beau is white!!! Grrrrrr!

But not all Filipino women responded this way. Interestingly, those who stated that they are Filipino nationalists (both men and women) also tended to portray Filipino women as "good wives" while at the same time fighting against the exploitation of Filipino women. Yen Le Espiritu's work in the San Diego area and K. A. Chang and Julian M. Grove's study in Hong Kong show that many Filipino women in communities outside the newsgroup embrace the stereotype of Filipinas as "good wives."[38] West and Espiritu, among others, have argued that this occurs because some Filipino women still want to differentiate themselves from American women.[39]

Although most posts concerning Asian or Filipino women have been written by self-defined men, many self-defined Filipino American women (including me) have expressed our opinions in just a few threads. One particular debate occurred when a Filipina feminist, Janet, attempted to reason with a man who posted this:

I have been to about 17 countries and have met people from all corners of the world. Filipina women seem to be the most perfect women for any man to have as a friend, wife, companion, lover etc ….

They are beautiful, they speak English, are moral and friendly but not promiscuous. Why would anybody ever want to look for a woman from another country? …

Janet warned against accepting the stereotype of Filipino women as "good wives." Instead, she wished to get rid of all stereotypes:

You seem to suggest to me that all Filipinas are beautiful, English speaking, moral, friendly and not promiscuous. I can think of specific Filipinas who do not possess one or more of the traits you so prize. Does that make them any less Filipina?

In this post, Janet offered counterexamples to undermine the essentialism and, at the end of her post, almost dared participants to characterize Filipino women who are not "beautiful, English speaking, moral, friendly, and not promiscuous" as not Filipina. Interestingly, no one publicly addressed her post. This, however, does not mean that she won the debate. What happened was that the other participants simply ignored this post, which in turn, caused this thread (and, therefore, Janet's voice) to die.

Meanwhile, the stereotyping of Filipino women did not cease after her letter. Despite this, Janet continued to reply to posts that contained essentialist images of Filipino women. In the following exchange, she attempted to reason with a man who posted a personal ad. As in the last post, she warned against accepting the stereotype of Filipino women as "good wives":

Well, I wish you luck in finding true love. Caveat emptor: not all Filipinas are as you describe. Make sure you get to know your future wife for an extended period of time before you marry her, don't just jump into marriage. What's worse: a bad marriage or divorce? The third time is a charm, especially if you make an honest effort to find out whether the person you're marrying is the right one for you. When you find the right person, no matter what her nationality, you shouldn't have to worry about divorce.

Despite her warning against stereotyping Filipino women, a participant whom I will call Scott chose to stereotype Janet based on her statements about divorce:

You see what I mean. Janet. If I were a betting man, I would bet it all that you are a Filipina. You are bright, sincere, concerned and caring for the future of a man and woman that you don't even know. You really feel that there is no need to worry about divorce. I do not believe that you would consider that as an option going into a marriage. I know a young, beautiful, intelligent American girl that talks with me about things from time to time. Just a couple of days ago, I was talking to her about marrying her boyfriend, which she plans to do. Her comment was: I hope, I hope it will be for the rest of my life. I pray we won't divorce. This is a wonderful girl, but do you see my point? She is going into marriage "hoping" there will be no divorce, but knowing it is a very distinct possibility. You will not even consider the possibility when you marry, of divorce. You will commit for life. Am I wrong?

Thus, Janet's warnings against stereotyping Filipino women were ignored, while her general statements about divorce were used to accentuate the differences between American and Filipino women. Janet replied to Scott's bet that she is a Filipina by stating, "Close. My parents are from the homeland; I was born and raised in the United States."

This part is interesting in and of itself because Janet, in all of her other posts, referred to herself either as a Filipina or a Pilipina. Although in her previous posts she frequently told the newsgroup that she was raised in the United States, she always made sure to refer to herself as a "*Filipina* raised in the United States" [emphasis added]. Her response to Scott, however, signaled a change in the way she identified herself. With the above statement, she differentiated herself from Filipinas located in the Philippines and, interestingly, did not use the terms *Philippine, Filipino,* or *Filipina* to refer to herself at all. This is significant because her most recent description emphasized her affiliation with the United States whereas previously she equalized her affiliation with the Philippines and the United States, which, I argue, is at least partially due to the discourse surrounding Filipino women in this newsgroup. She then responded to Scott's question about whether she would ever divorce: "I will commit for life. However, if I find myself stuck in a bad marriage, I will be *far* from passive about it."

Here Janet attempted to argue against the stereotype of Filipino women as good (dependent) wives by showing that she would not put up with a bad marriage. Her choice of words at the end is important because in stating that she, a Filipino woman, would be "far from passive," she attempts to invalidate the stereotype of Filipino women as submissive. However, by proclaiming that she is not a Filipina in the first part of her post and highlighting that she was born in the United States, she unintentionally allowed subsequent posters to "de-Filipinize" her and highlight her "Western" ways. One poster responded to her comments,

That's why I wouldn't marry a westernized Filipina, they're as bad as most white american women. Feel sorry for your boyfriend but that's his problem.

In the previous posts that I presented, participants accused Filipino and Asian women in general who chose to date white men as "whitewashed" women who were so ashamed of their culture that they were willing to sell out the race. But in this post, the person characterized Westernized Filipino women in general: all of them, regardless of their dating patterns, are to be avoided since they are just like white U.S. women. But, since the stereotype of Filipino women as "good wives" was initially created and is continually used to differentiate white U.S. women from Filipinas, Westernized Filipino women were marginalized from Filipinos (i.e., members of the culture) and not just from Filipinas.

Some participants were not as kind. Janet told the group that unfortunately she has been called a "feminazi" and "a white girl trapped inside a Filipina's body" because of her opposition to the "good wife" stereotype (and the other stereotypes). She contends that the most hostile responses have been from Filipino men because she's too independent and refuses to play along with the stereotype that Filipino women are "good wives" who would never divorce their husbands.

Again the dichotomy between [American] and Filipino is highlighted. *Filipina* serves as a marker between the two cultures, and Filipinas who fall between these cultures are not "real" Filipinas. In other words, Janet and other Filipino women who fight against all stereotypes (including stereotypes that differentiate them from American women) are marginalized and forced to ask whether they belong to the Filipino community. Neither fully American nor fully Filipino, they occupy a space somewhere in the periphery.

Conclusion

The focus on creating a unique cultural identity has created much confusion among the participants at soc.culture.filipino, especially among Filipino American women. I argue that this "strategic essentializing" of the Filipino woman has troubling implications because the participants fixed "Filipino woman" into one political position.

We have seen that in the struggle against the stereotypes and commodification of Filipino women, we need to take into account the positions of those expressing their opinions. Just because the participants joined the virtual Filipino community and/or consciously wanted to form a Filipino coalition does not mean that there were not socialized essentialist characterizations of races, genders, and cultures. In addition, since the participants (one hopes) spend most of their time engaging in real-life issues, we cannot expect them to leave their issues behind when they travel onto cyberspace. In this article, we saw that anticolonialism, though not explicitly discussed, affected the participants' definitions of what is or is not a Filipino. Here, as elsewhere, defining Filipino in opposition to American marginalized Filipino American women and upheld the gender hierarchy.

The promising thing about discussing issues like this on the Internet, however, is that the problems with using essentialist descriptions were somewhat exposed. Though there weren't a lot of posts that discredited the sexist essentialist descriptions of Filipino women, it is technically very easy to propose an alternative position. Also, the lack of moderation of most newsgroups ensures that alternative voices can he heard. Even in this newsgroup, for a while, it became very clear that a diasporic Filipino identity could not be formed using the old formula of dichotomizing two cultures. Partially because of this discussion on gender and another on the importance of citizenship in defining Filipino identity, participants tried to devise a classification system that would include Filipinos from around the world.[40] Through these discussions we all became more cognizant of the fact that Filipinos aren't all within the Philippines, cultural values aren't genetic, and culture isn't static. As postcolonial theorists have stated, we discovered (though temporarily) that to avoid marginalization, Filipino (and Kano for that matter) needed to be redefined in such a way that it both transcends national and racial boundaries and remains fluid. However, because of high turnover and the continuing proliferation of personal ads, the discourse revolving around Filipino women continued to be discussed using essentialist characterizations.

Identity is always in flux and created in relation to several political issues. When discussing identity in a transnational location, we can see the many inherent contradictions. Some participants (male and female), many of whom were interested in emphasizing the difference between the Philippines and America, did not view the "good wife" stereotype as problematic because it is used against the image of overly independent white Western woman. For many of them, the Westernization of the Philippines is the most pressing problem and, therefore, Filipinos should focus on retaining their culture and/ or protecting Filipinas from Western men. This goal clashed with the desire of others who wished to challenge essentialist images and who dismiss the distinction between Filipinas and American women that the former group wished to establish.

Emphasizing the fluidity of identities does not mean that we should not examine the power relationship between the United States and the Philippines. Cultural and economic colonialism are the root of various issues, including the commodification and stereotyping of Filipino women. However, as many feminists of color have stated, oppressions are linked, not hierarchical. Thus, we cannot choose between women's issues and anticolonialism but must address both simultaneously as well as racism, globalization, and other issues. As Audre Lorde has eloquently stated, "The master's tools will never dismantle the master's house."[41] Neither can we dismantle the master's house by remaining silent.

Acknowledgments

I would like to thank Greg Betzweiser, Norman K. Denzin, Yen Le Espiritu, John Lie, Judith Liu, Zine Magubane, Andy Pickering, Alice Ritscherle, Leigh Star, Judith Wittner, and two anonymous reviewers for their helpful comments during the preparation of this article.

Notes

1. Steven G. Jones, ed., *CyberSociety: Computer-Mediated Communication and Community* (Thousand Oaks, Calif.: Sage, 1995); Nancy Baym, "The Emergence of On-line Community," in *CyberSociety 2.0: Revisiting Computer-Mediated Communication and Community*, ed. Steven G. Jones (Thousand Oaks, Calif.: Sage, 1998), 35–68; Brenda Danet, "Text as Mask: Gender, Play, and Performance on the Internet," in Jones, ed., *CyberSociety 2.0*, 129–58.
2. Jones, *Cybersociety* (1995); Mark Poster, "Postmodern Virtualities," in *Cyberspace/Cyberbodies/Cyberpunk: Cultures of Technological Embodiment*, ed. Mike Featherstone and Roger Burrows (Thousand Oaks, Calif.: Sage, 1995), 79–96.
3. Vicente L. Rafael, *Contracting Colonialism: Translation and Christian Conversion in Tagalog Society under Early Spanish Rule* (Durham, N.C.: Duke University Press, 1993); Anne McClintock, "'No Longer in a Future Heaven': Gender, Race, and Nationalism," in *Sites of Desire, Economies of Pleasure: Sexualities in Asia and the Pacific*, ed. Lenore Manderson and Margaret Jolly (Chicago: University of Chicago Press, 1997), 89–112; Ann Stoler, "Educating Desire in Colonial Southeast Asia: Foucault, Freud, and Imperialist Sexualities," in Manderson and Jolly, eds., *Sites of Desire*, 271–317.
4. Stuart Hall, "Cultural Identity and Diaspora," in *Identity: Community, Culture, Difference*, ed. Jonathan Rutherford (London: Lawrence and Wishart, 1990), 222–37.
5. Ibid.; Paul Gilroy, *The Black Atlantic: Modernity and Double Consciousness* (Cambridge, Mass.: Harvard University Press, 1993); Rajagopalan Radhakrishnan, *Diasporic Mediations: Between Home and Location* (Minneapolis: University of Minnesota Press, 1996).
6. Arjun Appadurai, "Global Ethnoscapes: Notes and Queries for a Transnational Anthropology," in *Recapturing Anthropology: Writing in the Present*, ed. Richard G. Fox (Santa Fe: School of American Research Press, 1991), 191–210; Gilroy, *The Black Atlantic*; Hall, "Cultural Identity and Diaspora,"; Radhakrishnan, *Diasporic Meditations*.
7. Poster, "Postmodern Virtualities"; Mark Poster, "Virtual Ethnicity: Tribal Identity in an Age of Global Communications," in Jones, ed., *Cybersociety 2.0*, 184–211. Decentering subjects is a constant theme in postmodern, postcolonial, and sociology of science literature. In addition to Poster, other scholars in each of these areas have long debated whether technology will homogenize ("Americanize") people around the world or open up the arena, allowing multiple narratives; see, for example, Cheris Kramerae, "Feminist Fictions of Future Technology," in Jones, ed., *Cybersociety 2.0*, 100–28. On the Internet it is possible to see if, indeed, the decentering of subjects can help dismantle the grand narratives attributed to various races, sexes, cultures, and even sexualities. For example, in newsgroups there is the potential for thousands of people to contribute to one thread and—most important—especially on unmoderated newsgroups all of the posts have the "possibility" of assuming the same authority. It thus opens up the possibility for the proliferation of stories and local narratives, and the senders and addressees are on an equal plane. Given that within Internet newsgroups there is the promise that simultaneous posts can occur, that the authority of the senders and addresses are "flattened" and grand narratives can be broken down, and that diasporic members can create "virtual homelands," the Internet and computer-mediated communication are excellent routes to start studying how—or if—the "other" can re-create a nonessentialized subject/identity and, thus, redefine itself, a prime "goal" for colonized peoples.
8. Nira Yuval-Davis and Floya Anthias, *Woman-Nation-State* (Basingstoke, England: Macmillan, 1989).
9. There are various definitions of "identity politics"; Craig Calhoun, in the introduction to *Social Theory and the Politics of Identity*, ed. Craig Calhoun (Oxford: Basil Blackwell/Center for New Community, 1994), 21, notes that identity politics involves not only seeking recognition,

but also "refusing, diminishing or displacing identities others wish to recognize in individuals." However, Calhoun also describes new social movements that adopt a "soft relativism," a tendency to imply that "everyone is equally endowed with identity, equally entitled to their own identity, and equally entitled to respect for it" (24). Calhoun argues that this often naturalizes difference and fails to examine how difference is constructed. It is this type of identity politics that I refer to as "simple identity politics."

10. Bernice Reagon, "Coalition Polities: 'Turning the Century,'" in *Race, Class, and Gender*, ed. Margaret L. Andersen and Patricia Hill Collins (Belmont, Calif.: Wadsworth, 1992), 503–9.

11. Soc.culture.filipino, "List and Answers to Frequently Asked Questions," August 28, 1994.

12. Sherry Turkle, *The Second Self: Computers and the Human Spirit* (New York: Simon and Schuster, 1984).

13. Writing this article was an extremely difficult task. I know that I cannot remove myself from my writing; nonetheless, because I am an ethnographer, I tried very hard to distance myself from the posts. But, of course, I couldn't, especially since I was surrounded by my friends' stories about stereotyping, by negative media representations outside the newsgroup, and by my own experiences. In the two years that I participated on soc.culture.filipino, I became even more aware of my identity as a Filipino American woman and, quite unexpectedly, felt pain and anguish that I had never experienced before. As a sociologist, I have brought certain literatures and analytical frameworks to my ethnographic work. Specifically, I have been able to witness the effect of computer-mediated communication on the construction of racial, cultural, national, and gender identities. Thus, this study enabled me to link two different discourses together (computer-mediated communication and postcolonial studies) as well as to analyze the effects of new technologies on traditional identities.

14. George Psathas, *Conversation Analysis: The Study of Talk-in-Interaction* (Thousand Oaks, Calif.: Sage, 1995); Norman K. Denzin, "In Search of the Inner Child: Co-dependency and Gender in a Cyberspace Community," in *Emotions in Social Life*, ed. Gillian Bendelow and Simon J. Williams (London: Routledge, 1998), 97–119.

15. Mikhail M. Bakhtin, *Speech Genres and Other Late Essays*, trans. Vern W. McGee; ed. Caryl Emerson and Michael Holquist (Austin: University of Texas Press, 1986).

16. Before I began my research, I posted a letter on the newsgroup informing the participants of my study and encouraging them to e-mail me if they had any questions. Because of the large turnover of newsgroups, I reposted this letter every few weeks.

17. Lisa Law, "A Matter of 'Choice': Discourse on Prostitution in the Philippines," in Manderson and Margaret Jolly, eds., *Sites of Desire*, 233–61.

18. K. A. Chang and Julian M. Groves, "'Saints' and 'Prostitutes': Sexual Discourse in the Filipina Domestic Worker Community in Hong Kong," *Working Papers in the Social Sciences*, no. 20 (Hong Kong: Hong Kong University of Science and Technology, Division of Social Science, 1997).

19. Cynthia Enloe, *Bananas, Beaches, and Bases: Making Feminist Sense of International Politics* (Berkeley and Los Angeles: University of California Press, 1989), 39.

20. S. P. Sturdevant and Brenda Stolzfus, *Let the Good Times Roll: Prostitution and the U.S. Military in Asia* (New York: New Press, 1992).

21. Enloe, *Bananas, Beaches, and Bases*.

22. Ibid.

23. Ibid.; Chang and Groves, "'Saints' and 'Prostitutes.'"

24. Enloe, *Bananas, Beaches, and Bases*, 38.

25. Law, "'A Matter of Choice.'"

26. Ibid.

27. Ibid.

28. Raquel Z. Ordoñez, "Mail-Order Brides: An Emerging Community," in *Filipino Americans: Transformation and Identity*, ed. Maria P. P. Root (Thousand Oaks, Calif.: Sage, 1997), 121–42.

29. P. Azarcon de la Cruz, *Filipinas for Sale: An Alternative Philippine Report on Women and Tourism* (Manila: Aklat Filipino, 1985); Lois A. West, "Feminist Nationalist Social Movements: Beyond Universalism and towards a Gendered Cultural Relativism," *Women's Studies International Forum* 15, nos. 5–6 (1992): 563–79.

30. Chang and Groves, "'Saints' and 'Prostitutes.'"

31. Ibid.

32. West, "Feminist Nationalist Social Movements."

33. Gloria Anzaldúa, *Borderlands/La Frontera: The New Mestiza* (San Francisco: Aunt Lute Books, 1987).
34. In 1898, the United States "acquired" the Philippines, Cuba, and Puerto Rico from Spain as part of the Treaty of Paris for $20 million. They also annexed Hawaii and other Pacific islands in 1898 to increase sugar production. Soon after, the little-known Filipino-American War broke out as the United States attempted to establish control of the Philippines. The war lasted more than ten years and more than six hundred thousand Filipinos died as a result of fighting, disease, and starvation. Members of soc.culture.filipino often allude to this Filipino resistance, the Katipunan, and urge present-day Filipinos to get rid of their "colonial mentality" and resist the continuing cultural and economic influence of the United States. See Emily Noelle Ignacio, "The Quest for a Filipino Identity: Constructing Ethnic Identity in a Transnational Location," Ph.D. diss., University of Illinois at Urbana-Champaign, 1998.
35. Yuval-Davis and Anthias, *Woman-Nation-State.*
36. West, "Feminist Nationalist Social Movements."
37. Chang and Groves, "'Saints' and 'Prostitutes'"; Yen Le Espiritu, *Asian American Women and Men* (Thousand Oaks, Calif.: Sage, 1997). Law, "'A Matter of Choice'"; Ordoñez, "Mail-Order Brides."
38. Espiritu, *Asian American Women and Men;* Chang and Groves, "'Saints' and 'Prostitutes.'"
39. West, "Feminist Nationalist Social Movements"; Espiritu, *Asian American Women and Men.*
40. Ignacio, "The Quest for a Filipino Identity."
41. Audre Lorde, ed., "The Master's Tools Will Never Dismantle the Master's House," in *Sister/ Outsider: Essays and Speeches* (Freedom, Calif.: Crossing, 1984), 112.

16

"A-walkin' fo' de (Rice) Kake": A Filipina American Feminist's Adventures in Academia, or A Pinay's Progress

MELINDA L. DE JESÚS

This essay explores what I have come to regard as two sides of the same coin: my experiences as a diversity-initiative postdoctoral fellow at an intensely white New England university and as an assistant professor of Asian American studies in the San Francisco Bay Area. The title refers to Kake Walk, a University of Vermont (UVM) institution based on the minstrel shows of the 1890s.[1] Below, I delineate how my fellowship at UVM was predicated on a specific kind of "kake walk": I was to demonstrate my gratitude and appreciation for UVM's pursuit of "diversity" to its (white) administrators amid a climate of racial hostility and intimidation toward the small yet vocal and militant students of color and their supporters who were agitating for the establishment of ethnic studies programs and programs for the retention of students and faculty of color. Later will I outline how my former position in Asian American studies at San Francisco State University (SFSU) demanded a different kind of kake walk: the "rice kake" of my title was predicated on my demonstrating eternal obligation to Asian American studies' cultural nationalist agenda, as well as my ignoring the blatant misogyny, homophobic heteropatriarchy, and anti-intellectualism that my former colleagues promulgated in the name of "ethnic" solidarity.

My Postdoctoral Year in Vermont

In a packed gymnasium, five thousand white people, and perhaps two or three people of color, watch intently as two white college students put on a caricature of African Americans. Their hands and feet are white, exaggerating the fact that, to some whites, blacks have large hands and feet, whose palms and soles are not the same color as the rest of them. The students' faces are colored black, but it is not a human color. Rather, like the "pickaninny" dolls of the nineteenth century, this black is unnatural. Large, white eyes and mouth sockets exaggerate the perception whites have that the eyes and lips of African Americans are too big, stand out too vividly against their skin color. Outlandish kinky-haired wigs complete the effect, not so much comic as mildly repulsive, although the audience seems to view it with affection. The students now begin to strut and kick up their legs in a ritual called "a-walkin' fo' de kake." When they have finished, they bow humbly to a white couple with crowns on, seated in a place of honor. They shuffle off like Stepin Fetchit in the old Hollywood movies. The crowd shows its appreciation with wild applause. This is UVM Kake Walk, an eighty-year fascination with a stereotype of blacks in the whitest state in the Union.[2]

In 1995 and 1996, Citibank, the University of Vermont, and the New England Board of Higher Education brought eight predoctoral candidates and one postdoctoral candidate (me) to the UVM campus to increase "diversity." The Citibank Fellowship, according to the recruitment ad in *The Chronicle of Higher Education*, would "support an African American or Latino/a American for one or two years as he or she engages in teaching, research and scholarship at The University of Vermont. The fellowship experience is expected to contribute to the development of strong credentials for assuming a faculty position at The University of Vermont or another institution of higher education."

Most fellows worked on completing their dissertations while teaching a course or two in their field; some expected the fellowship to culminate into job offers at the university. That same year Citibank announced the reorganization of its fellowship program to support "international scholars."

In July, when I first came out to New England to look for an apartment, I was overwhelmed by the sea of green below my airplane window, the verdant carpet a soothing contrast to the dry, brown Northern California landscape I was used to. Once on the ground I was even more astounded by the state's incredible whiteness. Strolling along the main shopping plaza with my Anglo partner, we observed people wearing turtlenecks—and it was 85 degrees …. I was never so aware of my physical differences as when I moved within this sea of white faces. "Do you mind if I ask what you are?" the perky salesgirl inquired. "Yes," I replied. In mid-August, we drove out of Santa Cruz for Vermont, my little blue car crammed with my computer, books, CDs, and other necessities. The highway stretched before us like a shimmering ribbon. Once we left the Painted Desert, America took on a surreal sameness. Everything resembled Pennsylvania, my home state, replete with green rolling hills, acres and acres of corn shimmering in the afternoon sun, the ecstatic "Jesus is Lord!" billboards. We started playing a game called "¿Cuantas personas de color están aquí?" Each day the count

never amounted to more than three (including me). We drove into Burling-
ton in early autumn, when the trees had just begun to show their changing
colors, and my partner, after helping to settle me in, took the plane back to
California.

Prior to leaving Santa Cruz, I had read Kirin Narayan's delightful *Love Stars*
and All That, a coming-of-age story and tongue-in-cheek send-up of academic
life. Narayan's protagonist, Gita Das, a University of California–Berkeley graduate student, takes a one-year position at "Whitney" nee "Whitey," a fictional
private college in Vermont. Little did I know how closely Gita's experiences
would parallel mine:

> As an old and respected small liberal arts college, Whitney catered
> mostly to Caucasian students from wealthy families on the East Coast.
> Gita's first new classes left her with a blurred sense of blond hair,
> designer clothes, and ruddy health. Certainly the college was trying hard
> to bring in financial aid students from a diversity of backgrounds, but
> there was a certain truth to defacement of the *n* in the Whitney sign by
> the main gate. No matter how often campus authorities repainted that
> sign, or how often the small white campus security car patrolled past,
> that *n* continued to be missing.[3]

Once I was on campus, the English Department (which sponsored me)
was not quite sure what they wanted from me. My dissertation was finished
and filed, yet there were no opportunities for teaching. I affiliated myself
with the women's studies program; the feminist reading group; the fledgling
African, Latino, Asian, and Native American (ALANA) studies program; the
Office of Multicultural Affairs (OMA); and the Asian Student Union (ASU).
I joined the chamber chorus and sang Bach's *B-Minor Mass* in the middle
of a major snowstorm at Stowe, home of the Von Trapp family and its ski
resort. Through my association with ASU and ALANA students who were
headquartered at OMA, I learned more about the history of people of
color on campus and the events that lead to the founding of the Citibank
Fellowship Program itself: in 1991 ALANA students had staged a twenty-
two-day takeover of the president's office; later that year they established an
alternative Diversity University on the campus green, but it was destroyed by
fire.[4] In response, the Commission on Racial Equality and Multicultural
Education was formed and plans were set in motion for founding ALANA
Studies. In June 1995, Anthony Chavez was fired as director of the OMA for
alleged fiscal mismanagement, under great protest by ALANA students and
supporters. During my year at UVM, ALANA activists Shontae Praileau
and later Kei Kurihara went on a hunger strike to protest the university's

disregard for ALANA students' issues and its refusal to sign the ALANA Student Bill of Rights.

The ALANA activists at UVM are a core group of African American, Latino, Latino, Asian American, Native American, and mixed-race students (less than 5 percent of UVM students are of color). They are incredibly impressive: articulate, outspoken, focused; they model a truly multiracial coalition united to work for racial justice on campus. Organized, committed, eloquent, they are unafraid to challenge the administration. Never have I experienced such a sense of community and coalition.

As I began to ask questions about this history, I noticed that administrators and faculty alike were becoming defensive. How dare I ask colleagues how they situate their whiteness when attempting to do antiracist work, to teach ALANA studies? Two visions of ALANA/ethnic studies began to emerge: one based on personal experiences of institutional racism and/or the desire to dismantle all forms of oppression, the other a component of feel-good multiculturalism for the predominantly white student body. It became clear how ALANA studies would be co-opted by the multiculturalist stance of the university, just as the ALANA students feared.

Throughout a series of heated meetings between ALANA students and ALANA affiliated faculty and administrators, I find myself sitting exactly between the two groups, trying to build bridges. If forced to choose, with whom would I align myself: the militant ALANA undergraduates or the faculty members and administrators?

In "Black Image in White Vermont: The Origin, Meaning, and Abolition of Kake Walk," James Loewen writes, "The period of Kake Walk's founding, 1888 to 1893, saw more blacks lynched in the United States than any other time in our history …. Reflecting [the] white supremacist mentality [of this period], UVM students routinely built their skits around racial themes, including cannibals, lynchings, American Indians, 'Orientals,' Jews and the Ku Klux Klan. It was no accident that Kulled Koon's Kake Walk contained three Ks. Later, 'Kake Walk' was sometimes set in type that emphasized its three Ks."[5]

I contend that the institutionalization of Kake Walk at UVM's Winter Carnival, its eighty-year tradition, and the controversial banning of it from the campus, along with the history of the ALANA students' activism, say volumes about UVM's racial climate.

A Story: The Woman of Color's Burden

The biweekly feminist reading group was the highlight of my fellowship experience. I met many wonderful, brilliant men and women from all over campus, and our lively discussions were much more compelling than my graduate seminars had ever been. For one meeting in March we read and discussed Elizabeth Fox-Keller's "Making Gender Visible in the Pursuit of Nature's Secrets," which explored the androcentrism of scientific rhetoric.[6] Fox-Keller ends her article with the example of the Manhattan Project and how the creation of the atomic bomb is a salient example of gendered scientific knowledge: tracing the rhetoric of male birth throughout, she notes that women closest to the Manhattan Project were probably the secretaries of the great men building weapons of mass destruction; not even the wives of the bombs' creators knew about this top-secret project until the very end. Our discussion, as I recall, centered around how scientific and mathematical knowledge is deemed the domain of men, creating a vicious cycle of disempowerment for women. We brainstormed ideas on how we might reverse this trend. I listened for about an hour, then finally posed my questions: How are racism and sexism intertwined in this example? Why is Fox-Keller, so outraged that women were not privy to the Manhattan Project's information, so blasé about the intended victims of this knowledge? What did it mean that the bombs created to end the war were designed to be dropped on the people of Hiroshima and Nagasaki while simultaneously Americans of Japanese ancestry on the West Coast, two-thirds of them American citizens, were being held in concentration camps, denied their civil rights? How does Fox-Keller's whiteness privilege her relationship to this history of science, her demand for equal access to the power of this knowledge? What of coding the term women *here to mean* white *women? Moreover, how did our reading group's whiteness enable it to make the same assumption? Would white women scientists, if allowed on the Manhattan Project, oppose such an act of destruction or would they regard it as a necessary tool of nationalism and world peace? Isn't it more important to discuss how science is imbued with power (and by whom), power it then wields against those deemed "undesirable"—for example, the people of Hiroshima and Nagasaki, or even the working-class white women sterilized without their knowledge through eugenics experiments right here on UVM's campus? I spoke of the need for more complex analyses of the range of hegemonic affiliations and investments surrounding this historical moment, Fox-Keller's analysis of it, and our own reading strategies. But what I really wanted to ask was this: Why is it my job to problematize the intersection of race and gender in this reading group every time we meet?*

Loewen notes further that the Kake Walk "reminded slaves that planters controlled their lives, their leisure, and even their bodily motions. It told whites that they were powerful and important—the same conceit behind hiring only black waiters in fancy clubs today."[7] The same could be said about my fellowship experience. The university, by developing this program, expressed its desire for a specific kind of diversity fellow—scholarly, obliging, grateful and nonconfrontational, a controlled and controllable entity who resembles it in thought and deed, packaged in the body of a visible racial minority. In essence, UVM expected its fellows to perform in blackface: to appear "ethnic" on the *outside* but be sure to be white through and through (i.e., only "Oreos," "coconuts," "bananas," or "Twinkies" need apply). Because the program functioned like a revolving door, the fellows were fleeting images that lent the campus a hint of "color"; thus, the university would appear to have changed while the racist power structure of the campus remained intact. In this way, the fellowship program underscored who controlled academia and, hence, our careers.

This final anecdote best describes the day-to-day reality for people of color at UVM. I left Burlington in May 1996 to begin working at SFSU. A few months later I received e-mail from a black female colleague in UVM's administration concerning her harassment by a white student engaged in completing a course assignment called Diversity Scavenger Hunt. The well-meaning but naive Anglo instructor of the Race and Culture course, hoping to demonstrate to her students how few people of color worked for the university, assigned them the task of locating a specific number of staff/faculty of color all over campus and securing their signatures as "proof" of student interaction with each "target." Needless to say, the targets of the "hunt" found the exercise humiliating, embarrassing, and infuriating, just another example of UVM's racist status quo.

"Go West, Young Woman": My Job at San Francisco State University

But let me warn those who ally themselves too closely with the feminist movement: Feminism is a white women's movement, originally designed to reduce the voting power of black men [sic]. Alice Walker and Amy Tan are fine writers. But once they attack their own race, they become the worst traitors to their communities.

Even white cultural colonialists can't get away today with portraying men of color as animalistic. When supposedly enlightened women of color so willingly backstab their culture, it's unforgivable.

—Hoyt Sze, "Sexism in Asian American Studies"

This doesn't mean that we have placed our loyalties on the side of ethnicity over womanhood. The two are not at war with one another; we shouldn't have to sign a "loyalty oath" favoring one over the other. However, women of color are often made to feel that we must make a choice between the two.

—Mitsuye Yamada, "Asian Pacific American Women and Feminism"

I returned to California from Vermont in high spirits, with high hopes. Not only would I get to live with my partner and my four cats again, I had landed a tenure-track job in a tight market and I was excited to be back in the classroom. SFSU is an urban university with an enrollment of more than 28,000 students; more than 30 percent of this population is Asian American. This diverse campus witnessed the founding of the field of ethnic studies during the Third World Student Strikes of 1968 to 1969, and I would be part of the first Asian American studies program in the country. I was aware of some of the problems at SFSU—namely, the sexism, cultural nationalism, and anti-intellectualism outlined by Lane Ryo Hirabayashi and Marilyn Alquizola in "Asian American Studies: Reevaluating for the 1990s." Hirabayashi and Alquizola critique the program at San Francisco State, and Asian American studies in general, in the following way:

> What we remain sorely in need of … is a retheorization of a more diverse and inclusive field that also entails newly framed visions of relevance and accountability …. The bottom line is simple. We can no longer rely upon the exhausted tropes of cultural nationalism, whether these be "ethnic specificity," the essentialized unity of ethnic-specific experience, ethnic solidarity or even "the community". … The pursuit and evaluation of what constitutes Asian American Studies should be self-determined by a collective body of Asian American scholars, committed to a range of theoretically informed practices, rather than by distanced practitioners of traditional disciplines. Only then can the critical integrative field of Asian American Studies continue to grow and evolve in its own right as a component of Ethnic Studies, which was the very point of its creation in the first place.[8]

During my job interview, the current department chair assured me that things had changed significantly since the article was published in 1994.

I enter my very first classroom on this, my first day on the job, to teach my course in Filipino American literature. It is amazing for me, still Pennsylvanian after all these years, to step into a classroom and see so many Pinoy faces—and not one from my own family! From my hometown of about seventy Filipino Americans (in a town of 72,000) to a region with over 25,000 . … As I distribute the syllabus and prepare to present my course rationale, a Pinoy, possibly in his 40s and dressed like Che Guevara, beret and all, interrupts me and makes it clear that he's here to check up on "what I think I'm doing on campus, what I think I'm teaching" as "'they' don't know me," and I'm "just a name on a piece of paper." My heart begins to beat wildly, and my face is hot. More than the usual doubts ("I'm an academic fraud!" or "This student is old enough to be my dad!"), this is worse: suddenly I am

*in an indefensible position. My scholarship and pedagogy in Asian Ameri-
can studies have become eclipsed by the fact that I am just an "inauthentic"
Pinay from somewhere on the East Coast; I'm not really Filipino because
I'm not from Daly City (where many Filipinos live), and I'm not part of
the "community" (so loosely defined). Theories about the construction of
subject positions and identities are obscured by identity politics. Despite
thirty years of excellent scholarship, "Filipino" in this case still means male-
centered, straight, and manong- and California-centric .... The students
watch, some with grins, as he informs me that "everyone" knows him as a
"community activist." Che, who must make a nice living as he can afford
to come to my class midday and heckle me, continues to try to distract
me and my class. I'm rattled but go on with my course introduction. Later
I check with my department chair: he's somewhat sympathetic, tells me I
need to take care of it myself, and reminds me that I don't have to allow
unregistered students to audit my class. Next time Che appears, I'm ready.
Students stare as I demand that Che leave the room and speak to me in
the hall. Once I confront him, though, Che is suddenly meek; he won't look
me in the eye, he mumbles his name, his desire to sit in on my class this
semester. I firmly tell him "no"—that he's taking the seat of a paying
student. As Che slowly saunters down the hall, I practice breathing in and
out, in and out.*

Despite my former chair's assertions to the contrary, the cultural nationalist agenda is alive and well at San Francisco State. This time I'm "a-walking fo'
de *rice* kake": I am expected to perform my ethnicity or culture, but only
within the narrow confines of the prescribed role dictated by the senior members (all men, except for the wife of the chair). Rather than demonstrating the
solidity and depth of my training and pedagogy as a junior faculty member,
I am judged solely in terms of how I enact the role of "Filipina," how I teach
what I "am." My interests in "theory," particularly feminist, cultural, and queer
theories, are seen to "compromise" my allegiance to Asian American studies,
thus hindering my overall performance in the department.

*With two other junior faculty members, I attempt to start an Asian Ameri-
can studies reading group. I pick two articles—one by Colleen Lye on postmodernism, "Yellow Capital and Labor," and one by Evelyn Hu-de Hart on
the future of Ethnic studies. At our scheduled meeting time, only one other
faculty member arrives. He has not read the articles but is there to inform
us that we "can't just start a theory reading group," we "must consult with
members of the department who were present during the student strikes to
hear their ideas about Asian American studies." It is implied that the theory we desire to interrogate is "inauthentic," that "real" Asian American*

studies theory can only arise from "the community," from those moments in 1968 to 1969 ....

Attempting to bridge the gap between Ethnic studies and the English Department, I, with the support of the chair of the English Department, start a multicultural reading group. There is a flurry of interest from the English faculty; however only one faculty member from Asian American studies comes to the monthly meetings .... The reading group falters, unable to situate Asian American within its specific cultural context, its literary history. No one would think of reading William Shakespeare, William Faulkner, or even Toni Morrison without knowing about the time period in which each wrote! I am frustrated; why does this never change?

The following is from my second-year probationary review:

Asian American Studies does not have the luxury of being a traditional department to have built-in professional prestige or disciplinary recognition, nor does it enjoy enormous national academic support as the cases with feminist studies or African American studies. Being a new academic discipline of intellectual inquiry, Asian American Studies needs its faculty to commit their professionalism to advance its disciplinary mission. If ladder-rank faculty members in Asian American Studies do not have the professional and intellectual commitment to their employment discipline, it is fair to neither the department nor the individual. As department chair, I will not compromise this aspect of disciplinary integrity. I am concerned about this matter since Assistant Professor de Jesus has spoken to me about her preference to be a feminist literary critic and that Asian American Studies is a constraint.

My experiences at SFSU make my months at UVM seem like a slumber party. While I have come to expect insensitivity and racism from whites, I am greatly disappointed by my colleagues in the Asian American studies department there. It exists in the past, in an intellectual void: its preference for unexamined identity politics and cultural nationalism translates into wholesale denigration of contemporary critical race theory and research in general, and the promulgation of an intensely anti-intellectual climate that students embrace wholeheartedly. Similarly, while the senior members of my department disavow any intellectual investment, they are clear about their desire to maintain what the institutionalization of Asian American studies has afforded them: nice salaries, job security (tenure and full professorships), and gatekeeping power in regards to recruitment and curriculum development. How did this become the legacy of the Third World Student Strikes of 1968?

Lesson Learned (The Hard Way)

While my year in Vermont was characterized by loneliness and isolation, compounded by anxiety concerning the job market and the undefined nature of my presence in UVM's English department, I learned that not all white people are my enemies, that well-meaning people of all races often step on and over one another, that one can find good colleagues everywhere. What lives on in my mind and heart is the image of the truly cross-cultural, multiethnic solidarity of the ALANA students and the Committee for Racial Justice. They are my models for engaged, coalitional activism.

In contrast, I learned that having more faculty members of color on a campus is no guarantee of harmony or coalition. In addition to ignoring the innovations that cultural, women's, and queer studies bring Asian American studies, SFSU's Asian American studies department has splintered itself into discrete entities—Chinese, Vietnamese, Filipino, and Japanese American studies. This merely reinforces the idea that one's allegiance and identification is acceptable only along one sole trajectory—ethnicity—coded as "male," that theories of the construction identities and subjectivities (i.e., race, gender, class, and sexuality) are anathema. Indeed, the ideal of a Pan-Asian culture, so necessary to the formation of Asian American studies itself in 1969, has vanished along with any recognition of commonalities with other people of color.[9]

Additionally, SFSU's College of Ethnic Studies, the only college of its kind in the United States and the first-ever program in ethnic studies, is itself splintered, fractious. Its embarrassment of resources (more than thirty faculty lines!) seems to have bred arrogance and distrust rather than cooperation and coalition. Moreover, the ghettoization of faculty of color into one college (by choice or by the administration?) has created an atmosphere of competition for funding and resources, engendering bitterness and tension while the university's status quo is maintained.

Most of all, I've learned that the woman of color in academia is expected to be visible yet silent, seen but not heard. I defy that expectation. Moreover, I refuse to choose between loyalty to my "race" and loyalty to my gender; I refuse to disavow my intellectual interests, just as I am learning how I might best contribute to the Asian American community, a community I have never known until now.

Keeping Faith

The miracle is not to walk on water. The miracle is to walk on the green Earth in the present moment, to appreciate the peace and beauty that are available now.

—Thich Nhat Hanh, "Life Is a Miracle"

While revolution must begin with the self, the inner must be united with a broader social vision. Many people are deeply engaged in complicity with the very structures of domination they critique. Without critical vigilance there is no way to correct this mistake …. Militant resistance cannot be effective if we do not first enter silence and contemplation to discover—to have a vision of right action. The point is not to give up rage, rather that we use it to deepen the contemplation to illuminate compassion and struggle ….

A fundamental shift in consciousness is the only way to transform a culture of domination and oppression into one of love. Contemplation is the key to this shift. There is no change without contemplation. The image of Buddha under the Bodhi tree illustrates this—here is an action taking place that may not appear to be a meaningful one. Yet it transforms.

—bell hooks, "Contemplation and Transformation"

I will continue to work between the disciplines of literary, cultural, ethnic, women's, and queer studies, articulating tensions, seeking common ground. Scholars like myself are the dream, not the nightmare, of the student strikers who agitated for the establishment of ethnic studies back in 1968. As part of the first graduate school cohorts who *could* research and write about the intersections of these disciplines, I represent a new generation of scholars: women of color coming from a wide range of geographic, economic, and disciplinary backgrounds, interested in melding activism and theory, the personal, political, and intellectual.

Women scholars of color privilege models of scholarship and activism that emphasize multiple affiliations and coalitions, common struggles because we are working toward an ever-widening picture of social justice rather than just myopic cultural nationalism. Our work needs to be understood within this holistic, syncretic context. Furthermore, if we want more women of color to enter academia and *to survive once inside*, we need to make sure that there is adequate support and mentorship. And support must extend beyond diversity fellowship programs and job offers; we need to ensure intellectual and spiritual sustenance within an often debilitating, isolating system. Academia is exhilarating but often solitary: we write, grade, teach, prep, and research alone. We need to create networks of support, which will sustain us as we train the next generations.

Thus, I continue to struggle along this path, alone, without a map, without visible means of support. (Look Mom—no net!) I'm tired. But this is not my story alone. I've seen too many good friends, excellent teachers and scholars, walk away from the academy in disgust, near to breakdowns, tired of fighting—and for what? Success in the academy means nothing if we have to sacrifice our integrity, our self-esteem, and our psychological well-being.

> *Oftentimes I need to remind myself why I'm here: to study literature, to immerse myself in the complexity and beauty of language itself; my desire to teach and read works by authors who look like me, something I did not have as an undergraduate; my desire to nurture the minds and souls of students of color, as well as my own. What sustains me: great class discussion about Asian American aesthetics, reading a truly wonderful student essay, falling in love again with a novel I've taught four times before, the deluge of ideas when I begin to write a new essay.*

I remain homeless: between disciplines, generations, theoretical affiliations, ethnicities, and locations. I continue to seek coalition and refuge with others like me, a woman in the borderlands. I make and remake my intellectual and spiritual space as I struggle to transform this world into a place that can accept me, contradictions and all.

As women of color in an era of increasing hostility toward the already disenfranchised, we know that we cannot find strength in "kake walking" for anyone but in our ability to create and maintain multiple affiliations in our pursuit of social justice. Into the next century our work will be to resist any one ideology or movement that would demand our pledge of allegiance while we continue, as always, to voice our truths, to nurture ourselves and our communities, and to build coalitions with others engaged in liberation struggles—all in the name of creating a just and compassionate world.

Coda

I am now assistant professor of Asian Pacific American studies at Arizona State University and would like to elaborate upon the events leading to my resignation from SFSU. Sympathetic SFSU students had informed me that my "colleagues" had been searching for a Filipina to write a letter against me. In September 1998, the following letter, demanding reconsideration of my hire, was sent to my department chair, the dean of the College of Ethnic Studies, the president and the provost of SFSU, the Academic Senate, and the Equal Opportunity Program. The author was never a student of mine and I have never been introduced to her; nevertheless, her missive precipitated my request for a professional leave in spring 1999, and the rhetoric it represented fueled my search for a more amenable academic position. I have included the entire letter below as I believe it speaks volumes about the culture and values of SFSU's Asian American studies program and the atmosphere of intimidation and ill will which characterized my five semesters there.

September 8, 1998

Dear [dean of the College of Ethnic Studies and chair of Asian American Studies]:

I would like to bring to your attention that there is a professor in your department who does not emulate the standards towards positive learning by fostering students in learning basic facts needed particularly in order to progress in taking classes in Asian American Studies. The professor I am referring to is no [*sic*] other than Melinda De Jesus [*sic*].

Although I understand that S.F. State University is aimed to provide excellent education like the UC [University of California] system, by hiring and bringing in instructors with PhD's; however, I believe that though the intention is well, [*sic*] the results are detrimental. This is because S.F. State University is a feeder university to the surrounding bay area community. This means the professors at SFSU (most of them at least) are in touch with the issues within the community. The problem that comes ups [*sic*] when SFSU hires PhD graduates who are from a different locality or even graduated in a non-SFSU type of environment is that these professors tend to teach in a different style that tend [*sic*] to become a mismatch condescending teaching format to our students enrolled in Asian American Studies. In addition, because of this teaching format, the students tend to become withdrawn, rather than motivated towards the class material itself. Melinda De Jesus is one of three Filipino-Americans who teach Filipino-American classes. I am one of those students who [*sic*] currently serves [*sic*] my community outside of S.F. State University as a TV reporter for a local Filipino-American daily newscast and also in the capacity as a Commissioner for the S.F. Immigrant Rights Commission. Last year, I also served on the Academic Senate as the graduate representative for the entire school body. And the year prior, was [Associated Students] Vice-President for S.F. State University. I have vested interest to assure students who come up to me on a daily basis that this mistake will be corrected, and will be changed to ensure that ... [my copy of the page is cut off here].

As mentor to younger classmen, particularly those who take Asian American classes, I have noticed a drop of interest in these classes because of these new professors that [*sic*] really have no clue whatsoever in teaching S.F. State students. May I reiterate that I am not implying that S.F. State students are different from your average students at other universities, but I do know that most are on financial aid, have either immigrated here to the United States at an early age or most recently [*sic*], and are just finding out what it is to be part of America, as an Asian American student. With all this said, it is crucial that our students receive the best education possible because through these classes will they be able to become an asset to their communities.

Another aspect is that [Melinda De Jesus] teaches in the Filipino-American realm of Ethnic Studies, but is she really connected with the community? Quite honestly, it seems that she was hired under the false pretense that because she has a PhD from a UC, that she's capable of serving that part which lacks in the Filipino-American segment …. [The next sentences are blackened out in my copy of the letter] I think if S.F. State's answer to the necessity of bringing in a Filipino-American professor is Melinda De Jesus, then we are truly making a big mistake. What we (the Filipino-American students) need is a professor who is in-touch with the students in terms of community advocacy as well as academic theory which solely translates really to the reality of the question, "Upon completion of this course, What and how will this student apply knowledge learned within this class to outside these classrooms?" I say if the student cannot apply knowledge outside the classroom the course has failed. In this case, Melinda De Jesus has failed to teach her students what the reality of Philippine Literature really is.

I am requesting that each one of you look closely into this situation. It is not fair for the students to get mediocre education, most especially in areas pertaining to ethnic studies. I would be delighted to speak with you in person to offer more insight on the issue.

Maria-Lorraine F. Mallare

My goal in including this letter—indeed, in writing this article—is to air the dirty laundry of Asian American studies programs and to raise consciousness about the realities of women of color in the academy: too often, feminist scholars of color, construed as threats to ethnic studies' androcentric, cultural nationalist imperative and/or its "activist" roots, are vilified and disciplined by their own colleagues and communities for being "bad" daughters. It's time for a reality check: the field of Asian American studies has changed dramatically in thirty years and must acknowledge its growing pains. Only by confronting conflicts around professionalization, institutionalization, activism, and community, as well as the issues of cultural nationalism, the "old boy network," and its grudging acceptance of new Asian American studies scholars—particularly feminist scholars, will we create newer, more inclusive models of Asian American activism, theory, and pedagogy for the new millennium.

Dedication

This essay is dedicated in love and struggle to HHT, MCS, AA, BH, SS, and the ALANA student activists and their allies.

Notes

1. For an incisive history and analysis of this phenomenon and its repercussion, see James Loewen, "Black Image in White Vermont: The Origin, Meaning, and Abolition of Kake

Walk," in *The University of Vermont: The First Two Hundred Years*, ed. Robert V. Daniels (Hanover, Vt.: University Press of New England, 1991), 349–69.

2. Ibid., 349–50.
3. Kirin Narayan, *Love Stars and All That* (New York: Simon & Schuster, 1994), 171.
4. Tom Huntington, "UVM students protest firing of UVM official," *Vermont Collegian* 6, no. 1 (1995): 6–7.
5. Loewen, "Black Image in White Vermont," 354.
6. Evelyn Fox-Keller, "Making Gender Visible in Pursuit of Nature's Secrets," in *American Feminist Thought at Century's End: A Reader*, ed. Linda S. Kauffman (Cambridge, Mass.: Blackwell, 1994), 189–90.
7. Loewen, "Black Image in White Vermont," 351.
8. Lane Hirabayashi and Marilyn Alquizola, "Asian American Studies: Reevaluating for the 1990s," in *The State of Asian America*, ed. Karen Aguilar-San Juan (Boston: South End, 1994), 361.
9. For more information on the circumstances that led to founding Asian American Studies programs, see William Wei, *The Asian American Movement* (Philadelphia: Temple University Press, 1993); Yen Le Espiritu, *Asian American Panethnicity* (Philadelphia: Temple University Press, 1992); Ronald Takaki, *Strangers from a Different Shore* (Boston: Little and Brown, 1989); and Sucheng Chan, *Asian Americans: An Interpretive History* (Boston: Twayne, 1991).

17

Not White Enough, Not Filipino Enough:
A Young Mestiza's Journey

MICHELLE REMORERAS WATTS

Carl: What's up with the fancy clothing anyways?
Jack: I'm up for a promotion, that's what ….
Carl: You're in line for a promotion? I thought … I mean, you know?
Jack: They don't know. Everyone there thinks I'm Italian.

—Michael Arago, Pol Gravados, and Anthony Snow, *Silencio*

In the film *Silencio*,[1] a light-skinned mestizo rejects his Filipino-ethnic heritage and "passes" as Italian in order to get a promotion.[2] However, my experience as a brown-skinned, female mestiza has been much more complex than the stereotyped world of white-privilege from which certain "full-blooded" individuals accuse mestizos of benefiting.[3] Taking one glance at my silky dark-brown hair, brown skin, and rounded brown eyes, the majority of people I encounter immediately categorize me as Latino. As a result, I have received much derogatory treatment. Interestingly enough, as soon as people find out that I am part Asian, their disposition toward me changes and they make comments such as, "Oh, that's why you're so smart." These individuals dismiss my academic achievements as exclusively a result of my assumed racial inheritance, uninfluenced by my educational background, socioeconomic status, and personal investment. There is no doubt a racial hierarchy in America that draws hardly justifiable correlations between physical characteristics and certain intellectual, physical, and artistic skills and capabilities. As a mixed-race American, my position on the hierarchy fluctuates up and down based upon people's perceptions of "what" I am.

Gender also plays a significant role in affecting people's behavior toward me. As a driven and intelligent woman, I am perceived as a threat to men who are still unconsciously or consciously caught up in the mentality that men are innately more capable than women. They try to find ways to suppress my efforts so that they can remain or get ahead of me. The men who are supportive, however, more often than not have underlying sexual motives. This is a frustration, because I want people to support me for my academic and activist merits rather than lustful desires or curiosities.

Due to the rapidly increasing numbers of mixed-raced Filipinos in America, it is important that we develop a more in-depth understanding of the mestizo and mestiza experience. As a contribution to this focus area, this essay reflects on how socioeconomic status, educational and family background, race, and gender have interacted in my personal development as a mixed-race Filipina American.

The Earlier Years

I spent my childhood and adolescence living in a lower-economic-class area of Los Angeles, predominantly Latino and Southeast Asian, in a neighborhood with graffiti on the sidewalks and bars on every window. However, for the majority of my primary school education (grades K–12), I attended a very exclusive and expensive private school, the Buckley School. Embedded in the upper-middle-class hills of Sherman Oaks, just five minutes north of the illustrious cities of Beverly Hills and Bel Air, some of the school's most well-known graduates include the celebrities Tatiani Ali, Tevin Campbell, Sara Gilbert, Alyssa Milano, and Matthew Perry. Many rich and famous people, including Billy Idol, Tito Jackson, Quincy Jones, Will Smith, and Rod Stewart have sent or are currently sending their children there. Even though I was awarded a full scholarship from the tenth through twelfth grades, my parents and I had to spend numerous breakfasts, lunches, and dinners eating twenty-five-cent packages of Ramen noodles in order to afford my second- through ninth-grade education on partial scholarship. Some might judge my mother as irrational for insisting upon having me sent to a school our family could barely afford. However, all she wanted was what she perceived to be the highest-quality education for me at any and all costs.

My mother spent eight difficult years in the United States before I was born, struggling to secure the precious American Dream for herself. She never succeeded in accomplishing her initial expectations. In the Philippines, particularly in her *magandang-maganda* tropical hometown of Loon, Bohol, she was respected as a scholar. She was one of the few to be on a full scholarship to the University of the Philippines as an undergraduate; in addition, she continued to excel there as a law student. Nonetheless, despite her years of education, she was forced to become an overworked, underpaid paralegal in the United States. By the time she felt ready to bear a child, her ultimate goal in life was to have her child live the "American Dream" for her. As she would tell me, "I want you to have much more than I ever did. We may be sacrificing much for you to attend Buckley, but it's an investment; an investment in your future."

After a year in the United States, she married my father, a man of mixed ethnicity: French, English, and Native American. However, because of his fair-skinned complexion and blue eyes, U.S. racial categorizations would place him as "white." People of color may speculate why my mother, with beautifully thick black hair, deep-brown skin, and almond-shaped dark eyes chose to marry a phenotypically white man. They may accuse her of attempting to hasten the citizenship process or of finding a sellout means to insure that her offspring would be born into a higher status than she herself had. These people fail to realize the complexities behind my mother's choices in life. My mom's biological mother passed away when she was only seven months old. Consequently, my mom was raised by a physically and mentally abusive stepmother and a biological father who did not care enough to stop the abuse. In the Philippines, my mother was engaged to a Filipino medical doctor, but he was killed in the Vietnam War. She married my father because he was the first man who showed the care and affection she so needed and desired since Mark died. Many people of color have the tendency of pointing their finger at intermarried Asian women and yelling, "Whitewashed!" or "Traitor!" By doing this, they are viciously using our women as scapegoats without even taking into consideration their personal struggles and backgrounds. They are avoiding what we truly should be challenging, the societal structures and institutions that work against people of color. It is toward the mass media and the U.S. educational system that we should be directing our energy.

To my mother's misfortune, my father treated her very badly while they were married. His care and affection prior to marriage disappeared soon after the wedding vows were taken. I blame a large part of this on the movies and TV images my father grew up with, which taught him that third world women are sexual yet servile creatures, made to serve the white man's every wish. I blame this on the textbooks my father read as a child, which patronizingly described Filipinos as the "little-brown brothers" of the United States. My father did not physically abuse my mother but treated her as if she were a lower-class individual. He would find every possible way to criticize her and would talk badly about her to his relatives and to me. My parents would constantly fight. When I turned thirteen, they separated and finalized their divorce by the time I reached twenty. However, I was lucky, because the one thing they always agreed upon was that they wanted ultimate success for me in life. I saw my father every day after the separation until I went off to college, as he had moved into an apartment fewer than five minutes away. Both my parents wanted me to create waves in the world, to make a difference, and to be a good soul.

My father developed a career out of the U.S. Navy. After dropping out of high school to join the U.S. Naval Supply Corps for several years, he produced morale-building TV shows, which were broadcast at U.S. Naval Bases. He was particularly known for the Sailor of the Week, Month, and Year programs. Older than my mother by more than twenty years, my father was retired by the time I was born. So, while my mother worked full-time and, often, several hours overtime, he stayed with me at home. When I was very, very young, he read books with me; he taught me arithmetic before I even started kindergarten, drove me to gymnastics classes, told me about his world travels as a Navy man, and played softball with me in the park. On the weekends I would spend time with my mother. She would drive me an hour away to the University of Southern California School of Performing Arts, where I would take violin, dance, acting, and music theory lessons. Already, by the age of five, my parents had molded me into an extremely well-rounded individual, more than ready to begin my studies at an elite private school.

I did encounter racism and classism at the Buckley School. Many of my classmates lived in immense mansions with gorgeous views in Beverly Hills and Bel Air, and had two or more relatively new luxury cars. Their homes were equipped with swimming pools, tennis courts, large gardens with colorful and sweet-smelling flowers, and all the latest in electronic equipment. After visiting a friend's house, it would be difficult for me to go home to my neighborhood, filled with relatively tiny houses and apartments, unwatered brown grass, and old, barely functioning economy cars. The very same people who cleaned my classmates' immaculate homes everyday constituted a good percentage of my neighborhood's population. I was lucky enough to live in an actual house but was unable to appreciate it at the time because of the relativism. As students from wealthy backgrounds would make fun of students from upper-middle-class backgrounds, I dreaded inviting anyone from Buckley over to where I lived, which was to them a "poor" neighborhood.

Uniforms made it slightly easier to hide class difference, but I could not hide my brown skin color. I endured much discrimination due to my Latina appearance. The only other Latinos that these predominantly white and Middle Eastern American students knew were their housekeepers and gardeners and the janitors at school. As apparent from their conventions, several of these students looked down upon these hardworking service workers and blamed them for their lower-class status. This racism came down on me as well. People would point at the janitors, laughing hysterically, while asking, "Hey Rosarita! Is that your father? Are you going to end up like that? Cleaning up our shit?"

Despite all the harassment, because I excelled in my classes and demonstrated aptitude at both sports and performing arts, I was able to garner enough respect from my classmates to become a popular candidate for student government. I was elected as fifth-grade class president and to student government positions every year from then on through my senior year of high school. I was known as the "Renaissance Woman" of the Buckley School. In high school, I served as co-concertmaster of our concert orchestra, was on the varsity softball team and varsity cheerleading squad all four years, and excelled in all my honors and advanced placement (AP) courses. I completed a second year of AP calculus during my junior year and took linear algebra and ordinary differential equations classes at a local junior college during my senior year. I graduated as salutatorian and delivered the opening student address at my graduation. My high school experience, though with its extremely difficult challenges, seemed like an almost-too-good-to-be-true, rags-to-riches fairy tale.

Looking back, I recognize I am privileged to have attended an institution such as Buckley, which, despite the uncountable experiences of racial and class discrimination, supported my talents and assisted me in attempting to reach my academic and leadership potential. At Buckley, the faculty-to-student ratio was very low. My high school graduating class, which was considered large for Buckley, had fewer than seventy people, yet our class had two college counselors. Of course, not every student got accepted into the Ivy League schools, but on average, 100 percent of each year's graduating class matriculated into college. In comparison, the college matriculation rate of the public high school, which I would have attended had I not gone to Buckley, was less than 50 percent.

At Buckley, I noticed that the students from relatively less-well-off backgrounds tended to be the ones who got accepted into the most competitive collegiate institutions. I came to the conclusion that this is because we did not take our expensive, quality education for granted and worked very diligently in realization of this. Many of our extremely rich classmates seemed to forget their parents paid $13,000 annually—merely a small fraction of their gross family income—for their tuition. They spent the majority of their free time frolicking around Beverly Hills; spending money on extravagant clothes, parties, and cars; and mingling with other rich and famous people. For almost all of my rich classmates, an upper-middle-class future was the guaranteed minimum. For many of these students, one or both of their parents were legacies at an elite U.S. college. If "legacy" status was not enough, Daddy or Mommy had millions of dollars to fall back on. "Poor folk" like me did not have the status or money upon which to depend. I had little choice but to be a high achiever in my classes and extracurricular activities, or else my parents' economic sacrifice for my education would feel like a complete waste. My many accomplishments at a young age resulted in my acceptance into Stanford and Harvard universities and the Massachusetts Institute of Technology, among other top U.S. institutions.

My Experiences as a Pinay Activist at Stanford

Out of all the universities that I was accepted into, I matriculated into Stanford for several reasons. First of all, even though I wanted to get away from my home in Los Angeles, I did not want to go too far away. Flying to and from the East Coast takes at least five hours each way, while the flight from Los Angeles to San Jose, near Stanford, takes only an hour. Because of my many relatives and high school friends who lived in Los Angeles, and because of my father's heart condition, I wanted to make sure I could come home often. Second, I highly valued the more liberal and cutting-edge atmosphere, in addition to the golden sunny weather, of the West Coast. Even though Harvard was rated "number one" in *U.S. News and World Report's* annual college rankings, I saw more potential in Stanford, being located in the heart of the Silicon Valley and the activist-oriented Bay Area.

In autumn 1996, I arrived at Stanford with much drive, passion, and leadership experience. Searching for the ideal cause to which to direct all this, I became involved in several different activities during my first month there, including environmental activism, and the Stanford in Government and Dorm Government programs. I signed up for the Pilipino-American Student Union (PASU), but no one contacted me from the organization until my second month at Stanford. By then, my extracurricular plate was full; however, the organization's cochairpersons were persistent in calling me and inviting me to meetings. Finally, they got my attention when they told me PASU had a street dance group, which needed more dancers and, especially, a choreographer. I became very interested in making time to join and started going to the street dance practices. I became increasingly involved in PASU between 1996 and 1998. It was during this time that I began to educate myself more on political issues and injustices affecting Filipinos and Filipino Americans. Because of all that I learned, I became extremely motivated to do even more for PASU and the Filipino American community.

My First Experiences with Bay Area Activism: Coming to Terms with My Mestizaness

> But, should someone …
> question my credentials,
> how would I prove
> my qualifications?
> I could smile
> to slant my eyes,
> speak Spanish and disclose
> my Hispanic name …
> maybe pick up an accent
> and start bowing a lot.
>
> —Soto, "Women of Color"

In the spring of 1998, I slowly but surely began to escape the bubble of the Stanford campus and became more involved in Bay Area–wide activism. During the majority of my first two years at Stanford, I was more or less oblivious to the magnitude of opportunities in the Bay Area; only during the spring of my sophomore year did I begin to realize how much I had been limiting myself. Knowing that I was expected to succeed as chairperson of PASU, I wanted to be sure that I was well qualified and knowledgeable enough for the role. Consequently, I committed my spring quarter to becoming well versed in Filipino American community resources. I had huge plans for PASU. I knew that, as Filipino American students at Stanford, we had a tremendous amount of influence in the San Francisco Bay Area, and even nationwide, from which other Filipino Americans could benefit. Furthermore, we had tremendous potential to serve as role models for Filipino American youths. We just needed to be visible and active.

I didn't have a car in the spring of 1998, so I depended on public transportation or carpooling to get to various Bay Area Filipino American functions and events. Initially, breaking into the community scene was difficult. Several times I came home crying when people questioned why I was at a Filipino event, assuming I was a Latina or other non-Filipino. It shouldn't have mattered, anyway; a Latina has just as much of a right to attend a Filipino event as a Filipino does. Even when these people found out that I am a mixed-race Filipina, they still questioned my Filipino-ness yet admired my "mestiza beauty." It is ironic that while I experienced the initial difficulty of having my legitimacy as a Filipino American community organizer scrutinized, I was immediately accepted as a Filipino American community sex object. There is this odd conflict between suspicion and physical adoration, which often causes significant pain and identity conflict within mixed-race individuals.

Meeting Professor Maria P. P. Root, a fellow mestiza who teaches at the University of Washington, was one of the highlights of that spring. I had read her article "Contemporary Mixed-Heritage Filipino Americans" for an Asian American Studies class and was inspired by it.[4] When I found out she was giving a lecture at Stanford on multiracial identity, I pulled some strings with the school's newly established Comparative Studies in Race and Ethnicity (CSRE) Department to convince her to meet with me. I will never forget the time I was able to spend with her, talking two hours over coffee at the Stanford School of Education café. She was the first mestiza Filpino American community leader and intellect I had met. In my heart, I knew I wanted to commit myself to serving the Filipino American community, but I had not yet convinced myself that Filipino Americans outside Stanford would accept me as a community leader. Professor Root gave me the faith I needed in myself to carry on with all my Filipino American community work. I became confident that people would eventually come to appreciate the love I have for all I do and no longer dismiss my efforts because of my mestiza ethnic background.

During the summer of 1998, I finally had the freedom to blossom within the world of Bay Area Filipino American community activism. I began an internship at the Philippine Resource Center in San Francisco. I lived at Stanford, but would commute ninety minutes each way via Caltrain or the Samtrans bus five days a week. Through this internship, I began to create a state- and nationwide network of hundreds of Filipino American community leaders.

During the summer, I made a difficult decision: I would no longer be a pre-med student. I had done well in all my pre-med courses and was even top of the class in my organic chemistry courses, but my heart was not in medicine. I was pursuing a medical career solely to please my mother. As a young girl, she had wanted to become a medical doctor herself. However, her parents would not send her to medical school because it was *mahal na mahal* (too expensive). She went to law school where she was eligible for scholarship instead. Since she could not become a medical doctor, she wanted me to become one. But, experiencing one of the most empowering times of my life doing public relations and community work in San Francisco, I was forced to reflect upon where my true interests lay. I recognized that the majority of my favorite extracurricular experiences in both secondary school and college involved coordinating and working with large groups of people. Furthermore, as an Asian American studies major, I would be pursuing an academic field that had little to do with the health sciences. Taking all factors into consideration, I knew I would not be completely happy or fulfilled as a medical doctor.

In August 1998, I let my mother know that my heart was telling me to pursue a path other than toward medicine. Initially she was not happy with the idea and tried to convince me that becoming a medical doctor was undoubtedly the best route for me. I was finally able to persuade her to fly up from Los Angeles to the Bay Area for a few days and volunteer at the organization at which I worked. I thought that if she saw firsthand all the work I was doing she would understand why it had such a life-altering effect on me. She came up for a weekend in mid-August and volunteered at the Pistahan 1998 festival, held in the beautiful, green Yerba Buena Gardens of San Francisco, for which I served as one of the coordinators. Much to my happiness, my mother was very moved by all that I was doing and decided to support me in any career choice I would make.

Mobilizing the Masses

Back in June 1998, my goal was to make the name of Stanford PASU known throughout the San Francisco Bay Area by the time I graduated college. I wanted as many Bay Area Filipino Americans as possible to know that they could use Stanford PASU as a resource and for PASU members to serve as role models in the community. I made my presence known as a representative of Stanford at all the Bay Area Filipino American collegiate events I could possibly attend.

Nonetheless, as much as I tried to mobilize other Stanford PASU members to go out into the community, I could rarely get more than one or two people to join me at events and usually I just went by myself. This initial difficulty was due to several things. First of all, almost all of our "active" members had recently graduated. They came to our folk dancing practices and showed up at our bimonthly runs to Bay Area Filipino restaurants. I tried to focus efforts on member recruitment during the 1997–98 school year but was unsuccessful, as few others from PASU wanted to devote time to it. Thus, in the autumn of 1998, I had the extra pressure of having to start a club practically from scratch. I had to give the relatively few Stanford Filipino American undergraduates—fewer than forty—a reason and motivation to get involved. Most of these undergraduates did not see any potential in such a small club; they would rather get involved in larger, more established campus organizations. However, I believed that size should not hinder a club like Stanford PASU, which had so much potential as a statewide and national Filipino American resource. Especially, I knew that working with the multitude of Bay Area college and community organizations within a half-hour's drive, PASU could accomplish many amazing things.

Also in June 1998, I was determined to get PASU involved with the Northern California Pilipino American Student Organization (NCPASO) after more than a year of nonparticipation.[5] I was able to get the phone number for NCPASO's financial chair, Chris Cara. At our first phone conversation, we "clicked" immediately and talked for hours. Chris and I finally met in person at a Filipino American event in early July and our friendship grew dramatically over the course of the summer. Since Chris also happened to be the advisor for Pilipino Youth Coalition (PYC)–Alameda County—a group of Filipino American high school and college students devoted to community organizing—we started discussing the possibility of holding a PYC-PASU collaborative-youth conference. The conference would bring together Filipino American youth from across the Bay Area. Young-adult Filipino American community leaders would deliver workshops on politics, leadership, community organizing, Filipino culture and history, and college preparation.

Determined to have a 1999 Filipino Youth Conference at Stanford, I started attending the weekly PYC meetings across the bay in Union City. I offered Stanford's facilities and funding in exchange for PYC's woman- and man-power. PYC was excited about the offer, as they were unable to have their own 1998 conference because of lack of funding and facilities. It was mutually beneficial, as each of us had something that the other needed. We set a date for the PYC-PASU Filipino Youth Empowerment Conference (a.k.a. the Lugaw for the Pilipino Soul youth conference) in early spring of 1999.

Also in September 1998, I began to strengthen my bonds with other Bay Area student leaders by becoming a founding member of what would become known as the Tuesday Night Crew. Caroline Victorino and Melanie Fontanilla (of San Francisco State University), Chris Cara (of San Jose State University), and I began to meet every Tuesday night to not only get to know each other better as friends, but also with the idea that it would make collaboration on future projects much easier. We wanted a way to build our relationships outside monthly NCPASO meetings. For each Tuesday night gathering we would change locations, so that within a month, we would cover four corners of the Bay Area (Daly City, Berkeley, Fremont, and Stanford). We began to invite students from other Bay Area colleges to the Tuesday Night Crew, and soon enough, our group of student leaders snowballed.

In addition to the youth conference, I anticipated PASU hosting its first Pilipino-Cultural Night (PCN) within the school year. Sure, PASU held a mini-PCN during the 1997 to 1998 school year at one of the larger dorms on campus, but all that involved was performing the traditional *tinikling* and *sakuting* dances and serving Filipino food. I wanted to have a larger-scale PCN with skits and multiple folk dance suites. I thought about collaborating with the College of Notre Dame's Filipino club, Sanlahi. Their club was about twice as big as PASU's, but still small compared to those of the other Bay Area colleges. Sanlahi had hosted PCNs in past years, but they had been small ones due to the club's size. I approached Sanlahi's president, Fatima Valencia, about a possible collaboration and received a positive response from her.

In October 1998, I attended the NCPASO open house and met Wes Mercado and Louis Perez through one of my Tuesday Night Crew friends, Jeremy Rodis. Wes was the president of Ohlone College's Filipino American Student Association (OCFASA) and Louis was the Director of Ohlone's 1998 PCN. Jeremy had suggested that I talk with Wes and Louis about the collaborative PCN. Wes and Louis were very interested, especially because OCFASA was in need of an auditorium for their 1999 PCN. The OCFASA officer in charge of booking their usual auditorium did not do so in time. Wes and Louis started attending Tuesday Night Crew meetings, and during those initial meetings we would throw out skit ideas for the PCN. Louis very much wanted to direct a PCN about the assassination of former Philippines senator Begnino "Ninoy" Aquino. I supported Louis's artistic vision because it concerned an important event that many Filipino American college students were unfamiliar with despite its relatively recent occurence. If anything, Filipino American college students in the Bay Area knew about Filipino patriots José Protasio Rizal, Andres Bonifacio, and Lapu-Lapu, but very little about more recent heroes such as Senator Aquino.

The collaborative PCN was on. Sanlahi and PASU would prepare folk dances, and Wes and Louis would work on coordinating all the theatrical components. My job would be to take care of all the public relations, fund raising, and logistics; it was a huge undertaking, but I was more than willing to do it. I also brought up the idea of a collaborative PCN with the Filipino American club from the San Francisco Academy of Art College and Pinoy and Pinay Artists (PAPA). I had first met members of PAPA during an arts event hosted by Stanford's Filipino-faculty organization, the Filipino American Community at Stanford (FACS), in October 1997, and we had kept in touch. At first they hesitated to join the PCN since the commute to Stanford for theater and dance rehearsals was a long distance for them. We finally figured out that they could play an important role in program and publicity design. In fact, one of the PAPA members, ended up serving as stage manager and as one of the assistant theatrical directors.

Jeremy Rodis also had been talking to his fellow members of California State University Hayward's (CSUH's) Brown House about joining the collaborative effort. Brown House is not an official CSUH organization, but an offshoot of CSUH's official Filipino American club, the Pilipino American Student Association (PASA), consisting mostly of former PASA officers. Some members of Brown House choreographed and danced for Barangay Dance Company and Philippine Folkloric Arts, respectively. They were willing to instruct folk dances at Sanlahi's Filipino club on a weekly basis. The other members of Brown House would later become key extras and theatrical advisors for the PCN.

Six months later, on April 3, 1999, the first-ever Bay Area Collaborative Pilipino Cultural Night actually took place on the Stanford campus. The PCN was a success, despite moments of extreme stress in the weeks, days, and hours before the event. We received major sponsorship from Goldilocks Bakeshops and Restaurants, radio stations KTSF and KYLD, and Stanford University. The Filipino American pop group Kai made a cameo appearance. Comedians from the Tongue in a Mood theater group opened the first and second acts with stand-up and skit comedy. Members of the Barangay Dance Company and Philippine Folkloric Arts performed mountain and tribal dance suites, while students from Stanford PASU and College of Notre Dame Sanlahi performed the rural, Spanish, and Muslim suites. We sold out tickets for a theater with a capacity of 714 and raised $2,000 for a Filipino American youth cause, Project PULL (People United through Learning and Leadership) Academy. Our audience was filled with students and alumni from all over the Bay Area, including Stanford, University of California–Berkeley, San Francisco State University, Santa Clara University, Ohlone College, California State University–Hayward, College of Notre Dame, San Francisco Academy of Art College, and Sacramento State University. It was truly a night to remember.

On April 17, two weeks after the PCN, more young Filipino Americans would make their way to the Stanford campus for the Lugaw for the Pilipino Soul youth conference. Students attended workshops on combating Filipino American stereotypes, college preparation, and turning apathy into empowerment. The day ended with an amazing slam session that showcased local Filipino American youths' talent in spoken word and music. The next day we were featured in a San Jose *Mercury News* article, "Filipino American Youths Gather to Empower the Community."

The month of April 1999 was an unbelievable dream come true. All of my initial goals not only were accomplished but also exceeded expectations. Most important, Stanford PASU had made a huge mark on the Bay Area community scene, causing many Filipino American youths who had once believed that Stanford was not a place for Filipino Americans whatsoever to strongly consider attending Stanford as a goal to aspire to.

Sex and the Community

Are you willing to use the [erotic] power that you have in the service of what you believe?

—Audre Lorde, "Uses of the Erotic: The Erotic as Power"

Behind the success of the PCN and the youth conference, there was much intergender drama as well. Over the period of six months during which we worked on the events, the few other female coordinators and I had to ward off the advances of several of the male coordinators and participants. It got many of us, male and female, into a discussion of how sex can drive community activism. I initially had much pride in thinking that all the participants in the PCN and youth conference were involved because they believed in a vision of unity for the Filipino American community while exposing more youth to Stanford. The next thing I knew, and seemingly every week, at least one Pinoy admitted that sexual attraction was a strong motivating factor, if not the strongest factor, in getting him to join. Some of the female participants and coordinators reciprocated interest and some did not. I did not know whether to be sad and disappointed or be happy that sexual attraction provided incentive for people to get involved. Nonetheless, I still felt guilt, even though the female coordinators, including myself, were not consciously using the erotic. One of the male coordinators would often joke with me, "If you get a boyfriend, Michelle, it's all over." Despite his lighthearted manner, his statement made me extra conscious of interactions between the women and men involved in the events. At least the men who were unsuccessful at attracting the women they wanted stayed on with event planning. Perhaps this proves that sex was not their only incentive to get involved or that, maybe, they eventually came around to believing in a meaningful vision.

Talking with other women of color who also have been successful in mobilizing large numbers of people, I learned that many of them have experienced similar scenarios. It just so happens that many of their most loyal male constituents were initially or still were sexual admirers. Although sex can serve as a strong motivating force for female activists, the majority of male and female activists I have spoken to agree that, based upon their experience in community activism, sex is a much stronger driving force for men than for women.

At the suggestion of a visiting Pinay professor at Stanford University, Melinda de Jesús, I explored the writings of Audre Lorde, a pioneer of 1970s and 1980s feminist theory, who has argued that "the erotic is not only part of our spiritual power but a source of political power." Studying Lorde's theories of the erotic-as-power made me recognize that it was society's sexist expectations that caused me to feel undue guilt. As Lorde has noted, "We have been taught to suspect this resource, vilified, abused, and devalued within western society. On the one hand, the superficially erotic has been encouraged as a sign of female inferiority; on the other hand, women have been made to suffer and feel both contemptible and suspect by virtue of its existence."[6]

Although women leaders need not feel responsible for the hidden sexual agendas of certain constituents, I feel that it is important to ensure that those we lead truly appreciate the vision of the causes we devote ourselves to, as opposed to merely our physical selves. Doing so, however, will help ensure long-term, truly dedicated support of our constituency and that we will be taken seriously as true leaders, not just as trivialized sex objects.

Final Reflections: Glancing Ahead

Being able to sit back and reflect on how my ethnicity, gender, upbringing, and various experiences have interacted to create the person I am today has given me a clearer perspective on what I want from my life. I no longer want to feel that I have to prove my worthiness to anyone, just because I am not white, not of homogeneous racial ethnicity, and not male. This may take some time, and is easier said than done, because I cannot say that I am completely unaffected by the xenophobia that pervades our everyday lives. But, for me, it is something worth aiming for. By contributing my own thoughts and experiences to the dialogue on racism, sexism, and classism and continuing to educate myself on what scholars are currently discussing regarding these issues, I hope to lead by example for those who are not doing so already. Awareness of the imbalances of power in the world will put all of us in a better position to address inequalities and to pursue justice for our communities.

Notes

1. Michael Arago, Pol Gravados, and Anthony Snow, writers/dirs., *Silencio*, National Asian American Telecommunications Association, 1996, film.
2. Use of the terms *mestizo* and *mestiza* in this essay refers to offspring of a phenotypically Filipino parent and a phenotypically Caucasian parent.
3. Most Filipinos are actually part Spanish, Chinese, and/or Portuguese.
4. Maria P. P. Root, "Contemporary Mixed-Heritage Filipino Americans: Fighting Colonized Identities," in *Filipino Americans: Transformation and Identity*, ed. Maria P. P. Root (Thousand Oaks, Calif.: Sage, 1997), 80–94.
5. NCPASO is a coalition of all of the Filipino American collegiate organizations in Northern California.
6. Audre Lorde, "Uses of the Erotic: The Erotic as Power," in *Sister Outsider: Essays and Speeches by Audre Lorde* (Trumansburg, N.Y.: Crossing, 1984), 53.

VI
Peminist Cultural Production

18

Sino Ka? Ano Ka?: Contemporary Art by Eight Filipina American Artists

VICTORIA ALBA

Over the course of the century that began shortly after the declaration of Philippine independence in 1898, Filipino Americans—initially a negligible portion of the immigrants coming to the United States—emerged as the country's fastest-growing Asian American minority. Today, more than 250,000 Filipino Americans live in the San Francisco Bay Area; more than two million live in the entire country.

Despite these large numbers, Filipino Americans as a group have yet to be sufficiently recognized as part of America's artistic mainstream. It is within this context that *Sino Ka? Ano Ka?*, a group exhibition of Filipina American women artists, unfolds. While preparing for this essay, I was asked by a friend and former colleague—an artist himself—why such an exhibition was even worth undertaking. I was stunned because during the four years we had worked together at a local museum he had not only expressed pride in his own Jewish heritage but had also been interested in African American and Chicano art and the art of other ethnic Americans. At his request, I recited the names of the featured artists, of which he recognized only one, to which he responded, "How is her work Filipino?" This utterance makes clear the need for an exhibition such as *Sino Ka? Ano Ka?*—which fittingly translates as "Who are we? What are we?"

Well, we are everything and everywhere: young, old, poor, rich, straight, gay, lesbian, bisexual, transgender, neighbors, friends, artists, nurses, doctors, students, teachers, secretaries, managers, entertainers, software engineers, war veterans, newspaper vendors, and more. Statistically, we are one out of every twenty-five people in the San Francisco Bay Area. At times, it is not even apparent who we are: we can be light or dark, short or tall; we can be mistaken for Mexican, Indian, Indonesian, Malaysian, Samoan, Hawaiian, Japanese, Chinese, or European; what does a Filipino look like, anyway? My point is that Filipino Americans are a diverse group, little understood by the general public.

It is diversity, not homogeneity, that distinguishes *Sino Ka? Ano Ka?* Its participants have at least five things in common: they live in the Bay Area; have ties to Filipino culture, either through family or upbringing; are all women; are professional visual artists; and, above all, have chosen to exhibit their works alongside those of other Filipina American women (in the past, this might have been referred to as "solidarity"). Beyond this it would be difficult to make sweeping, across-the-board judgments about them or their art. The artists are from different backgrounds and have had unique experiences, each one the product and participant of a certain time and place; their works reflect a particular *zeitgeist* (spirit of the time) and w*eltanschauung* (worldview). Their ages range from twenty-four to forty-five. Three were born in the Philippines, five in the United States. Two of the women are of mixed racial heritage, while one of the women is self-described as "white."

It shouldn't surprise anyone that no two of the artists are alike. However, there are many that, when confronted with identity-based shows, assume this will be so. Furthermore, there are people like my friend who expect all the works to "look" Filipino.

The contemporary expressions featured here vary in content, media, and approach. Some of the artists operate collectively, others always alone. A few stick to one medium; most work in several media, among these, textiles, video, performance, and installation. Some have political agendas and engage in social protest and/or public art projects. Gender issues, feminist concerns, and Filipino American identity might be overtly addressed, submerged, or omitted. A lot of the artists inject humor into their work. Nearly all ask intelligent, challenging questions of their audiences.

Before discussing the individual artists and their work, I offer the words of twenty-nine-year-old artist Reanne Estrada, who notes, "I'm glad this exhibition is taking place. Hopefully, when people see the show they'll become aware of the variety of the work that's being done by artists who happen to be women and happen to be of Filipino origin. Because a lot of times the hardest thing about being a Filipina artist is that people want to pigeonhole you, they automatically assume that your work has to be overtly about your identity. No one necessarily expects this of a white male."

Terry Acebo Davis (b. 1953, Oakland, California)

Terry Acebo Davis says, "Our history as Filipino Americans exists as more of an oral history—we learn it through the stories of our parents, uncles, aunts, and fellow *kababayan* [countrymen]. As an artist, I believe it is my duty to pass these stories on through visual language."

For years, Acebo Davis has simultaneously balanced the careers of nurse, visual artist, arts educator, and activist. It is her artwork, however, that most passionately reflects her ethnic background. Her installations and works on paper continually evoke Filipino and Filipino American history and culture.

They are personal and political: sources range from her family's oral histories and photographic albums to materials gleaned from public archives and books.

Whether figurative or abstract, her works always allude to narrative. Her installations incorporate prints, manipulated photographs, and audio recordings, as well as actual objects invested with symbolic meaning such as field crates, thongs cast in bronze, and *banig,* woven sleep mats. Her prints are generally abstract and draw upon an array of printmaking processes and collage to call attention to form, color, and line. Text is as important as iconography, and letters and numbers are treated as discrete design elements. The surfaces to be printed on are equally critical: a Filipino theme might be paired with Philippine handmade paper fabricated from *cogon,* a native grass.

Many of her works address women's issues. And her reverence for art history is reflected in visual references to such trailblazers as Andy Warhol and Robert Rauschenberg. Meanwhile, her interests in medicine and art converge in numerous pieces depicting the body and its parts—anatomical references that at times enlist the tools of twentieth-century technology. A foot might appear as a drawing, photograph, or x-ray.

The haunting *73* (1997), a crosslike formation of screen prints rendered in black on brown, is based on a CAT SCAN (brain X-ray or computerized axial tomography) of her father's brain after a stroke at age seventy-three. The damaged brain tissue, roughly the size of a grapefruit, registers as hollow blank space. Acebo Davis conveys her sense of loss by filling the void with a photograph of her father in his youth.

The materials of *Dahil Sa Iyo* (Because of You; 1995) are domestic in origin: checkered plastic tablecloth and placemats, a wooden serving set, a nightlight, and crates with shoes. These are combined with life-size multiple screen prints of her mother to pay homage to the Filipinas of her mother's generation, immigrant women who held together their families and looked after the home. The reiterated figure is totemic, serving to emphasize the importance of the artist's female lineage.

Acebo Davis was born in Oakland and moved with her family to Fremont in the early 1960s. She received her first bachelor's degree in nursing from California State University–Hayward in 1976, then pursued a graduate degree in pediatric oncology at the University of California–San Francisco in 1985; she received a B.F.A. in printmaking from San Jose State University in 1991 and an M.F.A. in pictorial arts from San Jose State University in 1993. In 1997, she was the recipient of the James T. Phelan Award for Printmaking. Acebo Davis collaborates on installations and performances with the Filipino American artists collective DIWA (the word *diwa* is Tagalog for "spirit").

Eliza O. Barrios (b. 1968, San Diego, California)

A filmmaker, videographer, and installation artist, Eliza Barrios is clear about the consistent underlying theme of her personal art: "The work I deal with has

Fig. 18.1 Terry Acebo Davis. *Dahil Sa Iyo*, 1995. An installation: screened imagery on mixed media (66" x 84" x 18"). (Reprinted with permission of the artist.)

much to do with systems and processes, primarily how internal belief systems relate to external belief systems and how my Filipina heritage plays into this."

Although she was raised in San Diego, Barrios's upbringing was governed by the traditional values of her Philippine-born parents. She embraced many of these principles as her own but from an early age began questioning their expectations of her gender. Barrios remembers, "My parents raised my sister and I to be good Filipina girls and my sister picked up on that—she did hula and piano lessons, and slumber parties, whereas I wanted to be the boy, to play outside and do everything else. I was in my own world. I knew these feminine ideals and expectations were there, but I also knew I didn't want them. I wanted more freedom to be unconventional."

At sixteen, Barrios learned to express herself through photography, discovering a world of her own making. She continued to study photography through college and eventually moved beyond the two-dimensional plane by incorporating found objects and other sculptural elements. She also developed her content; in time, her art became a means for articulating her views concerning power and authority, society versus individual choice.

Barrios seized upon nails and hands as recurring motifs. She notes, "The hands can say as much about a person as the face. In the way they gesture, hold, clench, they can supply so many leads, yet at the same time, unlike a face, they're anonymous." Hands are a central metaphor in her elegantly minimalist piece *Solemn* (1996).

Solemn consists of eleven bare lightbulbs dangling on electrical cords suspended from above. Each bulb is positioned over a large steel funnel resting on a stand. At the base of the stand is a bowl containing water. In the bowl, visible at close range, is a projected image of a pair of hands. Moving from left to right, the hands, which are at first clasped together, open sequentially until they finally part. In this commentary on the dissemination or "funneling" of information and knowledge, the hands signify the human recipient, master of one's fate or passive object of control. With its austere symmetry, formal severity, and sleekness devoid of color, *Solemn* initially strikes the viewer as coldly industrial. Only as one approaches—that is, interacts with the work—can one discern its ultimately intimate message.

Solemn is deceptively neat, leading the viewer to believe that it was effortless to construct. In fact, it took Barrios two years to research and build the piece. While it meets her rigid standards—an admirer of Bauhaus and Japanese architecture, Barrios always strives for a clean, sharp look—its design is also practical. The highly symbolic funnels, for instance, are capacious enough to house slide projection mechanisms.

Barrios received her B.A. in photography and art in 1993 from San Francisco State University and her M.F.A. in 1995 from Mills College. Her installations have been shown extensively in Hawaii and California and her films screened at festivals internationally. Barrios has collaborated with DIWA

Fig. 18.2 Eliza O. Barrios. *Solemn* (detail), 1996. Metal funnel, tungsten light, ceramic bowl, photo negative plate, wood shelving (48" x 12" x 36"). (Reprinted with permission of the artist.)

and, along with Reanne Estrada and Jenifer Wofford, is one of the three members of Mail Order Brides.

Reanne Agustin Estrada (b. 1969, Manila, Philippines)

Perhaps none of the artists in *Sino Ka? Ano Ka?* are as engrossed with the artistic process as Reanne Estrada. Four years ago, Carlos Villa invited Estrada to create a "quilt of dreams" for an installation in conjunction with the Filipino Arts Expo at Center for the Arts. It would cover a bed in a room typical to one that might have been found at the International Hotel. A cultural fixture, the Kearny Street building constituted the heart of an area once known as Manilatown. During the first half of the twentieth century, the hotel was often the first stop for newly arrived Filipino immigrants. As its clientele aged, the hotel became an affordable, if modest, home for Filipino and Chinese seniors.[1]

Estrada was given free reign in terms of design, material, and mode of manufacture. Having little money but lots of time, she got her hands on some free fiber-optic cables, which she proceeded to gut. She untwisted the wires within, sorted them by color, and rolled them up like big balls of yarn. Then, by hand, she crocheted her bedspread: adjoined colored wires fashioned into hundreds of phrases that poignantly recalled the life of a *manong*, a Filipino old timer.

Although her current projects are much smaller in scale, they are almost as frugally produced and laboriously formed. Most recently, Estrada has been working with hair and Ivory Soap, which, in her capable hands, can remarkably resemble its namesake. Her carved pieces are reminiscent of antique Japanese *netsuke* sculpture. However, while these decorative miniatures imitate ancient Japanese or Chinese objéts d'art, they are contemporary in function (e.g., a contact lens case, a dental floss holder).

Sometimes Estrada leaves the soap intact and laces its surface with strands of hair collected from her brush and shower. The result is not unlike scrimshaw, as the bars look as if they have been finely etched. In an environment as dust-free as possible, Estrada has created complex patterns and designs, such as chevron stripes, labyrinths, and a Philippine flag. These "soap drawings" can take weeks to complete.

Estrada adds a final flourish of tongue-in-cheek by exhibiting the "soap drawings" in museum cases lined with black terry cloth, while the carvings sit like precious jewels in oval frames set with beveled glass. As she works, she methodically logs every detail, keeping track of the hours spent and number of hairs used. She says she maintains meticulous records "because people think the work artists do isn't labor, but it is, it takes a long time."

Born in Manila, Estrada moved with her family to Los Angeles when she was eight. She received her B.A. in visual and environmental studies from Harvard University in 1992 and soon thereafter moved to San Francisco. Her works have been shown in Hawaii, California, and Manila. She has collaborated on projects with DIWA and is one of the three members of the group Mail Order Brides.

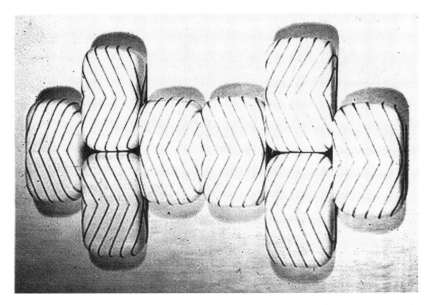

Fig. 18.3 Reanne Agustin Estrada. *VIII: One Hundred Thirty-Six* (detail), 1998. Hair on Ivory soap, in shadowbox on terrycloth-covered pedestal (37" x 21" x 17"). (Reprinted with permission of the artist.)

Johanna Poethig (b. 1956, Manila, Philippines)

Johanna Poethig declares, "In both the studio art and collaborative work I do, I'm motivated by examining culture and how cultures intersect. I'm also interested in looking at history and in creating works that are antithetical to the advertised life; that is, billboards, the marketplace, the commercial use of the urban landscape."

Poethig is an unlikely Filipina American: she's white, blond, and nearly six feet tall. Her parents, socially conscious American missionaries, relocated the family to Manila when Poethig was only three months old. While most foreign children were educated at American private schools, she attended Filipino public schools, spoke Tagalog, and, more important, saw the world through Philippine eyes. Although she often experienced a sense of being a minority or "the other," she strongly identified with her Filipino friends who looked at the United States as the "imperialist, colonialist nation." In elementary school, she acted out scenes from the Philippine Revolution with her schoolmates. Later, her high school history teacher led her class on field trips to anti-American demonstrations. Poethig grew up questioning not only the political consequences of the Philippine-U.S. relationship but also its social effects. She recognized that social privilege was linked to class and race, and noticed how images marketed to the public supported this scheme. She recalls, "I grew up with classically beautiful, graceful Filipinas—the ideal of beauty was not me, yet at the same time, advertising elevated the white girl."

A critical perspective resonates through her art, whether she's working on publicly funded large-scale projects or diminutive sculptures. During the last seventeen years she has painted vivid, forceful murals in the urban centers of Los Angeles, San Jose, and San Francisco, offering an aesthetic and thematic counterpoint to the cigarette and liquor ads generally encountered in such locales. Her works have celebrated Ferdinand Marcos's defeat, captured the plight of the homeless, saluted the beauty of multicultural artifacts, brightened playgrounds, and more. "The murals give public space a meaning beyond money," Poethig says.

Recently, Poethig has produced small ceramic sculptures that lambaste consumerism and commodity fetishism. She fights products with products by renaming, reinventing, and subverting common household goods. For example, a shapely ceramic bottle labeled "Liquid White Girl" looks suspiciously like Palmolive dish soap. The ubiquitous American icon Barbie is appropriated for a series of statuettes depicting Filipina archetypes and idols. The figurines are cast from the same mold, then Poethig individually manipulates, glazes, and fires them; Barbie as we know her is barely detectable in the end. In her wake there's *Kayumanggi*, a brown beauty; *Babaylan*, a shamaness, priestess, and healer; the strong and wild *Biker Manang*, who puffs on the lit end of a cigarette and sports a butterfly on her T-shirt instead of her sleeve; *Miss Binibining Balikbayan*, a beauty pageant queen; *Urduja*, a provincial princess; *Maria Clara*, a colonial mestiza in Spanish-style attire; *Pinky*, a trendy teenager; *Bulol Barbie*, after the eponymous Ifugao rice god; *Diwa*—all white, she's spirit personified; and the autobiographical *Puti Pinay*, a white Filipina in folkloric costume.

Poethig received her B.A. in 1980 from the University of California at Santa Cruz and her M.F.A. in 1992 from Mills College. She is on the faculty of the Visual and Public Art Institute of California State University–Monterey Bay and is artistic director of the Inner City Public Art Projects for Youth. She has won numerous awards, including a 1994 Bay Area Master Muralist Award. In her collaborations with DIWA, she performs the role of General Douglas MacArthur. She has also produced a satirical feminist CD and videos parodying exercise tapes and product infomercials.

Stephanie Syjuco (b. 1974, Manila, Philippines)

Stephanie Syjuco relates, "Raised in San Francisco, I didn't have much opportunity to run around in the wilderness. I'm very urban. My exposure to nature has been through parks, books, and sources like that. Then last summer, I spent some time in rural Maine. It was eye-opening, yet also very strange; I started making works that reflected my natural environment …. Even though they suggests organic forms and natural shapes, they are more my idea of nature. I make them up out of my head."

Fig. 18.4   Johanna Poethig. *Babaylan Barbie*, 1997. Ceramic (10" x 4" x 4"). (Reprinted with permission of the artist.)

Syjuco provides conclusive evidence that art imitates life. For several years now she has been interpreting and manufacturing objects that mimic articles found in nature, such as lichens, snowballs, moss, and grass swatches. She has also developed families of items that simulate recognizable phenomena or patterns that in real life are formed naturally. Some fall into the category of "portable accidents": these aggregate groups of blood or milk puddles can be arranged in any configuration but are more convincing if placed irregularly, as if they tumbled randomly like tossed dice. Others, like her version of the Rorschach inkblot test, must be precisely positioned for their oddly shaped components to make sense at all. Either way, Syjuco calls attention to the role of the human hand in shaping such formations or events—specifically a woman's hand, as underscored by her choice of media. Her biological specimens, portable accidents, and inkblots are crocheted or sewn, practices not widely thought of as art mediums, but as traditional domestic crafts.[2] Being raised in contemporary urban conditions, which were as removed from American traditions as from the American wilderness, Syjuco had to teach herself to crochet as an adult. She learned from a kit—packaged tradition, as it were.

Much of Syjuco's art has been inspired by her work at San Francisco's Exploratorium, a science museum. One of these pieces, *Ink Blot* (1997), refers to Hermann Rorschach's psychological test in which a subject's interpretations of ten standard symmetrical inkblots are analyzed as a measure of emotional and intellectual functioning. However, Syjuco has distorted the test. Magnified to a grotesquely imposing seven by fourteen feet, the zoomorphic inkblot recalls a colossal insect and strange fowl. Further, she has installed it in a corner to suggest "walls folding in on themselves or structural instability." Having taken on these new connotations, Rorschach's inkblot no longer seems to be an objective test but more the outward manifestation of a disturbed psychological state. Syjuco not only crochets and sews but also works in a variety of media, including painting and sculpture, and with more unusual materials such as blackboard paint; Formica; bread; hobbyists' model sets; and artificial flowers, fruit, and bugs.

Syjuco moved from Manila to San Francisco when she was a small child and later lived in Japan before returning to the Bay Area. In 1994, she participated in the Association of Independent Colleges of Art and Design New York Studio Program. In 1995, she received a B.F.A. in sculpture from the San Francisco Art Institute. In 1997, she attended the Skowhegan School of Painting and Sculpture. Her works have been featured in exhibitions in New York, Manila, and San Francisco—most notably, in a 1997 solo exhibition at John Berggruen Gallery and in the international touring exhibition *At Home and Abroad: Twenty Contemporary Filipino Artists* at the Asian Art Museum, June 13–August 30, 1998.

Lucille Lozada Tenazas (B. 1953, Aklan, Philippines)

Lucille Tenazas, principal of the San Francisco-based communication graphics and design firm Tenazas Design, notes, "Graphic design, to me, is the union of art and science, the combination of objective and subjective thinking. You use your left brain to be objective, analytical, and to solve problems while you use your right brain to be subjective, intuitive, and artistic."

It is easy to see why the highly respected *I.D.: The International Design Magazine* named Tenazas as one of the forty "leading-edge" designers in the United States. Her designs stand on their own as works of art. Deemed to be of museum quality, they were the focus of a retrospective exhibition at the San Francisco Museum of Modern Art in May 1997 and a solo exhibition at Manila's Ayala Museum in March 1998. Her long and varied list of clients ranges from corporations to nonprofit art organizations; among these are Apple Computers, Rizzoli Publications, the San Francisco International Airport, the San Francisco Center for the Arts, and the University Art Museum/ Pacific Film Archive.

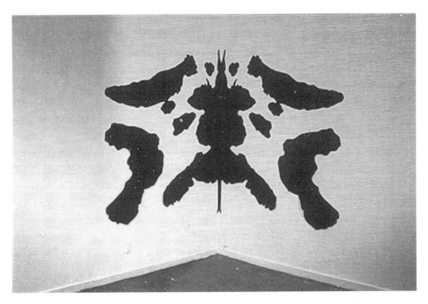

Fig. 18.5 Stephanie Syjuco. *Ink Blot (Corner)*, 1997. Felt with trim (168" x 84"). (Reprinted with permission of the artist.)

Some of the features of her distinctive style include collage, the innovative use of photography and type, the dispersion of text throughout the area of the design, layering and overlapping, and the use of "tertiary colors" that produce the illusion of transparency. But her art is more than the sum of its parts. What makes it work is Tenazas's philosophy toward design. She speaks of a "formal decorative surface" that gives way to "a deeper conceptual meaning." Her designs invoke aesthetic, intellectual, and visceral responses.

Tenazas's profound appreciation for language is evident. She learned English in the Philippines and mastered its subtleties after moving to the United States. Today, she delights in incorporating a certain amount of wordplay and text/language exercises into her design art. While accessibility is of concern to her, she notes that a work "should never be dull … if the text and design are well linked, people will want to read it …. I get involved editorially, the text shouldn't just sit there—text and design enhance each other and work in concert. I remember telling one of my students, 'What's the deal here? The words look like a caption.' They can't be placed randomly. My work is pragmatic in that the message is always there, but it is also poetic because I give it to you in layers."

Most amazing is Tenaza's ability to make the two-dimensional look three-dimensional. Combining various techniques, she fools the eye into perceiving depth. Her designs are akin to visual journeys; their elements become like rocks in a landscape or scrims in a stage set. She says, "It's like you are walking through the work."

Tenaza's method for teaching this lesson to her students exemplifies her unorthodox approach. She tells them to travel ten minutes from their home, but in a direction opposite to the one they are used to. She then asks that they translate this experience into the design of a product, such as a poster or a book, that becomes a record of their experience. The idea is to understand what it is about the place that engages them; this could be a sign, a billboard, or any other physical landmark. "I'm interested in their psychological connections to the place," she says.

Tenazas received her B.A. from the College of the Holy Spirit in the Philippines and her M.F.A. from the Cranbrook Academy of Art in Michigan (where she studied with the influential designer Catherine McCoy). She is adjunct professor of design at the California College of Arts and Crafts and has been a visiting faculty member at Yale University, the California Institute of the Arts, and the Rhode Island School of Design. A recipient of several design awards, she has exhibited her work at the Pompidou Center in Paris and the Fortuny Museum in Venice.

Catherine Wagner (b. 1953, San Francisco, California)

Catherine Wagner has achieved international renown for her conceptual photographs of construction sites, classrooms, and homes. For her project *Art and Science: Investigating Matter,* Wagner entered the exclusive world of scientific laboratories, photographing for four years at Los Alamos National Laboratory, Los Alamos, New Mexico; Washington University, St. Louis, Missouri; the Stanford Linear Accelerator, Stanford, California; and the Lawrence Livermore Laboratory, a division of the University of California, Livermore, California. Her subjects span the specter of human evolution, from prehistory to twenty-first-century cutting-edge biotechnology—from the sources of the past to the promises of the future. Equipped with a backdrop, lighting, and a four-by-five camera, she photographed fossils, moon rocks, genetically engineered tomatoes, and, most extensively, the Human Genome Project, a research program that has set as its goal the mapping of the three billion nucleotides in the human genome. (In more practical terms, this research isolates and identifies genes linked to human disease in hopes that such identification will eventually lead to preventions and cures.) The resulting photographs are beautiful, technically perfect, crisp, and exceptionally clear. However, this is not Wagner's sole aim; her photographs are intended to provoke questions regarding the social, spiritual, and physical impact such research will have on our culture. The outcome of this research will affect us all, and by presenting these images to nonscience audiences, she encourages a broader exchange. She writes, in her artist's statement, "I have tried to ask the kind of questions posed by philosophers, artists, ethicists, architects, and social scientists ... Who are we and who will we become? ... How, in the future, will we construct our individual and cultural identity?" She also makes a case for the restitution of the age-old relationship between science and art, noting, "Presently we are a society that compartmentalizes disciplines, which prohibits the opportunity to share in a dialogue that reinforces communality. Historically, art and science were not separate disciplines but worked collaboratively to inform one another."

People are absent from Wagner's work, yet the objects photographed are redolent of human activity. In some cases, objects pointing to human involvement help demystify the surroundings. For instance, notions of the scientific laboratory as ultrahygienic, hermetic, and irreproachably hi-tech are debunked with a photograph showing a bottle with a handwritten, makeshift tape label reading, "Definitely not sterile." Conversely, many of the images reveal the laboratory as an inscrutable, alien place. The piece *-86 Degree Freezers* (1995) depicts freezer cases containing "twelve areas of concern and crisis"; among these are blood and tissue samples of those with alcoholism, Alzheimer's disease, bipolar disorder (manic–depressive illness), breast cancer, and HIV. Although these diseases are among the most feared in and of themselves, the frost-lined shelves stacked high with test tubes, jars, and petri dishes provide no clue as to their content. The enigmatic objects lead us to ponder: are we looking at the secret weapons of a mysterious cabal or a treasure trove that will unlock the riddle of life?

Wagner received her B.A. in 1975 and her M.A. in 1977, both from San Francisco State University. She is the recipient of several major awards, including a Guggenheim Fellowship, National Endowment for the Arts Fellowships, a Mellon Foundation Grant, the Ferguson Award, and the Aaron Siskind Fellowship. She is affiliated with the Fraenkel Gallery in San Francisco and Gallery RAM in Santa Monica. She is currently professor of art at Mills College in Oakland, California.

Jenifer K. Wofford (b. 1973, San Francisco, California)

You can learn a bit about Jenifer K. Wofford by looking at her art. Five years ago, when she initially became interested in cultural heritage and identity, she mounted a room-size installation—centered around the emblematic butterfly-sleeve dress of the Philippines, the *terno*. A few years later, for the first time in her life, she worried about her weight. The fleeting anxiety inspired her to sculpt a series of curvaceous Italianate ceramic corsets. Then she bought a motorcycle and not long thereafter began sculpting motorcycle fuel tanks. In *Untitled: Sleeveless* (1997) she returns to the *terno*, this time reducing the dress to its defining feature, the sleeves. Usually made of indigenous *piña* fiber, Wofford's sleeves are cast from the New World material polyurethane. She displays them on a platform as if there were a dress, and/or person, between them. She says, "It's what's absent that defines the presence of the object. So this piece is about defining the space between the sleeves, defining my relationship to my Pinay heritage. At the same time, it is ambiguous, because I don't presume to claim this cultural identity as my own entirely; the piece

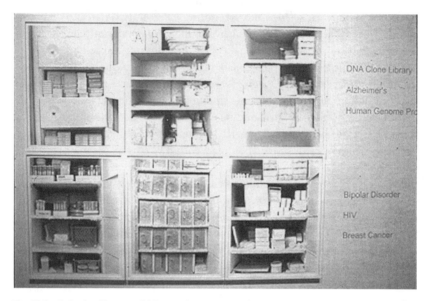

Fig. 18.6 Catherine Wagner. *-86 Degree Freezers (12 Areas of Concern and Crisis)*, 1995. Twelve-panel typology. (Reprinted with permission of the artist.)

can also be defined by what the viewer wants to bring to it. I'm creating a vacuum that someone else can inhabit."

Ambiguity is present in much of her work, due in part to her mixed racial heritage. Several years ago Wofford, whose father is Euro-American and whose mother is Filipina, created a series of ceramic busts with "vaguely Asian" or "hybrid" features. She explains, "Because I had no point of reference, I was trying to falsify my own history, create my own kind of iconography for the hybrid, a sort of heritage that doesn't exist historically. Say you're Italian and you grow up in Italy, you have the iconography of the Italian Renaissance and so forth. Yet while there's always been mixing, there isn't necessarily an iconography to go along with it, so I was, in a sense, solving a problem for myself."

This ambiguity also carries over into Wofford's noncultural identity-specific work. Although derived from an ostensibly "masculine" vehicle, her ceramic motorcycle fuel tanks are rounded, full, and sensual and sport natural buff finishes that convey a softness incongruous with the original object. Wofford, whose work largely focuses on the figure, designed the tanks to have allusions to the female form after noticing that they were analogous to the torso. But that wasn't the only reason she sculpted the tanks. "Basically, it's my love for pranksterism," she explains. "I think they're really funny."

Wofford received her B.F.A. in sculpture in 1995 from the San Francisco Art Institute. She also has studied at Diablo Valley College in Pleasant Hill, California, and at the Instituto Allende in San Miguel de Allende, Mexico. Her

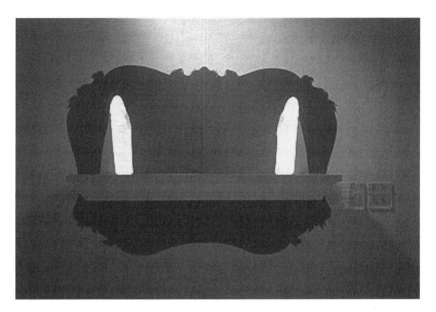

Fig. 18.7   Jenifer K. Wofford. *Sleeveless*, 1997. Resin, wood, pigment (20" x 48" x 13"). (Reprinted with permission of the artist.)

works have been shown in Hawaii, California, and Manila. Wofford is one of the three members of Mail Order Brides.

Mail Order Brides

On our own we tend to be hermits.

—Reanne Estrada of Mail Order Brides

A startling transformation takes place when Eliza Barrios, Reanne Estrada, and Jenifer Wofford come together: these normally sedate, introspective women go from observing their own private rituals to making themselves a collective public spectacle known as the MOB. That's the acronym for Mail Order Brides, the name the three of them have gone by since they first coined it for the title of a group exhibition at Los Medranos College in Pittsburg, California, in 1995.

MOB has attracted a local following for their lively performances, photo shoots, lectures, karaoke videos, and now their Market Street kiosks (in conjunction with the San Francisco Art Commission's Art in Transit Program) that lampoon Filipina stereotypes—particularly that of the mail-order bride. They always appear in "drag"—that is, makeup, attire, and wigs that conform to these stereotypes. Frequently, they structure their performances around food. Offering a feminist take on the Filipino obsession for beauty pageants, MOB delivered one of their most memorable spoofs as the Pinays on

Fig. 18.8 Mail Order Brides/MOB. *Have you eaten?* (1998). Left to right: Eliza Barrios, Reanne Estrada, Jenifer Wofford. Photo by Erik Nelson. (Reprinted with permission of the artist.)

Wheels—note the acronym, POW—in Oakland's 1997 Lunar New Year parade. Gussied up in wigs, gowns, and beauty contestant sashes, the MOB and several other Filipina American women autocaded through Oakland's Chinatown, just floats away from the "real" Miss Oakland Chinatown. From atop Barrios's truck, which was covered with Astroturf and flowers and trailed a long tulle train, some of the women smiled and waved while Barrios and Wofford circled on motorcycles below.

Reanne Estrada remarks, "MOB is not so much about making fun of the traditional role of the Filipina, but recontextualizing it. One of the reasons we picked up on the Mail Order Brides moniker was in response to how Filipina women are viewed, especially by the media. We wanted to turn this around on its head. Most Filipina women are not meek or subservient, but have a strong sense of self, and this can be traced directly to our pre-Hispanic matriarchies."

Author's Note

This essay was written in conjunction with the exhibition *Sino Ka? Ano Ka?* at the San Francisco State University Art Department Gallery from September 20 through October 21, 1998. Featured artists included Eliza O. Barrios, Terry Acebo Davis, Reanne Agustin Estrada, Johanna Poethig, Stephanie Syjuco, Lucille Lozada Tenazas, Catherine Wagner, and Jenifer K. Wofford.

Notes

1. Powerful real estate interests were behind the forcible eviction of the remaining International Hotel residents on August 7, 1977, by more than three hundred city marshals; the building itself was subsequently destroyed. However, a considerable number of West Coast Filipino Americans still regard the International Hotel as a symbol of cultural resistance and a painful reminder of the irreconcilable conflict between big business and the working class in the struggle for neighborhood control. For more information, see Curtis Choy, prod. and dir., *The Fall of the I-Hotel* (San Francisco: National Asian American Telecommunications Association, 1993), film; Beverly Kordziel, "To Be a Part of the People," in *Asian Americans: The Movement and the Moment,* ed. Steve Louie and Glenn Omatsu (Los Angeles: University of California–Los Angeles Asian American Studies Center, 2001), 241–47; and James L. Sobredo, "From Manila Bay to Daly City: Filipinos in San Francisco," in *Reclaiming San Francisco: History, Politics, Culture,* ed. James Brook (San Francisco: City Lights, 1998), 273–86.

2. The conflation of traditional domestic crafts and "high art" finds its precedent in feminist art practice of the 1970s. Feminist artists sought to challenge the male-dominated art elite by elevating the domestic arts (sewing, costuming, quilting, embroidery, weaving, and so on) to forms of expression as valid as painting or sculpture. As distinctions between crafts and fine arts diminished, women's traditional arts were not only explored for formal, decorative possibilities but also utilized as vehicles for metaphor. Judy Chicago, Miriam Schapiro, and members of the Womanhouse project were among the many artists who incorporated needlework into feminist statements. Faith Ringgold turned to the traditional patchwork quilt as a means for exploring cultural identity.

   Even before the feminist movement, twentieth-century women artists experimented with nontraditional materials. In the 1930s, surrealist Meret Oppenheim covered a teacup, saucer, and spoon with fur. In the 1960s and early 1970s, Magdalena Abakanowicz, Lee Bontecou, Barbara Chase-Riboud, and Eva Hesse were just a few of the sculptors to work with fabric. Men also combined nontraditional materials—more closely associated with the home than with the art studio—with "high art"; Judith E. Stein, "Collaboration," in *The Power of Feminist Art,* ed. Norma Broude and Mary R. Garrard (New York: Harry N. Abrams, 1994), 226–45, notes that Robert Rauschenberg included patchwork quilts in his paintings, while Arthur Dove utilized scraps of lace and cloth in his collages. The "Pattern and Decoration Movement" of the 1970s also involved both men and women. During this same epoch, Filipino American artist Carlos Villa, then an abstract painter, created magnificent painted and feathered cloaks that derived inspiration from religious ceremonies and traditional Pacific Islander costuming/art. For more information, see *Fiberarts Magazine* out of Asheville, North Carolina, which consistently reports on artists working with nontraditional materials.

19
Theory in/of Practice: Filipina American Feminist Filmmaking

CELINE PARREÑAS SHIMIZU

Movies mark and make memory. Beyond time, film captures relationships between and among people in many senses, including the psychic and physical. Movies can shape your life, move you to tears, cause fear, and arouse pleasure in melodramas, horror films, and romantic comedies. Within its production, film is a relational medium: writers, directors, producers, actors, and crew interact in order to produce the multiple layers of meaning in a film. As spectators we relate to the film and to each other: noisy people behind us, tall people in front of us, and people we laugh or cry with shape our viewing experience. Beyond the physical dimensions of watching a movie, we also bring our racialized, gendered, classed, and sexualized positions to bear on our spectatorships. Authors, spectators, and critics all anticipate each other in their relationships as historically situated subjects. That is, to understand a movie, we must always ask why is it being made now, for whom, why in this particular form, and what the implications are of our particular understanding.

Limited representations of Filipina women in U.S. movies infuriate me as a Filipina American spectator—enough to compel me to become an author, filmmaker, and theorist. This is not a reaction or opposition to stereotypes, but a creative response that makes the medium work for different ends. It is a creative act that speaks of a commitment to culture, as a living struggle and practice.

To make films focused on Filipina women as a Filipina American not only comes to mean speech in the sense of talking out loud, talking back, and articulating a life, position, or idea not usually represented in movies. Making movies within a Filipina American practice is about making oneself known as a subject shaped and formed by particular experiences—experiences as racialized, gendered, sexual, immigrant; these compel in me the need to find a visual voice, not only literal or spoken, but quite bodily a visual voice. I understand film to require the body in intense ways. When directing my camera operator, the body must move in precise ways in order to capture the other embodiment at work of the actor in front of the camera who externalizes the psychic state in physical form. To speak in ways that are seen is to use the very regimes of the visual to capture my experiences within this brown female body. I understand the power of occupying space in the movies—onscreen, it is about representation in the visual record relevant to the writing of U.S. history itself; in the scene of spectatorship, it is about confronting skewed versions of your subjectivity presented in larger cultures of representation. For example, in *On Cannibalism*, Fatimah Tobing Rony describes the process of recognizing the primitivized "other" speaking her language in *King Kong* as injurious.[1] In *Bontoc Eulogy*, Marlon Fuentes imagines the lives of the Filipina/o natives on display at the 1904 World's Fair.[2] He dramatizes the lives and experiences of Filipina/os in a film that explores important questions of culture, identity, and history. Like these filmmakers, I believe in utilizing its power for productive ends in a present context where Filipina/os and Filipina/os Americans continue to struggle for recognition within a medium that has so often disempowered us in U.S. cinema.

This essay defines a Filipina American feminist film practice committed to using the very technologies of power to articulate the complexities of Filipina American subjectivities. I aim to explore theory and practice that interrogate the very mechanisms and grammar of film language and knowledge. I do so ultimately to address the serious conundrum of why my feminist Filipina American film practice engages the shooting of explicit sex acts as necessary in order to address the multiplicity of racialized, classed, and gendered experiences of Filipina American women. To assert the political aesthetics of my approach is notable in a medium whose industry is so incredibly stratified in terms of gender, race, and class parity—very few women are active directors among multitudes of men registered with the Directors Guild of America. The amount of money and time required to work in this medium is staggering, so that few may enter the room in the first place in order to play a game where women are frequently supplementary and those of color too often peripheral. My political aesthetic goals are situated within an independent filmmaking arena that criticizes the exclusionary nature of the U.S. cinema industry itself.

In terms of the structure of this essay, I explain the choice of cinema—a tool of neocolonialism as captured in the adage of "four hundred years in the convent and one hundred years in Hollywood"—to express the experiences of Filipina Americans. In this first section I define Filipina American filmmaking practice as an aesthetic of expression that emerges from concrete bodily experiences. In the second section I discuss how the sexual subjection of race and gender experiences gives rise to a filmmaking practice I call *metaprocess*, which sees itself applied in the title of this essay as "theory in/of practice." It sees my trajectory as a filmmaker move from Filipina American subjects to a Filipina American analytic. In the third section I discuss the engagement of film as a struggle for recognition, in the larger project of culture and the personal project of the self, through a critical, multipronged, and explicitly sexual feminist practice.

Bodily Speech/Filipina American Films

So many stories need to be told about the dizzyingly varied array of Filipina American experiences in order to diversify how we understand what constitutes being American as well as what it means to speak as a marginalized subject. As a subject, being a Filipina American can illuminate what it means to be included and excluded in the national narratives of American culture industries today. In this section I will delineate my coming into the work of film as expression formed by my experience as a Filipina American immigrant.

Growing up in 1970s and 1980s Manila, my siblings and I would wind down for the prime-time television melodramas *Anna Lisa* and *Flor De Luna*. Perhaps soap operas based on teen stars led me to think so melodramatically about my own teen life, which I narcissistically understood to be epic and in need of recording. I observed my world obsessively in journals and notebooks, on candy wrappers, and in my school planner. Living in a gated metropolitan suburb, playing in the private streets, going to country clubs, taking vacations at hot springs, spending weekends at the mall, and socializing at formal teens-only parties since age twelve—the journals fill with images of meticulously rendered trees from my backyard and blond white people swimming in blue waves. I read poetry voraciously—Lord Byron, Walt Whitman, the classics. I jotted down the lines with love, finding the rhythms between the words and lines. I practiced performing them in public for our school elocution contests. In Manila, preoccupied by drawing and poetry, I felt grounded in generations of privilege and belonging.

Uprooting to the United States in the 1980s, poetry and painting helped me make sense of the suddenly confusing world in which I felt so out of context. My context disappeared from under my feet so that every step felt incredibly unsure. In Cambridge, Massachusetts, living in the housing projects with an incredible diversity of Asian, Caribbean, and African immigrants, the Bookmobile and the public library saved my life during an intense period of the browning of my skin. Sudden poverty aggravated my racialization. By age fourteen, I worked early shifts at Dunkin Donuts before school and during weekends. Drawn by the appellation *colored girl*, in the public library I found Ntozake Shange's choreopoems, which speak in an uncapitalized, rhythmic, and powerful language. I caressed with my fingers the pages and embraced with my hunched shoulders the book *For Colored Girls Who Have Considered Suicide/When the Rainbow is Enuf*, holding on as it changed my life.[3] My drawings changed and now focused on observing the view of my closet with the stripes and black blocks of my clothes among the great big boxes of our family's stuff barely contained therein. We lived in so little space: six kids, two parents, grandma, and other immigrants coming in and out of a two-bedroom apartment on the seventh floor of a high-rise. Visiting the building twenty years after our immigration, the place is harsher than I remember.

Since then, I attended the University of California–Berkeley to major in English and art in the heyday of incredible racial diversity. Among other women of color working in the arts, I found my way to Ethnic Studies to study poetry and movies concerned with making sense of race, class, and gender. These new terms, part of a mantra in the 1980s era of identity politics, came to illuminate the incredible psychic and experiential formation of my immigration, labor, and family. Ethnic Studies gave me a language to describe my experience and to understand the historical and institutional forces contextualizing a seemingly personal and private experience. My education gave me a context in which to become more sure-footed as a brown woman in the United States. Faculty members, other women of color, looked me in the eye with the commitment to help me develop a strong and informed voice. Through their work they helped me to assert the centrality of my brownness and femaleness as the face of America itself—in terms of both the privilege and underprivilege that entails. Through their lives I imagined the actuality of making movies and pursuing an intellectual life studying race, class, sex, and gender—as an important matrix for a better understanding of the world.

So much of my expression as a speaking subject came to be shaped by a kind of hypersexuality or excessive sexuality imbricating Filipina women in American fantasy life. The revelation of the Asian fetish all around me—white men fawning over Asian women— at first appealed in light of growing up in Boston, where Asian girls and women did not warrant attraction in my particular world. In terms of my growing feminism, the discourse of sex tourism and mail-order brides became more directly linked to the sexual fantasies attributed to Asian American women like me as I walked down the street. Lurid suggestions of men who attributed intimate relations with me in Southeast Asian bars during the Vietnam war resonated during my own sexual awakening. The totally impossible conflation of Southeast Asian women with me as an Asian American college student greatly formed my commitments to cinema.

My experience shapes my expression. As a Filipina American filmmaker, I obsess with what it means to be caught as a sexually racialized and gendered body. Bringing together the written/spoken word, visual images, and political organizing in producing film, this powerful medium is the one I choose to battle with for recognition.

Filmmaking for me is a pronged fork. I aim to accomplish these goals when making a film:

1. To access the grammar of the film industry, especially in an era saturated with moving-image visual culture, in order to celebrate, critique, and comment on lives in the margins.

2. To puncture the historical record with visual images that lay claim to Filipina women's history so that it is not simply about the romance of succumbing to the power of representation but the complexities of what Lisa Lowe calls the "heterogeneity, hybridity, and multiplicity" of the Asian American experience.[4]

3. To produce culture in a kind of confrontation with the self in order to transform, learn, and grow; that is, to isolate the historical moment that produces the Filipina body as student, daughter, and worker in relation to others so that the process itself becomes not only a historical record, but an engagement not only with technology but also with schools, family, and other industries and institutions.

4. To use the produced film object as a way to come into conversation with others beyond those who see and recognize Filipina/os in America and American history—in other words, to go to places where Filipina/os have varied levels of visibility and racializations.

The larger and overall political project that led me to filmmaking includes the following questions about the craft itself: What does film do, not only to me, but to what people know about people like me? How can I use it to move others as it moves me? The cross-cutting between two actors speaking and the camera placement rule of the 180-degree line, both devices that provide a seamless viewing experience for the audience in Hollywood film, challenged me as an ordinary viewer. Learning how to choreograph the camera, actor, and objects in production and build music and sound constituted film grammar I needed to learn (and already expected as a spectator). So I went to a major U.S. film school to learn how white men made movies. Along the way I encounter a larger culture deeming me improper to pursue such learning.

Every time I confront the medium in my own hands, whether as a filmmaker or film professor—the camera, the light meter, the gels, and the c-stands—I aim to revise the questions and raise the stakes of filmmaking to exceed profit or "it's just entertainment" agendas. Beyond learning the conventions of language, it is important to keep asking questions about how the very basic grammar of film can learn about Filipina women or how can I transform the medium in order to represent in their company the lives of Filipina women. If the language of Hollywood is to focus on one typically white male hero, what does it mean to tell a story of, say, seven Filipina sisters with varying degrees of heroism? While learning the rules of law for traditional filmmaking, keeping at the surface the need to innovate in order to better tell stories from the margins—with justice—is crucial in order to write Filipina women into history and to produce knowledge about why it matters.

With this in mind, I learned to claim the right to hold the camera as one that was proper for me—for the prioritization of Filipina American lives is worthwhile. I use that strange word *proper* since somehow the directorial role was designated to be less proper for me than it was for both men of color and white men at film school and at professional film sets. Every time I step forward to claim the camera, it is a claiming of vocabulary, literacy, and my own possibility—learning how to speak by knowing how to make the camera serve my authorial intentions. When I worked as assistant camerawoman on other directors' sets, tracking focus on the camera lens held really high stakes for me—not only to prove myself worthy of my job, but also to learn the logic of the beast. The stakes rode high for me as I perched precariously on the dolly with my fingers moving the lens, contorting my body to fit the movement of the camera. The whole time I was aware that this is the equipment that allows for voice, intervention, and legibility. While this surely sounds melodramatic, it was very much an up-against-the-wall coming of age and rising to the occasion of claiming presence—for me to be at film school and on film sets, to understand how the apparatus works historically and technically, so as to determine what it sees and what others see through it.

While other filmmakers with mainstream sensibilities concern themselves differently, films are a way for me to come into collision with others who both encounter and make them. As I make movies professionally, and in my work as a professional production designer on independent films, I feel the tremendous need to read about the cinema and the way others have engaged its power historically, in order to understand better where I want to go and how to be more effective politically. On two panels about Filipina and Asian American filmmaking, Linda Mabalot—the late Filipina American filmmaker, media activist, and longtime executive director of the nation's oldest Asian American media center, Visual Communications—and I both identified the academy and nonprofit media organizations as key sites where independent filmmakers of color work. While outside the industry, such arenas are also the sites of similar political challenges, especially in terms of funding. Many others face more uncertain financial demands associated with independent filmmaking so that the term *homeless filmmaker* is not surprising. Other Filipina American filmmakers like former activist/radio producer/independent filmmaker Veena Cabreros-Sud, finished New York University Film School, directed *The Real World* on MTV, garnered a Disney Writing Fellowship, and now works as a writer on prime-time television—after garnering several awards as an experimental filmmaker. Filipino American filmmaker and Columbia University–trained Ernesto Foronda works as a Hollywood screenwriter and producer as well as a record producer and film curator. Prominent Filipina American Claire Aguilar, who was schooled at the University of California–Los Angeles, works as programming director at the Independent Television Service.

After finishing UCLA Film School, the need to read and study did not subside, so I enrolled in Stanford University's Modern Thought and Literature Program in order to learn and write while continuing to make short films. This is how I came to work as a professor who teaches film production, criticism, and theory at a major research university and as an experimental filmmaker funded by the academy, activism, and various philanthropic organizations. While limited, there is some certainty about being in the academy that affords an experimental filmmaker the ability to work apart from logics and goals of profit and to remain informed—especially in the work of research and teaching. As I note in my listing of various filmmakers above, many fronts form the battle for recognition within the film industry. For many female filmmakers of color, the fights must occur on multiple fronts, not only do they struggle as screenwriters, producers, and directors, but also as sexual minorities of color. It is not simply a linear battle for inclusion in the industry, but identifying the fronts that are best for your specific passions and are worthy of your time in the face of resistance to presence deemed political, thus anti-profit and anti-art.

A question explored by many feminist and filmmakers of color is: What provokes the multiple speech of film production and theory I describe for myself? The filmmaker Helen Lee asks, "If theorist/maker Trinh T. Minh-ha is right in her formulation of the 'triple bind,' that women of color subject formations owe allegiances to many communities and multiple categorizations, do these shape women of color filmmakers' multiple visions?"[5] In "Women's Cinema as Counter Cinema," Claire Johnston advocates a similar platform for women to *work* on many fronts.[6] She writes, "A repressive moralistic assertion that women's cinema is collaborative filmmaking is misleading and unnecessary. We should seek to operate on all levels, within the male-dominated industry and outside it."[7] Johnston confirms that one's situation informs expression or authorship. In order to be heard as minority subjects, according to her feminist platform, women need to speak *on many fronts*.

While remembering the historical context of their writing within nationalist anticolonial revolutionary struggles in Latin America, Third Cinema filmmakers theorize the meeting of practice and theory directly in their central texts. Indeed, Third Cinema theory tends to present politics and aesthetics in a binary schism. Thus, while the theory may seem dated in the way it calls up oppositions out of favor in these poststructuralist times, I recuperate this work in order to highlight its sophisticated understanding of working in multiple forms and fronts. In the classic essay "Towards a Third Cinema," Fernando Solanas and Octavio Gettino describe filmmakers as intellectuals;[8] as intellectuals, they need to work on multiple sites of struggle. As Solanas and Gettino note, "Revolution begins when the masses sense the need for change and their intellectual vanguards begin to study and carry out this change through activities on different fronts."[9]

For Third Cinema, the aim of speaking on multiple fronts is to widen the reach of one's ideas as well as to find the forum where one speaks most effectively. Solanas and Gettino continue, "The intellectual must find through his action the field in which he can perform the most efficient work."[10] Notably, the primary subject in this discourse is gendered as male. Nonetheless, film practice and theory engage in the common task that is enriching to both.

Third Cinema prioritizes the importance of diffusing art in the life of society, to raise "the possibility for everyone to make films."[11] As Julio Garcia Espinosa confirms in "For an Imperfect Cinema," beauty as determined by the minority elite is not enough—but all should help to create our taste of culture by becoming artists and workers alike.[12] Stuart Hall of the Birmingham School of Cultural Studies also cites Frantz Fanon in his understanding of culture. While colonization "distorts, disfigures and destroys" the history of the colonized, what Hall calls "act[s] of imaginative re-discovery" create a resilient culture based on the present.[13] If the Third Cinema and Cultural Studies goals are to build institutions that dissolve aesthetics out of elitism and bring to the fore cultures of resilience relevant to everyday people, multiple speech helps to decolonize ideas and models established by colonialism. That is, theory and practice, together constituting what I define as Filipina American feminist filmmaking, help to dislodge colonial culture regarding cinema. Thus, engaging in film as the very technology that binds allows me to identify the potentialities and possibilities of speech in whatever forum feels best—theory and practice of explicit sexuality as a feminist film practice.

To speak from the place where one is or can be most articulate is a testament to the beauty of fear in making steps outside one's proper place. Filmmaking for me is the reclamation of fear and shame in order to get to a place of beauty, a place of saying what you want, no matter how awkward or tentative. It is beautiful because even if you are screaming it out loud, you are saying something that may feel incoherent so as to feel more coherent in the world. Filipina/o American films with feminist and postcolonial sensibilities, like Ernesto Foronda's *Back to Bataan Beach* and Veena Cabreros-Sud's *Sisters N Brothers* and *Stretchmark*,[14] transform the way I understand the experiences of Filipina/os in America. *Back to Bataan Beach* illustrates hybrid sensibilities of the postcolonial Filipino condition through a rendering of American and Spanish colonialisms both humorous and indicative of traumatic injury. Cabreros-Sud's rendition of the gendered encounter of a Filipina and Filipino American man and woman colliding on the street in *Sisters N Brothers* captures the varied, competing, and contradictory versions of the racial experience. *Stretchmark* moves the viewer with its intensely personal representation of the public and private struggles of a brown single mother. The filmic record in these works helps to frame everyday lives for Filipino Americans in resonant ways. This process, in turn, helps to make what we know and what we imagine in our futures; that is, the burdens of colonialism, racism, and injustice do not preclude the act of imagining many possibilities in making meaning out of our lives—envisioned and executed in movies that move, thrill, affirm, and question us. Movies offer new possibilities, forms, and structures of legibility for imagining and recognizing Filipina/o Americans.

Explicit Sex Acts in Filipina American Feminist Film Practice

In my own film work, I attempt to investigate the moving-image, visual production of race and sexuality onscreen and the scenes of its making, reception, and criticism. In this section I focus on moments in my films where I present racialized sex acts as a productive force and discuss the feminist practice of shooting sex acts. It seems extremely novel for a Filipina American to shoot explicit racialized sex acts, especially in light of the medium, which portrays Filipina women so sexually in popular transnational discourse.[15] Subjected by sexuality in popular cinema, my own articulations of subject position are constituted by a long history of sex acts on screen: *made by* sexual imagery, I *make* sexual imagery. This equation of experience informing expression is an important formulation in my work that is most apparent in my commitment to theorizing race and sexuality.

Here I will discuss, within my work, scenes that posit sex as productive in telling the specificities of a racial context or community. The first film, *Mahal Means Love and Expensive*, is based on ethnographies of Filipina American students regarding colonialism, immigration and sexuality;[16] *Super Flip* emerges from the experimental ethnographies of Filipina/o American low-wage workers in San Francisco, wherein I discover a narrative of sex and shopping as coping mechanisms. In *Mahal*, a young Filipina American artist recognizes the emotions and aesthetics called upon by sexual engagement within a history of colonialism and immigration. In *Super Flip*, a young immigrant maid cleans up her life by leaving her philandering husband and exposing the messy morass of her home life.

Informed by interviews with Filipina American students for *Mahal Means Love and Expensive*, I constructed an experimental narrative around locating racial truth in sexual experiences. Choosing to push the Kodak film stock to saturated colors of redness and skin to become so brown, the mood and design of the film reflected the colonial memory of the homeland imposed over the experience of sexual awakening for my protagonist, a subject who engages simultaneous self-objectification and subject formation occurring in the sex act. As a feminist filmmaker, it was very difficult to arrange shooting the explicit sex acts on my set. A minimal number of people—the director of photography, the actors, and I shot the scene. I wanted to empower the actors to demand whatever conditions necessary to feel safe in their nakedness. The simulation of the sexual act worked within the narrative as a site of volcanic eruption—red-lava paint rubbing all over brown skin expressed bodies meeting, but somehow colliding and not connecting. Rather than solely express pleasure in sex, I express the importance of trauma in a visual field of movies and print media otherwise saturated with Filipina women as prostitutes and mail order brides.

The first scene from *Super Flip* features a Filipina immigrant maid having sex with her husband; his fist punches the camera and, in effect, the spectator as I establish patriarchy.[17] Against a representational field that shows Asian women in nondiscerning enjoyment of sex, my shot prioritizes the maid's subjectivity and illustrates her nonenjoyment. My interviews with Filipino men, friendly bragging sessions about sexual escapades, reflected Asian American historical narratives about the prowess of Filipino men as exceptional in light of the feminization of Asian American men. The parallel to the 1920s and 1930s world of Filipino sexual masculinity, discussed by Ron Takaki in *Strangers from a Different Shore* and whose group aesthetics are represented well in Fred Cordova's *Filipinos: The Forgotten Asian Americans*,[18] informed my production design. I shot in pool halls and nightclubs, some the very sites of early Filipino American history in San Francisco. In the sex scenes, however, I wanted to bring in the women and men's varied, racially based, sexual, and gendered narratives. Working with the actors, we shot the Latina–Filipino sexual encounter between the husband and his girlfriend in Spanish and Tagalog in a scene exploring a shared Catholic sensibility regarding the sexual experience. The scene between the white woman and the patriarchal Filipino man contrasts directly with the opening sex scene. The white woman achieves satisfaction even if the man refuses to participate. The sexualities of the Filipina and white women come into conversation and collision with the men.

In these films, sex is a site of power relations. As a site of cultural meeting, it is also where racialization forms and transforms in relation to others. Sexual pleasure in my films counters nationalist and racial discourses that advocate a particularly negative sexuality for racial subjects. Rather than understanding racial subjects to be dominated by the objectifying force of sexuality—or simplifying the role of race in the visualization of sex—I show the productive encounter of these two powerful social forces. Filmmaker Lindsey Jang characterizes the phenomenon of filmmakers of color trafficking in sexual images as compliant to dominant cultural scripts. The framework of compliance, complicity, or capitulation is inadequate, for it renders the subjecthood of the marginal as totally powerless. While power may be imbalanced, to diagnose objectification as complete so no resistance occurs is more dehumanizing. Case in point: the situation is more complicated, for I shoot sex scenes aiming for the transformation of established ideas about racial sexuality. My larger aesthetic aims to express living experience by finding ways in which to speak, respond, and create new cultures from that lived experience. I recast sex in order to move it away from discourses of subjugation to those of productive, volatile, and even life-changing self-formation.

My most recent work aims to further expose the process of dominant cinema—particularly its ability to naturalize fantasies of Asian women into visible fact. Following Frantz Fanon in "The Fact of Blackness,"[19] *The Fact of Asian Women* shows how the sight of the racially and sexually marked Asian woman in American popular film shows the centrality of sex in her representation.[20] *The Fact of Asian Women* is a documentary about the bind of being an

Asian American actress in Hollywood. Within the project, contemporary actresses reenact scenes from Hollywood films in order to comment on, criticize, and evaluate them within and beyond the framework of racial and sexual stereotypes. Dressed in costumes that evoke famous emblematic characters of Asian female hypersexuality, the actors perform published quotations and reenact scenes from Hollywood movies featuring actresses Anna May Wong, Nancy Kwan, and Lucy Liu—in order to evaluate them. The film was shot in San Francisco in 2001 with a professional crew of independent women of color, filmmakers whose lighting and camera work interrogated the "sexual lighting" and "male gaze" of Hollywood films. In editing, I created a layering of voices that included my critical voice as well as the actors and crew coming together to critique Hollywood images. As a whole, the documentary dissects and reimagines the grammar of representation composing Asian women in popular culture in order to alter their traditional morphology in cinema.

The Fact of Asian Women illustrates the relationship of young contemporary Asian American actresses to the Hollywood Asian American femme fatale as fantasy. In the film I argue that racialized sexuality and the male gaze organize the performance, lighting, and camera framing of three generations of Asian American femme fatales in Hollywood. My objects of study are emblematic scenes from *Shanghai Express*, featuring Anna May Wong;[21] *The World of Suzie Wong*, starring Nancy Kwan;[22] and *Charlie's Angels*, costarring Lucy Liu.[23] The film is organized into three parts: the studio, the streets, and the stores. In the

Fig. 19.1 From *The Fact of Asian Women* (2002). Left to right: Lena Zee, Angelina Cheng, Celine Parreñas Shimizu, and Kim Jiang in *The Fact of Asian Women*. Photo by Stephanie Chen. (Reprinted with permission.)

studio, the contemporary actors perform interview transcripts of the original actors' published interviews. In directing the young actors to reenact movie scenes, I expose our conversation when creating the opposite performance. In the streets, the hired actors recast the endings of the original films. Finally, I interview the contemporary actors about the entire shooting experience while in stores. The stores express the individual styles of the actors; after choosing their own clothes, they look very different from the characters they play, a method of exposure Trinh T. Minh-ha pioneers in her film *Surname Viet Given Name Nam* (1989).[24] Through this process, in my context I show how the actors do have power, although quite limited, in shaping the images we consume. By taking them to the streets, I aim for the screen and scene to collide.

The film is an exploration of the Asian woman's depiction in the cinema as a fantasy rather than a real figure that is ethnically specific to Chinese women. As a Filipina American, and thus marginalized within the Asian American grouping, I note how, nonetheless, the images stand in for Asian American women as a whole. It is important to address and interrogate the monolithic production of classifying Asian American women for their similarities, but how exactly is that sexuality different for other Asian women? It is interesting that this film enjoyed programming within a Filipina/o American program at Visual Communications' Asian American International Film Festival in Los Angeles. I surmise that it falls under the curatorial categorization for it offers a Filipina American feminist critique of the classification of hypersexuality for Asian women in the U.S. cinema industry, an image that is actually based on Chinese Americans, a specific and more dominant ethnic group. This film critiques the production of hypersexuality for the whole as constituted by the few. As a Filipina American filmmaker, I begin by making films specific to Filipina American women and move to consider the broader categorization of Asian women. I believe that *Asian women* is a term that does not capture the heterogeneity of women who fall under that sign but it is wielded in order to gain legibility in the industry where casting frequently operates using limited categorized breakdowns such as female, Asian, or 20s. Actors of color must break through the limited roles designated for Asians and try for unmarked roles meant for whites.

When my contemporary Asian American female actors reenact scenes from popular Hollywood films in order to reexamine the construction of image, and when they perform the characters of Anna May Wong, Nancy Kwan, and Lucy Liu on the streets, young contemporary actors collide with these "ghosts." In both scenes we hear the young actresses comment on what it felt like to perform these characters and roles. Through this method in these scenes, I employ the elements of the cinematic language I call *metaprocess*. This method allows me to actually film my favorite part of the process—working with actors as they challenge my vision for the work. I formulate this language in order to break the edification of these Hollywood images, following what Loni Ding calls the "showing of the opposite" in her film strategy,[25] and what Julio Garcia Espinosa describes further as the Third Cinema mission, that "above all ... imperfect cinema must show the process which generates the problems. It is thus the opposite of a cinema principally dedicated to celebrating results ... the opposite of a cinema which 'beautifully illustrates' ideas or concepts which we already possess."[26] I take Espinosa's demand to "show the process which generates the problems." In dissecting the very language producing Asian female hypersexuality, I expose the grammar and technology of film in order to reimagine and reutilize them.

The reason I quote from this masculinist, Marxist movement of Third Cinema is because of its clear engagement with theory and practice that matters to people. While adhering to the political beliefs of a decolonizing practice, I aim for metaprocess to capture how visual production emerges from a mutual imbrication of dominant cinema and experimental voice.

In the second part of the film, I bring together the past and the present in order to remove the actors from the screen by taking them from the studio and streets to the stores to question their legitimacy and believability among the living, and then through interviews that capture the creative work that occurs behind the scenes. My director of photography, Yun Jong Suh, and gaffer Serene Fang both considered their assignments "sexual lighting" and "male-gaze–framing." Like the actors, the cinematographers took on what they describe as the painful process of learning what it means to shoot Asian women in traditional ways. Through the process of reenactment in cinematography, directing, and performance, I isolate the creative process as a site of authorship that captures the social world's poetics or what white men seemingly intended Asian women to appear to be. By showing the production of scenes as encounters of power, I hope that viewers see that the encounter continues with them, whether they simply accept the roles as passive viewers or to counter those images with their response, such as in the possibility of becoming authors of actual film works themselves. In my future work, I look forward to more embodiments of metaprocess, which most precisely exposes the procedure by which images are made.

Theory in/of Practice

In this final section, I evoke how social categorizations provoke multiple forms of speech in the form of theory and practice informed by the spirit of experimentation. I keep at the surface the need to ask questions about the limits and possibilities of existing forms. The multiple speech of production and theory allows me to see the social problem from multiple angles—that is, reading, writing, interview, ethnography, archival research, and production keep focused on the tensions of pain and pleasure in experiencing images as well as how images come from experience within a brown female body. Through the assertion of aesthetics based on experience and the method of the metaprocess

I describe above, I aim to provide an episteme regarding theory and practice, or a "theory in/of practice." A term that comes from Michel Foucault's *The Archaeology of Knowledge* and *Aesthetics, Method and Epistemology*,[27] an *episteme* indicates the "totality of relations that can be discovered, for a given period."[28] Creative practice articulates a theory of the world; theory in itself is and emerges from creative practice. Theory is practice. Creative activity is theory. Both are political projects.

Accordingly, I speak in these multiple forums in order to ensure the applicability of my findings regarding the productive relationships among race, sex, and the moving image. In reflecting on my work as a film theorist, I discover that my films aim to ensure closeness to people: actors, viewers, and producers working together in a process that isolates painful implications of experiencing racial sexual images as well as the pleasure in expressing or making these images. This important question always rises when it comes to playing with fire, that is, speaking in a language that has disenfranchised Filipina/os and Filipina/o Americans. Paying attention to the relationships constituting the cinema such as those of director-actor and actor-spectator maintains a certain kind of accountability to people and their experiences regarding these images. Such attention to relations with others helps me to make existing scholarship more relevant—that is, the assertion of creative agency to actors within a framework of relationality emerges only from my actual film practice. I collaborate with actors and my crew in order to shape my authorship. For example, when directing Lena Zee to "show the opposite" during rehearsals for *The Fact of Asian Women*, I told her to find pleasure in avenging the rape of Anna May Wong's character in *Shanghai Express*. To perform pleasure would, however, further marginalize the character. The strategy of "showing the opposite" here reminds me of the damaging social implications of "play" in the creative world.

My more traditional scholarly work, archival research, ethnographic methods, and close readings help me to formulate my creative process in production. While the performances in scenes of *The Fact of Asian Women* are not composed of kissing, touching, or copulating, they are racialized sex acts. While the original scenes did not feature traditional sex acts, the exteriority of Asian women promises an interiority overdetermined by sexuality so that walking on the streets, for these women, becomes a testament to the saturation of sexuality onscreen that does not make sense in the scenes of real life. For the actresses in my film, that is, moving like Anna May Wong constitutes a kind of pathological asexuality for Lena Zee; strutting like Nancy Kwan results in a particular kind of sexual availability for Angelina Cheng that leaves her shaken on the streets; and Kim Jiang's donning dominatrix gear to evoke Lucy Liu reveals the caricature quality of contemporary Asian female roles. Racialized sex acts are not just about performing various acts as Asian females, but in being the very repository of perverse sexuality. That bisexual acts emanate from an already perverse being. Extending Homi Bhabha's argument—that

Fig. 19.2 From *The Fact of Asian Women* (2002). Kim Jiang performs a fantasy of the dominatrix near Maiden Lane in San Francisco, CA. Photo by Stephanie Chen. (Reprinted with permission of the artist.)

"'skin' in racist discourse," itself based on Fanon's "epidermal schema," is a prime signifier of racial difference—The *Fact of Asian Women* explores how Asian women's visibility in film indicates a primarily sexual ontology.[29]

In terms of the multipronged approach to a Filipina American feminist practice, there's a dance involved in playing with fire in the belly of the beast. That is, when engaging the technology of film in Los Angeles—it is a struggle not quite captured in the binary of resistance/opposition or capitulation to power typically characterizing such battles. A feminist Filipina American film practice recognizes one's position as both subject and object. While it is important to understand one's history of objectification and marginalization, it is equally important to note that one is absolutely not powerless or completely objectified and marginalized as a Filipina American filmmaker. Actually, precisely because of their marginalized status, Filipina women are always at risk of being appropriated and commodified when coming into speech and subjection. If representations of explicit sexuality risk particular interpretations that may reaffirm hypersexuality or docility, my answer is a question, a resounding "So what?"—especially if it allows the discussion of trauma, injury, pleasure, and self-affirmation as central experiences for Filipina American women in sex. My movement from films specific to Filipina women to an analytic of questioning the categorization of Asian women as hypersexual beings is informed by a concern and commitment to experimenting with form in order to say something more about cultures that classify, exclude, and fetishize.

Production and theory are both creative processes of relevance to culture and society. We are all producers of culture and knowledge whether we see, are seen, write, are written, read, shoot, laugh, or cry in the movies. To work in multiple realms critically is to explore social problems from many lenses and technologies in order to evaluate how we may best contribute to struggles for recognition in moving-image media. At the same time, multiple speech expands our ability to envision solutions and widen our capacities to feel the implications of what we think and write.

Notes

1. Fatimah Tobing Rony, prod. and dir., *On Cannibalism* (New York: Women Make Movies, 1994), 6 min. videocassette; Merian C. Cooper, prod., Ernst B. Schoedsack, dir., *King Kong* (USA: RKO Pictures, 1933) 105 min.
2. Marlon Fuentes, prod. and dir., *Bontoc Eulogy* (San Francisco: National Asian American Telecommunications Association, 1995), videocassette.
3. Ntozake Shange, *For Colored Girls Who Have Considered Suicide/When the Rainbow Is Enuf: A Choreopoem* (San Lorenzo: Shameless Hussy, 1975).
4. Lisa Lowe, "Heterogeneity, Hybridity, and Multiplicity: Marking Asian American Differences," *Diaspora* 1, no. 1 (1991): 44.
5. Helen Lee, "A Peculiar Sensation," in *Dangerous Women,* ed. Elaine Kim and Chungmoo Choi (London: Routledge, 1998), 293; Trinh T. Minh-ha, *Woman Native Other* (Bloomington: Indiana University Press, 1989).
6. Claire Johnston, "Women's Cinema as Counter Cinema," in *Film and Feminism,* ed. E. Ann Kaplan (London: Oxford University Press, 2000), 22–34.
7. Ibid., 33.
8. Fernando Solanas and Octavio Gettino, "Towards a Third Cinema," in *New Latin American Cinema,* ed. Michael Martin (Detroit: Wayne State University Press, 1997), 44–63.
9. Ibid., 46.
10. Ibid., 47.
11. Julio Garcia Espinosa, "For an Imperfect Cinema," in Martin, ed., *New Latin American Cinema* (London: BFI, 1983), 28.
12. Ibid., 29.
13. Stuart Hall, "Cultural Identity and Cinematic Representation," *Framework,* no. 36 (1989): 69.
14. Ernesto Foronda, dir. and prod., *Back to Bataan Beach* (San Francisco: National Asian American Telecommunications Association, 1995), videocassette; Veena Cabreros-Sud, dir. and prod., *Sisters N Brothers* (San Francisco: National Asian American Telecommunications Association, 1994), videocassette. Veena Cabreros-Sud, dir. and prod., *Stretchmark* (San Francisco: National Asian American Telecommunications Association, 1996), videocassette.
15. Roland Tolentino, "Bodies, Letters, Catalogs: Filipinas in Transnational Space," *Social Text,* no. 48 (1996): 49–76.
16. Celine Parreñas Shimizu, dir. and prod., *Mahal Means Love* and *Expensive* (San Francisco: Celine Parreñas Shimizu, 1993), film; Shimizu@asamst.ucsb.edu.
17. Celine Parreñas Shimizu, dir. and prod., *Super Flip* (San Francisco: Celine Parreñas Shimizu, 1997), film; Shimizu@asamst.ucsb.edu.
18. Ronald Takaki, *Strangers from a Different Shore* (Boston: Back Bay, 1998); Fred Cordova, *Filipinos: The Forgotten Asian Americans* (Dubuque, Iowa: Kendall/Hunt, 1983).
19. Frantz Fanon, "The Fact of Blackness," in *Black Skin, White Masks,* trans. Charles Markmann and Constance Farrington (New York: Grove, 1967).
20. Celine Parreñas Shimizu, dir. and prod., *The Fact of Asian Women* (San Francisco: Celine Parreñas Shimizu, 2002), digital film.
21. Adolf Zukor, prod., Josef Von Sternberg, dir., *Shanghai Express* (USA: Paramount Pictures, 1932), 80 min. videocassette.
22. Ray Stark, prod., Richard Quine, dir., *The World of Suzie Wong* (USA: Paramount Pictures, 1960), 126 min. videocassette.

23. Drew Barrymore, prod., (McG) Joseph McGinty Nichol, dir., *Charlie's Angels* (USA: Columbia Pictures, 2000), 90 min. videocassette.

24. Trinh T. Minh-ha, dir., *Surname Viet Given Name Nam* (New York: Women Make Movies, 1989), 108 min.

25. Loni Ding, "Strategies of an Asian American Filmmaker," in *Moving the Image: Independent Asian Pacific American Media Arts 1970–1990*, ed. Russell Leong (Los Angeles: University of California Asian American Studies Center Press, 1992), 47.

26. Espinosa, "For an Imperfect Cinema," 32.

27. Michel Foucault, *The Archaeology of Knowledge*, trans. A. M. Sheridan Smith (New York: Pantheon, 1972); Michel Foucault, *Aesthetics, Method, and Epistemology*, ed. James D. Faubion, trans. Robert Hurley (New York: New Press, 1998).

28. Foucault, *Aesthetics*, xxviii.

29. Homi K. Bhabha, *The Location of Culture* (London: Routledge, 1994), 78, 82.

20

Resisting Appropriation and Assimilation via *(a)eromestizaje* and Radical Performance Art Practice

GIGI OTÁLVARO-HORMILLOSA

(a)eromestizaje is my concept for subversive hybridity that celebrates the aerodynamic, sex-positive, and ethereal manifestations of identities grounded in shifting notions of community, desire, and cultural resistance. The root word, *mestizaje*, is a term used to describe the race mixture of Spanish and indigenous blood that is prevalent in Latin America and the Philippines. I see *mestizaje* as simultaneously a fortunate and unfortunate consequence of colonialism, in that the genocide and rape of indigenous races led to the creation of a new group of mixed-race people, such as the large majority of Latin Americans and Filipinos today who acknowledge both their indigenous and European roots. Being of Filipino and Colombian heritage myself, I embrace the many cultures of conflict that make up my complex identity born out of a moment of world transformation, as in the case of colonial conquest. Furthermore, I recognize the way in which colonial gender constructs continue to manifest themselves in contemporary communities of color, specifically via machismo as a mechanism for men of color to continually prove themselves because of the conquest of their masculinity. For this reason, I believe that queers of color have immense potential for dismantling binary constructs of race, gender, and sexuality that continue to oppress our communities locally and globally. I have developed my own strategies and art practice around this vision of cultural resistance by way of *(a)eromestizaje*, which is both the queering of *mestizaje* as well as the racial hybridization of queerness.

In the process of resisting dominant cultural practices, I feel that it is important to avoid getting caught up in the deconstruction of representations of our communities (and the people who continue to perpetuate such negative cultural stereotypes), in order to preserve the creative energy that is necessary to develop new possibilities and visions. As a performance artist, I attempt to do so by integrating movement, theory, video, and percussion. I see interdisciplinary form as a parallel to the content of my work that references the multiple discourses and community borders I perpetually cross in an effort to encourage understanding among people-of-color communities and queer communities. One of my video/performance pieces, *Inverted Minstrel*, is a good example of this difficult task of attempting to merge multiple discourses that have a specific entry point into interrogating heteropatriarchal hegemony. The concept for *Inverted Minstrel* came about because of my thought process, which began when I first arrived in the Bay Area. I began to develop a critical essay about the politics of hip-hop within queer communities of color, particularly Filipino and Latino communities. I chose to focus, or "be inspired," by popular hip-hop culture (as opposed to conscious, progressive, or underground hip-hop that is developed from antiracist, antisexist, and anticapitalist politics) because of the the sexism and homophobia that is so prevalent in this genre, as well as the privileged status hip-hop enjoys due to its centrality in American pop culture, which is one of the primary vehicles of U.S. imperialism. As a mixed-race artist disillusioned by mass-produced pop culture and disgusted by the way in which people of color have been represented and represent themselves in such forms as pop hip-hop culture, I feel that it is critical for queer artists and artists of color to challenge these representations while creating new possibilities.

In the creation and development process for *Inverted Minstrel*, I used the concept and imagery of an inverted minstrel (in terms of race, gender, and sexuality) to write an essay that would illustrate my ideas and questions about cultural appropriation, inversions of hierarchy, Afrophallocentrism, Europhallocentrism, black/white sexual supremacist ideals, relational patriarchies, U.S. racial formation, and the way in which U.S. imperialism influences racial constructions around the world. I decided to create a video of the essay and deliver the text in the voice of Frantz Kafka's ape, from "Address to the Academy," who is overcome by various contemporary voices (the Filipino; the *vato*—a Mexican/Chicano term that is the equivalent to a "thug" or a "homeboy" in American slang; the redneck; the dyke, and so forth) as he/she performs the act of thinking out these issues and writing a paper with the help of Curious George (my performance partner/puppet).

Throughout the majority of the video, the camera is set in front of this character, who is sitting behind a laptop and writing the essay, while channeling the various voices pertaining to these stereotypical characters. I am dressed in a white shirt and tie, with a goatee painted on my face. To a certain degree, the appearance of the character implies that he/she is an assimilated, well-educated, privileged person of color who is on his/her way to corporate America. The scenes of the character in the process of writing and speaking, are interspersed with scenes of the inverted minstrel's performance sequence (described in the following paragraph), anthropological images of various Filipinos, images of popular culture from Elvis to Eminem, Snoop Dogg and Foxy Brown, and text screens that highlight the critical sections of the essay that is being written and spoken. *Inverted Minstrel* exists as a video, and was also performed as a live piece in conjunction with the video. During the live performance, I play a version of the video that does not include the images of the inverted minstrel's performance sequence, since this is performed live. Throughout the performance, the video and the live actions illustrate one another. The video stops at various points throughout the performance, while the inverted minstrel performs a series of actions, and at other times plays while the inverted minstrel is either frozen in tableau or in the process of performing a subtle action that does not interfere with the video.

The video starts to play as I enter and perform in drag as a *vato* by painting a goatee on my face; I begin to gesticulate accordingly with a boom box to my ear. I then deconstruct this image by disrobing (under my boxing robe, I am in full body paint—half black/half white—with the exception of my face, and I am wearing a dildo-less, politicized harness loincloth along with American flag–printed panties) and posing as a *vato* playmate, which embodies the juxtaposition of extreme representations of masculinity and femininity. I then bind my breasts and unravel my gigantic phallus prop, which has been hidden from audience view under a small red blanket. The gigantic phallus prop is half black and half white. I stylistically strap it on so that the colors of the tool appear to be the inverse of the colors on my body. A series of acts follow involving the phallus and two small, funny-looking, plastic male figures resembling a white Ken doll and a black Ken doll posing for *Play Girl*.

Later on in the creative process, I developed another piece, which provided the historical context to the diorama piece. I took on the persona of a traditional minstrel by putting on blackface paint and dancing in a distorted manner with a bamboo stick. The minstrel performance takes place before the video/performance diorama described previously. The fictional character (partially based on the history of blackface performance) performed with a description that was slide-projected as a backdrop. The text read

> *Iggy*: Hello der. Ma name is Ignacio Balinguit, but you can call me Iggy, das ma stage name anyways. Ma grea, grea, grea, great grampappy, Pedro Balinguit, was as a chief from de Visayan Island ob de Philippines. He done jumped a slave ship dat was on'is way ta Spain from Acapulco, Mexico. He landed in N'Orleans, Louisiana, and married an Injun-black woman der. Ma family's been roun'ere eber since. Folks, dey say I dance real good. I hear dat de white men up North, dey becoming popular and making big bucks by paintin' dey faces black and doin' Ethiopian dances. Well, hot dawg! I'ma fixin' to make me some bucks like so!

The traditional minstrel character functioned as a meeting point between the past and the present. It was important for me to connect my observations about Filipino American identity formation in the Bay Area to the history of blackface performance. When I first moved to the Bay Area in 1998, I began to notice Afrocentric trends among Filipino American culture, particularly youth culture. One of my first observations occurred when I attended my first Filipino festival in 1998 at Yerba Buena Gardens in San Francisco. For the first time, I became exposed to a Filipino American youth culture, which I perceived to be a Filipino American version of hip-hop/pop. I assumed then that this had been a subject of concern to Filipino Americans who had been here longer, observing with critical eyes these practices of appropriation of black American cultural forms on the part of our people. However, it is important to acknowledge differences in appropriation of black culture and other non-white cultures by whites who might do so in a colonizing manner (as a historically consistent sense of entitlement over "other" cultural practices and artifacts) as opposed to other people of color who might do so as a shared practice of resistance against the white power structure.

Fig. 20.1 From *Inverted Minstrel.* Photo by Nancy Ericsson. (Reprinted with permission of the artist.)

These initial observations came as a surprise to me, given that I had never come into contact with such a large number of Filipinos. Growing up in Miami, where the dominant culture is Latino, I had very little exposure to anything Asian other than my mother's or grandmother's Filipino cooking or their Tagalog conversations. It didn't help that we were raised in such a way that our Asian heritage was secondary. Consequently, as a child, I unconsciously experienced patriarchy in a racialized manner in which I was unable to fully explore my Asian self. Given the structures of racism that perpetuate the notion that *Asian* means "submissive" while *Latino* means "macho and aggressive," it's as if cultural stereotype triumphed in our household. Due to this absence of Filipino—much less, Asian—culture during my coming of age, these first observations of the Bay Area, Filipino, hip-hop head phenomenon were somewhat shocking, despite the fact that on some level I could identify with it in that there was a time during my college years when I became involved in hip-hop music culture. It was a period during which I unconsciously adopted an Afrocentric approach in the cultivation of my critical perspective. I hadn't really questioned the consequences of Afrocentrism within cross-racial coalition work, since that seemed to be the model that most people of color embraced within Third World campus activism. However, toward the end of my college years, I began to question my own Afrocentrism, in terms of both my appropriation of Afrocentric models of resistance as well as my neglect of my own history and the creation of my own cultural practices of resistance. By the time I finished college and headed to the Bay Area, the wheels of this thought process were beginning to roll.

Once I arrived in the Bay Area, I was overwhelmed and excited by the incredible level of *mestizaje* I encountered, which manifested itself in such identities as Filipino Puerto Rican, African American Korean, Iranian Guatemalteco, or Japanese Nicaraguense, to name a few. In addition, I became more aware of the way in which the historical forces of colonialism had created enormous mixed-race communities such as the African/Latino/Asian populations that had emerged as distinct cultures throughout the Americas. Therefore, as a disclaimer, I want to add that in using blanket terms such as Asian, Latino/a, or nonwhite/nonblack, I intend to use "strategic essentialism" (as in Gayatri Spivak's use of the term[1]) as a way to isolate racial and cultural forces in order to illustrate their impact on each other rather than exclude multiracial identities, myself included.*

---

*When addressing race relations in a U.S. context throughout this essay, my use of the term "blacks" refers to people of African descent in the United States (i.e., African American, Jamaican, Puerto Rican, etc.). I consciously do not use "African American" because I feel that this term privileges African *Americans* while excluding Afro-Latinos, Afro-Caribbeans, and other non-American people of African descent who share similar experiences with African Americans in the United States, but are also culturally distinct.

I also want to make an important note that in the past, I have written pieces in response to narcissistic claims by black-identified writers who were accusing Asians of "copying blacks" and limiting the issue of cultural appropriation to the Asian/black hip-hop issue (and other instances of appropriation of black American culture specifically), while ignoring the influence of Asian and Latino culture on black-American culture. One of these particular instances occurred in college when I responded to a piece written by a Latina student in which she denied that racism or any other structure of oppression affected Asians in a substantial way. Clearly, in my opinion, she was writing from a perspective that supports the Asian "model minority" myth, which ultimately denies the reality of the diverse range of histories of oppression experienced by various Asian populations throughout the Americas. This incident revealed the way in which my mixed-race identity could be a point of identification or disidentification, depending on context. It also revealed the level of complexity in approaching issues of cultural appropriation and the manner in which one's alliances determine one's justification (or lack thereof) in the process of (mis)appropriating culture. For example, since Latino/as and blacks are assumed to share more cultural similarities than Asians and blacks, I might feel more "justified" in being a hip-hop head as a result of identifying more with my Latina self as opposed to my Asian self; but then, I think to myself, how do Filipinos fall into this picture, given their cultural similarity to Latinos as a result of a shared Spanish colonial history? What about their connection to the African diaspora as evidenced by the *negritos*, Filipinos living in the Visayan region whose physical features are similar to those of Africans?

Though hip-hop is often perceived as a culture that is perpetually (mis)appropriated, one could argue that hip-hop itself has partly been created by multiple communities, particularly if one traces the roots of hip-hop to jazz. For instance, the heavy influence of South Asian musical and spiritual traditions on jazz artists such as Alice and John Coltrane, Eric Dolphy, Sonny Rollins, and Pharoah Sanders, and other examples, such as Wu Tang Klan, or Willie Ninja, the well-known 1980s New York City drag diva featured in the film *Paris Is Burning*,[2] are often not acknowledged, nor is the fact that Nuyoricans (Puerto Ricans living in New York City) played a significant role in the development of hip-hop as a musical form. (And let's not forget the series of orientalist commercials that were played throughout the Source hip-hop Awards 1999 in which black hip-hop artists performed their own version of orientalism.[3]) These forms of appropriation of Asian culture on the part of black jazz artists reveal the way in which Asian and Latino appropriation of hip-hop puts the very idea of appropriation into question and renders itself legitimate in the sense that these communities can claim some ownership to the origin of hip-hop; however, due to the binary way in which race is conceptualized in a U.S. context, cultural appropriation is more often talked about in relation to the appropriation of black culture by all other cultures. Appropriation is a multifaceted and complex issue that must not be taken out of context or attributed to one culture. This essay is only meant to address one of the many examples and complexities of appropriation in addition to how my mixed-race identity formation has influenced these opinions that I am continually reformulating through video, writing, and performance.

My first reaction to what I perceived to be an Afrocentric Filipino American youth culture was pure disappointment, and I don't mean disappointment in relation to black culture per se, but in relation to my people's negligent acts of appropriation (again, I refer to it as appropriation due to the fact that we live in a country that has created binary systems of thought in terms of race and has rendered Asian American and Latino experiences, influences, and perspectives invisible). It's sad to question and/or admit, but are these youths performing the ultimate act of a colonized mentality, which has been created by our American oppressors? Have we become so completely immersed in American culture that we have accepted and fallen into a pattern of performing identities that are totally consistent with the paradigm of race that has made us invisible by forcing us to be black or white by virtue of our location in the middle of this color spectrum, this detrimental linear way of perceiving colored experiences? Maybe these questions explain why I went from being a hippie to a hip-hop head during part of my coming of age in college.

These experiences have led me to a point at which I am easily angered and frustrated by listening to Latino or Asian kids call each other "nigga" or "bitch" while they sport their Tommy Hilfiger gear or listen to their badass tunes on their portable boom boxes. To me, this is a very clear example of an act of misappropriation. Despite the fact that the term *nigger* has been used against other nonwhite people by white colonial forces, its origins in African American slavery as well its reappropriation is specific to black-American culture. It's as if Asians and Latinos need to prove how "down" they are by showing how "ebonically linguistic" (to borrow a term from Q-Tip) they are. In addition, it is an indication that they have adopted an example of black-American culture's internalized racism as a way to express their own internalized racism in reaction to both white supremacy and black supremacy (hence the hippie turned hip-hop head). I use black supremacy to describe the power of black cultural representations in the media and in music, in addition to the way in which inversions of hierarchy create black/white sexual supremacist ideals, which I will go into further in this essay. Furthermore, with respect to the common usage of *bitch* in popular hip-hop culture, non-blacks' use of this term is an indication that they are adopting a patriarchal black cultural form of sexism.

When I think about the process of Asian and Latino youth coming into a racialized and resistant consciousness to the white American power structure while identifying with black American youth and their own struggles of resistance, I hope that the creation of Latino and Asian cultural forms and resistance practices can originate from spaces that are more specific and authentic to their experiences and histories; however, I do not intend to use the term *authenticity* in a way that invalidates choices people make in expressing themselves (which has often been used against "whitewashed" or "not Asian/Latino/black enough" queers of color). Rather, I use *authenticity* in relation to Latino and Asian cultures that originate within themselves and are not primarily influenced by Afrocentrism. I do not intend to deny the global influence of African culture on Asian or Latino cultures since, historically, these cultures have always influenced each other. For instance, the Philippines is an archipelago of 7,000 islands that conceptually intersects with the African diaspora in the sense that there exist many mixed-race Filipinos of African descent due to the presence of African-American soldiers who participated in various wars throughout the 20th century. One might also argue that the *negritos,* to which I referred earlier, from the southern region of the Philippines share cultural similarities to people of African descent by way of their physical attributes. Furthermore, the Spanish/Asian/African/indigenous *mestizaje* of Latin America has resulted in an array of beautiful cultures that manifest this racial and cultural mixing in distinct ways that are specific to each Latin American country in South America, Central America, and the Caribbean.

I'd like to revisit the issue of "nigga" and "bitch" usage. Various people to whom I've spoken about this issue have primarily attributed it to class and claim that within the "ghetto" (I place "ghetto" in quotes to indicate my resistance to using this term at a time when so many people romanticize it) there is a shared common experience among all "ghetto" youth—though I would argue that this trend is also common among middle-class Asian and Latino youth, specifically those who are economically privileged enough to be college students. With respect to the "ghetto," I still wonder why gravitation toward black American culture specifically still dominates the "ghetto" as opposed to a genuine reciprocity and representation of all cultures. Could it have something to do with the fact that since this country operates on the all-powerful racial binary, black culture is made more visible by the media and by mainstream commodification practices of black culture, which has been bought and sold since and before the time of minstrelsy? The only difference now is that those in power realize they can sell black American culture not only to the white voyeur but also to a more expansive urban "multicultural" audience consisting of youth of all colors. This is ultimately a function of capitalism, which allows the United States to maintain itself as the number one imperial power of the world. Furthermore, the international status of the United States justifies a sense of arrogance among a particular group of African Americans who assume that the African American experience must be at the center of all oppression. (Unfortunately, most Americans, in general, are incapable of seeing beyond themselves.) This leads to a system of ranking oppression in which all other struggles are defined in relation to African American resistance. As Chicana lesbian playwright Cherríe Moraga has stated in various interviews, it is absurd to rank oppression because power is constantly shifting. For instance, how can anyone claim that a working-class or poor, white, disabled lesbian, or a queer Chicano, or a straight black man has more power over the other when each of them can act as the other's oppressor depending on the social space in which they find themselves, be it one that is heterosexist, ableist, white supremacist, classist, or queer-centric?

One of the major dangers I see in black appropriation trends is the fact that the United States, as a world superpower, influences the ways in which race is viewed worldwide and can potentially justify Afrocentrism in an international context for nonwhite people. Seen in this light, hip-hop becomes a vehicle for the global conquest of binary racial models that are constructed in the United States. "Communities of color" in the United States, including new arrivals of immigrant youth, continue to take on black American hip-hop culture as a means to define them against whiteness. I do not intend to deny agency in this process, since resistant hybrid practices can potentially arise from intercultural spaces. For instance, at the Filipino festival to which I referred earlier, indigenous ritual performances were performed/juxtaposed alongside Filipino American youth performances of R & B and hip-hop. The performance of these cultural forms and identities allows for possibilities for transformation and, I would add, hybridized artistic and cultural practices; however, the problem that I have observed is that the origin continues to be Afrocentric due to the fact that communities have accepted and bought into the paradigm of race that regulates Asian and Latino identities to either blackness or whiteness. This ultimately prevents the development of artistic practices and cultural styles that originate from and are specific to other nonwhite/nonblack cultures and histories.

The fact that Asian/Latino youth practices of appropriation are occurring within the sexual realm (i.e., forms of music that can potentially be sexist and/or homophobic) is completely consistent with the historical patterns in which racial oppression has been sexualized in the sense that white supremacy has and continues to maintain itself by the sexual exploitation of people of color—specifically women of color as evidenced by the global trafficking of female workers from Asia, Latin America, and Africa. In the deconstruction of the white supremacist ideals that have created a sexual color spectrum in which blacks are hypersexualized and Asians are desexualized,[4] a risk exists in which Afrocentric models of race will ultimately replace rather than transform this sexual color spectrum by creating a black supremacist ideal that exists in reaction to white supremacy. When excessively macho and heterosexist "gangsta" rap or hip-hop music is appropriated by Asian and Latino youth (and I don't mean to ignore similar politics that are implicit in many examples of Latino music and music in general), they perpetuate these sexual color spectrums, which are informed by the white supremacist ideal as much as they are by the black supremacist ideal. This manifests itself in the appropriation of black hypermasculinity (as it is portrayed in American pop culture) by Asian and Latino men who see this version of masculinity (which often goes hand in hand with misogyny, sexism, and homophobia) as one that is more desirable and valid than Asian or Latino masculinity; hence, Afrophallocentrism.

As Tomas Amalguer, as well as Kobena Mercer and Isaac Julien have written, machismo and hypermasculinity can be seen as reactions by men of color to the colonial exploitation in which their masculinity had initially been questioned. Consequently, the colonial violence ingrained in men of color is projected in sexist and homophobic ways onto women and queers.[5] I have come to the conclusion that one possible way to shift these paradigms is through coalition building with our allies. I am specifically referring to progressive straight men of color who understand that machismo is detrimental to our communities and who can convey these ideas to their brothers who feel that they can only react to racism and classism in a hypocritical manner that denies the sexism and homophobia, which they thus continually perpetuate.

On a less pessimistic note, I do believe that there is much beauty and potential in the sharing of and identification with other cultures of resistance. After all, there is a historical reality of shared experience in the oppression of colonized cultures, though each has its own specificity, which must be acknowledged and respected. I feel that my queer Filipina Colombian subjectivity has allowed me to see that the African/Latino/Asian diasporas intersect in real, imagined, geographic, and cultural ways; however, it is also disappointing to see the melding of all of these cultures in a way that is not as balanced or as mutual as it should and can be.

As many of us who are queer and of color have learned, dominant cultures reproduce themselves within queer communities and "communities of color"—a term which, though useful for strategic purposes and depending on context, must also be problematized, as evidenced by this article; however, it is the seeming juxtaposition of radical identities (in this case, queer and hybrid) that can lead to progressive and subversive practices within hybrid space as well as in each of our individual communities. Queerness informs my ideas about race in a similar way that race informs my ideas about sexuality and gender. That is why I strongly believe that queers of color have a crucial role in deconstructing the oppressive, rigid gender systems that have been created by colonialism.

We have learned the lesson that our oppressors have many different faces. Most of my disidentification with the youth cultures to which I have referred arises from my deep ambivalence to patriarchal and heterosexist black musical forms in American pop culture that exacerbate the sexism and homophobia within all communities of color, including those that are queer (and this I find to be particularly ironic and extremely contradictory in light of our resistance to heteronormativity). I do not mean to essentialize black patriarchy as being more extreme than white patriarchy. It should be clear that sexism and homophobia permeate all cultures and that, historically, nonwhite men have been physically, economically, and sexually exploited by white patriarchy,[6] but there needs to be a better way for men of color to react to the white power structure than by projecting sexist and homophobic violence in their cultural manifestations of resistance.

Colonial violence maintains itself by the creation of black/white paradigms of race that render other cultures and colors invisible or prone to locating themselves on either side of this paradigm. These paradigms must be challenged in order to reveal the shared—though distinct—histories of oppression and resistance, which can result in representations of race that are not dominated by any one culture but manifest the potential of many different cultures. Hence, my concept for (a)eromestizaje is influenced by previous generations of queer feminists of color such as Gloria Anzaldúa and Cherríe Moraga. I recognize the need for women of color—particularly mixed-race women of color who are conscious of our complex role in the world in negotiating the voices of our many ancestors—to participate in sexual healing and to reclaim the erotic power that has been taken away from us by our colonizers and our own brothers and fathers (before, during, and after colonialism).

These realizations are my primary motivation for creating the performances that I do. Many of the ideas around appropriation that I have presented in this essay make up the concept behind *Inverted Minstrel*, while my ideas around *(a)eromestizaje* form the basis of one of my other major works, *Cosmic Blood*, which explores *mestizaje* as a function of and metaphor for world transformation. From 2000 to 2002, I toured *Inverted Minstrel* to various conferences and universities; the video version has also screened at various festivals in the United States and abroad.[7] Since the piece is grounded in academic discourse and community-organizing strategies, it has been appropriate for many different spaces, yet this has also posed a great challenge since oftentimes academic and conference venues do not offer much in terms of the aesthetic and technical aspects of theatrical production. Despite these challenges, I have received critical, theoretical feedback about the content of the work that I would have otherwise not received in an artistic venue where feedback relates more to the form and aesthetic of the work.

Inverted Minstrel has received very mixed reactions, which is expected considering that my attempt was to merge various antihegemonic discourses while challenging accepted notions of identity and community. The negative responses often came from people who felt that I was trying to say too much or focus on too many complex issues at once, while the positive responses came from people who were hungry for more artists and activists to voice these concerns. This sort of response is what motivates me to continue to do the work that I do because I still feel that there is not enough understanding across cultures of resistance. Furthermore, merging academics with art practice is a necessary and challenging task, especially for someone such as myself who comes from both worlds, yet there is also a part of me that wants to get away from academic discourse in order to reach people on a more community-based level as well as on a global level, which is what has influenced my other works, such as *Cosmic Blood*.

I began to develop *Cosmic Blood* at a time when I was starting to feel overwhelmed by the language and discourse that dictated my work, as in the case of *Inverted Minstrel*. It was also inspired by apocalyptic feelings that surfaced after the events of September 11, 2001, and my own motivation to create work from a spiritual perspective that offered hope for the future. Since my previous work had relied so much on language, I felt that it was important to develop a piece that was primarily based on images, though still heavily concept driven. In addition, I think that creating work that does not rely on the English language offers more possibilities in reaching audiences worldwide. In Peru during the summer of 2001, where I presented excerpts of the work, *Mestiza/o Beast* and *Bliss, Devotion, and the Cosmic Mestiza*, at a performance event that was part of the Hemispheric Institute on Performance and Politics, it felt very rewarding when people told me that they responded positively on a completely visceral level. When I first started to present this work, I was apprehensive because I was still attached to language as a means of communicating my concepts, which can be theoretically complex. I was also using my body in an explicit manner to present images that I was afraid might perpetuate the ultimate ethnic freak show. I guess that's the risk we all have to take, particularly as artists who are women, queer, and/or of color, since so much of our experience as individuals and as a community throughout history relates to sexual violence and distorted images relating to our racial and gender "otherness." I find that presenting these two particular pieces from *Cosmic Blood* is effective in that *Mestiza/o Beast* references the history of conquest and rape while *Bliss, Devotion, and the Cosmic Mestiza* points to possibilities for transformation in the process of turning to ancestors and creative cosmic forces for hope, especially at a time when so many people are filled with cynicism.

In *Mestiza/o Beast* I literally act out the conquest and rape of the indigenous "savage" beast while turning around the concept of the savage and imposing it on the conquistador. My costume is a fur cloak, and I perform (first as the Indian savage) a sequence of actions that simulate rape while a video that parallels my actions on stage is projected as a backdrop. The video involves my interaction (as the conquistador) with multiple characters—a Filipina woman and a Latino man, both of whom are raped and who together reference the connection between the Philippines and Latin America due to Spanish colonialism. During the live performance, I transform into the conquistador savage by putting on a different color fur cloak and a conquistador helmet. I perform as the conquistador, and at the end of the piece, my actions mirror the narrative on the video, during which the Filipina indigenous woman rises up and kills the conquistador.

In *Bliss, Devotion, and the Cosmic Mestiza* I present an image of what I speculate to be a *mestiza* from the future. In the same way that Filipinos and Latin Americans who are mixed with European and indigenous blood are the physical manifestation of colonialism as world transformation, the cosmic *mestiza* is a physical manifestation of the hybridization of humans and extraterrestrial, cosmic, and/or ancestral forces that may come about as a result of the impending world transformation. On the video animation that introduces the live performance, the world blows up during Armageddon, and the character that becomes the cosmic *mestiza* travels through time and space while undergoing a process of hybridization. She lands on another planet, and in the same way that during various colonial encounters indigenous "savages" were literally put on display for Western audiences,[8] the cosmic *mestiza* is captured and put on display at a sci-fi circus freak show. Later, with the help of her ancestors who suffered in a similar way, she breaks free and continues to travel through time and space in her process of hybridization as a survival mechanism.

In creating *Cosmic Blood* and *Inverted Minstrel,* I have learned that as an artist and activist, I perpetually feel honor, responsibility, pressure, and risk due to the fact that there exists so much disillusionment, cultural misunderstanding, and lack of trust among the public. However, I am hopeful and willing to continue developing my art practice as a way to create ritual in bringing people together to celebrate the queering of *mestizaje* and the hybridization of queerness. Queerness is sexuality in constant motion in a similar way that *mestizaje* functions as world transformation.

Notes

1. See Gayatri Chakravorty Spivak, "Subaltern Studies: Deconstructing Historiography," in *In Other Worlds: Essays in Cultural Politics* (New York: Methuen, 1987), 197–221.
2. Jenny Livingston, prod. and dir., *Paris Burning* (New York: Off White Productions, 1991), videocassette.
3. These commercial breaks are reminiscent of the way in which minstrel shows (a form of popular entertainment during the early nineteenth century in which primarily Irish working-class men painted their faces black and performed their version of "blackness" to white working-class audiences) initially emerged as short acts between the main acts of a theater program. For a rich theoretical and historical account of minstrelsy, see Eric Lott, *Love and Theft* (New York: Routledge, 1994).
4. For articles and books that address these racialized constructions of masculinity, see Richard Fung, "Looking for My Penis: The Eroticized Asian in Gay Video Porn," in *How Do I Look?* ed. Bad-Object Choices (Seattle: Bay, 1991); and Frantz Fanon, "The Negro and Psychopathology," in *Black Skin White Mask* (New York: Grove, 1967).
5. See Tomas Amalguer, "Chicano Men: A Cartography of Homosexual Identity and Behavior," in *The Lesbian and Gay Studies Reader,* ed. Henry Abelove, Michael Barale, and David Halperin (New York: Routledge, 1982); and Isaac Julien and Kobena Mercer, "True Confessions," in *Black Male,* ed. Thelma Golden (New York: Whitney Museum of American Art, 1994).
6. See Hazel Carby, "White Women Listen! Black Feminism and the Politics of Sisterhood," in *The Empire Strikes Back: Race and Racism in Seventies Britain,* ed. Hazel Carby and Paul Gilroy (London: Hutchinson/University of Birmingham Center for Contemporary Cultural Studies, 1982), 212–35.

7. *Inverted Minstrel* can be viewed as a streaming video on my website, www.devilbunny.org.
8. For a historical timeline of various examples of the ethnographic exhibition of human beings—and particularly people of color—that has occurred over the last five centuries, see Coco Fusco, "The Other History of Intercultural Performance," in *English Is Broken Here* (New York: New Press, 1995).

21

The Herstory of *Bamboo Girl* Zine

SABRINA MARGARITA ALCANTARA-TAN

I write, edit, and publish a zine— an independent publication that often challenges mainstream points of view; does not break even in sales; is personal,
sometimes political, sometimes both; and is purely done out of passion; it
speaks from my point of view as a queer, mixed-blood Filipina/Asian woman
who confronts issues of racism, sexism, and homophobia in an in-your-face
kind of way. I started it in 1995 for many reasons: because I couldn't find publications that spoke to me, because I was getting totally disenchanted with the
punk and hardcore scene, because I was sick of explaining my heritages when
fielding the constant "Where are you from?" or "What are you?" questions,
and because I was experiencing way too much street harassment in New York
City that led to catcalls based on stereotypes. I didn't have a constructive way
of expressing my annoyance, anger, and rage, and it didn't help that I was
brought up in a traditionally Filipino household in which you only spoke
when spoken to and young women were groomed at an early age to just sit
there and look pretty. It is often the norm for girls in Filipino households to be
groomed for the numerous beauty pageants held in the Filipino community
and to learn how to be graceful in cotillion gowns at coming-out parties. Special attention is taken as to how one dresses, applies makeup, walks, and so
forth. I myself was put through finishing school, where I was taught to run the
runway and learn makeup application until I finally acted out and wore my
steel toe boots during rehearsal one day. I had also taken ballet since the age of
four (which I can now thank for my lack of clumsiness). In addition to these
restrictions on outward appearances, in traditional Filipino households, it is,
as I have mentioned, undesirable to be vocal—especially toward one's parents,
and in particular the father figure. Therefore, this type of upbringing doesn't
always foster much of a backbone when one is faced with people who step over
the line and when exploring what one believes in (since one is not supposed to
question that in the first place!).

Growing up, I searched like crazy for publications that spoke to me one is
but decided that my unique voice was too specific or—worse—even wrong (as
I was taught to think by mainstream culture) after reading Asian American

Fig. 21.1 A Public Service Announcement from *Bamboo Girl*. Page 2 from *Bamboo Girl* #4, 1996. (Reprinted with permission of the artist.)

and Filipino American magazines like *A. Magazine*, *Filipinas*, and others that appealed to the general population. These magazines only showed Filipinas (and Asian in general) as kitschy, cute, fun to make fun of; Asian girls and women as the daughters of *senseis* (martial arts masters/teachers); sex kittens;

and dominatrices. We were portrayed in porno anime—and all with a lack of command of the English language. There were also martial arts magazines published by white guys with gigantic egos and Asiaphile fantasies. I was sick of it. I was looking for a publication about fierce Filipina or Asian women to look up to, and it would've been even cooler if she were of mixed race like me so I could read and feel validated. But no luck.

Now in 2004, there are realistic role models out there for young Filipina and Asian girls, but when I ask them who their idols are, they usually say "my mom." So it seems that it's not necessarily the media influence that's nourished their hunger for identity-crisis revelations. There are successful Filipina women like Loida Nicholas Lewis and Josie Natori, and even more local heroes in New York like Amy Besa of Cendrillion Restaurant and activist Ninotchka Rosca, but for our young folks there's the need to see our representations onscreen, on television, and on the cutting edge without having to use "ethnic" punches to get in.

Back then I was into punk and hardcore, which seemed to really speak for me: rebelliousness, expressive clothes to match the "fuck-everything!" motto I upheld for a long time. But this scene just became a tired one for me after hearing all the straight white guys (who headed the majority of bands) whine about their oppression while they mocked gay men and lesbians and didn't include many people of color as part of the "regular scene" at their shows. These were the same guys who would eventually grow up to be middle-aged, white yuppies heading large companies that make the glass-and-bamboo ceiling that was so hard to break through for women like me; not only did women have to deal with the proverbial "glass ceiling," but Asians and anyone considered Asian also had to meet head on with the "bamboo ceiling," made especially for those of Asian descent. Sometimes it stopped us from progressing any further in our careers because of perceived language and cultural barriers; in other cases, unless you were a semiattractive woman your barrier was your beauty, and most non-Asians would find it difficult to look past that. I was incredulous that the people who had labeled themselves "punks"—mainly because it symbolized being different and celebrated that difference—were making fun of others who were different from them. It became a total double standard. When punk began, it was truly an art form, an act of rebellion against the norm, a celebration of being an individual; now it's mutated into a form of nostalgia for youth to hang onto: the Mohawk hairstyle (which I did wear for a while, and in a beautiful blue hue, I might add), the clothes, the belts, the chains, and the boots. Now it's all about clothes and if you look the part. There is hardly any examination of privilege (which many white punks have—even the Riot Grrrls, who were the feminist response to punk, to describe them in a nutshell), true oppression, or acknowledgment of women of color or of those from different countries. Everything has become *uber*-heterosexual and has remained white-dominated (in both male and female realms). For example, during a Take Back the Night march a few years ago, as we passed St. Marks Place—a haven for many punks in New York City—I saw a punk jump through his friends on the sidewalk and scream at us, "*You're* the freaks!" I was taken aback, because if this kid really knew what he was talking about and was a "real" punk, he wouldn't have been mocking queers, especially on a night that we were protesting violence and gay bashing. So it wasn't too long until I became disenchanted with punk in general and quickly disappeared from the scene. I hardly go to shows anymore—I used to be a regular in nightclubs and the people at the door already knew to let me in.

I very much enjoyed my punk days—I loved the surge of creativity it infused in me, the loud concerts, the chaos on the stage, the slamming into others on the dance floor. Fun! Fun! Fun! I started *Bamboo Girl* at this time to let out my rage against the injustices I saw in the world—the injustices I experienced as a mixed-blood, vocal Filipina on the streets of New York. (I was being hypersexualized, of course, as I was ethnically ambiguous to most passersby.) I ended up connecting with others through my zine, creating dialogue with others whose views were both similar and unlike mine, and even came into my full queerness during this time. This growing mentally brought with it a sense of peace, a sense of belonging, and a stronger sense of ethnic pride.

In terms of my ethnic identity, I grew up in a nearly all-white suburb of Pittsburgh, Pennsylvania. I was one of four Asian Americans for miles and there was one African American guy. It was painfully clear that these minority students so desperately wanted to be accepted into the "in" crowd, which to them meant disowning their perceived culture and "whitifying" their manner-isms, speaking patterns, personality, and so forth. I just felt out of sync with everyone, especially the fellow minority students, because although I would desperately try to connect with them, I was shunned by them; and those who shunned me the most were my fellow Asian Americans. I felt like I was the only one proud of who I was—a woman of color with much culture and history. I wasn't even sure of what country I came from or what it meant, but I knew that I was "different," and I was proud of it. I remember my mom saying of clothes that I thought were too risqué or strange, "I like that. That's differ-ent." It became something I heard myself saying often: that things that are different are beautiful.

Earlier on, I thought I was Chinese, since all my classmates, even up until high school, called me "chink." Sometimes the teasing was so intense I'd run home crying; one time my classmates told everyone else I ate dog. According to my mother, I often ran home crying. She'd try to alleviate the situation by saying the boys just had a crush on me.

Later, my mom corrected the "chink" assumptions by informing me that I was Filipino; and not only that, I was *mestiza* as well, which for a Filipino usually means that you're mixed with either white, Spanish, or Chinese blood.

In my case, it's all three. I would soon learn that the words *mestiza* or *tisay* would hold some baggage, considering that the Philippines was colonized by Spain for more than five hundred years, who burned much of our written history, and had many illegitimate children with the *indios*, or native peoples. There were also trading routes that connected us with China, India, and other countries; then came the war, when the Americans came and left many Amerasian children. It is well known that whiter-skinned Filipinos are often more celebrated and popular than darker-skinned Filipinos, and for years, whitening creams have sold off the shelves (keep in mind most of us Filipinas are *kayumanggi* [naturally brown complexioned]). Most entertainers and actors/actresses are more often pale-skinned, and commercials push whitening products all the time. So there is obviously a double standard as to what Filipinos naturally are in complexion and what is considered beautiful. I have often dealt with the backlash based on my skin color, because in the Philippines it represents privilege, easy living, getting what you want. In the United States, however, there is no concept of what it means to be tisay. Some people became confused, and almost obsessed, trying to fit me into tight, neat boxes because there was no room for me on the check-one-ethnicity application forms. "What are you?" became a constant question I'd be asked. Now I can understand others' need to categorize me, though it still is annoying; a few years ago, however, I wasn't so tolerant because I was questioning what it meant to be mixed myself. I still do sometimes, and it's important for me to validate my ethnic backgrounds as well as others who identify as having a mixed ethnic heritage.

Additionally, street harassment became a big issue for me. My blossoming feminism came with my daily use of miniskirts; many men felt the need to vocalize their Asian fantasies to me while I was walking home or to work. I was bubbling with rage, especially since, for a time, some men even invited themselves to grab my thighs or arms in passing. So I took up Filipino martial arts, specifically *pananandata* (weapon fighting), Marinas style. Pananandata itself is a Northern style of Filipino martial arts that originated in the Tagalog regions of Central Luzon. Pananandata Marinas style is a style of this that uses weapons and methods—*arnis* sticks, *balisongs* (butterfly knives), *yantok at daga* (knife fighting), *latikos* (whips), and empty hands—that were passed down through the family of Punong Guro Amante P. Marinas Sr. In 1973, Marinas introduced it to this country. Learning this form of martial arts was essential to gaining a sense of confidence on the street, where previously I had none. It also confirmed that the Pinay blood coursing in me really responded to this ancient art of defense. Although it didn't cure my apprehension of harassment on the street, it made me feel more at peace. I thought, "Why should I even deal with this crap?" Some men would say that I'm asking for it because of my hefty tattoos and because of how I look or dress. So I *ask* for the harassment by wearing clothes that men can't handle by keeping their flies zipped? When woman are attacked or raped, often the perpetrators say the women asked for it because of what they were wearing. I think it's a plain case of lack of control—theirs! Although I don't wear miniskirts as often now, I think it's a bunch of bull that men use that excuse to feel free to say things to me or to touch me without my permission. What makes them think I'm attracted to men in the first place? Is that something they could've ever considered? I have no doubts that many of them felt more at ease touching me and getting in my personal space without asking because since I'm Filipina or Asian they think that I won't mind, that I may even like it, or even that I may be grateful for the attention. When I open my mouth to tell them that their advances are not appreciated, their rose-colored shades are ripped off and they spout hatred my way and call me "bitch" or "dyke." Could it be that these harassers are flabbergasted that a petite Pacific flower such as I would actually stand up for herself? that she doesn't condone the behavior and could patiently voice it? that we're not giggling *arigatos* (thank yous) with mouth covered to these losers that think we should be grateful for the attention?

Take one day in the train station on a hot summer's day. I'm wearing a nice nonrevealing mini dress, big-holed net stockings, and open-laced Doc Marten boots. A man stops right in front of me and looks me up and down like it's going out of style. I tell him firmly, "I don't appreciate the way you're staring at me." He calls me a "fucking bitch." The train comes. I get off at the next stop, going up the stairs with everyone else. The same guy comes up behind me and whispers into my ear, "Next time don't wear that shit." I yelled loudly, stopping traffic, "Next time don't wear this shit? Next time, don't be a sexist asshole!" He seemed shocked, and in an effort to regain his manhood, started yelling, "Bitch, you're crazy! Cunt!" Meanwhile, my hand in his face, I leave him to fester in his embarrassment. Everyone saw him in his lunacy and that was good enough for me.

For the majority of my life, people have told me that I shouldn't feel what I feel, that I can't be a certain way because I don't look like it, that I'm not "feminine" enough because of my tattoos or because I've cut my long locks. Of course, my confusion about my ethnic background(s) led the way—and the only thing that kept me sane was writing in my diary; I got my first one as a gift on the day of my First Holy Communion. (That's second grade, for those of you who can't remember that far back!) It was easiest for me to express my ideas in writing rather than to vocalize them. Although someday I wanted to be good at vocalizing, I thought I should at least start somewhere—and that was through writing. The diary had the Twin Star Sanrio angels on it, and it was a gift from my *tito* (uncle) as my First Holy Communion gift. It became a precious place for me to write my feelings, feelings that I couldn't disclose to my parents or closest relatives. It became my sanctuary.

A friend at the time, Barbara—who did a zine herself—finally said one day, "If you can't find something to read that addresses your issues, why don't you do your own zine?" My thought was, "No way. I can't do that." But then one day, I just started cutting and pasting, writing on my computer, and *Bamboo Girl* issue number 1 was pushed out of the oven. It turned out being one of the most cathartic things I've ever done, and I haven't stopped publishing it since. Many ask me why I chose the name *Bamboo Girl* for my zine. There is absolutely no deep meaning; I just wanted an Asian-related name that also reflected my femaleness. It was extremely personal and angry and, for the first time, I felt validated, like my words had weight—after all, they were printed officially on paper! That began a feeling of confidence in my own words.

When I started doing my zine, it was mainly a selfish act, as I just wanted to write stuff down to get things off my chest or else I'd end up doing something heinous and end up in jail. I didn't even think that anyone would want to read my writings. But I just passed a few issues out to friends of mine who were all really supportive. By word of mouth, it became something to which some people, especially Asian and mixed-race women, could relate. I was amazed at the thought that other people agreed with some of the things I was thinking, and then the mail started coming in. That's when I started making friends with all types of people who read, or wanted to read, my zine, and it wasn't only mail from women of color—straight white guys wrote to me, too. Most of the readers were usually young, college-aged Asian American women, and most definitely, Filipinas and Filipino Americans were very supportive of *Bamboo Girl*. Surprisingly, those on the West Coast, specifically California, were most supportive. I think it had to do with the large Filipino and Asian populations there, since they seemed to "get" my zine the most. The East Coast, on the other hand, is not as up to speed on Filipino issues, but then, that's where I have gotten many feminist readers and mixed-blood readers. Most were supportive and interested in what I was putting out. Then one day I really looked at what I had written and realized that I'd created my own truths by printing my zine. Now, finally, there was some validation for myself, but also for other women and men who saw similarities in things I talked about in my issues.

Now that my reader base is somewhat larger (my first issue was of 100 copies; now my print run is 2,000 to 3,000), I try to keep in mind that I need to focus a little more on exactly what I'm talking about. It's still more or less a collection of different things: herstory; cultural facts; exercises to keep your queer, feminist, colored-gal self in check; and interviews with Filipinas, Asians, and Asian mutts who are doing significant things but may or may not be getting as much press in the mainstream. There are always things to help empower yourself, no matter if you're a queer, colored woman or a straight, white guy.

So my zine started as something to do on the side at my boring day job. I even copied my first couple of issues on their heavy-duty copiers. However, it became something that now has to be printed offset because quantity makes it cheaper that way. Although my format constantly changes and grows in different ways, I've already resolved not to give in to the "diva-zinester attitude" that some people have adopted (that is, zinesters who think they're superstars in their own self-publishing bubble). I've met some really great people who do zines, but I have to admit I've met a couple of nutcases and egomaniacs whom I definitely wouldn't want to be caught in a dark alley with, let alone a zine convention!

Both the format and layout and the content and tone of *Bamboo Girl* zine have changed over the past couple of issues. It first began as a cut-and-paste format, half-legal-sized photocopied zine, and has grown since into a full size zine (8.5" x 11") that contains more computerized layouts. In the beginning, my content focused much on punk rock female bands, but as the issues progressed, I started expanding into the greater Filipino and Asian community as interviewees. Through experience, I came to realize I was having an impact on younger readers, so I tried to still keep my voice but to give some guidance as well—guidance I could have used at their age. My zine began as a venting tool for my anger at violence I had experienced in my past and my present, and my frustrations at trying to find myself. Now older, I still think that anger is a precious tool in creating and propelling change, and my readers, and friends I've met through my zine, have helped me grow as well. I think I will always have that anger at injustice and the determination to want to do something about it, but at least my rage has been tamed and redirected so I don't fall off the deep end and physically attack someone like I used to. When you don't have control over things in your life and are feeling most powerless, physically attacking others becomes second nature—unless, obviously, you're defending yourself, which is another story. I've learned this one thing from personal experience: I wouldn't say that writing *Bamboo Girl* has given me control over certain aspects of my life, but it definitely has helped me get things off my chest in a more constructive way. And, in the process, I've been inwardly growing as well. I learned Filipino martial arts, and having a confidence that's backed by one's own culture is powerful in itself. That is, in its distilled form, none of this Tiger Shulman show-off, let-me-break-boards-with-my-head-to-show-my-virility crap. In Tagalog (the main Filipino language), that's called being *hambog*.

I still have a way to go to achieve inner peace, but in the meantime, my zine has been a wonderful way for me to work out my mental clutter as well as help me hook up with others who share similar and different views.

I am constantly accused or praised, depending on where it comes from, for things I say in my zine. I guess the bottom line is that I'm always pushing the envelope because there needs to be dialogue. But I don't bring up certain issues just to create controversy, which is what I think some people misunderstand; it's just that some of my viewpoints are innately different from others, and that's fine. In fact, I celebrate the fact that I can learn from others' viewpoints—as long as they're also open to hearing mine. Write me at: P.O. Box 507, New York, NY 10159-0507, or BambooGirl@aol.com.

22

Through Our Pinay Writings:
Narrating Trauma, Embodying Recovery

MARIE-THERESE C. SULIT

The trauma is a repeated suffering of the event, but it is also a continual leaving of its site. The traumatic reexperiencing of the event thus carries with it … the impossibility of knowing that first constituted it. And by carrying that impossibility of knowing out of the empirical event itself, trauma opens up and challenges us to a new kind of listening, the witnessing, precisely, of impossibility …. To listen to the crisis of a trauma, that is, is not only to listen for the event, but to hear in the testimony the survivor's departure from it; the challenge of the therapeutic listener, in other words, is how to listen to departure.

—Cathy Caruth, "Introduction" in *Trauma: Explorations in Memory*

Mister,
Unceasing difficulty.
Unceasing challenge
Gropes me.

— Elynia S. Mabanglo, "Invitation of the Imperialist"

These particular lines from Elynia S. Mabanglo's poem "Invitation of the Imperialist"[1] speak to me on a number of levels: as a Filipina American, as a doctoral candidate (i.e., a literary and cultural studies critic) in English, and as a reader. First, I place myself in the role of the female poetic persona who writes of her own personal traumatic encounter (i.e., torture and rape), which allegorizes the traumatic history of the Philippines/U.S. imperial and colonial encounter. The speaker's particular challenge lies in the ambivalence of using the English language to narrate her trauma, a tool of colonialism that the "Mister" (i.e., the American imperialist) uses to mock her. Second, I place myself as the reader—the witness—to this encounter painstakingly detailed throughout the poem, realizing that my own tenuous position walks a fine line between loving and hating both the Filipino and American cultures that

351

constitute my process of reading and responding to literature. And last, I place myself as a literary and cultural studies critic at this historical juncture, one that witnesses the violent realities of the global community around me, most of which implicate the insidious, avaricious, and specious actions of the current governmental administration in the United States. These violent realities, the "Unceasing difficulty. / Unceasing challenge" that "Gropes me," necessarily impact my personal, communal, national, and transnational understandings of history and literature through these particular slices of life.

However, this understanding betrays its limits because, as Cathy Caruth reminds me, "the traumatic reexperiencing of the event thus carries with it ... the impossibility of knowing that first constituted it."[2] An understanding that is true to the actuality of the violent reality remains deferred by virtue of the historicity and the historiography of the "empirical event"—that is, the U.S.–Philippines encounter that began more than a hundred years ago. Still, the possibilities, not of *revising* but of *reviving* history, become manifest in this process of recuperation, of recovery, or what Caruth heralds as a "new kind of listening, the witnessing, precisely, of impossibility." For me, this process may no longer be simply a choice; in fact, it entails a submission to rather than a mastery of the speakers of these writings, as represented through the writers of the Philippine diaspora. Just as the reading process requires me to listen to "the repeated suffering of the event," the interpretive process makes manifest the ways in which I, and we, as witnesses, can listen to—indeed, imagine—the departure from this state of suffering.

Introduction: The Intersection between Trauma Studies and Filipino/a American Studies

From the war between Palestine and Israel over the Holy Land to the embattled situation in Iraq—events that implicate the biased involvement, indeed the complicity, of the United States in subtle and overt ways through their foreign policies—one undoubtedly sees the violence that imbues these violent realities without ostensibly forming and shaping an understanding of the trauma that underscores these historical events.

A violent event occurs once, but a traumatic experience of that event occurs repeatedly. Thus, Caruth explains, the classical meaning of the word *trauma*, which denotes a wound or "injury inflected on a body," significantly shifts in the early twentieth century through medical and psychiatric usage to denote "the wound of the mind."[3] This wound of the mind thus manifests in breaches in a survivor's sensibility, particularly regarding time and place, as well as personal, political, and communal identity. Caruth notes that "it is this inherent latency of the event, that paradoxically explains the peculiar, temporal structure, the belatedness, of historical experience .... For history to be a history of trauma means that it is referential precisely to the extent that it is not fully perceived as it occurs; or to put it somewhat differently, that a history can be grasped only in the very inaccessibility of its occurrence."[4] Thus, Caruth explains, where immediate understanding of a violent event remains elusive, as contemporary historical events show, "the possibility of a history that is no longer straightforwardly referential" arises in the aftermath of a violent event: the traumatic memory, or testimony, of a traumatic experience.[5]

Furthermore, the notion of memory or testimony implies a survivor (in the rendering of the story) and a listener (in the listening to it—that is, witnessing) who can be understood as a proxy survivor; in fact, this encounter of rendering and listening constitutes the sense of witness.[6] In an interview with Caruth, psychologist Robert Jay Lifton—some of whose work centered on trauma of American soldiers in the Vietnam War—makes a careful distinction between true and false witness. He notes that "false witness tends to be a political and ideological process. And really false witness is at the heart of most victimization."[7] In refusing a narrative of victimization and espousing a true witness narrative, an ethical responsibility falls on a survivor's rendering of a violent event and a listener's choice to bear witness. Here, the contexts of nation and culture—of war and peace—embrace this encounter between a survivor and a witness. In the introductory quotation, Caruth then offers three fundamentally paradoxical ideas of trauma: the continual return and departure of the event for a survivor of trauma—a movement that defers a complete knowing and understanding of the event; the connection between the survivor and the listener in the traumatic testimony of the violent event; and the impossibility for the victim and the listener to fully know, and understand, the violent event. However, this kind of understanding creates the possibility for recovery—indeed, for revision—of history, that is, of healing.

The intersection between trauma studies, as presented by Caruth, and Filipino/a and Filipino/a American studies provides particularly fertile ground with which to know and understand, as much as possible, the Philippines as a colony of Western powers—of Spain, and especially of the United States. If trauma is understood as a history of trauma, then a series of violent realities specifically marks the history of the Philippines as a traumatic one: from the uprisings against Magellan in the sixteenth century, through the wars between the United States and Spain and the United States and the Philippines in the late nineteenth century, through the period of colonial rule under the United States and World War II with the Japanese occupation of the Philippines in the mid-twentieth century, through the 1986 revolution against the regime of Ferdinand Marcos, to the present, through the "war on terror" instigated by the administration of U. S. president George W. Bush.

Such historic and ideological movements reflect the states of neocolonialism and the promise of postcolonialism that shape the Philippines and its encounters today. If trauma is also understood as a series of tensions, then the study of this encounter between the peoples of the Philippines and the history of the Philippines offers a productive, useful, and illuminating means to understand a greater global history stained by such violent events in the past and present. In short, understanding the encounters of the Philippines enables a greater understanding of historic and contemporary events, yet these levels of understanding remain elusive. Thus, the intersection between trauma studies and Filipino/a American studies significantly broaches the oscillations between violence and recovery; the immediacy of violent events and the belatedness of understanding such events; cultural amnesia and cultural remembrance; reticence, even silence, and modes of articulation; and last, death and life.

Filipino/a and Filipino/a American literature imparts a collage of perspectives that frames historical events in ostensibly accessible ways, depicting and representing the series of tensions that run throughout traumatic narratives. Through these depictions of characters and representations of historical moments, writers and readers can listen to—indeed, witness—the varied and aforementioned vacillations that haunt narratives of trauma, thereby proffering the possibility for recovery of different and alternate perspectives of history that indelibly connect the memory of an individual character, or set of characters, into a kind of collective memory. However, one uneasy caveat outlines this last point: the slippage between the individual and collective sensibility of memory. Narratives of trauma, I believe, rely upon this connection between the individual and collective memory without subordinating either one to the other.

However, Caruth also notes the negative dynamics of trauma: the potential for the witness to become traumatized through listening, and for the individual to become retraumatized in the rendering. Surviving and witnessing ironically hold the risk for crisis as well. How can the survivor and the witness avoid this dangerous pitfall of retraumatization? Perhaps it is through the recognition of the space between the violent reality and the period of trauma. As Caruth posits, "the language of trauma … and the stories associated with it" carry with them "complex ways … of knowing and not knowing," and as trauma subsumes characters and witnesses in the literality of a violent event, then it is precisely this literality that necessitates interpretation.[8] Thus, the mode of interpreting—that is, of listening—sustains the chance for the recovery of history (i.e., healing) similar to the mode of storytelling itself.

Contemporary women writers of the Philippine diaspora, such as Merlinda Bobis, M. Evelina Galang, Elynia S. Mabanglo, and Lara Stapleton, portray slices of life of various female personae. They also present hard and poignant angles of Philippine colonial and neocolonial history, projecting—indeed, imagining—a latent, perhaps limited, restoration of hope for a postcolonial future for these characters and their impoverished situations (literally, emotionally, and intellectually) throughout the Philippine diaspora. While they offer meditations on gender and class as well as nation formation, interpreting their stories through the concept of trauma infuses an affective—distinct from reactive—layer of interpretation necessary when discussing violence and recovery. Caruth's encounter of witnessing necessarily entails the ethical role of rendering and listening to a story. In short, the sense of responsibility and empathy infuses the writings by these contemporary women writers of the Philippine diaspora necessary for the greater recovery of this particular history of violence—in the hopes of understanding and envisioning a transformation for the lives of the survivors.

Several questions surface at this point. First, does language, in rendering and interpreting, reenact a kind of symbolic violence that parallels the literal violence of imperialism and colonialism? Second, rather than infusing a sense of the visceral or corporeal into narratives of trauma, does language perform a kind of disembodiment or demystification process? Finally, does emphasizing the place of the affective in these traumatic narratives reiterate the connection between emotions or passions with the feminine realm, thereby reinforcing the age-old dichotomy between the mind and the body? Rather than asserting an interpretation that further engenders clear categories of the feminine and masculine, the rich and poor, and the Philippines and the United States, these writings offer the opportunity for nuanced readings that blur such dichotomies. In this essay, I resist submitting a hard and fast teleology of trauma and works by contemporary women writers of the Philippine diaspora. Instead, Caruth's concept of trauma fittingly provides a malleable structure for ways of understanding and attempting to understand the reality of violence in modern times. Thus, by interpreting narratives of trauma—considering the stops and starts, the gaps and connections, and the ways in which form and content mirror each other—readers (that is, witnesses) are given perspectives or realities that combine consciousness with vulnerability. Rather than calling into question the ways in which the reality of a violent event may be perceived as inaccurate or false, Caruth instead acknowledges the move on the part of the survivor and the witness to actively engage in that reality, and in the process, she highlights the double-sided nature of discourse to depict the violence, to capture the trauma and, in the end, offer the cure.[9] Thus, narratives of trauma, I believe, translate into narratives of resiliency.

The Violence of the Wound: Imperialism, Colonialism, and NeoColonialism

From her collection *Invitation of the Imperialist/Anyaya ng Imperyalista*, the poem "Invitation of the Imperialist" by Filipina poet Elynia S. Mabanglo strikingly represents the more-than-one-hundred-year encounter between the Philippines and the United States through the dyads of patron/client and employer/employee, a troubling dynamic that indicates the hierarchical, patriarchal, and capitalistic structures that frame this encounter. The speaker states:

> Your invitation is persistent
> The card says that I must attend

> My future will be discussed
> Truly, when the poor are being honored
> Wisdom leaves their body
> In the outburst of excitement, reason vanishes
> Ignorance prevails. (6–7)

Mabanglo also adds a layer of irony around these dynamics by posing these dyads as an attempted seduction that shifts into a torture and rape: "A dinner is what I've attended / I am, in fact, the food to be consumed" (11). In this poem, Mabanglo compresses the violent reality of this long encounter between the United States and Philippines by staging it in this manner as a means through which readers witness the symbolic rape of the Philippines through the rape of the female persona. While the speaker concedes that "the fragrance of metaphor was lost in the air," thus suggesting the ways in which language mystifies and disembodies experience, the speaker's voice moves between the literality of the torture and rape with her figurative understanding of the experience:

> I am first split at the stomach
> The liver of need is disgorged
> Apparently pleased by my distending entrails
> He begins to gnaw on my gall bladder and intestines.
> My resolution rooted in the bitterness
> My desire shaped by the sourness. (11)

These rhetorical moves refuse a simplistic downward spiral of victimization as the Filipina persona adamantly voices her greater awareness of the motives of "the wealthy patron," "the gentleman host," the "foreigner," "the man," and "Mister imperialist," as well as her own complicit desire (6, 7, 8, 12).

The speaker, manipulated by the American male persona, acknowledges the gift and curse of education and the English language:

> Your literature is now what I write.
> My tongue searches for your food.
> Once I was even fluent in my own language
> Where your words are now inextricably intertwined. (10)

As representative of those Filipino peoples who ostensibly benefit from their access to education, the speaker also underscores her own complicity in her, and their, still-oppressed situations:

> You are the shadow I drag
> I can only hide you when there is no light.

> I might annihilate you from my humanity
> I must lose my shadow. (10)

The very articulation of her, and their, complicity finds itself mirrored and mocked by the male persona:

> They say, you Pinoys, okey makisama,
> Even borrowing money to entertain visitors.
> You know how to accrue debts of gratitude,
> All your life paying, though you can never repay.
> This is the basis of my alluring program. (9)

Profound poverty strongly resulted from the corrupt Marcos Regime, a particularly strong period of neocolonialism as Marcos borrowed exorbitant funds from the International Monetary Fund/World Bank and exploited the Filipino citizens, thus re-creating a cycle of exploitation and dependency inherited as part of the colonial legacy from the United States (i.e., cronyism).

Significantly, the speaker recognizes the annihilation of her country and her own identity in these lines, and this annihilation thus attests to the state of trauma that still permeates the land, a trauma that finds itself embodied in the female persona's body:

> I could see,
> I could touch
> Yet I could not comprehend.
> It was then I wished to renounce the experience. (9)

Mabanglo moves the reader through the violent reality, adding flourishes that strongly suggest the process of understanding the trauma: "My mind refuses to yield, / … Consciousness is a framed painting / Refusing to die, I am its subject" (12). These articulations then spur the female persona to write, and in doing so, to resist:

> The finger is the other of all words
> The finger shapes this metaphor.
> Unceasing difficulty.
> Unceasing challenge. (12–13)

To counter the violence of this rape, which represents the violence of the U.S.–Philippine encounter, Mabanglo ends this poem a resistant, vital voice, albeit one also dying:

> You will be able to completely kill me …
> But my hatred will flourish

> Burgeoning luxuriantly
> In the womb of thousands of rising hands …
> They will seethe, becoming thousands of eyes and mouths
> Until they produce different sounds,
> Rhythm and imagination
> On millions of paper,
> Until they become rising fists
> Hands that cannot be counted:
> Subverting you,
> Suffocating you,
> Smothering you. (13)

While Mabanglo depicts hatred and anger as disturbing yet mobilizing forces in this poem, she also portrays the inherent responsibility of the female persona to understand her own complicity in the process of colonialism and neocolonialism. Only in recognizing this complicity can the speaker establish and maintain her "consciousness," which also implicates those of her fellow countrypeople to become one in solidarity. Furthermore, Mabanglo offers two surrogates for her readers: the female and the male personae, which in spite of their strict dichotomy compel the readers to identify with these speakers. And last, as much as Mabanglo grants her readers the opportunity to role play in active, almost tangible, and critical ways to gain greater understanding of this encounter, she also insists that readers stand as witnesses to these layers of violent reality, thus enacting a process of recovery of this history.

In "A Conjectural Poem by Flor Contemplacion," Mabanglo astutely walks readers through layers of discourse—indeed, through conjecture upon conjecture—of the life and death of the overseas contract worker (OCW), Flor Contemplacion, who, upon conviction of the murders of a fellow Filipina OCW and her ward in Singapore, was executed by hanging on March 17, 1995. Once again, Mabanglo imagines herself in the female persona—in this instance, a far more specific speaker—in order to meditate upon the dangers of representation: of one's identity (personal, communal, and national); of one's relationship to another identity; of the limits of perception; and, most important, of the disavowal of responsibility. Mabanglo's deliberate gloss of the word *conjecture* suggests the numerous conjectures of and around Contemplacion: her impoverished childhood, her state of mental health, her relationships with her family in the Philippines, her motivations for committing the murders, her tenuous (at best) legal position in relation to the Singaporean and Filipino governments, her presumed abuse and torture at the hands of the Singaporean officials, the eleventh-hour witness who asserted Contemplacion's innocence in vain, and her symbolic resonances (both positive and negative) in life and in death (in large part promulgated by the media).

Divided into five parts, the poem imitates the steps of trauma, much akin to the symptoms of posttraumatic stress disorder, through striking imagery (hallucinations, nightmares, and events) that plays itself repeatedly in one's mind, immersing the reader-as-witness through her series of violent realities as captured by media images and imagined by Mabanglo. Of Contemplacion's exploited position as a housemaid and the state of OCWs, Mabanglo writes, "dust / became salt / of thousands of existences."[10] Of Contemplacion's execution by hanging, she writes,

> Arraigned
> by accusation
> by promise
> by need
> … empty as it descended
> but instantly it ascended
> with my lifeless body. (40)

And of her childhood and adolescence,

> in school I am the child the teacher scolded
> … a teenage girl spanked by my father
> … cursed at by mother
> … slapped by my older brother
> … insulted by a wealthy classmate
> … forced to kneel on salt. (42)

Of Contemplacion's torture she writes,

> I wished to become deaf
> … I wished to be bald
> … I wished to become numb
> … I wished to become a corpse. (43–44)

And of her use as an election issue by Ramos and her tragic situation as the catalyst for protest,

> on the face of placards
> on computer screens
> in the speeches of legislators
> became the sparks of anger
> became an election issue
> became the poison of wind.
> All of which produce a narrative of trauma. (46–47)

The poem begins and ends with Contemplacion's death, though Maban-glo's first-person narration also conjures her up, as if alive, in a kind of living death. Akin to the female persona in "Invitation of the Imperialist," this image of Contemplacion aptly mirrors her life as a manual laborer, with little suste-nance, literally and figuratively:

> a pot of dust
> diffused to the plazas
> of Singapore
> of Laguna
> of Manila
> of different cities
> inside and outside
> of my country, the Philippines
> … cleaved
> by foreigners
> in the shadow of marriage
> in the shade of dollars
> in the promised
> quiet nap. (37–38)

Mabanglo draws on Christian imagery as a way to portray Contemplacion's devout faith as a Catholic and, more acutely, to explore her marginal position between life and death, thereby redefining the Christian concept of dying in order to eternally find peace and live. Thus, Contemplacion's persona in this poem refuses any facile meaning as a Christ figure. According to the principles of Christianity, Jesus Christ accepts his paradoxical fate as the Son of God. He is perceived as a radical by the Jewish community, betrayed by Judas for thirty pieces of silver, sentenced to death by Pontius Pilate, and ultimately, sacrificed for the sins of all of humanity. Mabanglo revises the imagery of eternal justice in order to also show the profound extent of material injustice committed against Contemplacion, and decidedly, Mabanglo ensures that her representa-tion of Contemplacion in five parts defies such a precise chronology:

> I am a night hunting for stars
> … … … … … … … ….
> I am a night
> without a last supper
> … … … … … … … ….
> I am a night
> which does not pass by Pilate
> … … … … … … … ….
> I am a night

in Golgotha

… … … … … … … …..

I am a night

of resurrection. (37, 38, 40, 43, 46)

Contemplacion is deprived of opportunity and nourishment ("hunting for stars" and "without a last supper"), ignored by the Philippine government until too late and tortured by the Singaporean government and thus denied her human rights by both ("which does not pass by Pilate"), and left for dead ("in Golgotha"); the poem's closing lines, "I am a night / of resurrection," echo the life and death of the female persona in "Invitation of the Imperialist." Various media objectify Contemplacion—in fact, three Filipino films claim to represent her life and death accurately:

Prostituted

Prostituting

(by) the issue

(by) the story

(by) the remains

(they say) in the name of truth

(they say) in the name of justice

(they say) in the name of honor. (47)

Mabanglo's portrayal of Contemplacion gives her subjectivity in death, suggesting a community of deaths, and calls for readers to become witnesses. Contemplacion's life and death necessarily represents the lives of overseas contract workers—once ironically referred to by Corazon Aquino as "modern-day heroes" whose revenue of seven billion dollars per year subsidizes the Philippine government—who experience violent realities with little form of recompense (legally, monetarily, personally, and communally) and sustain lives filled with trauma, and who still await some kind of salvation or redemption through the form of national and transnational empathy and responsibility.

Inertia and Repetition as the Symptoms of Trauma: The State of Neocolonialism

Shifting the terrain, Filipina American writer Lara Stapleton, in her short story "So Much," presents a single, working-class mother (a counterpart of sorts to the Filipina OCW) named Ina and her fourteen-year-old daughter Lian in an unknown urban city in the United States. The story works allegorically by opening with Lian's heartache over a breakup—which to anyone in their mid-teens feels excessively "traumatic"—in order to explore the violent realities of Ina's life in an unknown province in the Philippines at an unknown time when, presumably, guerrilla forces kidnapped citizens. "Lian's misery," writes Stapleton, "has a name. It is 'I was so much in love,'" an observation that Ina echoes: "When Ina was a girl, she was so much in love, like Lian is now. Ina was crazy for love. She loved him so much .... He was a soldier and he died."[11] However, Stapleton uses these ostensibly tragic stories of love for the daughter and the mother as a way to tap into the tough, even sparing, love that exists between Ina and Lian, whose emotionally impoverished lives shape the ways in which they respond to each other and how readers, in turn, respond to them.

Stapleton positions her readers as witnesses, albeit playful ones, from the onset of the story: "Lian likes to sit with her misery on the front stoop. She wants to have witnesses .... Lian knows from the way they look away that they have made note of her quiet and noble suffering" (99). She carefully draws readers into this story through the daughter's "trauma" and ends the story with the rather surprising series of violent events of the mother. Thus, these two female characters of "So Much" depict two particular symptoms, if you will, of trauma: (1) the inertia embodied by survivors of violence, as in Ina's case, and (2) the tendency to unconsciously commit, to varying degrees, violent acts, as in Lian's case.

Throughout the story, Ina and Lian act as foils for each other. Weary from work and "hungry for the stuffed chair," Ina remains relatively inert throughout the story: "Ina is tired when she gets home from work. Ina has spent the whole day longing for this moment, this getting in the door and setting down her things .... Ina is waiting for her own boredom to grow stronger than her weariness" (99, 101). To counter Ina's inertia, Stapleton describes Lian in energetic, almost violent, ways: "Lian cannot control her hands, her slim and tapered fingers. When she is angry, or even just startled, her hands fly, backhand, forehand .... She listens to her daughter throw things and growl—a pillow, a shoe, nothing breakable ..." (99, 101, 103). Ina's proclivity toward inertia, readers learn, stems from her earlier life in her province as guerrillas systematically kidnap her family members for unknown reasons. Her love affair with "the soldier," who presumably opposes the guerrillas, keeps her out of favor with her family but, as Stapleton writes, "Ina's greatest regret is the relief it brought .... She took the tragedy for herself, thought of the redemption it could bring .... They came, and it was her sister they took, and Ina knew her own wrongdoing was erased. Her petty offenses were forgiven. They came for her sister and this was Ina's first thought. Her second thought was, no, please, but nothing she thought or felt afterward would erase the fact that she had taken this suffering for her own ends" (104).

The story, as it appears in print, indicates a large break on the page between another "traumatic" moment of Lian's heartache and Ina's flashback, the moment when Ina's trauma begins. This break visually depicts the flashback but, more important, emphasizes Ina's inertia. Part of this inertia arises from the guilt she feels for being spared. Ironically, Ina's seeming redemption in that one instance comes at the cost of her long-term recovery.

However, Stapleton immediately intensifies this "redemption" with another visual break on the page that brings Ina back to another traumatic moment when a guerrilla inevitably comes for her. In that moment, a physically starving Ina, who "for four days" dreams "of fistfuls of lard," foils her kidnapping by sleeping with her kidnapper: "So this is what Ina did. His breath smelled distinctly of fat .... She licked his gums and cheeks and tongue, and this gave her strength for two days" (104–5). This strange action heightens Ina's sexuality and connects it to violent events, this last event presumably resulting in her pregnancy with Lian. At this moment, this visual break on the page indicates a flash forward as Stapleton writes, "And so Lian" (105). Thus, Stapleton connects the traumas of mother and daughter and ends the story with a kind of tableau: Ina comforts Lian,

> at the same time admonishing herself for contributing to Lian's weakness .... Ina must teach Lian to love like a person labors .... Loving like a person labors, like when you work and are weary and work on, and the stomach pains come, thirst or exhaustion, the cramps, and you breathe a certain way, contract certain muscles to lessen it as much as possible. But at the same time you accept the pain and expect that it will pass .... In life, those you love will be gone, and even when you do love with such fierceness—because you will, everyone will love with such fierceness—you must breathe a certain way until it passes. (105)

Stapleton layers the violent events of Ina's life in a manner that explains the trauma of Ina's working-class existence as a single mother. Ironically, the one moment when she takes action to save herself, using her sexuality to do so (in contradistinction to the female persona in Mabanglo's "Invitation of the Imperialist"), results in Lian, whose trauma of heartache over a guy actually unmasks a more poignant trauma: the tough love of her mother. This ending suggests a moment of recovery for Ina, a point of connection between mother and daughter, and a deeper resiliency embodied by both of them. If anger and hate act as mobilizing forces in Mabanglo's "Invitation of the Imperialist" for violence and trauma, then Stapleton's "So Much" meditates upon the limitations and possibilities for guilt in moving characters out of trauma into recovery.

Similar to Stapleton, Filipina American writer M. Evelina Galang, in her short story "Miss Teenage Sampaguita," muses upon the states of inertia of an aunt, Tita Baby, and her niece Millicent (Millie) in a Midwestern suburb in the United States; their trauma involves the everyday asides that limit the range of experiences simply because of their gender, a contradictory cycle of repression that repeats with each generation and results in inertia. Thus, this story's conception of trauma connects the original definition of trauma as a wound of the body with its contemporary definition of trauma as a wound in the mind. Galang, however, makes quick reference to another trauma, the Japanese occupation of the family's village in the Philippines, to underscore this one. Tita Baby's brother and Millie's father Frank, as representative of strict masculine ideals and practices, acts as the channel that inherits and perpetuates this cycle of repression.

Galang shows the contradictions of the double standard regarding gender as both Tita Baby and Millie, the youngest siblings in their respective families, suffer from the dogmatic control of Frank, who emulates his own father during the Japanese occupation of their village. Clearly, the powerlessness of the male figures throughout their homeland during the occupation inaugurates the illusory sense of power that they assume within their home. Frank's shift into the role of patriarch seems both surprising and unsurprising to Tita Baby, who recalls, "I can still hear the way his [their father's] voice entered the house, took hold of all of us, invaded our peace like the Japanese had when they invaded our village years before. It was as though he were the enemy."[12] Likewise, Tita Baby notes Frank's booming voice as she connects the apparent sense of power he copies from their father with the professional accomplishments—that is, middle-class existence in the United States—of her siblings: "My brother is the fourth doctor in our house. There are four attorneys and three dentists. I'm the only one who isn't a professional. I am a mother" (145). Even though Galang notes the opportunity for Millie, an excellent student, to follow in her father's footsteps as a doctor, unlike Tita Baby, she also highlights Millie's position as the dutiful daughter in seeming preparation for her role as a devoted wife someday, much akin to Tita Baby. Tita Baby makes significant note of the ways in which she and Millie also perpetuate their own complicity in their repression as they still follow Frank's voice. Tita Baby asks herself, "God, it's that voice, I think. Why can't I walk away from it?" and she also remarks: "Millie acts out her role, little miss beauty queen," acquiescing to the myth of the superwoman (150, 148). Compressing the two traumas—the Japanese occupation and the everyday repression of Millie—Galang calls attention to the unjust practices of Frank. Tellingly, perhaps too naively, Millie quietly refers to herself as "a prisoner of war" to her mother Lettie and Tita Baby, who understand this place only too well (143).

Galang uses Tita Baby's observations of Millie to emphasize Millie's inertia, thus reflecting her own inertia. Galang writes, "I [Tita Baby] can't tell how she [Millie] feels about these things. She says them without any emotion. She's too young to date. She's too old to babble on the phone. The whole thing makes me nervous ..... She never smiles. She doesn't laugh like the other girls .... She keeps her mouth closed, hides her braces like her feelings" (142, 150). Furthermore, Galang stresses the trauma that Millie experiences in the ordinary repetition of household tasks: "Her work is perfectly choreo-graphed as she slips in and out of view, sometimes with a rag in her hands and sometimes with a broom .... Millie keeps moving, laying down silver-ware—fork, spoon, knife, fork, spoon, knife" (141, 140). This repetition seems almost hypnotic to Tita Baby, Millie, and thus, the readers as witnesses. However, Tita Baby breaks out of this hypnosis by asking significant critical questions of Millie and herself: "Why doesn't she say no? Why doesn't she speak up? Why am I so upset?" (152). In this pivotal moment, inertia gives way to consciousness as Millie confides in her aunt and her aunt responds in kind, giving voice to herself and their situations:

> Her stories fill me up. Start from the bottom of my soles and rise high into my throat. Her stories wring my insides and my heart and I find myself choking .... And her mother, like my mother, like myself, our voices are so small sometimes, and the work that must get done is so interminable. And what I hate most of all is seeing her, Miss Teenage Sampaguita, withering like the rest of us. Growing faint. Dying like white petals fraying from the vine, and slipping silently from walls and fences, and falling like compost onto fertile ground. (154–55)

Strikingly, the idea that "our voices are so small sometimes, and the work that must get done is so interminable" reiterates the conditions of the female characters of the other narratives of trauma considered throughout this essay. Galang's short story highlights the necessity of giving voice, and sharing sto-ries as a means through which they understand their repressed situations though the depiction of their middle-class existence affords these Filipina Americans a significant privilege denied to their literary counterparts. Galang's description of the national flower of the Philippines, the sampaguita, aptly defines the contradictory status and location—of limitation and prom-ise—of these female personae across temporal and spatial planes:

> I remember looking up at the walls so high, I thought they [the flowers] crossed blue boundaries, clouds and morning stars, and I realize it wasn't just that the walls were covered with Sampaguitas; it's that they grew to be wild and abundant ... the white petals stretched along the walls, scaled over them, and escaped down the sides into the neighbor's yard .... In my memory, I am alone in a corner of the garden, pulling flowers from the wall and sucking nectar from the petals and my mother and her mother, sitting on the bench under one of the mango trees, whisper to each other. (147–48)

Galang's thoughtful description strongly suggests the restrictions that surround these flowers, as representative of women, as she also accentuates the transgressive and communal qualities embodied by these flowers. Counter to the emotions of anger, hate, and guilt that act as catalysts for recovery and change in the previous writings, Galang's "Miss Teenage Sampaguita" stresses the need for empathy and communication which, in turn, highlights the reciprocal nature of the encounter in witnessing for the understanding violent realities and recognizing trauma in the hopes of recovering from it.

The Possibility for Recovery as the Projection of Postcolonialism

Throughout her collection *The Kissing*, Filipina Australian writer Merlinda Bobis infuses the necessity of empathy and communication as well as the obligation and responsibility that constitute the dynamic between a survivor and a witness. Bobis presents the mystical storyteller Selma of the North and South in her short story "Before the Moon Rises," a title that communicates danger and threat. In this first-person narrative, readers learn that soldiers have issued orders for the "whole village to evacuate" since the government "only believes in catching rebels."[13] Quoting the rhetoric of the soldiers, a deaf Selma—an outsider continually mocked by the villagers—still "hears" (i.e., understands) the soldiers' orders: "Away, away, the guns waved towards the forest. Quick, before the moon rises. And no one must come back" (132). Selma strikes them "as a strange vision. A very old woman, shriveled and dark as a coconut husk, trailing long white hair to her ankles as she carried trunks of bamboo from the forest" (133). Selma, Bobis writes, knows "one hundred years of grief" (138), a time period that spans the U.S.–Philippines confrontation and moves from colonialism to neocolonialism as the soldiers dominate and terrorize their fellow countrypeople.

If one legacy of neocolonialism rests in inertia, Bobis explores the apathy that also results from this confrontation. Selma initially refuses to help the villagers during the military occupation because she makes a promise to herself: "Didn't I promise myself that, on my hundredth year, I would wait for my last days peacefully in a hut apart from people and their stories? I promised not to care any more. I had seen and heard too many stories by now and had told them many times over" (138). Selma, however, feels obligated to break her promise to herself, opting to help the community that shuns her after a young, male soldier severely injures a young, female child who previously accused Selma of stealing her dog. Selma chants to the soldier, making him submissive, and tends to the child, noting, "The whole village follows them to my hut—ay, I have done it again .... Now I have the village in my hut. Another people must be told stories, so they can hear the forgotten tale in each drop of blood that they spill. Every tale which dries up and dies when it leaves the body. What nuisance! On my hundredth year, I will be asked to sing their blood again, so they can understand and change their history. So they can keep the moon from rising" (138).

If Galang suggests the importance of sharing stories, Bobis states it outrightly as she also details the ephemeral quality of these stories: "Every tale ...

dries up and dies when it leaves the body." Selma informs the villagers just as she tells the readers as witnesses of the greater need to tell stories continually, particularly the stories of violent realities, these narratives of trauma, "so they can understand and change their history." By the end of the piece, the villagers and the soldiers ask, indeed beg, for these stories that recount these violent realities, calling her "Nanay" and "Mother Selma": "'[T]ell us a story' .... 'Tell us a story about wounds' .... 'A story about tears' .... 'About going away.' 'About the forest.' 'About the moon before it rises.'" (138). Selma begins this story by showing reluctance, resistance, and awareness in her quiet mission and she ends this tale with a joyous, communal, and wryly humorous image:

> The hushed voices are drowned by several babies bawling in synchro-nized hunger. The mothers bare their breasts. A young man farts too loudly. The children giggle and tease. Some of the soldiers suggest that the grief-stricken boy lie down to keep his tears from spilling. A grand-father says it's a good idea. Everyone talks all at once, trying to give advice. The hut trembles with all their home-noises holding back the rising of the moon .... It occurs to me that I had burnt the rice and that there is not enough dried fish and tomatoes for everyone. (139)

Selma revises the miracle of multiplication by Jesus Christ through ironic observation, "It occurs to me that I had burnt the rice and that there is not enough dried fish and tomatoes for everyone," a rhetorical move that also underlines the deep hospitality inherent in her and their demeanors. Thus, by portraying this imagined community to her readers, she makes equal the villagers, soldiers, and Selma, envisioning the promise of a postcolonial period. Thus, Bobis signifies the importance of accepting responsibility, thus disavowing apathy and storytelling. Presumably, the process of recovery begins.

In her short story "Fish-Hair Woman," Bobis makes this process of recov-ery literal by unearthing an aspect of recent history in the Philippines: the military purge during the Aquino era, from 1986 to 1992. This was an era in which, surprisingly, more people were killed than under the Marcos adminis-tration of more than twenty years—at least as documentation attests. This angle of history echoes earlier periods of Philippine history that summon up the role of the United States in the Philippines—from its annexation in 1898 from Spain through the Marcos and Aquino administrations to the training of Filipino soldiers today for the "war on terror." These filters of Philippine history are shown through the figure of the fish-hair woman, who acts as the literal embodiment of history and memory. As Bobis writes,

> Hair. How was it linked with the heart? I'll tell you—it had something to do with memory. Every time I remembered anything that unsettled my

heart, my hair grew at least one handspan … very tricky hair, very tricky heart …. You see … history hurts my hair, did you know that? Remembering is always a bleeding out of memory, like pulling thread from a vein in the heart, a coagulation so fine, miles of it stretching upwards to the scalp, then sprouting there into the longest strand of red hair. Some face-saving tale to explain my twelve metres of very thick black hair with its streaks of red and hide my history.[14]

And further, she incarnates the theme of grief, the missing crucial step between trauma and healing since her village, she notes, "had forgotten how to cry" (16).

In this mystical story, the fish-hair woman pulls bodies from the river with her hair in a village in Iraya, "in the south of Luzon during that purge by the military" (10). Clearly disavowing the present moment's inclination toward historical forgetfulness and selective memory, the representation of the fish-hair woman, like Selma, rests at the cusp of life and death, sustenance and destruction, human and godlike as she states, "After I fished out a boy's body, which nobody claimed, the cracks began to show …. I screamed, and for the first time the village that had forgotten how to cry, saw that perhaps I was beginning to remember how, behind all sockets, there can be no real drought for the eye. You who read this and shiver at this macabre war, may you never pretend that you have forgotten" (16–17). The fish-hair woman indicts her local community for their sense of apathy and the soldiers for their ruthlessness just as Bobis exhorts her readers to "never pretend you have forgotten." Tellingly, Bobis refuses an ambivalent position as storyteller, just as the fish-hair woman continues this gruesome process of recovery.

Significantly, Bobis goes beyond having readers witness the trauma and moves these witnesses through the stages of trauma through the fish-hair woman's pointed address to "you." She writes, "And may you never know the kinship between fishing for the dead and actual killing. The first time you do either, you break. You, too, die within, thus you begin to practice the art of uncaring, teach your gut to behave for the sake of your own salvation, so that the next time and the next, it becomes easier to cross with mortality …. But, somewhere at the tail-end of that numbed routine, you give once more. You break, and no amount of practice can put you back together again" (17).

Experiencing violent realities through anger and hatred—whether as the recipient or as the instigator of these events—translates into guilt and a general state of inertia that finally gives way to confronting these realities. Thus, a space opens for recovery, a process that anticipates the necessity for one to break with, yet be aware of, the old history and the old identity in order to forge a different history and a new identity and imagining a period of postcolonialism.

To reiterate, one step reveals itself as the key step in the process of recovery: grief. Bobis makes grief a literal stage in this process of recovery by actually having the villagers cry, as "all hearts marking time at the bank, nearly breaking in unison as I, hair undone like a net, descended into the dark waters to fish out another victim of our senseless war" (14). The ending ironically suggests the tragic death of the fish-hair woman's Australian lover, Tony, and his subsequent recovery from the river by her. Thus, this process of recovery, Bobis suggests, exempts no one in the end. As a repository of history and memory, the fish-hair woman poignantly represents the necessary processes of remembering and recalling this silenced history and presents the possibility for recovery, a period of postcolonialism, through the process of grief, as she muses, "The disappeared could at least be found for a decent burial. And the river would be restored to its old taste, sweetened again by the hills. Then we could fish again or wash our clothes there again, or gather the kangkong and gabi leaves at its bank again. It meant sustenance" (18).

Conclusion

The interplay among these contemporary works of literature and particular moments of Philippine history, which implicate the United States as an empire, attest to the mutual yet uneven construction of both nations in relation to and against each other. This notion harks back to the now-famous exchange between Fredric Jameson and Aijaz Ahmad, both of whom, at that academic moment, intervened in the directions of multiculturalism vis-à-vis postcolonial studies. In his article "Third-World Literature in the Era of Multinational Capitalism," Jameson ostensibly submits the concept of national allegory, wherein a character of a third world nation represents the voice of the nation.[15] However, Jameson makes this assertion in order to address the shift in literary and cultural studies toward a reductive, multicultural agenda; thus, his original argument for national allegory is, in fact, not the point. Ahmad, in *In Theory: Classes, Nations, Literatures*, challenges Jameson's argument for national allegory, posing the troublesome ways in which the conflation of an individual and collective identity, particularly regarding third world nations, limits the ways for understanding the complicated dynamics of colonial relationships.[16] In response, Jameson uses this interpretive move on Ahmad's part in order to highlight precisely the credibility of his own argument. The Jameson–Ahmad exchange emphasizes one central idea: the different usages and analyses of postcolonial narratives by literary and cultural critics in service of particular agendas. For the purposes of this essay, the recounting of this interplay between Jameson and Ahmad addresses the question of voice (i.e., that of the character, the author, the critic); the depicted realities of the character; and, most important, the layers of history that shape the narrative vis-à-vis the memory—that is, the testimony—of a character. The role of the critic, or the reader, thus translates into the role of the witness who listens to the testimony of the character as a repository for individual and collective memory. In this collapsing of the personal and the political, a national and transnational literature emerges, thus offering the possibility for understanding the ways in which nations construct one another, the motivations and intentions of these kinds of agendas, and the consequences of these sorts of actions. Narratives of trauma, as the female personae of these particular writings consistently show, thus become narratives of resiliency. Embodied in this resiliency lies the promise of recovery and of peace.

To briefly return to the Jameson–Ahmad discussion, the concept of allegory perhaps holds too singular a meaning, one in keeping with the traditional definition of allegory as a story that stands for another story (typically religious and didactic). In short, one story acts as a screen for the other. The religious and didactic purposes of allegory prove useful, especially regarding the writings from the Philippine diaspora, given its strong religious and spiritual sensibility. However, by offering one *ur*-reading of a story, this traditional definition of allegory also seems too limiting in its scope, dangerous in its disavowal of historical significance and literary possibility. Thus, a revision of the term *allegory* as stories that represent past histories of violent encounters—that is, as narratives of trauma—presents a productive and significant opportunity to explore many interpretive possibilities in writings from the Philippine diaspora that broach the religious and spiritual with the historical and literary. This sensibility, I believe, reveals a timely notion in the religious and spiritual rhetoric that runs throughout the media discourse of contemporary events. These works of literature from the Philippine diaspora allegorically invoke a different kind of religiosity and spirituality, thus offering a different language to understand this historical moment. If language acts as a tool of colonialism, then it also acts as the tool of transformation, a means of departure, if you will—a message conveyed by these women writers of the Philippine diaspora.

For these various female personae, annihilation of their history—layers of violent events—results in a negative sensibility, a general state of inertia in one's identity (personal, communal, and national) that necessitates creative ways for working through trauma and for understanding their—indeed, *our*—history as a history of trauma. The act of writing becomes an act of surviving just as the act of listening becomes an act of witnessing. It is hoped that this essay disavows a fixed teleology through these works of literature by these select women writers and suggests the usefulness for this methodology of trauma in considering works of world literature—in particular, works of the Philippine diaspora—that, in turn, exhort the United States and the greater world to express empathy, increase communication, and bear responsibility for others. These women writers give voice, particularly through female personae, to explore the problems within and throughout the Philippine diaspora, writing creative riffs on a history of trauma as they also suggest the promise of recovery on multiple levels. In listening to the crisis of trauma, as Caruth reminds us, we, as readers and witnesses, also can listen for the departure from it.[17] Only through the imagination of this kind of encounter can a reckoning or an awakening happen within an individual and throughout a community.

Acknowledgments

For their encouragement and inspiration, I am greatly indebted to my family, immediate and extended, especially my parents and my sisters; my advisor Dr. Josephine Lee and committee members; my friends and colleagues in the Departments of English and American Studies at the University of Minnesota–Twin Cities and the University of Wisconsin–Madison, especially those at the latter's Center for Southeast Asian Studies; to Melinda L. de Jesús, the editor of this timely anthology, for this wonderful opportunity; and last, to the Pinay writers discussed herein for their exquisite works of literature.

Notes

1. Elynia S. Mabanglo, "Invitation of the Imperialist," in *Invitation of the Imperialist/Anyaya Ng Imperyalista* (Quezon City: University of Philippines Press, 1998), 6–13; hereafter, page numbers will be cited parenthetically in the text.
2. Cathy Caruth, "Introduction" in *Trauma: Explorations in Memory* (Baltimore and London: Johns Hopkins University Press, 1995), 10.
3. Cathy Caruth, *Unclaimed Experience: Trauma, Narrative, and History* (Baltimore: Johns Hopkins University Press, 1996), 4.
4. Caruth, *Trauma*, 7–8.
5. Caruth, *Unclaimed Experience*, 11.
6. Caruth, *Trauma*, 145.
7. Robert Jay Lifton, *Home from the War: Vietnam Veterans, Neither Victims nor Executioners* (New York: Simon and Schuster, 1973), 139.
8. Caruth, *Unclaimed Experience*, 4.
9. Caruth, *Trauma*, 34.
10. Elynia S. Mabanglo, "A Conjectural Poem by Flor Contemplacion," in *Invitation of the Imperialist*, 37; hereafter, page numbers will be cited parenthetically in the text.
11. Lara Stapleton, *The Lowest Blue Flame before Nothing* (San Francisco: Aunt Lute, 1998), 98, 100; hereafter, page numbers will be cited parenthetically in the text.
12. M. Evelina Galang, "Miss Teenage Sampaguita," in *Her Wild American Self* (Minneapolis, Minn.: Coffee House Press, 1996), 140; hereafter, page numbers will be cited parenthetically in the text.
13. Merlinda Bobis, "Before the Moon Rises," in *The Kissing* (San Francisco: Aunt Lute, 2001), 132; hereafter, page numbers will be cited parenthetically in the text.
14. Merlinda Bobis, "Fish-Hair Woman," in *The Kissing*, 10; hereafter, page numbers will be cited parenthetically in the text.
15. Fredric Jameson, "Third-World Literature in the Era of Multinational Capitalism," *Social Text* 15 (Fall 1986): 65–88.
16. Aijaz Ahmad, *In Theory: Classes, Nations, Literatures* (London and New York: Verso Books, 1992).
17. Caruth, *Trauma*, 10.

23

Filipinas "Living in a Time of War"

NEFERTI XINA M. TADIAR

In an essay written for an exhibit of some forty Philippine women artists called *Ang Babae,* Thelma Kintanar asks: "*Ang babaeng Filipina: sino at ano siya*?" (The Filipina woman: who and what is she?[1]) The posing of *ang babaeng Filipina* as a question can be seen as a political act of resistance against a pressing situation. For Kintanar, that situation is the imprisonment of Filipina women in their gender. *Babae* is, in her view, the name of a prison made up of *de-kahong paglalarawan,* or confining portraits, that serve to represent only the traditional roles women play in a colonialist, patriarchal society. *Babae* is a prison house of images of beautiful, fragrant, shy, and weak women; images that obscure and limit the human capacities and powers they actually and historically have performed.

In "Ang Maging Babae" (To Be a Woman),[2] the poet Elynia Mabanglo provides a similar view of the predicament that is *babae*:

> Kasumpa-sumpa
> ang maging babae sa panahong ito.
> Depinisyong pamana
> ng nakaraa't kasalukuyan.
> Anyong hinulma
> ng pag-aasam at pangangailangan.
> [What a curse
> to be a woman in these times.
> A definition inherited
> from the past and the present.
> A form molded
> out of longing and need.][3]

The cursed form of woman consists, however, of images that are also actual functions:

> Ikaw ang pundiya ng karsonsilyo,
> ang kurbata, maging ang burda sa panyo't kamiseta.

Susukatin ang ganda mo sa kama,
ang talino'y sa pagkita ng pera.
[You are a brief's bottom
a necktie, the embroidery on a handkerchief and an undershirt.
Your beauty will be measured on the bed,
your mind, by money earned.]⁴

What Mabanglo expresses is what many feminists have condemned as the being-for-others (particularly being-for-men) of women, their apprehension as *kasangkapan*, domestic belongings: household utensils, clothing, adornment, land, and food. The "What" in the question "What is she?" is thus also an answer: "She is what?"—an object for useful and profitable consumption, a thing. *What* refers to the form and function of *babae* as a commodity.

The predicament of *babae* is not transhistorical; it is a prevailing condition "in this time." For Filipina poet Joi Barrios, this time is a time of war. Indeed, to be a woman is to live in a time of war ("*Ang pagiging babae ay pamumuhay sa panahon ng digma*").⁵ In this poem, the fear that stems from a woman's future resting in the hands of men is linked to the cruelty of poverty and the ever-present threat of violence that presides over her home and her country. The condition of women as living in a time of war is thus inextricable from the condition of the country that bears the same name as its women: Filipinas.

I might describe this gendered, sexual, racial, and national war as principally the very long war that is at once what enables and *is* development. Spanish and U.S. colonialism, U.S. neocolonialism, World Bank– and International Monetary Fund–backed authoritarian modernization, export-oriented industrialization, and globalization: these are some of the ways that this war has been called and waged. Filipina women not only have borne the costs of this war of development but also have literally become the bodily price paid for it. Prostituted women, domestic and service-sector workers, homeworkers, and rural and agricultural workers as well as factory workers are the most visible, primary, national commodities that the Philippines has marketed vigorously since the 1970s in order to buy its share of economic development.

The focus on Filipinas and their relationship to development, which the regime of Ferdinand Marcos institutionalized, demonstrates the academic and technocratic participation in this objectification of Filipinas for the intertwined interests of multi- and transnational capital, national governments, and national elites. The year 1975 was declared the International Women's Year by the United Nations, which also declared the next ten years as the International Decade for Women. It was in the context of this international event that the Marcos government established, in the same year, the National Commission on the Role of the Filipino Woman and installed Imelda Marcos as its honorary chairwoman for the next ten years. Two goals of the UN declaration demonstrate to what end Filipinas were to be put:

to support the integration of women in the total economic, social and cultural development effort.

and

to recognize the contribution of women to the promotion of friendly relations and cooperation among nations and to the strengthening of world peace.[6]

In what way are these declared ideals of total development and world peace declarations of war? In the same way that global capitalism, on which these goals tacitly depend, is war—war against the vast majority of people in the world, including Filipinas. Friendly relations and cooperation among nations depend on the acceptance and maintenance of oppressive divisions of labor and prevailing exploitative processes of capitalist production. War is the means by which that acceptance and maintenance is secured. It is also the everyday condition under which countless lives are depleted, deprived, and simply used and used up in order to secure the development of a few. In the Philippines, the International Decade for Women was undoubtedly the decade for the incorporation of Filipinas in the state-sponsored prostitution and tourism industries of the new hospitality economy.

"The woman question" for which countless studies made in the 1970s and 1980s about Philippine women and development were answers—can thus be posed in a way that divests it of its radically transformative possibilities. This question loses its potentially subversive and resistant spirit when it is asked and answered in a simple, empirical way and thereby fails to interrogate the very realities it investigates. To ask, "The Filipina woman: who and what is she?" in a radical way is to see her status, and the state of affairs in which she holds that status, as in a state of emergency—indeed, a state of war. It is to inquire into the ways that being a Filipina means living in a time of war.

Pamumuhay means not only "to live" but also "a means of living," that is, work. Being a Filipina is, in the context of the second meaning, a form of work. The vast majority of Filipinas make their living out of being Filipina as well as being women. By this I mean that the work Filipinas do, and the violence, fear, and racial and sexual oppression and exploitation they experience as part of this living have at once resulted from and enabled the global economy that the Philippines services as a provider of cheap domestic and sexual labor. Whether they are nurses here in the United States; mail-order brides in the United States, Australia, or Germany; domestic workers in Hong Kong, Italy, or Saudi Arabia; or entertainers in Japan, Filipinas suffer the consequences of, even as they create the conditions for, the national and international structures and processes that constitute the commodified identity *Filipina* in the warring world market.

Never has there been a time when Filipinas have been so alone yet so crowded in this global identity. Many numbers attest to the crowdedness and self-selling labor power of the Filipina. There are more than two million Filipina overseas contract workers in 125 countries all over the world: 50,000 Filipina mail-order brides in the United States, about the same number of Filipina entertainers in Japan, 100,000 Filipina domestic workers in Italy, and so on and so forth.[7] These are not only numbers; they are also images. In a summary of statements made by American men about Filipinas, based on more than 1,500 pages of Usenet news posts and material from seventy-five pen pal services, Filipinas were portrayed as ideal women because of their eagerness to marry, their youthful looks (their "exceptionally smooth skin and tight vaginas"), their real enjoyment of sex, their loyalty, and their dispensability.[8] They are low-maintenance wives, fully domesticated and convenient, and one can always be returned and replaced by a younger model. Filipinas are status symbols, bodily signs of their husbands'/proprietors' worldly experience, cultural sophistication, sexual prowess, and liberal racial attitudes. They are things and signs whose meanings and devaluation are the product of a long history of "special relations" between the United States and the Philippines.

In this time of globalization, we witness and experience the detachment of nationality from nation, as the historical crises that define and shape the Philippines become sedimented in the bodies of Filipinas. In the United States, E. San Juan Jr. describes the predicament of this nationality as "the predicament and crisis of dislocation, fragmentation, uprooting, loss of traditions, exclusion, and alienation."[9]

Until recently, the predicament of Filipino Americans largely has been portrayed through the experiences of Filipino-American men. However, it is Filipina Americans *as Filipinas* that are made to embody and bodily bear the consequences of the crisis of a floating nationality, as evidenced by the alarming rate of suicides among young Filipina Americans, especially in California.[10] While I cannot possibly understand nor explain what we can only so inadequately read as the individual despair signified by such suicides, I will venture to suggest a connection between these suicides and the great tension that Filipina Americans are made to live under. On the one hand, they are symbolic bearers, defenders, and keepers of a besieged, original-national culture. On the other hand, they are accommodating, cooperative, and embracing members of a present culture that is of their adoptive home. These suicides, as well as the mysterious deaths of Filipina overseas contract workers whose corpses are shipped back to the Philippines in both increasing and increasingly unremarked-upon numbers; the murder and mutilation of Filipinas in the hands of strangers, lovers, husbands, fathers, brothers, friends, clients, and employers; and the systematic gendered, sexualized, racialized, and class-based killing and injuring of Filipinas everywhere are to me material testaments of wars for which Filipinas are the casualties and the means, the fuel, the fodder, and the weaponry. These deaths may, however, also be, very importantly for us, testaments that Filipinas are fighters, warriors in and against these wars.

What is the task of feminist Filipina art and cultural production in the midst of these wars? It is not merely to represent the existing realities of Filipinas, which the prevailing images belie. Nor is it merely to represent the subjective experiences of Filipinas living in such realities. It is, rather, to radically put to doubt the "givenness," necessity, and legitimacy of objective reality, the reality in which Filipinas can and do serve as objects for the profit, pleasure, and power of others.

To ask "*Sino ang Filipina?*" (Who is the Filipina?) is to call into question the completion of her objectification, which is expressed in the question, "What is she?" It is therefore also to foreground the subjective dimension of this labor, which is objectified in and as the commodity Filipina. It is to recognize and reappropriate the creative, living labor that Filipinas carry out in the production of themselves and the world.

As the content of the question "Who?", Filipina subjectivity consists of modes of experience—that is, modes of understanding, feeling, and relating—through which women make themselves into Filipinas. In its idealized and therefore commodifiable form, it consists of practices of caring for others, of extending oneself to others, of serving and accommodating others. But even within that form, it also consists of longing for better things, better worlds for oneself and for one's own and of bravely venturing out into the world with little or no guarantees of safety in search of new possibilities for life. Filipina subjectivity consists of those practices of dreaming in action that are indispensable to the work and commodity identity that Filipinas are called upon, *as Filipinas*, to perform. It consists of the desires and dreams of Filipinas used to fuel multinational garment, electronic, and sex industries as well as individual neocolonial fantasies of the "American" way of life and collective U.S. dreams of worldly conquest, power, and success. Just as imprisoning images of Filipinas both result from and contribute to the conditions of war in which they live, so is the identity function of Filipinas as *ano* (what) constituted by their subjective agency as *sino* (who). That agency is the capacity of Filipinas to determine and exercise will and desire over the conditions that appear to rule, regulate, and transcend our lives.

The dispersed and yet common existence of Filipinas all over the world foregrounds at once the profound sameness and the profound differences of our situations and lives. This situation has urged many to ask, "*Sino ka? Sino tayo? Sino ako?*" (Who are you? What are we? Who am I?)

While there are many ways to understand and respond to such questions, more often than not they are taken as paths toward a hegemonic notion of identity. A review in *Asian Art News* of the 1998 exhibit of the works of eight Filipina American artists held at San Francisco State University, for example, understands the exhibit's title, *Sino Ka? Ano Ka?* (Who Are You? What Are

You?) to be about "the Filipina American"—that is, to be about the "concept of being Filipina-American."[11] As a matter of "identity issues," the exhibit can thus be read for the "distinctive sensibility" and "distinctive modern aesthetic" expressed by the works of self-identified Filipina Americans. Whatever the artworks might *do* as artworks (and here I am thinking of them as instantiations, rearticulations, and disarticulations of that other form of work of *making a living*), they all become, within this rubric, answers to "the challenge of the Filipina-American: How to establish a sense of self within the confusing era of increasing pluralism."[12]

While a sense of self is a necessary means of Filipina struggles in these times, given the tendency toward the subsumption of systems of political representation by market logics, an identitarian sense of self easily becomes the final object of such struggles, making the question of the Filipina American another image function for capitalist time—"the global poster girl of our millennial, cross-cultural age."[13] Viewed as exemplary instances of "cultural fusion," the artworks thus are taken as indications of an economically valorized "hybrid" identity that bourgeois Filipino nationalists have long been peddling to gain respectable acceptance in international society.

It is not my intention to join the specious dismissive "critiques" of identity politics. I do, however, want to call attention to the way "identity" has a habit of turning into another commodity. That in itself is not a politically debilitating thing, for indeed commodities are things containing, as Filipinas show, subjective activity and therefore immanent agency. But it is too easy for that activity to become lost in the search for political *representation* and, moreover, for that activity to become converted into universally exchangeable values, such as the values of cross-culturalism in today's "good" globalizing art.

One might argue that art "itself," without the industry of art for which galleries and art magazines are essential instruments, does more than this and that it is simply the way art is read in reviews such as this one that makes it into a commodity reflecting an imaginary wholeness and integrity of identity for its interpellated audience. But how we read or view art very much shapes how and for what art is made and what it might do. *Look, it's me* (or not) is the expression of a dominant viewing relation to the world, including art. This habit of looking for whether something is or isn't me but someone else—that is, for what and who something *represents* (as its value)—is a habit formed under the regime of capitalist-subsumed, racialized, and sexualized relations of hierarchy and appropriation, a regime under which "people have become things." It is this habit of looking that compels the oppressively competitive, utilitarian, and subjugating ways we look at each and every other, and the harsh and punitive ways we regard ourselves (where "we" indicates any identifiable collective "someone" within this regime).

The putative identity of Filipinas is clearly no guarantee against Filipinas looking at Filipinas in this way: seeking a value to extol, subordinate, or deny in people-become-things in an attempt to negotiate their own value. Consider, for example, these statements by Filipina domestic helpers in Germany about other Filipinas (which were culled by Maria Carmen Domingo-Kirk in her research)[14]:

Ligaya: My employers were concerned about my social life. They invited another Filipina who has lived here for five years and is employed as a nurse. I looked forward to what she and I could do, like go to the movies or shopping. When she arrived, she gave me a look I could never forget the rest of my life. *Nanliit ako sa tingin niya, datapwa't utusan lang ako* [I was debased by the look she gave me because she regarded me as merely one who is ordered about]. While we were having dinner she would give that look. She did not say anything bad to me personally, it was just that look she gave me. I decided I did not want to see her again.

Floring: I have had too many bad experiences with other Filipinas. When they find out I do not have a legal working visa (I came on a tourist visa), they look down on me. *Mababa ang tingin nila sa akin, para akong tae* [They regard me very lowly, as if I were shit]. I smile when I am introduced to other Filipinas. But those with legal working visas would usually acknowledge me by giving me that look. *Napapahiya tuloy ako, gusto ko nang magtago sa kanilang tingin* [In this way I am shamed, I want to hide from their look].

Pacing: I do not socialize with other Filpinas because I have had too many bad experiences. The worst experience is when I see other Filipinas in the trains, stores, or markets and they give me that look. *Masakit sa aking kalooban ang kanilang pagtingin* [The way they look is painful to my inner self]. So my companion and I just stick together and eat in inexpensive restaurants or go shopping. Filipinas look down on us because we do not come out up to their level.

Zeny: *Masama ang nangyayari sa mga Pilipina sapagkat nagkakaroon nang sama ng loob* [What happens to Filipinas is harmful because bad feelings become harbored among them]. I know this because I have experienced this feeling too often. I am talking about how Filipinas here regard each other. *Minamata nila ang kapwa nila Pilipina* [They look down on fellow Filipinas].

Gloria: When I finally found a job as a domestic worker, other Filipinas did not accept me as their own kind. As soon as they found out I was only a domestic worker, their whole attitude changed. I have a college degree from the Philippines and worked for the government, but it does not mean anything here. *Ang napakasamang naranasan ko dito ay ang tingin ng kapwa Pilipina-para kang hindi tao, para kang baliwala* [The worst thing I've experienced here is the look of fellow Filipinas—as if you weren't human, as if you were nothing].

These domestic workers experience the failure of a Filipina identity to create congenial social relations among those encompassed by it. What they experience—not instead of, but rather *through* identity—is the active wielding of microclass differences among their "kind."[15] This wielding is done through the "look" (*tingin*), which is at once product and action of the "eye" (*minamata*, translated as "to look down on"; literally, it means "to eye" or, better, "to make an eye at or to"). The "eye" effects both an objectification and a reduction of the object, experienced as debasement (making into shit), humiliation (shaming, making one want to disappear), and devaluation (dehumanization, annihilation). The "look of fellow Filipinas" is therefore not a look of "kindness"; it is an infliction of pain, a violent insistence on difference in the face of sameness.

I offer these testimonies in part to demonstrate that there is no natural experience of sharedness even within the "same" national, gender, and class identity. Indeed, it is primarily the claims to identity, not the putative "differences" cutting across and covered over by this identity, that shape the exchanges of looks, inducing *sama ng loob* (bad feelings), among Filipinas. As a means of equivalence shaped by exchanged value, identity helps to create the differences it is said to gloss over or homogenize. I am not saying that there are no disparities and discordances among the life experiences and conditions of people prior to claims of their identity, only that identity serves as the background against which the singularities of lives become perceivable as indices of alterity (which, using another axis—say, of race or class—can congeal into another identity).

It is not surprising that the Filipina identity should provoke the contradictory responses expressed above: familiarity and repulsion. On one side, the Filipina identity is the achievement of integration of women in development, which is part of this ever-present war. It is the national means of exchange, the national commodity export par excellence, which supports the peso, and "the Filipino" for which it stands, against ever-threatening devaluation. It is the name for the histories that have shaped its production and that continue to be lived by the women who go by that name. As such, the Filipina is what the everyday social struggle of Filipinas directs itself against, most often at the expense of other Filipinas. Hence the "look of fellow Filipinas" is an act of differentiation from the Filipina identity, which in the very act of this differentiation only becomes confirmed in the one looked at: "it's as if I weren't human, as if I were nothing." Never has there been a time when Filipinas have been so alone and yet so crowded in this identity.

On the other side, the Filipina identity is composed of creative strategies of living against this war, the war that is the reality of racialized development and sexualized commodification. As such, the Filipina is the very means and process of political struggle. To the extent that it is an instrument of social stratification, it can serve as the instrument of mobilization and the means of new social relations. However, the reification of the processes of production, which constitutes this identity and allows it to be used for social stratification, continues to dog its use as a means of struggle. This is what explains the constant breakdown of "identity" in the midst of political mobilization: what is appropriated as an affirmative, liberative signifier threatens constantly to turn into a confining, essential social marker.[16] This is also what partly explains the failure of "identity" to elicit an immediate response of "identification" on the part of those it represents, particularly those for whom struggle is principally a matter of economic production and survival, and less a matter of political representation.[17] With the apparent severance of production from consumption, it is not surprising that these two spheres of practice should fail to connect in the daily experiences of those subsumed in one or the other.

It is precisely the tendency toward abstraction and reification that can make "identity" a politically divisive rather than a socially transformative means of struggle. Celine Parreñas rightly notes "the radical limits of empathy" between Filipina American feminists and Filipina sex workers.[18] These limits should not be equated, however, with the profound sociohistorical "differences" obtaining between these two positional inflections of "Filipina." These limits are, rather, shaped by the commodity form of personhood on which the very notion of empathy is predicated. Empathy is the act of identification with another, which presupposes the bourgeois notion of the individual self.[19] For Walter Benjamin, it is what is characteristic of the commodity world, the "unlimited tendency to represent the position of everyone else, every animal, every dead thing in the cosmos."[20]

The gaze of empathy is thus the gaze of equivalence, a form of looking that makes the world into images of one's experiences as objects of consumption. It is this gaze that forms the violent aspect of "that look" that Filipinas inflict on each other—on one side, it is emphatic identification; on the other side, repulsive indifference. That "look" is a reifying form of regard that casts these Filipinas' painful experience of absolute and essential finitude.

To ask "*Sino ka?*" "*Sino ako?*" "*Sino tayo?*" should not, therefore, be a demand for the representation of Filipina identity. It should not be to look for what we might identify with. Rather, it is to probe into the historical experiences out of which dominant images of Filipinas have been produced. It is to break the world of semblances in which people have become things. It is to de-reify our forms of regard and to discover new ways of relating to one another. Indeed, it is in asking these questions, as a way of remediating social relations among Filipinas, that artists and cultural producers can exercise their transformative potential. Cultural production is a form of mediation that activates and intervenes in prevailing structures of society. It thus has the capacity to alter the dominant forms of looking that support oppressive and exploitative social relations. Exhibitions of Filipina and Filipina American art are occasions for the re-visioning and revising not only of oppressive images of Filipinas but also of the experiential practices—particularly forms of regard—by means of which Filipinas help to perpetuate both those images and the conditions for their production.

The task of feminist writers, artists, and critics is therefore to reinvent experiential strategies for re-creating the realities we inherit and take as "givens." We can reinvent if we recognize the dimensions of our experiential practices that are not already subsumed by capitalist structures. Hence, even "that look" of Filipinas is not fully the consequence and instrument of the reifying gaze. Its capacity to inflict pain on the self's interior (*kalooban*), to be experienced as a form of action on oneself, indicates a kind of visual-social practice that is at once inside and outside capitalist command. The visual-social practice of *minamata* is the practice whereby the eye serves as an instrument of a force that is not equivalent to individualist human agency.[21] It is a tangible form of regard that invokes and depends on a notion of self as a permeable material substance with an inner sentient surface. This other visual-social practice subsisting within the look of commodification might be revitalized as a means of altering prevailing relations among Filipinas and, further, of transforming the processes of production supported by those relations.

If we look at art less in terms of representation than as practices of mediation, we can recognize the ways in which specific works might begin to alter our habitual forms of regard and release other possibilities. In the exhibit, *Sino Ka? Ano Ka?* I was struck, for example, by Reanne Agustin Estrada's hair-and-soap sculptures. These translucent, soft-colored soaps with strands of hair painstakingly pressed into them in various decorative as well as representational designs elicited in me both repulsion and attraction for their redemptive, aesthetic embossing of dead bodily matter on the instruments of cleanliness and beauty with which women are identified. As Joi Barrios's poem "Sabon" (Soap) expresses, "Ang babae'y nakakahong / parang baretang sabon / sa telebisyon" (Women are placed in boxes / like bars of soap / on television).[22] Whether they are beauty soaps or laundry soaps, they work for men and the gaze that men represent. Estrada's work, however, returns this alienated labor to women by making visible and tangible the creative potential of that labor for them. Inscribing the necessary but disavowed issue of their corporeality on the implements of women's work, Estrada's soaps do not only reappropriate the domestic labor-time that they represent for creative pleasure. In remediating women's relations to their own bodies through a tangible form of regard (a form of looking that is also a form of touching and experiencing touch), these creative works begin to alter the objectifying commodity relations expressed by the injunction, "Look, but don't touch!"

The alteration of our habitual forms of regard is one of the ways by which Filipinas can pierce through the "boxes" of representational identity functions that are imprisoning us. To ask "*Sino?*" is to put into question the very reality framework with which we understand our identities. The reconstitution of reality often means the proposition of new myths, new dreams, as well as the recuperation and revitalization of dreams that are already at work in the making of the world. In mentioning Filipina American suicides, I was not trying to portray Filipina Americans as the greatest victims of the prevailing war. Rather, I was trying to express the great violence of power over life that Filipinas and Pinays both contend with and wield. That power over life stems, however, from an even stronger life power, a power *for* life, that is the force that courses through us as Filipinas and Pinays in struggle. Indeed, it is the latter who have revitalized the historical myth of the *babaylan*, the priestesses of precolonial times who were mediators between earthly desires and unearthly powers. Today, Filipinas and Pinays reinvent the role of the *babaylan*, reclaiming the spirit of the male warriors who superseded them to create a new meaning for Filipina/Pinay. As an example, Barrios's subjective reconstitution of reality as a war enables a new role for women that makes them warriors of and for life, in a renewed context where living is a creative struggle for freedom. I want to end with the conclusion of her meditation on being a woman in a time of war, a meditation that is itself a realization of new, resistant, and transformative forms of mediating the world in which Filipinas find themselves:

> Kay tagal kong pinag-aralan
> ang puno't dulo
> ng digmaan.
> Sa huli'y naunawaan,
> na ang pagiging babae
> ay walang katapusang pakikibaka
> para mabuhay at maging malaya.
> [How long have I studied
> the depths and extent
> of this war.
> In the end, I understand
> that to be a woman
> is a never-ceasing struggle
> to live and be free.][23]

Author's Note

This is a revised version of a talk given at the closing symposium for *Sino Ka? Ano Ka?* (Who Are You? What Are You?), an exhibition of contemporary Filipina American art, at the San Francisco State University Art Department Gallery, October 21, 1998.

Notes

1. Thelma B. Kintanar, "Babae: Bilanggo ng Kasarian o Babaylan?" in *Ang Babae,* ed. Thelma B. Kintanar (Manila: Cultural Center of the Philippines, 1992), 1. The exhibit was organized by Kababaihan sa Sining at Bagong Sibol na Kamalayan (Kasibulan) and held at the Bulwagang Juan Luna, Sentrong Pangkultura ng Pilipinas (Cultural Center of the Philippines) in 1992.
2. Elynia S. Mabanglo, "Ang Maging Babae," in *Mga Liham ni Pinay* (Manila: De La Salle University Press, 1990), 3–4; the translation is mine.
3. Ibid., 3.
4. Ibid., 4.
5. Joi Barrios, "Ang pagiging babae ay pamumuhay sa panahon ng digma," in *Ang Pagiging Babae ay Pamumuhay sa Panahon ng Digma* (Manila: Institute of Women's Studies, St. Scholastica's College, 1990), 90.
6. Amaryllis T. Torres, "The Filipina Looks at Herself: A Review of Women's Studies in the Philippines," in *The Filipino Woman in Focus: A Book of Readings,* ed. Amaryllis T. Torres with M. Lisa, T. Carnagy et al. (Quezon City: University of the Philippines Office of Research Coordination/University of the Philippines Press, 1995), 14.
7. Roland Tolentino, "Bodies, Letters, Catalogs: Filipinas in Transnational Space," *Social Text,* no. 48 (1996): 49–76.
8. Quoted in Juno Parreñas, unpublished student paper, University of California, Santa Cruz, 1999.
9. E. San Juan Jr., "The Predicament of Filipinos in the United States: 'Where Are You From? When Are You Going Back?'" in *The State of Asian American: Activism and Resistance in the 1990s,* ed. Karin Aguilar-San Juan (Boston: South End, 1994), 207.
10. This information was relayed to me by Cristina Szanton-Blanc in conversation at the Southeast Asian Diasporas Conference, Singapore, December 1996.
11. Reena Jana, "Unfolding Identities," *Asian Art News* 9, no. 2 (1999): 42–45.
12. Ibid.
13. Ibid.
14. Quoted in Maria Carmen Domingo-Kirk, "Victims Discourses: Filipina Domestic Workers in Germany," *Journal of the American Association for Philippine Psychology* 1, no. 1 (1994): 24–37, 28–29.
15. Domingo-Kirk, "Victims Discourses," 35n8, translates *kapwa* (fellow or co-) as "kind," which conveys shared characteristics rather than shared circumstances. However, *kapwa* can refer to both kinds of sharedness and it is modern context that impels the interpretation of it in terms of the former as a definition of "identity."
16. See Margarita Alcantara, Leslie Mah, and Selena Whang, "Yellowdykecore: Queer, Punk 'n' Asian: A Roundtable Discussion," in *Dragon Ladies: Asian American Feminists Breathe Fire,* ed. Sonia Shah (Boston: South End, 1997), 216–32. Cultural activists Alcantara, Mah, and Whang talk about having to rid themselves of whatever identity they claimed in the process of struggle once they came across its constraining possibilities.
17. Marivic R. Desquitado, "A Letter from the Philippines," in *The Persistent Desire,* ed. Joan Nestle (Boston: Alyson, 1992), 295–98. I am not saying these are different or even separable forms of struggle. However, this is the conventional polarity dividing revolutionary nationalist and liberal, democratic approaches to social oppression, a polarity whose prevailing significance can be gleaned in the difficulty of Marivic Desquitado in enjoining other Filipina lesbians to participate in the internationalist politics of sexuality, to which she was drawn.
18. Celine Parreñas, Presentation at the Closing Symposium for *Sino Ka? Ano Ka?* San Francisco State University Art Department Gallery, October 21, 1998.
19. The term *empathy* is said to have been first introduced by a Munich professor of psychology and aesthetics, Theodor Lipps (1851–1914), who was an important influence on Sigmund Freud. See James Strachey, "Editor's Preface," in Sigmund Freud, *Jokes and Their Relations to the Unconscious,* trans. and ed. James Strachey (New York: W. W. Norton, 1960), 4–5.
20. Walter Benjamin, quoted in Susan Buck-Morss, "The Flaneur, the Sandwichman and the Whore: The Politics of Loitering," *New German Critique,* no. 39 (second special issue on Walter Benjamin; 1986): 122.

21. Hence the notion of the "evil eye," which one can "give" to others through ways similar to the ways "witches" or "sorcerers" (*mangkukulam*) can inflict a curse. With the prevalence of Western medicine, this phenomenon is commonly understood through notions of contagion (though one might also say the reverse: that people's understanding of contagion is shaped by persistent notions of "magic").
22. Barrios, "Ang pagiging babae ay pamumuhay sa panahon ng digma," 90.
23. Ibid.

Contributors

Delia D. Aguilar held joint appointments in the Departments of Women's Studies and Ethnic Studies at Bowling Green State University in Ohio and at Washington State University in Pullman, Washington. She now teaches women's studies at the University of Connecticut.

Karin Aguilar-San Juan is an assistant professor of American studies at Macalester College in St. Paul, Minnesota. She edited the collection *The State of Asian America: Activism and Resistance in the 1990s* (1994). Prior to graduate school, she was an editor at *Dollars and Sense*, a progressive economics monthly, and at South End Press, an independent publisher of trade, nonfiction books.

Victoria Alba is a freelance arts writer in the San Francisco, California Bay Area.

Sabrina Margarita Alcantara-Tan is a queer, Filipina mestiza. She is editress of the zine *Bamboo Girl* (www.bamboogirl.com, under the auspices of Pinay Power Productions), which is by and for—but not exclusive to—young, loud women of color. It deals with issues of racism, sexism, and homophobia, much from the mixed-blood Filipina point of view. Her work has been published in the collections *Dragon Ladies: Asian American Feminists Breathe Fire* (1997) and *That Takes Ovaries* (2002), and in *Maganda* magazine, and her video work has been screened at the Mix Gay and Lesbian Film Festival. She studies *Pananandata*, the Filipino martial art of weapon fighting, and her favorite weapon is the *balisong*. She is dedicated to what Filipinas, Asians, and Asian mutt women face on a daily basis and works constantly to give those who stereotype her and other Asian women a very hard time. She is an alumna of New York University.

Rachel A.R. Bundang is a doctoral candidate in Constructive Theologies, Praxis, and Ethics at Union Theological Seminary in the City of New York. She is a scholar of Asian/Pacific American religions, Catholic moral theology, and feminist social ethics. Also trained in violin, piano, and voice, she is a working musician and vocalist active in several jazz/funk and classical collectives.

Catherine Ceniza Choy is associate professor of ethnic studies at the University of California–Berkeley. She is the author of *Empire of Care: Nursing and Migration in Filipino American History* (2003). Her current book project focuses on the history of Asian international adoption in the United States.

Perla Paredes Daly graduated from the College of Fine Arts at the University of the Philippines–Diliman in 1986. A multimedia artist, she works in digital art and collage, graphic design, interactive design, photography, painting, sculpture, and *baybayin* jewelry. Perla writes spiritual prose and poetry and a cybercolumn called *Halin sa Tagipusuon (From the Heart)*, and she is the creator of newfilipina.com. She believes the Internet's force can empower by connecting people with each other and with progressive, life-changing ideas. She also loves gardening, yoga, reiki, and working via the Internet. Perla, her husband Kenneth, their sons Skyler, Brennan, and Greg, and Lola Jo live in the Connecticut boondocks these days.

Melinda L. de Jesús is assistant professor of Asian Pacific American studies at Arizona State University–Tempe, where she writes and teaches about Asian American literature and culture, Filipina/American feminisms, and new media pedagogies. Her work has appeared in *Meridians:Feminism, Race, Transnationalism*; *Radical Teacher*; *MELUS Journal*; the *Children's Literature Association Quarterly*; the *Journal of Asian American Studies*; *LIT: Literature, Interpretation, Theory*; the *Sisters of Color International Online Journal*; *Works and Days*; and the collection *Delinquents and Debutantes: Twentieth Century American Girls' Culture* (1998). She is an Aquarian and admits an obsession with Hello Kitty.

M. Evelina Galang is the author of *Her Wild American Self*, a collection of short fiction (1996). Her collection's title story has been short-listed by both *The Best American Short Stories* and the Pushcart Prize. Her novel *One Tribe* won the 2004 Association of Writers and Writing Programs (AWP) Prize in the novel category and is forthcoming. Galang is also the editor of *Screaming Monkeys: Critiques of Asian American Images* (2003); this collection won *Fore-Word* magazine's Gold Book of the Year Award for 2003. In 2001, she was the Fulbright Senior Research Scholar in the Philippines, where she continued to explore the stories of surviving Filipina comfort women of World War II for her upcoming collection of essays, *Lola's House: Women Living with War*. Galang teaches in the MFA Creative Writing Program at the University of Miami.

Emily Noelle Ignacio is assistant professor of sociology at Loyola University, Chicago. She is the author of *Building Diaspora: Filipino Community Formation on the Internet* (2004). Her work on the effect of media technologies on communities has also appeared in the *Sociological Quarterly, Cultural Studies/ Critical Methodologies,* the *Journal of the American Society for Information Science,* and *Library Trends.* She is currently examining the role of home masses in racial and cultural formation processes within a Filipino American community in Chicago.

Christine T. Lipat was born and raised in New Jersey. Currently she is acting executive director of the Asian Arts Alliance and a founding member of Kilawin Kolektibo, a Pinay lesbian-identified collective of women based in New York City.

Dawn Bohulano Mabalon is a third-generation Pinay born and raised in Stockton, California, where she is the chair of the Little Manila Foundation. She is an assistant professor of history at San Francisco State University. She received a Ph.D. from Stanford University and an M.A. from the University of California–Los Angeles.

Gigi Otálvaro-Hormillosa, also known as the Devil Bunny in Bondage, is a San Francisco–based, interdisciplinary performance artist, video artist, cultural activist, curator, and percussionist of Filipino and Colombian descent. She is originally from Miami, Florida, and received her B.A. from Brown University, where she created an independent concentration, Hybridity and Performance. She has worked on various artistic collaborations under the mentorship and direction of performing artists such as Elia Arce, Guillermo Gomez-Peña, Pearl Ubungen, and Afia Walking Tree. Her work in performance, video, and writing has been presented nationally and internationally, and her writing has been published in the *Social Justice Journal, Shellac, Antithesis Journal: Sex 2000,* online at artistmanifesto.com, and in the collection *Postcolonial and Queer Theories: Intersections and Essays* (2001). Awards include grants from the Franklin Furnace Fund for Performance Art, the San Francisco Art Commission Cultural Equity Grants Program, and the Potrero Nuevo Fund Prize. For more information about Gigi and to view performance video clips and images, visit www.devilbunny.org.

Trinity A. Ordona is cofounder and co-coordinator of Asian and Pacific Islander Family Pride, the first and only nonprofit organization to provide cultural, linguistic, and peer support to families of Asian and Pacific Islander lesbian, gay, bisexual, and transgender people. She has a thirty-five-year history of civil rights activism and has received several awards for her grassroots organizing strategies. Ordona is an instructor in the Gay and Lesbian Studies Department at the City College of San Francisco and the associate director of the Lesbian Health Research Center at the University of California–San Francisco. She has spoken widely in academic and community venues in the United States, Canada, Japan, India, and the Philippines on race, gender, sexuality, and health.

Rhacel Salazar Parreñas is associate professor of Asian American studies at the University of California–Davis. She is the author of *Servants of Globalization: Women, Migration, and Domestic Work* and the forthcoming book *Children of Global Migration: Transnational Families and Gendered Woes.* She is currently at work on a coedited volume on Asian Diasporas. She writes on gender, migration, and globalization.

Linda M. Pierce is an Assistant Professor at the University of Southern Mississippi where she teaches multiethnic American literature with emphases in Filipino/a American, Asian American, and African American studies; critical race theory; postcolonial literature and theory; feminist theory and women's studies. Her introductions to *Carlos Bulosan* and *America Is in the Heart* are forthcoming in the *Encyclopedia of American Ethnic Literature* (2005). She edited the summer 2003 issue of *Arizona Quarterly* (59.2), which features her introduction, "Questions of Identity: Complicating Race in American Literary History." Her article "Pinay White Woman" appears in *Whiteness: Feminist Philosphical Reflections* (Rowman & Littlefield, 1999). Linda is currently working on her book-length manuscript, *Displaced Memory: Oscar Micheaux, Carlos Bulosan, and the Process of U.S. Decolonization.*

Frank L. Samson is currently a Ph.D. candidate in sociology at Stanford University. He holds degrees from the University of California–Los Angeles and Harvard University and teaches courses in sociology and ethnic studies.

Celine Parreñas Shimizu, film scholar and film/videomaker, works as assistant professor in Asian American studies and film at the University of California–Santa Barbara. She has a Ph.D. from Stanford University, an M.F.A. from the University of California–Los Angeles, and a B.A. from the University of California–Berkeley (1992). She is finishing *The Hypersexuality of Race: Screening Asian Women in America,* which analyses the production of sexuality for Asian women in the U.S. cinema industry—including stag films, contemporary pornography, Hollywood blockbusters, musicals, and independent sexually explicit media by Asian American women. Her publications include "Unashamed to Be So Beautiful," coauthored with Theo Gonzalves in *Countervisions: Asian American Film Criticism* (2000) and "Sex Acts: Asian American Film Feminisms," coauthored with Helen Lee, in the journal *Signs* (2004). An internationally screened and award-winning filmmaker, her works include *Mahal Means Love and Expensive* (1993), *Her Uprooting Plants Her* (1995), and *Super Flip* (1997). Her latest film, *The Fact of Asian Women* (2002) received awards for Best Documentary Short at the Big Mini DV Festival 2002, Best

Picture for Women's Issues at Zoie Fest 2003, and Best of Festival Documentary at the 2003 Berkeley International Film and Video Festival, and was Winner in Long Format-Education at the 2003 DV Awards. Shimizu has received many prestigious awards, fellowships, grants, and honors, including the University of California Institute for Research in the Arts Award; the Social Science Research Council Sexuality Research Fellowship; the Edie and Lew Wasserman Directing Fellowship; and the Eisner Prize, the University of California–Berkeley's highest award in the creative arts.

Cianna Pamintuan Stewart graduated from Wesleyan University, where she studied theater. She divides her time between theater directing and organizing around Asian/Pacific Islander gender and sexual diversity through the Visibility Campaign and the Asian/Pacific Islander Wellness Center Community HIV/AIDS Services in San Francisco.

Leny Mendoza Strobel is assistant professor of American multicultural studies at Sonoma State University in San Francisco. She is the author of *Coming Full Circle: The Process of Decolonization among Post 1965 Filipino Americans* (2000) and the coeditor, with Roshni Rustomiji-Kerns and Rajini Srikranth, of *Encounters: People of Asian Descent in the Americas* (1999). Her writings have appeared in *Postcolonial Theory and the U.S.: Race, Ethnicity and Literature* (2000); *Filipino Americans: Transformation and Identity* (1997); *Not Home but Here: Filipino Writings in the Diaspora* (2003); and various journals and magazines.

Marie-Therese C. Sulit is a doctoral candidate in the Department of English at the University of Minnesota–Twin Cities. Her research interests include twentieth-century American and world literature, American popular culture, twentieth-century minority and ethnic literatures, Asian American studies, and, especially, Filipino studies and Filipino American studies. She has written essays on the writers Theresa Hak Kyung Cha, Li-Young Lee, and Carolyn Forché in the forthcoming *Companion to Twentieth Century American Poetry*. Her dissertation is titled "Hunger for Home: The Filipina and Filipina American Writer Imagining Community in the Diaspora," and an overview will appear in article form in the upcoming collection *National, Communal and Personal Voices in Asian America and the Asian Diaspora*.

Neferti Xina M. Tadiar is associate professor in the Department of History of Consciousness at the University of California–Santa Cruz. She received Ph.D. from Duke University, earned under the direction of Frederic Jameson. Her work is concerned with the relations between cultural production and political economy within third-world and postcolonial contexts. Publications include *Fantasy-Production: Sexual Economies and Other Philippine Consequences for the New World Order* (2004).

Allyson Goce Tintiangco-Cubales is assistant professor of Asian American studies at San Francisco State University. She received her B.A. from the University of California–Berkeley and her Ph.D. from the University of California–Los Angeles. She works in the fields of Filipina feminism, youth programming, and community service and is a new mom to daughter Mahalaya.

Mary Ann Ubaldo graduated from the University of the Philippines and is a cofounder of Kilawin Kolektibo, a Pinay lesbian-identified collective of women based in New York City. A musician and photographer, she runs a jewelry business named after the legendary Filipina tribal warrior Urduja, in which she creates unique pieces that incorporate Filipino motifs using the ancient Philippine script known as *alibata*.

Michelle Remoreras Watts is a law student at the University of California–Berkeley (Boalt Hall). While at Boalt Hall, she codrafted the *Internet Communication Protection Act of 2003* (California Assembly Bill 1143) and received the Raymond L. Ocampo Jr. Scholarship from the Filipino Bar Association of Northern California. In 2001, Michelle received a B.A. in Asian American Studies with honors from Stanford University.

Permissions

I am grateful to the authors and/or publishers for giving me permission to reprint selections that originally appeared in the following publications in slightly different forms:

Leny Mendoza Strobel, "A Personal Story: Becoming a Split Filipina Subject." *Amerasia Journal* 19, no. 3 (1993): 117–129.

Melinda L. de Jesús, "Fictions of Assimilation: Nancy Drew, Cultural Imperialism, and the Filipina American Experience." In *Delinquents and Debutantes: Twentieth-Century American Girls' Culture*, ed. Sherrie Inness (New York: New York University Press, 1998), 227–246.

Rachel A. R. Bundang, "'This Is Not Your Mother's Catholic Church:' When Filipino Catholic Spirituality Meets American Culture." *Brown Papers* (Women's Theological Center, Boston) 3, no. 1 (1996): 1–14.

Catherine Ceniza Choy, "Asian American History: Reflections on Imperialism, Immigration, and 'The Body.'" *Amerasia Journal* 26, no. 1 (2000): 119–140.

Rhacel Salazar Parreñas, "Migrant Filipina Domestic Workers and the International Division of Reproductive Labor." *Gender and Society* 14, no. 4 (2000): 560–580.

Christine T. Lipat, Trinity A. Ordona, Cianna Pamintuan Stewart, and Mary Ann Ubaldo. "Tomboy, Dyke, Lezzie, and Bi: Filipina Lesbian and Bisexual Women Speak Out." In *Filipino Americans: Transformation and Identity*, ed. Maria P. P. Root (Thousand Oaks, Calif.: Sage, 1997), 230–246.

M. Evelina Galang, "Deflowering the Sampaguita." In *Filipino Americans: Transformation and Identity,* ed. Maria P. P. Root (Thousand Oaks, Calif.: Sage, 1997), 219–229.

Trinity A. Ordona, "The Long Road Ahead." In *Tibok: Heartbeat of the Filipina Lesbian,* ed. Anna Leah Sarabia (Manila: Anvil, 1998), 147–159.

Emily Noelle Ignacio, "Ain't I a Filipino (Woman)? An Analysis of Authorship/Authority through the Construction of 'Filipina' on the Net." *Sociological Quarterly* 41, no. 4 (2000): 551–572.

Melinda L. de Jesús, "'A walkin' fo' de (Rice)Kake': A Filipina American Feminist's Adventures in Academia, or A Pinay's Progress." *Sisters of Color International Online Journal* 1, No. 1 (2000); http://www.ac.wwu.edu/~womenstd/SOCI/cakewalk.html>

Sabrina Margarita Alcantara-Tan, "The Herstory of *Bamboo Girl* Zine." *Frontiers: Journal of Women's Studies* 21, nos. 1–2 (2000): 159–163.

Ruth Elynia S. Mabanglo, "Invitation of the Imperialist" and "A Conjectural Poem by Flor Contemplacion" in *Invitation of the Imperialist/Anyaya Ng Imperyalista* (Quezon City: The University of Philippines Press, 1998).

Neferti Xina M. Tadiar, "Filipinas: 'Living in a Time of War.'" In *Body Politics: Essays on Cultural Representations of Women's Bodies,* ed. Odine de Guzman (Quezon City: Center for Women's Studies, University of the Philippines, 2002).

Index